The Accumulation of Capital

'*The Accumulation of Capital* is arguably the most important advance on Marx's political economy to date. Written by a working-class revolutionary leader who begins by critically analyzing Marx's draft Volume 2 of *Capital* and ends by relating to militarism, Luxemburg develops a theoretical foundation for the global drive and structural crisis of capitalism. Although opposed by contemporaries Lenin and Bukharin, her book has passed historical test and can be avoided only at our peril.'

Paul Zarembka

Rosa
Luxemburg

The Accumulation of Capital

Translated by Agnes Schwarzschild

With a new introduction by Tadeusz Kowalik

 London and New York

Die Akkumulation des Kapitals first published 1913

English edition first published 1951
by Routledge & Kegan Paul

First published in Routledge Classics 2003
by Routledge
2 Park Square, Milton Park, Abingdon, Oxon, OX14 4RN
711 Third Avenue, New York, NY 10017

Routledge is an imprint of the Taylor & Francis Group

This edition © 2003 Routledge
Introduction to the Routledge Classics edition © 2003 Tadeusz Kowalik

Typeset in Joanna by RefineCatch Limited, Bungay, Suffolk
Printed and bound in Great Britain by
CPI Antony Rowe, Chippenham, Wiltshire

British Library Cataloguing in Publication Data
A catalogue record for this book is available from the British Library

Library of Congress Cataloging in Publication Data
A catalog record for this book has been requested

ISBN 978–0–415–30445–0

CONTENTS

Introduction to the
Routledge Classics Edition

Rosa Luxemburg has been known not only (perhaps even not so much) as an economic theoretician, but also as one of the leaders of the German Social Democratic Party and founder of the Social Democratic Party in the Kingdom of Poland. In non-communist socialist circles her political pamphlet criticising the Russian Revolution remains most popular. In the academic milieu the reception of Luxemburg's economic works came rather late as they were written in Marxian (Marxist) language and deeply involved in the controversies amongst the socialists. The first English edition (1951) of her book *The Accumulation of Capital* was vindicated as one of the pioneering works of the effective demand theory and Joan Robinson's introduction attempted to translate the main message of this Polish–German economist into the language of Keynesian economics.

Rosa Luxemburg was born in 1870, in Zamość (a part of Polish territory under Russian occupation). She went to university in Zurich, moving from the study of philosophy and natural sciences to economics. Her PhD dissertation, presented there in 1897, was on the industrial development of the Kingdom of Poland (*Die industrielle Entwicklung Polens*). A year later she moved to Germany for good, in order to be active in a leading European socialist party. Her name became widely known not only in Germany, but also within The Socialist

International, due to her polemical essays against the 'revisionism' and 'reformism' of Eduard Bernstein, in which she defended revolutionary Marxism (they were published in a book *Sozialreform oder Revolution*, 1900). Since then these two names have long symbolised the two opposing wings of the socialist movement not only in Germany, but in the whole of continental Europe. Luxemburg was murdered in Berlin during the German revolution in 1919.

The Accumulation of Capital, probably the best book produced by a Marxist and socialist thinker since Karl Marx's *opus magnum*, emerged from her sudden revelation. Until January 1912 Rosa Luxemburg was an orthodox follower of Marx, believing that political economy had found its 'crowning achievement' in *Das Kapital* and may be perfected by his followers only in details. In this vein she began writing a textbook for popular consumption, but while struggling with its last chapter on the general tendencies of capitalist development, she suddenly discovered a problem solved neither by Marx nor anybody else. It was clear to her that capitalism is a historical phenomenon, but that the answer to what its future economic limits were had not been found. This was a question she tried to answer.

Her revelation was so strong that she wrote the treatise as if in *extasis*. As she put it in a letter to her friend: 'The period in which I wrote the *Accumulation* belongs to the happiest of my life. I lived in a veritable trance. Day and night I neither saw nor heard anything as that one problem developed so beautifully before my eyes. I don't know which gave me more pleasure: the process of thinking ... or the literary creation with pen in hand. Do you know that I wrote the whole 900 pages in 4 months at one sitting? An unheard-of thing! Without checking the rough copy even once, I had it printed'.[1]

These 'rush and Rausch' methods had their advantages and disadvantages. From these emotions stem a colourful literary text, which is a pleasure to read, particularly the historical chapters. But as an analytical study, it has flaws, repetitions, and even contradictions. Understandably, such a work has been interpreted in many different

---

[1] The Letters of Rosa Luxemburg, edited and with an Introduction by Stephen Eric Bronner, New Edition, Humanities Press, New Jersey, 1993, p. 204 (this was a letter to Hans Dieffenbach, 12 May 1917).

ways and it, in fact, provoked most controversy amongst Marxists, although less so within academic circles.

Rosa Luxemburg was enlightened not only by the new unsolved problem, but also by a discovery of an analytical tool for solving it. She starts her analysis by acknowledging Marx's important contribution to political economy by grasping, in one formula, the problem of the reproduction of global social capital. In his famous schemata of reproduction, Marx shows an exchange (proportions) between two aggregate divisions of the national economy: the means of production and consumption products. The usefulness of this tool lies in facilitating a theoretical consideration of the dynamics of the capitalist economy in most general terms, using such aggregate categories, like global capital, wage fund and the total sum of profits for the whole capitalist class. One has to remember that, in the times of Rosa Luxemburg, economics was almost totally caught up in microanalysis. Even such notions as gross domestic product or national income, nowadays regarded as elementary, were as yet unknown.

However, Luxemburg was convinced that Marx had managed to create only a very general, abstract (mathematical) formula, which should be seen as the starting point of analysing the real problems of capitalist economic development as a whole. Moreover, she thought that Marx had made several assumptions in his formula, which prevented him from seeing the real contradictions in the process of capitalist development.

Her analysis, with its polemical digressions, not only criticised these assumptions, but also showed up some contradictions in Marx's reasoning, particularly differences expressed in the second and third volumes of his *opus magnum*. Her criticism, however, did not transform itself into an elaboration of general schemata, free of the very assumptions she regarded as wrong. She did not succeed in including in her model the pre-capitalist environment or money. But she did manage to articulate, through a dialogue with Marx, some very important and stimulating ideas, both theoretically and through historical analysis.

The most general problem, which was in a way self-evident for Marx but bothered Rosa Luxemburg, was a question: what are the incentives and stimuli for capitalist economic development? Are they intimately connected with a very nature of capitalist entrepreneurs, or dependent on environment? In contemporary terms (introduced by J.M. Keynes and M. Kalecki) the problem was how to explain the process of transformation of savings into real investment. Marx saw the historical limits of capitalism as lying in the tension and class conflict created by rapid economic development, which laid the ground for social revolution. But he explained economic expansion by a constant thirst for profits and the rivalry between individual capitalists for its maximisation (cf. his famous exclamation: 'Accumulate! Accumulate! That is Moses and the Prophets'). According to this view, the transformation of world economies into a global capitalist system was only a matter of time.

In his opinion, 'The bourgeoisie, by the improvement of all instruments of production, by the immensely facilitated means of communications, draws all, even the most barbarian nations, into civilization. The cheap prices of its commodities are the heavy artillery with which it batters down all Chinese walls, with which it forces the barbarians' intensely obstinate hatred of foreigners to capitulate'.[2]

This approach, which Joan Robinson summed up as the 'animal spirit' of capitalist entrepreneurs, was for Rosa Luxemburg too one-dimensional. Capitalist entrepreneurs expand their activity into backward regions not only because they generally have a thirst for profits anywhere, and not only because of rivalry among them. They are compelled to do so because they as a class, as global capital of a given country, have declining opportunities to sell their products profitably in their own country. Hence the process of exchange between the capitalist and non-capitalist environment acts as a feeding ground of accumulation, and is a *sine qua non* of the existence of the capitalist economy.[3] This explains the roots of imperialist rivalry between the superpowers for colonies. Imperialism was for her 'the political

[2] K. Marx and F. Engels, The Communist Manifesto, 1848, quoted after Bottomore and Rubel, Karl Marx, Selected Writings in Sociology and Social Philosophy, McGraw-Hill Book Company, New York, Toronto and London, 1964, p. 137.

[3] A similar view was expressed by the French historian Fernand Braudel. In his seminal three-volume work he accepted I. Wallerstein's view, that 'there can be coexistence of "modes of production" from slavery to capitalism, that the latter can only live if it is surrounded by the other modes, and indeed at their expense. Rosa Luxemburg was right.' Fernand Braudel, Civilization and Capitalism, 15th–18th Century. Vol. III, The Perspective of the World, translated from the French by S. Reynolds, Collins, London, and Harper & Row, New York, 1984, pp. 64–65. I thank Prof. Paul Zarembka for sending me English sources in this and the first footnote and for valuable remarks.

expression of the accumulation of capital in its competitive struggle for what remains still open of the non-capitalist environment' (p. 426). But her definition also contained the struggle by colonial countries for liberation. Marx was, in her eyes, wrong when he only stressed the crucial role of political power and of violence in the early phase of so-called primitive capital accumulation. In reality, political power is nothing but a vehicle for the economic process (p. 433).

Rosa Luxemburg's attempt to develop a theoretical explanation for the role of the non-capitalist environment in capitalist development was preceded by her empirical study. In the above-mentioned PhD dissertation, a statistical and economic analysis led her to the conclusion that industrial development in the Polish Kingdom very much depended on its expansion to the more backward 'eastern markets' (in Russia). It had become inextricably entwined with the Russian economy and that is why she believed that the fight for Poland's independence would be against the historical tendencies of capitalist development. Because of this conclusion she was blamed, not only by nationalists, but also by more patriotically oriented socialists for creating a cosmopolitan theory of the 'organic inclusion of Poland into Tsarist Russia'.

There is some other evidence that the above-mentioned revelation was a culmination in her mind of one big theoretical problem from some earlier raised questions. Traces of these types of questions can also be found in her widely known polemics with Edward Bernstein (her *Social Reform or Revolution?*). Here she describes the process of the rapid concentration of production and the centralisation of capital (cartels, trusts and concerns) which goes together with the decline of small and medium firms. Simultaneously, she treated this process of concentration as leading to the monopolisation of advanced economies on the one hand, while small and medium-sized firms remained the most entrepreneurial and innovative. Thus, without smaller firms the capitalist economy would become, as she writes, 'stagnant and drowsy'. Since she rather overestimated the pace and degree of 'monopolisation', she had to face the question about why the most advanced economies were still growing rather rapidly. There must exist some other, perhaps external, stimuli for a highly concentrated economy. A non-capitalist environment was to provide the bulk of the answer.

Seen from today's perspective, Rosa Luxemburg's stress on a break-down of capitalism, as the result of the exhaustion of the pre-capitalist systems, seems one-sided. More convincing were theoreticians, like Michal Kalecki and Joseph Steindl, arguing that without some semi-external factors capitalist economy would be stagnant (one may add that stagnation would have led to the collapse of capitalism only if an alternative system was at hand, as Rosa Luxemburg deeply believed). However, many economists and historians would agree that the expansion by the most advanced economies to the backward regions (and exploitation of them) has been one of the most important factors determining the exceptional boom which has lasted for over two hundred years.

Some other stimuli, however, did not entirely escape her attention. The last chapter of *The Accumulation of Capital*, entitled 'Militarism as a Province of Accumulation', in many instances sounds as if it were written during the Cold War, explaining a long boom in the American economy. In her opinion, armament production, in the imperialist era, is one of the most important ways of solving difficulties related to the selling of stocks from a rapidly growing productive sphere. The attractiveness of expanding this sphere of the economy also consists in the fact that expenditure by the state in military equipment is 'free of the vagaries and subjective fluctuations of personal consumption, it achieves an almost automatic regularity and rhythmic growth' (p. 446). At one point Luxemburg writes about 'contradictory phenomena' and that 'the old capitalist countries provide ever larger markets for . . . one another' (p. 347).

The Accumulation of Capital is a thorough study of connections and contradictions between developed economies and what today is called The Third World. For Rosa Luxemburg this was a fertile soil for wars, revolutions, or at least for a permanent instability of world economy. After almost one century of bitter experiences there are not many political and economic analysts who would deny that these questions continue to be of utmost importance.

TADEUSZ KOWALIK

Translator's Note

This is an original translation not only of the main body of the work but also of a number of quotations from foreign authors. Page references thus usually indicate the original foreign sources.

In so far as possible, however, I have availed myself of existing translations and have referred to the following standard works:

Karl Marx: *Capital*, vol. i (transl. by Moore-Aveling, London, 1920); vol. ii (transl. by E. Untermann, Chicago, 1907); vol. iii (transl. by E. Untermann, Chicago, 1909).
—— *The Poverty of Philosophy* (translator's name not given, London, 1936).

Sismondi's introduction to the second edition of *Nouveaux Principes* is quoted from M. Mignet's translation of selected passages by Sismondi, entitled *Political Economy and the Philosophy of Government*, London, 1847. No English translation exists of Marx's *Theorien über den Mehrwert*.

Unfortunately, not all the West European texts, and none of the Russian—except Engels' correspondence with Nikolayon—were accessible to me, and I regret having been unable to trace some quotations and check up on others. In such cases, the English version follows the German text and will at least bring out the point the author wanted to make.

To save the reader grappling with unfamiliar concepts, I have converted foreign currencies and measures into their English equivalents, at the following rates:

20 *marks*—25 *francs*—$5—£1 (gold standard); 1 *hectare*—(roughly) 2.5 acres; 1 *kilometre*—$\frac{5}{8}$ mile.

I am glad of this opportunity to express my gratitude to Dr. W. Stark and Mrs. J. Robinson for the helpful criticism and appreciation with which my work has met.

AGNES SCHWARZSCHILD

A NOTE ON ROSA LUXEMBURG

Rosa Luxemburg was born on 5 March 1870, at Zamosc, a little town of Russian Poland, not far from the city of Lublin. She came from a fairly well-to-do family of Jewish merchants, and soon showed the two outstanding traits which were to characterise all her life and work: a high degree of intelligence, and a burning thirst for social justice which led her, while still a schoolgirl, into the revolutionary camp. Partly to escape the Russian police, partly to complete her education, she went to Zurich and studied there the sciences of law and economics. Her doctoral dissertation dealt with the industrial development of Poland and showed up the vital integration of Polish industry with the wider economic system of metropolitan Russia. It was a work not only of considerable promise, but already of solid and substantial achievement.

Her doctorate won, Rosa Luxemburg looked around for a promising field of work and decided to go to Germany, whose working-class movement seemed destined to play a leading part in the future history of international socialism. She settled there in 1896, and two years later contracted a formal marriage with a German subject which secured her against the danger of forcible deportation to Russia. Now, at that moment the German Social-Democratic Party was in the throes of a serious crisis. In 1899, Eduard Bernstein published his well-known work *Die Voraussetzungen des Sozialismus und die Aufgaben der Sozialdemokratie*, which urged the party to drop its revolutionary jargon and to work henceforth for tangible social reforms within the given economic set-up, instead of trying to bring about its final and forcible overthrow. This 'reformism' or 'revisionism' seemed to Rosa Luxemburg a base as well as a foolish doctrine, and she published in the same year a pamphlet *Sozialreform oder Revolution?* which dealt with Bernstein's ideas in no uncertain fashion. From this moment onward, she was and remained one of the acknowledged leaders of the left wing within the German working-class movement.

The events of the year 1905 gave Rosa Luxemburg a welcome opportunity to demonstrate that revolution was to her more than a subject of purely academic interest. As soon as the Russian masses began to move, she hurried to Warsaw and threw herself into the fray. There followed a short span of feverish activity, half a year's imprisonment, and, finally, a return journey to Berlin. The experiences of the Warsaw rising are reflected in a book entitled *Massenstreik, Partei und Gewerkschaften*, which was published in 1906. It recommends the general strike as the most effective weapon in the struggle of the proletariat against the bourgeoisie.

The International Socialist Congress which met at Stuttgart in 1907 prepared and foreshadowed the sorry history of Rosa Luxemburg's later life. On that occasion she drafted, together with Lenin, a resolution which demanded that the workers of the world should make any future war an opportunity for the destruction of the capitalist system. Unlike so many others, she stuck to her resolution when, seven years later, the time of testing came. The result was that she had to spend nearly the whole of the first World War in jail, either under punishment or in protective custody. But imprisonment did not mean inactivity. In 1916, there appeared in Switzerland her book *Die Krise der Sozialdemokratie*, which assailed the leaders of the German labour party for their patriotic attitude and called the masses to revolutionary action. The foundation of the Spartacus League in 1917, the germ cell out of which the Communist Party of Germany was soon to develop, was vitally connected with the dissemination of Rosa Luxemburg's aggressive sentiments.

The collapse of the *Kaiserreich* on 11 November 1918, gave Rosa Luxemburg her freedom and an undreamt-of range of opportunities.

The two months that followed must have been more crowded and more colourful than all her previous life taken together. But the end of her career was imminent. The fatal Spartacus week, an abortive rising of the Berlin workers, led on 15 January 1919, to her arrest by a government composed of former party comrades. During her removal to prison she was attacked and severely beaten by soldiers belonging to the extreme right, a treatment which she did not survive. Her body was recovered days later from a canal.

A type not unlike Trotsky, Rosa Luxemburg had her tender and sentimental side, which comes to the surface in her correspondence, especially in the *Briefe aus dem Gefaengnis* printed in 1922. As a thinker she showed considerable honesty and independence of mind. *The Accumulation of Capital*, first published in 1913, which is undoubtedly her finest achievement, reveals her as that rarest of all rare phenomena—a Marxist critical of Karl Marx.

W. STARK

INTRODUCTION

Academic economists have recently returned from the elaboration of static equilibrium to the classical search for a dynamic model of a developing economy. Rosa Luxemburg, neglected by Marxist and academic economists alike, offers a theory of the dynamic development of capitalism which is of the greatest interest. The book is one of considerable difficulty (apart from the vivid historical chapters), and to those accustomed only to academic analysis the difficulty is rendered well-nigh insurmountable by the Marxist terminology in which it is expressed. The purpose of this preface is to provide a glossary of terms, and to search for the main thread of the argument (leaving the historical illustrations to speak for themselves) and set it out in simpler language.

The result is no doubt too simple. The reader must sample for himself the rich confusion in which the central core of analysis is imbedded, and must judge for himself whether the core has been mishandled in the process of digging it out.[1]

Our author takes her departure from the numerical examples for simple reproduction (production with a constant stock of capital) and

---

[1] For a totally different interpretation see Sweezy; *The Theory of Capitalist Development*, chap. xi, Section 9.

expanded reproduction (production with capital accumulating) set out in volume ii of Marx's *Capital*. As she points out,[2] Marx completed the model for simple reproduction, but the models for accumulation were left at his death in a chaos of notes, and they are not really fit to bear all the weight she puts on them (Heaven help us if posterity is to pore over all the backs of old envelopes on which economists have jotted down numerical examples in working out a piece of analysis). To follow her line of thought, however, it is necessary to examine her version of Marx's models closely, to see on what assumptions they are based (explicitly or unconsciously) and to search the assumptions for clues to the succeeding analysis.

To begin at the beginning—gross national income (for a closed economy) for, say, a year, is written $c + v + s$; that is, constant capital, variable capital and surplus. Variable capital, v, is the annual wages bill. Surplus, s, is annual rent, interest, and net profit, so that $v + s$ represents net national income. (In this introduction surplus is used interchangeably with rent, interest and net profit.) Constant capital, c, represents at the same time the contribution which materials and capital equipment make to annual output, and the cost of maintaining the stock of physical capital in existence at the beginning of the year. When all commodities are selling at normal prices, these two quantities are equal (normal prices are tacitly assumed always to rule,[3] an assumption which is useful for long-period problems, though treacherous when we have to deal with slumps and crises). Gross receipts equal to $c + v + s$ pass through the hands of the capitalists during the year, of which they use an amount, c, to replace physical capital used up during the year, so that c represents costs of raw materials and wear and tear and amortisation of plant. An amount, v, is paid to workers and is consumed by them (saving by workers is regarded as negligible[4]). The surplus, s, remains to the capitalists for their own consumption and for net saving. The professional classes (civil servants, priests, prostitutes, etc.) are treated as hangers-on of the capitalists, and their incomes do not appear, as they are not regarded as producing *value*.[5] Expenditure

---

[2] See p. 139.
[3] Cf. The quotation from *Capital*, vol. iii, p. 331.
[4] See p. 104.
[5] See p. 107.

upon them tends to lessen the saving of capitalists, and their own expenditure and saving are treated as expenditure and saving out of surplus.

In the model set out in chapter 6 there is no technical progress (this is a drastic simplification made deliberately[6]) and the ratio of capital to labour is constant (as the stock of capital increases employment increases in proportion). Thus real output per worker employed is constant (hours of work per year do not vary) and real wages per man are constant. It follows that real surplus per man is also constant. So long as these assumptions are retained Marxian *value* presents no problem. *Value* is the product of labour-time. *Value* created per man-year is constant because hours of work are constant. Real product per man year being constant, on the above assumptions, the *value* of a unit of product is constant. For convenience we may assume money wages per man constant. Then, on these assumptions, both the money price of a unit of output and the *value* of a unit of money are constant. This of course merely plasters over all the problems of measurement connected with the use of index numbers, but provided that the technique of production is unchanging, and normal prices are ruling, those problems are not serious, and we can conduct the analysis in terms of money values.[7] (Rosa Luxemburg regards it as a matter of indifference whether we calculate in money or in *value*.[8])

The assumption of constant real wages presents a difficulty which we may notice in passing. The operation of the capitalist system is presumed to depress the level of wages down to the limit set by the minimum subsistence of the worker and his family. But how large a family? It would be an extraordinary fluke if the average size of family supported by the given wage of a worker were such as to provide for a rate of growth of population exactly adjusted to the rate of accumulation of capital, and she certainly does not hold that this is the case.[9] There is a reserve army of labour standing by, ready to take employment when the capitalists offer it. While they are unemployed the

[6] See p. 102.

[7] Exchanges between industries, however, must take place at 'prices of production' not at *values*. See below, p. xxiv, note.

[8] See p. 85.

[9] See p. 341.

workers have no source of income, but are kept alive by sharing in the consumption of the wages of friends and relations who are in work.[10] When an increase in the stock of capital takes place, more workers begin to earn wages, those formerly employed are relieved of the burden of supporting some unemployed relations, and their own consumption rises. Thus either they were living below the subsistence minimum before, or they are above it now. We may cut this knot by simply postulating that real wages per man are constant,[11] without asking why. The important point for the analysis which we are examining is that when employment increases the total consumption of the workers as a whole increases by the amount of the wages received by the additional workers.[12]

We may now set out the model for simple reproduction—that is, annual national income for an economy in which the stock of capital is kept intact but not increased. All output is divided into two departments: I, producing capital equipment and raw materials, (producers' goods), and II, producing consumption goods. Then we have

$$\text{I}: c_1 + v_1 + s_1 = c_1 + c_2$$
$$\text{II}: c_2 + v_2 + s_2 = v_1 + v_2 + s_1 + s_2$$

Thus

$$c_2 = v_1 + s_1$$

This means that the net output of the producers' goods department is equal to the replacement of capital in the consumers' goods department. The whole surplus, as well as the whole of wages, is currently consumed.

Before proceeding to the model for accumulation there is a difficulty which must be discussed. In the above model the stock of capital exists, so to speak, off stage. Rosa Luxemburg is perfectly well aware of the relationship between annual wear and tear of capital, which is part of c,

---

[10] See p. 106.
[11] Later it is assumed that real wages can be depressed by taxation (p. 435).
[12] See p. 88.

and the stock of fixed capital,[13] but as soon as she (following Marx) discusses accumulation she equates the addition to the stock of capital made by saving out of surplus in one year to the wear and tear of capital in the next year. To make sense of this we must assume that all capital is consumed and made good once a year. She seems to slip into this assumption inadvertently at first, though later it is made explicit.[14] She also consciously postulates that v represents the amount of capital which is paid out in wages in advance of receipts from sales of the commodities produced. (This, as she says, is the natural assumption to make for agricultural production, where workers this year are paid from the proceeds of last year's harvest.)[15] Thus v represents at the same time the annual wages bill and the amount of capital locked up in the wages fund, while c represents both the annual amortisation of capital and the total stock of capital (other than the wages fund). This is a simplification which is tiresome rather than helpful (it arises from Marx's ill-judged habit of writing $\dfrac{s}{c+v}$ for the rate of profit on capital), but it is no more than a simplification and does not invalidate the rest of the analysis.

Another awkward assumption, which causes serious trouble later, is implicit in the argument. Savings out of the surplus accruing in each department (producers' and consumers' goods) are always invested in capital in the same department. There is no reason to imagine that one capitalist is linked to others in his own department more than to those in the other department, so the conception seems to be that each capitalist invests his savings in his own business. There is no lending by one capitalist to another and no capitalist ever shifts his sphere of operations from one department to another. This is a severe assumption to make even about the era before limited liability was introduced, and becomes absurd afterwards. Moreover it is incompatible with the postulate that the rate of profit on capital tends to equality throughout the economy,[16] for the mechanism which equalises profits is the flow of

[13] See p. 57.
[14] See p. 335.
[15] See p. 49, note 1.
[16] See p. 51.

new investment, and the transfer of capital as amortisation funds are reinvested, into more profitable lines of production and away from less profitable lines.[17]

The assumption that there is no lending by one capitalist to another puts limitation upon the model. Not only must the total rate of investment be equal to the total of planned saving, but investment in each department must be equal to saving in that department, and not only must the rate of increase of capital lead to an increase of total output compatible with total demand, but the increase in output of each department, dictated by the increase in capital in that department, must be divided between consumers' and producers' goods in proportions compatible with the demand for each, dictated by the consumption and the investment plans in each department.

There is no difficulty, however, in choosing numbers which satisfy the requirements of the model. The numerical examples derived from Marx's jottings are cumbersome and confusing, but a clear and simple model can be constructed on the basis of the assumptions set out in chapter vii. In each department, constant capital is four times variable capital.[18] (Constant capital is the stock of raw materials which is turned over once a year; variable capital is the wages bill, which is equal to the capital represented by the wages fund.) Surplus is equal to variable capital (net income is divided equally between wages and surplus) and half of surplus is saved.[19] Savings are allotted between constant and variable capital in such a way as to preserve the 4 to 1 ratio. Thus

---

[17] In the numerical example quoted in chap. 6 (p. 90) the rate of profit is much higher in Department II than in I. Marx has made the rate of exploitation equal in the two departments, and the ratio of constant to variable capital higher in Department I. This is evidently an oversight. The two departments must trade with each other at market prices, not in terms of *value*. Therefore s_1 must represent the profits accruing to Department I, not a proportion (half in the example) of the *value* generated in Department I. $\frac{s_1}{v_1}$ should exceed $\frac{s_2}{v_2}$ to an extent corresponding to the higher organic composition of capital in Department I. The point is interesting, as it shows that when off guard Marx forgot that he could make prices proportional to *values* only when the organic composition of capital is the same in all industries.

[18] See p. 102.

[19] See p. 103.

four-fifths of savings represents a demand for producers' goods, and is added to constant capital each year, and one-fifth represents a demand for consumers' goods, and is added to the wages fund (variable capital). These ratios dictate the relationship between Department I (producers' goods) and Department II (consumer's goods).[20] It can easily be seen that the basic assumptions require that the output of Department I must stand in the ratio of 11 to 4 to the output of Department II.[21] We can now construct a much simpler model than those provided in the text.

	c	v	s	Gross Output
Department I	44	11	11	66
Department II	16	4	4	24
			Total	90

In Department I, 5.5 units are saved (half of s) of which 4.4 are invested in constant capital and 1.1 in variable capital. In Department II 2 units are saved, 1.6 being added to constant and 0.4 to variable capital. The 66 units of producers' goods provide 44 + 4.4 constant capital for Department I and 16 + 1.6 constant capital for Department II and the 24 units of consumers' goods provide 11 + 4 wages of labour already employed, 5.5 + 2 for consumption out of surplus, and 1.1 + 0.4 addition to variable capital, which provide for an addition to employment.

After the investment has been made, and the labour force increased in proportion to the wages bill, we have

	c	v	s	Gross Output
Department I	48.4	12.1	12.1	72.6
Department II	17.6	4.4	4.4	26.4
			Total	99

[20] Since, in this model, the organic composition of capital is the same in the two departments, prices correspond to *values*.

[21] Of total gross output, $\frac{2}{3}$ is replacement of constant capital; surplus is $\frac{1}{6}$ of gross output, and of surplus half is saved; thus savings are $\frac{1}{12}$ of gross output; of saving $\frac{4}{5}$ is added to constant capital; thus $\frac{1}{15}$ of gross output is added to constant capital. The output of Department I is therefore $\frac{2}{3} + \frac{1}{15}$ or $\frac{11}{15}$ of total gross output. Similarly, the output of Department II is $\frac{4}{15}$ of total gross output.

The two departments are now equipped to carry out another round of investment at the prescribed rate, and the process of accumulation continues. The ratios happen to have been chosen so that the total labour force, and total gross output, increase by 10 per cent per annum.[22]

But all this, as Rosa Luxemburg remarks, is just arithmetic.[23] The only point of substance which she deduces from Marx's numerical examples is that it is always Department I which takes the initiative. She maintains that the capitalists in Department I decide how much producers' goods to produce, and that Department II has to arrange its affairs so as to absorb an amount of producers' goods which will fit in with their plans.[24] On the face of it, this is obviously absurd. The arithmetic is perfectly neutral between the two departments, and, as she herself shows, will serve equally well for the imagined case of a socialist society where investment is planned with a view to consumption.[25]

But behind all this rigmarole lies the real problem which she is trying to formulate. Where does the demand come from which keeps accumulation going?

She is not concerned with the problem, nowadays so familiar, of the balance between saving and investment. Marx himself was aware of that problem, as is seen in his analysis of disequilibrium under conditions of simple reproduction (zero net investment).[26] When new fixed capital comes into existence, part of gross receipts are set aside in amortisation funds without any actual outlay being made on renewals. Then total demand falls short of equilibrium output, and the system runs into a slump. Contrariwise, when a burst of renewals falls due, in excess of the current rate of amortisation, a boom sets in. For equilibrium it is necessary for the age composition of the stock of capital to be such that current renewals just absorb current amortisation funds. Similarly, when accumulation is taking place, current investment must absorb current net saving.[27]

---

[22] This model bears a strong family resemblance to Mr. Harrod's 'Warranted rate of growth'. *Towards a Dynamic Economics*, lecture III.

[23] See p. 91.

[24] See p. 97.

[25] See p. 100.

[26] See p. 63.

[27] See p. 87.

It is in connection with the problem of effective demand, in this sense, that Marx brings gold-mining into the analysis. When real output expands at constant money prices, the increasing total of money value of output requires an increase in the stook of money in circulation (unless the velocity of circulation rises appropriately). The capitalists therefore have to devote part of their savings to increasing their holdings of cash (for there is no borrowing). This causes a deficiency of effective demand. But the increase in the quantity of money in circulation comes from newly mined gold, and the expenditure of the gold mining industry upon the other departments just makes up the deficiency in demand.[28]

Rosa Luxemburg garbles this argument considerably, and brushes it away as beside the point. And it is beside the point that she is concerned with. She does not admit the savings and investment problem, for she takes it for granted that each individual act of saving out of surplus is accompanied by a corresponding amount of real investment, and that every piece of investment is financed by saving out of surplus of the same capitalist who makes it.[29] What she appears to be concerned with is rather the inducement to invest. What motive have the capitalists for enlarging their stock of real capital?[30] How do they know that there will be demand for the increased output of goods which the new capital will produce, so that they can 'capitalise' their surplus in a profitable form? (On the purely analytical plane her affinity seems to be with Hobson rather than Keynes.)

Needless to say, our author does not formulate the problem of the inducement to invest in modern terminology, and the ambiguities and contradictions in her exposition have left ample scope for her critics to represent her theory as irredeemable nonsense.[31] But the most natural way to read it is also the clearest. Investment can take place in an ever-accumulating stock of capital only if the capitalists are assured of an

---

[28] See p. 74. The phrase '*zahlungsfähige nachfrage*', translated 'effective demand', is not the effective demand of Keynes (roughly, current expenditure) but appears often to mean demand for new capital, or, perhaps, prospective future demand for goods to be produced by new capital.

[29] This assumption is made explicit later (p. 322).

[30] See pp. 103 et seq.

[31] See Sweezy, loc. cit.

ever-expanding market for the goods which the capital will produce. On this reading, the statement of the problem leads straightforwardly to the solution propounded in the third Section of this book.

Marx has his own answer to the problem of inducement to invest, which she refers to in the first chapter.[32] The pressure of competition forces each individual capitalist to increase his capital in order to take advantage of economies of large-scale production, for if he does not his rivals will, and he will be undersold. Rosa Luxemburg does not discuss whether this mechanism provides an adequate drive to keep accumulation going, but looks for some prospective demand outside the circle of production. Here the numerical examples, as she shows, fail to help. And this is in the nature of the case, for (in modern jargon) the examples deal with *ex post* quantities, while she is looking for *ex ante* prospects of increased demand for commodities. If accumulation does take place, demand will absorb output, as the model shows, but what is it that makes accumulation take place?

In Section II our author sets out to find what answers have been given to her problem. The analysis she has in mind is now broader than the strict confines of the arithmetical model. Technical progress is going on, and the output of an hour's labour rises as time goes by. (The concept of *value* now becomes treacherous, for the *value* of commodities is continuously falling.) Real wages tend to be constant in terms of commodities, thus the *value* of labour power is falling, and the share of surplus in net income is rising ($\frac{s}{v}$, the rate of exploitation, is rising).

The amount of saving in real terms is therefore rising (she suggests later that the proportion of surplus saved rises with surplus, in which case real savings increase all the more[33]). The problem is thus more formidable than appears in the model, for the equilibrium rate of accumulation of capital, in real terms, is greater than in the model, where the rate of exploitation is constant. At the same time the proportion of constant to variable capital is rising. She regards this not as something which is likely to happen for technical reasons, but as being necessarily bound up with the very nature of technical progress. As

[32] See p. 12.
[33] See p. 282.

productivity increases, the amount of producers' goods handled per man-hour of labour increases; therefore, she says, the proportion of c to v must increase.[34] This is an error. It arises from thinking of constant capital in terms of goods, and contrasting it with variable capital in terms of *value*, that is, hours of labour. She forgets Marx's warning that, as progress takes place, the *value* of the commodities making up constant capital also falls.[35] It is perfectly possible for productivity to increase without any increase in the *value* of capital per man employed. This would occur if improvements in the productivity of labour in making producers' goods kept pace with the productivity of labour in using producers' goods to make consumers' goods (capital-saving inventions balance labour-saving inventions, so that technical progress is 'neutral'). However, we can easily get out of this difficulty by postulating that as a matter of fact technical progress is mainly labour-saving, or, a better term, capital-using, so that capital per man employed is rising through time.

Rosa Luxemburg treats the authors whom she examines in Section II with a good deal of sarcasm, and dismisses them all as useless. To some of the points raised her answers seem scarcely adequate. For instance, Rodbertus sees the source of all the troubles of capitalism in the falling proportion of wages in national income.[36] He can be interpreted to refer to the proportion of wages in gross income. In that case, she is right (on the assumption of capital-using inventions) in arguing that a fall in the proportion of wages is bound up with technical progress, and that the proportion could be held constant only by stopping progress. He can also be taken to refer to the share of wages in net output, and this is the more natural reading. On this reading she argues that the fall in share of wages (or rise in rate of exploitation) is necessary to prevent a fall in the rate of profit on capital[37] (as capital per man employed rises, profit per man employed must rise if profit per unit of capital is constant). But she does not follow up the argument and

---

[34] See p. 234.

[35] This point is, however, later admitted (p. 317).

[36] See p. 228.

[37] See p. 235. Marx himself failed to get this point clear. Cf. my *Essay on Marxian Economics*, chap. v.

inquire what rise in the rate of exploitation is necessary to keep capitalism going (actually, the statisticians tell us, the share of wages in net income has been fairly constant in modern industrial economies[38]). It is obvious that the less the rate of exploitation rises, the smaller is the rise in the rate of saving which the system has to digest, while the rise in real consumption by workers, which takes place when the rate of exploitation rises more slowly than productivity in the consumption good industries, creates an outlet for investment in productive capacity in those industries. The horrors of capitalism, and the difficulties which it creates for itself, are both exaggerated by the assumption of constant real-wage rates and, although it would be impossible to defend Rodbertus' position that a constant rate of exploitation is all that is needed to put everything right, he certainly makes a contribution to the argument which ought to be taken into account.

Tugan-Baranovski also seems to be treated too lightly. His conception is that the rising proportion of constant capital in both departments (machines to make machines as well as machines to make consumers' goods) provides an outlet for accumulation, and that competition is the driving force which keeps capitalists accumulating. Rosa Luxemburg is no doubt correct in saying that his argument does not carry the analysis beyond the stage at which Marx left it,[39] but he certainly elaborates a point which she seems perversely to overlook. Her real objection to Tugan-Baranovski is that he shows how, in certain conditions, capitalist accumulation might be self-perpetuating, while she wishes to establish that the coming disintegration of the capitalist system is not merely probable on the evidence, but is a logical necessity.[40]

The authors such as Sismondi, Malthus and Vorontsov, who are groping after the problem of equilibrium between saving and investment, are treated with even less sympathy (though she has a kindly feeling for

---

[38] Cf. Kalecki, *Essays in the Theory of Economic Fluctuations*, pp. 14 et seq.

[39] See p. 302.

[40] See p. 293. Marx did not find himself in this dilemma because he held that there is a fundamental 'contradiction' in capitalism which shows itself in a strong tendency for the rate of profit on capital to fall as technical progress takes place. But Rosa Luxemburg sees that the tendency to a falling rate of profit is automatically checked and may even be reversed if real-wage rates are constant (p. 318).

Sismondi, to whom she considers that Marx gave too little recognition[41]) for she is either oblivious that there is such a problem, or regards it as trivial.[42] We leave the discussion, at the end of Section II, at the same point where we entered it, with the clue to the inducement to invest still to find.

Section III is broader, more vigorous and in general more rewarding than the two preceding parts. It opens with a return to Marx's model for a capitalist system with accumulation going on. Our author then sets out a fresh model allowing for technical progress. The rate of exploitation (the ratio of surplus to wages) is rising, for real wages remain constant while output per man increases. In the model the proportion of surplus saved is assumed constant for simplicity, though in reality, she holds, it would tend to rise with the real income of the capitalists.[43] The ratio of constant to variable capital is rising for technical reasons. (The convention by which the annual wear and tear of capital is identified with the stock of capital now becomes a great impediment to clear thinking.) The arithmetical model shows the system running into an *impasse* because the output of Department I falls short of the requirements of constant capital in the two departments taken together, while the output of Department II exceeds consumption.[44] The method of argument is by no means rigorous. Nothing follows from the fact that one particular numerical example fails to give a solution, and the example is troublesome to interpret as it is necessary to distinguish between discrepancies due to rounding off the figures from those which are intended to illustrate a point of principle.[45] But there is no need to paddle in the arithmetic to find where the difficulty lies. The model is over-determined because of the rule that the increment of capital within each department at the end of a year must equal the saving made within the same department during the year. If capitalists from Department II were permitted to lend part of

[41] See p. 192, note 12.

[42] One passage suggests that she sees the problem, but thinks it irrelevant to the real issue (p. 322).

[43] See p. 318.

[44] See p. 317.

[45] In this model the rate of exploitation is different in the two departments. This means that the numbers represent money value, not *value*.

their savings to Department I to be invested in its capital, a breakdown would no longer be inevitable. Suppose that total real wages are constant and that real consumption by capitalists increases slowly, so that the real output of Department II rises at a slower rate than productivity, then the amount of labour employed in it is shrinking. The ratio of capital to labour however is rising as a consequence of capital-using technical progress. The output of Department I, and its productive capacity, is growing through time. Capital invested in Department I is accumulating faster than the saving of the capitalists in Department I, and capitalists of Department II, who have no profitable outlet in their own industries for their savings, acquire titles to part of the capital in Department I by supplying the difference between investment in Department I and its own saving.[46] For any increase in the stock of capital of both departments taken together, required by technical progress and demand conditions, there is an appropriate amount of saving, and so long as the total accumulation required and total saving fit, there is no breakdown.

But here we find the clue to the real contradiction. These quantities might conceivably fit, but there is no guarantee that they will. If the ratio of saving which the capitalists (taken together) choose to make exceeds the rate of accumulation dictated by technical progress, the excess savings can only be 'capitalised' if there is an outlet for investment outside the system. (The opposite case of deficient savings is also possible. Progress would then be slowed down below the technically possible maximum; but this case is not contemplated by our author, and it would be irrelevant to elaborate upon it.)

Once more we can substitute for a supposed logical necessity a plausible hypothesis about the nature of the real case, and so rescue the succeeding argument. If in reality the distribution of income between workers and capitalists, and the propensity to save of capitalists, are such as to require a rate of accumulation which exceeds the rate of increase in the stock of capital appropriate to technical conditions, then there is a chronic excess of the potential supply of real capital over the demand for it and the system must fall into chronic depression.

---

[46] Rosa Luxemburg seems to regard this process as impossible, but for what reason is by no means clear (p. 321).

(This is the 'stagnation thesis' thrown out by Keynes and elaborated by modern American economists, notably Alvin Hansen). How then is it that capitalist expansion had not yet (in 1912) shown any sign of slackening?

In chapter xxvi Rosa Luxemburg advances her central thesis—that it is the invasion of primitive economies by capitalism which keeps the system alive. There follows a scorching account of the manner in which the capitalist system, by trade, conquest and theft, swallowed up the pre-capitalist economies,—some reduced to colonies of capitalist nations, some remaining nominally independent—and fed itself upon their ruins. The thread of analysis running through the historical illustrations is not easy to pick up, but the main argument seems to be as follows: As soon as a primitive closed economy has been broken into, by force or guile, cheap mass-produced consumption goods displace the old hand production of the family or village communities, so that a market is provided for ever-increasing outputs from the industries of Department II in the old centres of capitalism, without the standard of life of the workers who consume these commodities being raised.[47] The ever-growing capacity of the export industries requires the products of Department I, thus maintaining investment at home. At the same time great capital works, such as railways, are undertaken in the new territories.[48] This investment is matched partly by savings from surplus extracted on the spot, but mainly by loans from the old capitalist countries. There is no difficulty here in accounting for the inducement to invest, for the new territories yield commodities unobtainable at home.[49] We might set out the essence of the argument as follows: Cloth from Lancashire pays for labour in America, which is used to produce wheat and cotton. These provide wages and raw materials to the Lancashire mills, while the profits acquired both on the plantations and in the mills are invested in steel rails and rolling stock, which open up fresh territories, so that the whole process is continuously expanding. Moreover, apart from profits earned on capital actually invested in the new territories, great capital gains are made simply by acquiring

[47] See p. 332.
[48] See p. 332.
[49] See p. 338.

possession of land and other natural resources.[50] Labour to work the resources may be provided by the local dispossessed peasantry or by immigration from the centres of capitalism.[51] Investment in equipment for it to use is more profitable than in that operated by home labour, partly because the wretched condition of the colonial workers makes the rate of exploitation higher,[52] but mainly just because they are on the spot, and can turn the natural resources seized by the capitalists into means of production. No amount of investment in equipment for British labour would produce soil bearing cotton, rubber or copper. Thus investment is deflected abroad[53] and the promise of profit represented by the natural resources calls into existence, by fair means or foul, the labour and capital to make it come true. The process of building up this capital provides an outlet for the old industries and rescues them from the contradictions inherent in deficiency of demand.

The analysis of militarism in the last chapter over-reaches itself by trying to prove too much. The argument is that armaments are built up out of taxes which fall entirely on wages.[54] This can be regarded as a kind of 'forced saving' imposed on the workers. These savings are extra to the saving out of surplus. They are invested in armaments, and that ends the story. On this basis the armaments, in themselves, cannot be held to provide an outlet for the investment of surplus (though the use of the armaments, as in the Opium War,[55] to break up primitive economies is a necessary condition for the colonial investment already described) and capital equipment to produce armaments is merely substituted for capital formerly producing consumers' goods. The analysis which best fits Rosa Luxemburg's own argument, and the facts, is that armaments provide an outlet for the investment of surplus (over and above any contribution there may be from forced saving out of wages), which, unlike other kinds of investment, creates no further problem by increasing productive capacity (not to mention the huge new investment opportunities created by reconstruction

[50] See p. 350.
[51] See p. 408.
[52] See p. 415.
[53] See p. 401.
[54] See p. 437.
[55] See p. 367.

after the capitalist nations have turned their weapons against each other).

All this is perhaps too neat an account of what our author is saying. The argument streams along bearing a welter of historical examples in its flood, and ideas emerge and disappear again bewilderingly. But something like the above seems to be intended. And something like it is now widely accepted as being true. Rosa Luxemburg, as we have seen, neglects the rise in real wages which takes place as capitalism develops, and denies the internal inducement to invest provided by technical progress, two factors which help to rescue capitalism from the difficulties which it creates for itself. She is left with only one influence (economic imperialism) to account for continuous capital accumulation, so that her analysis is incomplete. All the same, few would deny that the extension of capitalism into new territories was the mainspring of what an academic economist has called the 'vast secular boom' of the last two hundred years,[56] and many academic economists account for the uneasy condition of capitalism in the twentieth century largely by the 'closing of the frontier' all over the world.[57] But the academic economists are being wise after the event. For all its confusions and exaggerations, this book shows more prescience than any orthodox contemporary could claim.

JOAN ROBINSON

Cambridge.

---

[56] Hicks, *Value and Capital*, p. 302, note. Mr. Hicks himself, however, regards the increase in population as the mainspring.

[57] Cf. *A Survey of Contemporary Economics* (ed. Ellis), p. 63.

Section I

The Problem of Reproduction

1

THE OBJECT OF
OUR INVESTIGATION

Karl Marx made a contribution of lasting service to the theory of economics when he drew attention to the problem of the reproduction of the entire social capital. It is significant that in the history of economics we find only two attempts at an exact exposition of this problem: one by Quesney, the father of the Physiocrats, at its very inception; and in its final stage this attempt by Marx. In the interim, the problem was ever with bourgeois economics. Yet bourgeois economists have never been fully aware of this problem in its pure aspects, detached from related and intersecting minor problems; they have never been able to formulate it precisely, let alone solve it. Seeing that the problem is of paramount importance, their attempts may all the same help us to some understanding of the trend of scientific economics.

What is it precisely that constitutes this problem of the reproduction of total capital? The literal meaning of the word 'reproduction' is repetition, renewal of the process of production. At first sight it may be difficult to see in what respect the idea of reproduction differs from that of repetition which we can all understand—why such a new and unfamiliar term should be required. But in the sort of repetition which we shall consider, in the continual recurrence of the process of production, there are certain distinctive features. First, the regular repetition of reproduction is the general *sine qua non* of regular consumption which in its turn has been the precondition of human civilisation in every one of its historical forms. The concept of reproduction, viewed in this way, reflects an aspect of the history of civilisation. Production can never be resumed, there can be no reproduction, unless certain prerequisites such as tools, raw materials and labour have been established during the preceding period of production. However, at the most primitive level of man's civilisation, at the initial stage of man's power over nature, this possibility to re-engage in production depended more or less on chance. So long as hunting and fishing were the main foundations of social existence, frequent periods of general starvation interrupted the regular repetition of production. Some primitive peoples recognised at a very early stage that for reproduction as a regularly recurring process certain measures were essential; these they incorporated into ceremonies of a religious nature; and in this way they accepted such measures as traditional social commitments. Thus, as the thorough researches of Spencer and Gillen have taught us, the totem cult of the Australian negroes is fundamentally nothing but certain measures taken by social groups for the purpose of securing and preserving their animal and vegetable foodstuffs; these precautions had been taken year by year since time immemorial and thus they became fossilised into religious ceremonials. Yet the circle of consumption and production which forms the essence of reproduction became possible only with the invention of tillage with the hoe, with the taming of domestic animals, and with cattle-raising for the purpose of consumption. Reproduction is something more than mere repetition in so far as it presupposes a certain level of society's supremacy over nature, or, in economic terms, a certain standard of labour productivity.

On the other hand, at all stages of social development, the process of production is based on the continuation of two different, though closely connected factors, the technical and social conditions—on the precise relationship between man and nature and that between men and men. Reproduction depends to the same degree on both these conditions. We have just seen how reproduction is bound up with the conditions of human working techniques, how far it is indeed solely the result of a certain level of labour productivity; but the social forms of production prevailing in each case are no less decisive. In a primitive communist agrarian community, reproduction as well as the whole plan of economic life is determined by the community of all workers and their democratic organs. The decision to re-engage in labour—the organisation of labour—the provision of raw materials, tools, and man-power as the essential preliminaries of labour—the arrangement of reproduction and the determination of its volume are all results of a planned co-operation in which everybody within the boundaries of the community takes his part. In an economic system based on slave labour or *corvée*, reproduction is enforced and regulated in all details by personal relations of domination. Here the volume of reproduction is determined by the right of disposal held by the ruling *élites* over smaller or larger circles of other people's labour. In a society producing by capitalist methods, reproduction assumes a peculiar form, as a mere glance at certain striking phenomena will show us. In every other society known to history, reproduction recurs in a regular sequence as far as its preconditions, the existing means of production and labour power, make this possible. As a rule, only external influences such as a devastating war or a great pestilence, depopulating vast areas of former cultural life, and consequently destroying masses of labour power and of accumulated means of production, can result in a complete interruption of reproduction or in its contraction to any considerable extent for longer or shorter periods. A despotic organisation of the plan of production may on occasion lead to similar phenomena. When in ancient Egypt Pharaoh's will chained thousands of fellaheen for decades to the building of the pyramids; when in modern Egypt Ismail Pasha ordered 20,000 fellaheen to forced labour on the Suez Canal; or when, about two hundred years before Christ, the Emperor Shi Hoang Ti, founder of the Chin dynasty, allowed 400,000 people to perish of hunger and exhaustion and thus sacrificed a whole generation to his purpose of consolidating the Great Wall at China's northern frontier, the result was always that vast stretches of arable land were left fallow and that regular economic life was interrupted for long periods. In all these cases the causes of these interruptions of reproduction obviously lay in the one-sided determination of the plan of reproduction by those in power.

Societies which produce according to capitalist methods present a different picture. We observe that in certain periods all the ingredients of reproduction may be available, both labour and means of production, and yet some vital needs of society for consumer goods may be left unfulfilled. We find that in spite of these resources reproduction may in part be completely suspended and in part curtailed. Here it is no despotic interference with the economic plan that is responsible for the difficulties in the process of production. Quite apart from all technical conditions, reproduction here depends on purely social considerations: only those goods are produced which can with certainty be expected to sell, and not merely to sell, but to sell at the customary profit. Thus profit becomes an end in itself, the decisive factor which determines not only production but also reproduction. Not only does it decide in each case what work is to be undertaken, how it is to be carried out, and how the products are to be distributed; what is more, profit decides, also, at the end of every working period, whether the labour process is to be resumed, and, if so, to what extent and in what direction it should be made to operate.[1]

In capitalist society, therefore, the process of reproduction as a whole, constitutes a peculiar and most complicated problem, in consequence of these purely historical and social factors. There is, as we shall see, an external characteristic which shows clearly this specific historical peculiarity of the capitalist process of reproduction. Comprising not only production but also circulation (the process of exchange), it unites these two elements. Capitalist production is primarily production by innumerable private producers without any planned regulation. The only social link between these producers is the act of exchange. In taking account of social requirements reproduction has no clue to go on other than the experiences of the preceding labour period. These experiences, however, remain the private experiences of individual producers and are not integrated into a comprehensive and social form. Moreover, they do not always refer positively and directly to the needs of society. They are often rather indirect and negative, for it is only on the basis of price fluctuations that they indicate whether the aggregate of produced commodities falls short of the effective demand or exceeds it. Yet the individual private producers make recurrent use of

[1] 'If production be capitalistic in form, so, too, will be reproduction' (*Capital*, vol. i, p. 578).

these experiences of the preceding labour period when they re-engage in reproduction, so that glut or shortage are bound to occur again in the following period. Individual branches of production may develop independently, so that there may be a surplus in one branch and a deficiency in another. But as nearly all individual branches of production are interdependent technically, glut or shortage in some of the larger branches of production lead to the same phenomenon in most of the others. Thus the general supply of products may alternate periodically between shortage and surplus relative to the social demand.

Herein lies the peculiar character of reproduction in a capitalist society, which differs from all other known forms of production. In the first place, every branch of production develops independently within certain limits, in a way that leads to periodical interruptions of production of shorter or longer duration. Secondly, the individual branches of reproduction show deviations from social requirements amounting to all-round disparity and thus resulting in a general interruption of reproduction. These features of capitalist reproduction are quite characteristic. In all other economic systems, reproduction runs its uninterrupted and regular course, apart from external disturbance by violence. Capitalist reproduction, however, to quote Sismondi's well-known dictum, can only be represented as a continuous sequence of individual spirals. Every such spiral starts with small loops which become increasingly larger and eventually very large indeed. Then they contract, and a new spiral starts again with small loops, repeating the figure up to the point of interruption. This periodical fluctuation between the largest volume of reproduction and its contraction to partial suspension, this cycle of slump, boom, and crisis, as it has been called, is the most striking peculiarity of capitalist reproduction.

It is very important, however, to establish quite firmly and from the very outset that this cyclical movement of boom, slump, and crisis, does not represent the whole problem of capitalist reproduction, although it is an essential element of it. Periodical cycles and crises are specific phases of reproduction in a capitalist system of economy, but not the whole of this process. In order to demonstrate the pure implications of capitalist reproduction we must rather consider it quite apart from the periodical cycles and crises. Strange as this may appear, the method is quite rational; it is indeed the only method of inquiry that is scientifically tenable. In order to demonstrate and to solve the problem of pure value we must leave price fluctuations out of consideration. The approach of vulgar economics always attempts to solve the problem of value by reference to fluctuations in demand and supply. Classical economists, from Adam Smith to Karl Marx, attack the problem in the opposite way, pointing out that fluctuations in the mutual relation between demand and supply can explain only disparities between price and value, not value itself. In order to find the value of a commodity, we must start by assuming that demand and supply are in a state of equilibrium, that the price of a commodity and its value closely correspond to one another. Thus the scientific problem of value begins at the very point where the effect of demand and supply ceases to operate.

In consequence of periodical cycles and crises capitalist reproduction fluctuates as a rule around the level of the effective total demand of society, sometimes rising above and sometimes falling below this level, contracting occasionally even to the point of almost complete interruption of reproduction. However, if we consider a longer period, a whole cycle with its alternating phases of prosperity and depression, of boom and slump, that is if we consider reproduction at its highest and lowest volume, including the stage of suspension, we can set off boom against slump and work out an average, a mean volume of reproduction for the whole cycle. This average is not only a theoretical figment of thought, it is also a real objective fact. For in spite of the sharp rises and falls in the course of a cycle, in spite of crises, the needs of society are always satisfied more or less, reproduction continues on its complicated course, and productive capacities develop progressively. How can this take place, leaving cycles and crises out of consideration? Here the real question begins. The attempt to solve the problem of reproduction in terms of the periodical character of crises is fundamentally a device of vulgar economics, just like the attempt to solve the problem of value in terms of fluctuations in demand and supply. Nevertheless, we shall see in the course of our observations that as soon as economic theory gets an inkling of the problem of reproduction, as soon as it has at least started guessing at the problem, it reveals a persistent tendency suddenly to transform the problem of reproduction into the problem of crises, thus barring its own way to the solution of the question. When we speak of capitalist reproduction in the following exposition, we shall always understand by this term a mean volume of productivity which is an average taken over the various phases of a cycle.

Now, the total of capitalist reproduction is created by an unlimited and constantly changing number of private producers. They produce independently of one another; apart from the observation of price fluctuations there is no social control—no social link exists between the individual producers other than the exchange of commodities. The question arises how these innumerable disconnected operations can lead to the actual total of production. This general aspect of our problem indeed strikes us immediately as one of prime importance. But if we put it this way, we overlook the fact that such private producers are not simply producers of commodities but are essentially capitalist producers, that the total production of society is not simply production for the sake of satisfying social requirements, and equally not merely production of commodities, but essentially capitalist production.

Let us examine our problem anew in the light of this fact. A producer who produces not only commodities but capital must above all create surplus value. The capitalist producer's final goal, his main incentive, is the production of surplus value. The proceeds from the commodities he has manufactured must not only recompense him for all his outlay, but in addition they must yield him a value which does not correspond with any expense on his part, and is pure gain. If we consider the process of production from the point of view of the creation of surplus value, we see that the capital advanced by the capitalist is divided into two parts: the first part represents his expenses on means of production such as premises, raw material, partly finished goods and machinery. The second part is spent on wages. This holds good, even if the capitalist producer does not know it himself, and in spite of the pious stuff about fixed and circulating capital with which he may delude himself and the world. Marx called this first part constant capital. Its value is not changed by its utilisation in the labour process—it is transferred in toto to the finished product. The second part Marx calls the variable capital. This gives rise to an additional value, which materialises when the results of unpaid labour are appropriated. The various components which make up the value of every commodity produced by capitalist methods may be expressed by the formula: $c + v + s$. In this formula c stands for the value of the constant capital laid out in inanimate means of production and transferred to the commodity, v stands for the value of the variable capital advanced in form of wages, and s stands for the surplus value, the additional value of the unpaid part of wage labour. Every type of goods shows these three components of value, whether we consider an individual commodity or the aggregate of commodities as a whole, whether we consider cotton textiles or ballet performances, cast-iron tubes or liberal newspapers. Thus for the capitalist producer the manufacture of commodities is not an end in itself, it is only a means to the appropriation of surplus value. This surplus value, however, can be of no use to the capitalist so long as it remains hidden in the commodity form of the product. Once the commodity has been produced, it must be realised, it must be converted into a form of pure value; that is, into money. All capital expenses incorporated in the commodity must shed their commodity-form and revert to the capitalist as money to make this conversion possible so that he can appropriate the surplus value in cash. The purpose of production is fulfilled only when this conversion has been successful, only when the aggregate of commodities has been sold according to its value. The proceeds of this sale of commodities, the money that has been received for them, contains the same components of value as the former aggregate of commodities and can be expressed by the same formula $c + v + s$. Part c recompenses the capitalist for his advances on means of production that have been used up, part v recompenses him for his advances on wages, and the last part, s, represents the expected surplus, the capitalist's clear profit in cash.[2]

This conversion of capital from its original form, from the starting point of all capitalist production, into means of production, dead and living, such as raw materials, instruments, and labour; its further conversion into commodities by a living labour process; and its final reconversion into money, a greater amount of money indeed than at the initial stage—this transformation of capital is, however, required for more than the production and appropriation of surplus value. The

[2] Surplus value in our exposition is identical with profit. This is true for production as a whole, which alone is of account in our further observations. For the time being, we shall not deal with the further division of surplus value into its component parts: profit of enterprise, interest, and rent, as this subdivision is immaterial to the problem of reproduction.

aim and incentive of capitalist production is not a surplus value pure and simple, to be appropriated in any desired quantity, but a surplus value ever growing into larger quantities, surplus value *ad infinitum*. But to achieve this aim, the same magic means must be used over and over again, the means of capitalist production—the ever repeated appropriation of the proceeds of unpaid wage labour in the process of commodity manufacture, and the subsequent realisation of the commodities so produced.

Thus quite a new incentive is given to constantly renewed production, to the process of reproduction as a regular phenomenon in capitalist society, an incentive unknown to any other system of production. In every other economic system known to history, reproduction is determined by the unceasing need of society for consumer goods, whether they are the needs of all the workers determined in a democratic manner as in an agrarian and communist market community, or the despotically determined needs of an antagonistic class society, as in an economy of slave labour or *corvée* and the like. But in a capitalist system of production, it is not consideration of social needs which actuates the individual private producer who alone matters in this connection. His production is determined entirely by the effective demand, and even this is to him a mere means for the realisation of surplus value which for him is indispensable. Appropriation of surplus value is his real incentive, and production of consumer goods for the satisfaction of the effective demand is only a detour when we look to the real motive, that of appropriation of surplus value, although for the individual capitalist it is also a rule of necessity. This motive, to appropriate surplus value, also urges him to re-engage in reproduction over and over again. It is the production of surplus value which turns reproduction of social necessities into a *perpetuum mobile*. Reproduction, for its part, can obviously be only resumed when the products of the previous period, the commodities, have been realised; that is, converted into money; for capital in the form of money, in the form of pure value, must always be the starting point of reproduction in a capitalist system. The first condition of reproduction for the capitalist producer is thus seen to be a successful realisation of the commodities produced during the preceding period of production.

Now we come to a second important point. Under a system of

private economy, it is the individual producer who determines the volume of reproduction at his discretion. His main incentive is appropriation of surplus value, indeed an appropriation increasing as rapidly as possible. An accelerated appropriation of surplus value, however, necessitates an increased production of capital to generate this surplus value. Here a large-scale enterprise enjoys advantages over a small one in every respect. In fine, the capitalist method of production furnishes not only a permanent incentive to reproduction in general, but also a motive for its expansion, for reproduction on an ever larger scale.

Nor is that all. Capitalist methods of production do more than awaken in the capitalist this thirst for surplus value whereby he is impelled to ceaseless expansion of reproduction. Expansion becomes in truth a coercive law, an economic condition of existence for the individual capitalist. Under the rule of competition, cheapness of commodities is the most important weapon of the individual capitalist in his struggle for a place in the market. Now all methods of reducing the cost of commodity production permanently amount in the end to an expansion of production; excepting those only which aim at a specific increase of the rate of surplus value by measures such as wage-cutting or lengthening the hours of work. As for these latter devices, they are as such likely to encounter many obstacles. In this respect, a large enterprise invariably enjoys advantages of every kind over a small or medium concern. They may range from a saving in premises or instruments, in the application of more efficient means of production, in extensive replacement of manual labour by machinery, down to a speedy exploitation of a favourable turn of the market so as to acquire raw materials cheaply. Within very wide limits, these advantages increase in direct proportion to the expansion of the enterprise. Thus, as soon as a few capitalist enterprises have been enlarged, competition itself forces all others to expand likewise. Expansion becomes a condition of existence. A growing tendency towards reproduction at a progressively increasing scale thus ensues, which spreads automatically like a tidal wave over ever larger surfaces of reproduction.

Expanding reproduction is not a new discovery of capital. On the contrary, it had been the rule since time immemorial in every form of society that displayed economic and cultural progress. It is true, of course, that simple reproduction as a mere continuous repetition of the process of production on the same scale as before can be observed over long periods of social history. In the ancient agrarian and communist village communities, for instance, increase in population did not lead to a gradual expansion of production, but rather to the new generation being expelled and the subsequent founding of equally small and self-sufficient colonies. The old small handicraft units of India and China provide similar instances of a traditional repetition of production in the same forms and on the same scale, handed down from generation to generation. But simple reproduction is in all these cases the source and unmistakable sign of a general economic and cultural stagnation. No important forward step in production, no memorial of civilisation, such as the great waterworks of the East, the pyramids of Egypt, the military roads of Rome, the Arts and Sciences of Greece, or the development of craftsmanship and towns in the Middle Ages would have been possible without expanding reproduction; for the basis and also the social incentive for a decisive advancement of civilisation lies solely in the gradual expansion of production beyond immediate requirements, and in a continual growth of the population itself as well as of its demands.

Exchange in particular, which brought about a class society, and its historical development into the capitalist form of economy, would have been unthinkable without expanding reproduction. In a capitalist society, moreover, expanding reproduction acquires certain characteristics. As we have already mentioned, it becomes right away a coercive law to the individual capitalist. Capitalist methods of production do not exclude simple or even retrogressive reproduction; indeed, this is responsible for the periodical phenomenon of crises following phases, likewise periodical, of overstrained expansion of reproduction in times of boom. But ignoring periodical fluctuations, the general trend of reproduction is ever towards expansion. For the individual capitalist, failure to keep abreast of this expansion means quitting the competitive struggle, economic death.

Moreover, there are certain other aspects to be considered. The concept of expanding reproduction applies only to the quantity of products, to the aggregate of manufactured objects. So long as production rests solely or mainly upon a natural economy, consumption determines the extent and character of the individual labour process, as well as that of reproduction in general, as an end in itself: this applies to the agrarian and communist village communities of India, to the Roman *villa* with its economy of slave labour, and to the medieval feudal farm based on *corvée*. But the picture is different in a capitalist economic system. Capitalist production is not production for the purpose of consumption, it is production for the purpose of creating value. The whole process of production as well as of reproduction is ruled by value relationships. Capitalist production is not the production of consumer goods, nor is it merely the production of commodities: it is pre-eminently the production of surplus value. Expanding reproduction, from a capitalist point of view, is expanding production of surplus value, though it takes place in the forms of commodity production and is thus in the last instance the production of consumer goods. Changes in the productivity of labour during the course of reproduction cause continual discrepancies between these two aspects. If productivity increases, the same amount of capital and surplus value may represent a progressively larger amount of consumer goods. Expanding production, understood as the creation of a greater amount of surplus value, need not therefore necessarily imply expanding reproduction in the capitalist meaning of the term. Conversely, capital may, within limits, yield a greater surplus value in consequence of a higher degree of exploitation such as is brought about by wage-cutting and the like, without actually producing a greater amount of goods. But in both cases the surplus value has a twofold aspect: it is a quantity of value as well as an aggregate of material products, and from a capitalist point of view, its elements in both instances are thus the same.

As a rule, an increased production of surplus value results from an increase of capital brought about by addition of part of the appropriated surplus value to the original capital, no matter whether this capitalist surplus value is used for the expansion of an old enterprise or for founding a new one, an independent offshoot. Capitalist expanding reproduction thus acquires the specific characteristics of an increase in capital by means of a progressive capitalisation of surplus value, or, as Marx has put it, by the accumulation of capital.

The general formula for enlarged reproduction under the rule of capital thus runs as follows: $c + v + \frac{s}{x} + s'$. Here $\frac{s}{x}$ stands for the capitalised part of the surplus value appropriated in an earlier period of production; s' stands for the new surplus value created by the increased capital. Part of this new surplus value is capitalised again, and expanding reproduction is thus, from the capitalist point of view, a constantly flowing process of alternate appropriation and capitalisation of surplus value.

So far, however, we have only arrived at a general and abstract formula for reproduction. Let us now consider more closely the concrete conditions which are necessary to apply this formula.

The surplus value which has been appropriated, after it has successfully cast off its commodity-form in the market, appears as a given amount of money. This money-form is the form of its absolute value, the beginning of its career as capital. But as it is impossible to create surplus value with money, it cannot, in this form, advance beyond the threshold of its career. Capital must assume commodity-form, so that the particular portion of it which is earmarked for accumulation can be capitalised. For only in this form can it become productive capital; that is, capital begetting new surplus value. Therefore, like the original capital, it must again be divided into two parts; a constant part, comprising the inanimate means of production, and a variable part, the wages. Only then will our formula $c + v + s$ apply to it in the same way as it applied to the old capital.

But the good intent of the capitalist to accumulate, his thrift and abstinence which make him use the greater part of his surplus value for production instead of squandering it on personal luxuries, is not sufficient for this purpose. On the contrary, it is essential that he should find on the commodity market the concrete forms which he intends to give his new surplus value. In the first place, he must secure the material means of production such as raw materials, machines etc. required for the branch of production he has chosen and planned, so that the particular part of the surplus value which corresponds to his constant capital may assume a productive form. Secondly, the other, variable part of his surplus value must also be convertible, and two essentials are necessary for this conversion: of first importance, the labour market must offer a sufficient quantity of additional labour, and secondly, as the workers cannot live on money alone, the commodity market, too, must offer an additional amount of provisions, which the workers newly to be employed may exchange against the variable part of the surplus value they will get from the capitalist.

All these prerequisites found, the capitalist can set his capitalised surplus value to work and make it, as operating capital, beget new surplus value. But still his task is not completely done. Both the new capital and the surplus value produced still exist for the time being in the shape of an additional quantity of some commodity or other. In this form the new capital is but advanced, and the new surplus value created by it is still in a form in which it is of no use to the capitalist. The new capital as well as the surplus value which it has created must cast off their commodity-form, re-assume the form of pure value, and thus revert to the capitalist as money. Unless this process is successfully concluded, the new capital and surplus value will be wholly or partly lost, the capitalisation of surplus value will have miscarried, and there will have been no accumulation. It is absolutely essential to the accumulation of capital that a sufficient quantity of commodities created by the new capital should win a place for itself on the market and be realised.

Thus we see that expanding reproduction as accumulation of capital in a capitalist system is bound up with a whole series of special conditions. Let us look at these more closely. The first condition is that production should create surplus value, for surplus value is the elementary form in which alone increased production is possible under capitalist conditions. The entire process of production must abide by this condition when determining the relations between capitalist and worker in the production of commodities. Once this first condition is given, the second is that surplus value must be realised, converted into the form of money, so that it can be appropriated for the purposes of expanding reproduction. This second condition thus leads us to the commodity market. Here, the hazards of exchange decide the further fate of the surplus value, and thus the future of reproduction. The third condition is as follows: provided that part of the realised surplus value has been added to capital for the purpose of accumulation, this new capital must first assume its productive form of labour and inanimate means of production. Moreover, that part of it which had been exchanged for labour must be converted into provisions for the workers. Thus we are led again to the markets of labour and commodities. If all these requirements have been met and enlarged reproduction of com-modities has taken place, a fourth condition must be added: the additional quantity of commodities representing the new capital plus surplus value will have to be realised, that is, reconverted into money. Only if this conversion has been successful, can it be said that expanding capitalist reproduction has actually taken place. This last condition leads us back to the commodity market.

Thus capitalist production and reproduction imply a constant shift-ing between the place of production and the commodity market, a shuttle movement from the private office and the factory where unauthorised persons are strictly excluded, where the sovereign will of the individual capitalist is the highest law, to the commodity market where nobody sets up any laws and where neither will nor reason assert themselves. But it is this very licence and anarchy of the com-modity market which brings home to the individual capitalist that he is dependent upon society, upon the entirety of its producing and con-suming members. The individual capitalist may need additional means of production, additional labour and provisions for these workers in order to expand reproduction, but whether he can get what he needs depends upon factors and events beyond his control, materialising, as it were, behind his back. In order to realise his increased aggregate of products, the individual capitalist requires a larger market for his goods, but he has no control whatever over the actual increase of demand in general, or of the particular demand for his special kind of good.

The conditions we have enumerated here, which all give expression to the inherent contradiction between consumption and private pro-duction and their social interconnection, are nothing new, and it is not only at the stage of reproduction that they become apparent. These conditions express the general contradiction inherent in capitalist pro-duction. They involve, however, particular difficulties as regards the process of reproduction for the following reasons. With regard to reproduction, especially expanding reproduction, the capitalist method of production not only reveals its general fundamental character, but, what is more, it shows, in the various periods of production, a definite rhythm within a continuous progression—the characteristic interplay of individual wills. From this point of view, we must inquire in a general way how it is possible for every individual capitalist to find on the market the means of production and the labour he requires for the purpose of realising the commodities he has produced, although there exists no social control whatever, no plan to harmonise production and demand. This question may be answered by saying that the capitalist's greed for surplus value, enhanced by competition, and the automatic effects of capitalist exploitation, lead to the production of every kind of commodity, including means of production, and also that a growing class of proletarianised workers becomes generally available for the purposes of capital. On the other hand, the lack of a plan in this respect shows itself in the fact that the balance between demand and supply in all spheres can be achieved only by continuous deviations, by hourly fluctuations of prices, and by periodical crises and changes of the market situation.

From the point of view of reproduction the question is a different one. How is it possible that the unplanned supply in the market for labour and means of production, and the unplanned and incalculable changes in demand nevertheless provide adequate incalculable changes in demand nevertheless provide adequate quantities and qualities of means of production, labour and opportunities for selling which the individual capitalist needs in order to make a sale? How can it be assured that every one of these factors increases in the right proportion? Let us put the problem more precisely. According to our well-known formula, let the composition of the individual capitalist's production be expressed by the proportion $40c + 10v + 10s$. His constant capital is consequently four times as much as his variable capital, and the rate of exploitation is 100 per cent. The aggregate of commodities is thus represented by a value of 60. Let us now assume that the capitalist is in a position to capitalise and to add to the old capital of this given composition half of his surplus value. In this case, the formula $44c + 11v + 11s = 66$ would apply to the next period of production.

Let us assume now that the capitalist can continue the annual capitalisation of half his surplus value for a number of years. For this purpose it is not sufficient that means of production, labour and markets in general should be forthcoming, but he must find these factors in a proportion that is strictly in keeping with his progress in accumulation.

2

QUESNAY'S AND ADAM SMITH'S ANALYSES OF THE PROCESS OF REPRODUCTION

So far we have taken account only of the individual capitalist in our survey of reproduction; he is its typical representative, its agent, for reproduction is indeed brought about entirely by individual capitalist enterprises. This approach has already shown us that the problem involves difficulties enough. Yet these difficulties increase to an extraordinary degree and become even more complicated, when we turn our attention from the individual capitalist to the totality of capitalists.

A superficial glance suffices to show that capitalist reproduction as a social whole must not be regarded simply as a mechanical summation of all the separate processes of individual capitalist reproduction. We have seen, for instance, that one of the fundamental conditions for enlarged reproduction by an individual capitalist is a corresponding increase of his opportunities to sell on the commodity market. But the individual capitalist may not always expand because of an absolute increase in the absorptive capacity of the market, but also as a result of the competitive struggle, at the cost of other individual capitalists. Thus one capitalist may win what another or many others who have been shouldered from the market must write off as a loss. This process will enable one capitalist to increase his reproduction by the amount that it compels others by losses to restrict their own. One capitalist will be able to engage in enlarged reproduction because others cannot even achieve simple reproduction. In the same way, one capitalist may enlarge his reproduction by using labour power and means of production which another's bankruptcy, that is his partial or complete retirement from reproduction, has set free.

These commonplaces prove that reproduction of the social capital as a whole is not the same as the reproduction of the individual capitalist raised to the nth degree. They show that the reproductive activities of individual capitalists ceaselessly cut across one another and to a greater or smaller degree may cancel each other out.

Therefore we must clarify our concept of reproduction of capital as a whole, before we examine the laws and mechanisms of capitalist total reproduction. We must raise the question whether it is even possible to deduce anything like total reproduction from the disorderly jumble of individual capitals in constant motion, changing from moment to moment according to uncontrollable and incalculable laws, partly running a parallel course, and partly intersecting and cancelling each other out. Can one actually talk of total social capital of society as an entity, and if so, what is the real meaning of this concept? That is the first question a scientific examination of the laws of reproduction has to consider. At the dawn of economic theory and bourgeois economics, Quesnay, the father of the Physiocrats, approached the problem with classical fearlessness and simplicity and took it for granted that total capital exists as a real and active entity. In his famous *Tableau Économique*, so intricate that no one before Marx could understand it, Quesnay demonstrated the phases of the reproduction of aggregate capital with a few figures, at the same time taking into account that it must also be considered from the aspect of commodity exchange, that is as a process of circulation.[1]

---

[1] 'Quesnay's *Tableau Économique* shows . . . how the result of national production in a certain year, amounting to some definite value, is distributed by means of the circulation in such a way, that . . . reproduction can take place. . . . The innumerable individual acts of circulation are at once viewed in their characteristic social mass movement— the circulation between great social classes distinguished by their economic function' (*Capital*, vol. ii, p. 414).

Society as Quesnay sees it consists of three classes: the productive class of agriculturists; the sterile class containing all those who are active outside the sphere of agriculture—industry, commerce, and the liberal professions; and lastly the class of landowners, including the Sovereign and the collectors of tithes. The national aggregate product materialises in the hands of the productive class as an aggregate of provisions and raw materials to the value of some 5,000 million livres. Of this sum, 2,000 millions represent the annual working capital of agriculture, 1,000 millions represent the annual wear and tear of fixed capital, and 2,000 millions are the net revenue accruing to the land-owners. Apart from this total produce, the agriculturists, here conceived quite in capitalist terms as tenant farmers, have 2,000 million livres cash in hand. Circulation now takes place in such a way that the tenant class pay the landowners 2,000 millions cash as rent (as the cost of the previous period of production). For this money the landowning class buy provisions from the tenants for 1,000 millions and industrial products from the sterile class for the remaining 1,000 millions. The tenants in their turn buy industrial products for the 1,000 millions handed back to them, whereupon the sterile class buy agricultural products for the 2,000 millions they have in hand: for 1,000 millions raw materials etc., to replace their annual working capital, and provisions for the remaining 1,000 millions. Thus the money has in the end returned to its starting point, the tenant class; the product is distributed among all classes so that consumption is ensured for everyone; at the same time the means of production of the sterile as well as of the productive class have been renewed and the landowning class has received its revenue. The prerequisites of reproduction are all present, the conditions of circulation have all been fulfilled, and reproduction can start again on its regular course.[2]

---

[2] Cf. *Analyse du Tableau Économique*, in *Journal de l'Agriculture, du Commerce et des Finances*, by Dupont (1766), pp. 305 ff. in Oncken's edition of *Œuvres de F. Quesnay*. Quesnay remarks explicitly that circulation as he describes it is based upon two conditions: unhampered trade, and a system of taxation applying only to rent: 'Yet these facts have indispensable conditions; that the freedom of commerce sustains the sale of products at a good price, . . . and moreover, that the farmer need not pay any other direct or indirect charges but this income, part of which, say two sevenths, must form the revenue of the Sovereign' (op. cit., p. 311).

We shall see later in the course of our investigation that this exposition, though showing flashes of genius, remains deficient and primitive. In any case, we must stress here that Quesnay, on the threshold of scientific economics, had not the slightest doubt as to the possibility of demonstrating total social capital and its reproduction. Adam Smith, on the other hand, while giving a more profound analysis of the relations of capital, laid out what seems like a maze when compared with the clear and sweeping outlines of the Physiocrat conception. By his wrong analysis of prices, Smith upset the whole foundation of the scientific demonstration of the capitalist process as a whole. This wrong analysis of prices ruled bourgeois economics for a long time; it is the theory which maintains that, although the value of a commodity represents the amount of labour spent in its production, yet the price consists of three elements only: the wage of labour, the profit of capital, and the rent.

As this obviously must also apply to the aggregate of commodities, the national product, we are faced with the startling discovery that, although the value of the aggregate of commodities manufactured by capitalist methods represents all paid wages together with the profits of capital and the rents, that is the aggregate surplus value, and consequently can replace these, there is no component of value which corresponds to the constant capital used in production. According to Smith, $v + s$ is the formula expressing the value of the capitalist product as a whole. Demonstrating his view with the example of corn, Smith says as follows:

'These three parts (wages, profit, and rent) seem either immediately or ultimately to make up the whole price of corn. A fourth part, it may perhaps be thought, is necessary for replacing the stock of the farmer, or for compensating the wear and tear of his labouring cattle, and other instruments of husbandry. But it must be considered that the price of any instrument of husbandry, such as a labouring horse, is itself made up of the same three parts: the rent of this land and the reared, the labour of tending and rearing him, and the profits of the farmer who advances both the rent of this land and the wages of this labour. Though the price of the corn, therefore, may pay the price as well as the maintenance of the horse, the whole price still resolves itself either immediately or ultimately into the same three parts of rent, of labour and profit.'[3]

Sending us in this manner 'from pillar to post', as Marx has put it, Smith again and again resolved constant capital into $v + s$. However, he had occasional doubts and from time to time relapsed into the contrary opinion. He says in the second book:

'It has been shown in the first Book, that the price of the greater part of commodities resolves itself into three parts, of which one pays the wages of the labour, another the profits of the stock, and a third the rent of the land which had been employed in producing and bringing them to market ... Since this is the case ... with regard to every particular commodity, taken separately; it must be so with regard to all the commodities which compose the whole annual produce of the land and labour of every country, taken complexly. The whole price or exchangeable value of that annual produce must resolve itself into the same three parts, and be parcelled out among the different inhabitants of the country, either as the wages of their labour, the profits of their stock, or the rent of their land.'[4]

Here Smith hesitates and immediately below explains: 'But though the whole value of the annual produce of the land and labour of every country is thus divided among and constitutes a revenue to its different inhabitants, yet as in the rent of a private estate we distinguish between the gross rent and the neat rent, so may we likewise in the revenue of all the inhabitants of a great country.

'The gross rent of a private estate comprehends whatever is paid by the farmer; the neat rent, what remains free to the landlord after deducting the expense of management, of repairs, and all other necessary charges; or what, without hurting his estate, he can afford to place in his stock reserved for immediate consumption, or to spend upon his table, equipage, the ornaments of his house and furniture, his private enjoyments and amusements. His real wealth is in proportion, not to his gross, but to his neat rent.

'The gross revenue of all the inhabitants of a great country

---

[3] Adam Smith, *An Enquiry into the Nature and Causes of the Wealth of Nations* (ed. McCulloch, Edinburgh London, 1828), vol. i, pp. 86–8.

[4] Op. cit., vol. ii, pp. 17–18.

comprehends the whole annual produce of their land and labour; the neat revenue, what remains free to them after deducting the expense of maintaining, first, their fixed; and, secondly, their circulating capital, or what, without encroaching upon their capital, they can place in their stock reserved for immediate consumption, or spend upon their subsistence, conveniencies, and amusements. Their real wealth too is in proportion, not to their gross, but to their neat revenue.'[5]

Here Smith introduces a portion of value which corresponds to constant capital, only to eliminate it the very next moment by resolving it into wages, profits, and rents. And in the end, the matter rests with this explanation:

'As the machines and instruments of trade, etc. which compose the fixed capital either of an individual or of a society, make no part either of the gross or the neat revenue of either, so money, by means of which the whole revenue of the society is regularly distributed among all its different members, makes itself no part of that revenue.'[6]

Constant capital, the fixed capital of Adam Smith, is thus put on the same level as money and does not enter into the total produce of society, its gross revenue. It does not exist within this total product as an element of value.

You cannot get blood out of a stone, and so circulation, the mutual exchange of the total product constituted in this manner, can only lead to realisation of the wages (v) and of the surplus value (s). However, as it cannot by any means replace the constant capital, continued reproduction evidently must become impossible. Smith indeed knew quite well, and did not dream of denying, that every individual capitalist requires constant capital in addition to his wages fund, his variable capital, in order to run his enterprise. Yet the above analysis of commodity prices, when it comes to take note of capitalist production as a whole, allows constant capital to disappear without a trace in a puzzling way. Thus the problem of the reproduction of capital is completely muddled up. It is plain that if the most elementary premise of the problem, the demonstration of social capital as a whole, were on the rocks, the whole analysis was bound to fail. Ricardo, Say, Sismondi

[5] Ibid., pp. 18–19.
[6] Ibid., p. 23.

and others took up this erroneous theory of Adam Smith, and they all stumbled in their observations on the problem of reproduction over this most elementary difficulty: the demonstration of social capital.

Another difficulty is mixed up with the foregoing from the very outset of scientific analysis. What is the nature of the total capital of a society? As regards the individual producer, the position is clear: his capital consists of the expenses of his enterprise. Assuming capitalist methods of production, the value of his product yields him a surplus over and above his expenses, that surplus value which does not replace his capital but constitutes his net income, which he can consume completely without encroaching upon his capital and which is thus his fund of consumption. It is true that the capitalist may save part of this net income, not consuming it himself but adding it to his capital. But that is another matter, a new step, the formation of a new capital which again must be replaced by subsequent reproduction and must again yield him a surplus. In any case, the capital of an individual always consists of what he requires for production, together with his advances on the running of his enterprise, and his income is what he himself actually consumes or may consume, his fund of consumption. If we ask a capitalist: 'What are the wages you pay your workers?' his answer will be: 'They are obviously part of my working capital.' But if we ask: 'What are these wages for the workers who have received them?'—it is impossible that he should describe them as capital, for wages received are not capital for the workers but income, their fund of consumption.

Let us now take another example. A manufacturer of machinery produces machines in his factory. The annual output is a certain number of machines. In its value, however, this annual output contains the capital advanced by the manufacturer as well as the net income that has been earned. Part of the manufactured machines thus represent income for the manufacturer and are destined to realise this income in the process of circulation and exchange. But the person who buys these machines from the manufacturer does not buy them as income but in order to use them as a means of production; for him they are capital.

These examples make it seem plausible that an object which is capital for one person may be income for another and *vice versa*. How can it be possible under these circumstances to construct anything in the nature of a total capital of society? Indeed almost every scientific economist up to the time of Marx concluded that there is no social capital.[7] Smith was still doubtful, undecided, vacillating about this question; so was Ricardo. But already Say declared categorically:

'It is in this way, that the total value of products is distributed amongst the members of the community; I say, the *total* value, because such part of the whole value produced, as does not go to one of the consuming producers, is received by the rest. The clothier buys wool of the farmer, pays his workmen in every department, and sells the cloth, the result of their united exertion, at a price that reimburses all his advances, and affords himself a profit. He never reckons as profit, or as the revenue of his own industry, anything more than the *net* surplus, after deducting all charges and outgoings; but those outgoings are merely an advance of their respective revenues to the previous producers, which are refunded by the *gross* value of the cloth. The price paid to the farmer for his wool is the compound of the several revenues of the cultivator, the shepherd and the landlord. Although the farmer reckons as *net* produce only the surplus remaining after payment of his landlord and his servants in husbandry, yet to them these payments are items of revenue—rent to the one and wages to the other—to the one, the revenue of the land, to the other, the revenue of his industry. The aggregate of all these is defrayed out of the value of the cloth, the whole of which forms the revenue of some one or other, and is entirely absorbed in that way.—Whence it appears that the term *net* produce applies only to the individual revenue of each separate producer or adventurer in industry, but that the aggregate of individual revenue, the total revenue of the community, is equal to the *gross* produce of its land, capital and industry, which entirely subverts the system of the economists of the last century, who considered nothing but the net produce of the land as farming revenue, and therefore concluded, that this net produce was all that the community had to consume; instead of closing with the obvious inference, that the whole of what had been created, may also be consumed by mankind.'[8]

Say proves his theory in his own peculiar fashion. Whereas Adam

---

[7] As to the concept of 'national capital' specific to Rodbertus, see below, Section II.

[8] J. B. Say, *A Treatise on Political Economy* (transl. by C. R. Prinsep, vol. ii, London, 1821), pp. 75–7.

Smith tried to give a proof by referring each private capital unit to its place of production in order to resolve it into a mere product of labour, but conceived of every product of labour in strictly capitalist terms as a sum of paid and unpaid labour, as $v + s$, and thus came to resolve the total product of society into $v + s$; Say, of course, is cocksure enough to 'correct' these classical errors by inflating them into common vulgarities. His argument is based upon the fact that the entrepreneur at every stage of production pays other people, the representatives of previous stages of production, for the means of production which are capital for him, and that these people in their turn put part of this payment into their own pockets as their income and partly use it to recoup themselves for expenses advanced in order to provide yet another set of people with an income. Say converts Adam Smith's endless chain of labour processes into an equally unending chain of mutual advances on income and their repayment from the proceeds of sales. The worker appears here as the absolute equal of the entrepreneur. He has his income advanced in the form of wages, paying for it in turn by the labour he performs. Thus the final value of the aggregate social product appears as the sum of a large number of advanced incomes and is spent in the process of exchange on repayment of all these advances. It is characteristic of Say's superficiality that he illustrates the social connections of capitalist reproduction by the example of watch manufacture—a branch of production which at that time and partly even to-day is pure 'manufacture' where every worker is also an entrepreneur on a small scale and the process of production of surplus value is masked by a series of successive acts of exchange typical of simple commodity production.

Thus Say gives an extremely crude expression to the confusion inaugurated by Adam Smith. The aggregate of annual social produce can be completely resolved as regards its value into a sequence of various incomes. Therefore it is completely consumed every year. It remains an enigma how production can be taken up again without capital and means of production, and capitalist reproduction appears to be an insoluble problem.

If we compare the varying approaches to the problem from the time of the Physiocrats to that of Adam Smith, we cannot fail to recognise partial progress as well as partial regression. The main characteristic of the economic conception of the Physiocrats was their assumption that agriculture alone creates a surplus, that is surplus value, and that agricultural labour is the only kind of labour which is productive in the capitalist sense of the term. Consequently we see in the *Tableau Économique* that the unproductive class of industrial workers creates value only to the extent of the same 2,000 million livres which it consumes as raw materials and foodstuffs. Consequently, too, in the process of exchange, the total of manufactured products is divided into two parts, one of which goes to the tenant class and the other to the landowning class, while the manufacturing class does not consume its own products. Thus in the value of its commodities, the manufacturing class reproduces, strictly speaking, only that circulating capital which has been consumed, and no income is created for the class of entrepreneurs. The only income of society that comes into circulation in excess of all capital advances, is created in agriculture and is consumed by the landowning class in the form of rents, while even the tenant class do no more than replace their capital: to wit, 1,000 million livres interest from the fixed capital and 2,000 million circulating capital, two-thirds being raw materials and foodstuffs, and one-third industrial products. Further it is striking that it is in agriculture alone that Quesnay assumes the existence of fixed capital which he calls *avances primitives* as distinct from *avances annuelles*. Industry, as he sees it, apparently works without any fixed capital, only with circulating capital turned over each year, and consequently does not create in its annual output of commodities any element of value for making good the wear and tear of fixed capital (such as premises, tools, and so on).[9]

In contrast with this obvious defect, the English classical school shows a decisive advance above all in proclaiming every kind of labour as productive, thus revealing the creation of surplus value in manufacture as well as in agriculture. We say: the English classical school, because on this point Adam Smith himself occasionally relapses quietly

---

[9] Attention must be drawn to the fact that Mirabeau in his *Explications* on the *Tableau Économique* explicitly mentions the fixed capital of the unproductive class: 'The primary advances of this class, for the establishment of manufactures, for instruments, machines, mills, smithies (ironworks) and other factories . . . (amount to) 2,000 million livres' (*Tableau Économique avec ses Explications*, 1760, p. 82). In his confusing sketch of the *Tableau* itself, Mirabeau, too, fails to take this fixed capital of the sterile class into account.

into the Physiocrat point of view. It is only Ricardo who develops the theory of the value of labour as highly and logically as it could advance within the limits of the bourgeois approach. The consequence is that we must assume all capital investment to produce annual surplus value, in the manufacturing part of social production as a whole no less than in agriculture.[10]

On the other hand, the discovery of the productive, value-creating property of every kind of labour, alike in agriculture and in manufacture, suggested to Smith that agricultural labour, too, must produce, apart from the rent for the land-owning class, a surplus for the tenant class over and above the total of their capital expenses. Thus, in addition to the replacement of capital, an annual income of the tenant class comes into being.[11]

Lastly, by a systematic elaboration of the concepts of *avances primitives* and *avances annuelles* introduced by Quesnay, which he calls fixed and circulating capital, Smith has made clear, among other things, that the manufacturing side of social production requires a fixed as well as a circulating capital. Thus he was well on the way to restoring to order the concepts of capital and revenue of society, and to describing them in precise terms. The following exposition represents the highest level of clarity which he achieved in this respect:

'Though the whole annual produce of the land and labour of every

---

[10] Smith accordingly arrives at this general formulation: 'The value which the workmen add to the materials, therefore, resolves itself in this case into two parts, of which the one pays their wages, the other the profits of their employer upon the whole stock of materials and wages which he advanced' (op. cit., vol. i, p. 83). Further, in Book II, chap. 8, on industrial labour in particular: 'The labour of a manufacturer adds generally to the value of the materials which he works upon, that of his own maintenance and of his master's profit. The labour of a menial servant, on the contrary, adds to the value of nothing. Though the manufacturer has his wages advanced to him by his master, he in reality costs him no expense, the value of those wages being generally restored, together with a profit, in the improved value of the subject upon which his labour is bestowed' (op. cit., vol. ii, pp. 93–4).

[11] 'The labourers ... therefore, employed in agriculture, not only occasion, like the workmen in manufactures, the reproduction of a value equal to their own consumption, or to the capital which employs them, together with its owner's profit, but of a much greater value. Over and above the capital of the farmer and all its profits, they regularly occasion the reproduction of the rent of the landlord' (ibid., p. 149).

country is, no doubt, ultimately destined for supplying the consumption of its inhabitants and for procuring a revenue to them, yet when it first comes either from the ground or from the hands of the productive labourer, it naturally divides itself into two parts. One of them, and frequently the largest, is, in the first place, destined for replacing a capital, or for renewing the provisions, materials, and finished work, which had been withdrawn from a capital; the other for constituting a revenue either to the owner of this capital, as the profit of his stock, or to some other person, as the rent of his land.'[12]

'The gross revenue of all the inhabitants of a great country comprehends the whole annual produce of their land and labour; the neat revenue, what remains free to them after deducting the expense of maintaining, first, their fixed, and secondly, their circulating capital; or what, without encroaching upon their capital, they can place in their stock reserved for immediate consumption, or spend upon their subsistence, conveniencies, and amusements. Their real wealth too is in proportion, not to their gross, but to their neat revenue.'[13]

The concepts of total capital and income appear here in a more comprehensive and stricter form than in the *Tableau Économique*. The one-sided connection of social income with agriculture is severed and social income becomes a broader concept; and a broader concept of capital in its two forms, fixed and circulating capital, is made the basis of social production as a whole. Instead of the misleading differentiation of production into two departments, agriculture and industry, other categories of real importance are here brought to the fore: the distinction between capital and income and the distinction, further, between fixed and circulating capital.

Now Smith proceeds to a further analysis of the mutual relations of these categories and of how they change in the course of the social process, in production and circulation—in the reproductive process of

---

[12] Ibid., pp. 97–8. Yet already in the following sentence Smith converts capital completely into wages, that is variable capital: 'That part of the annual produce of the land and labour of any country which replaces a capital, never is immediately employed to maintain any but productive hands. It pays the wages of productive labour only. That which is immediately destined for constituting a revenue, either as profit or as rent, may maintain indifferently either productive or unproductive hands' (ibid., p. 98).

[13] Ibid., p. 19.

society. He emphasises here a radical distinction between fixed and circulating capital from the point of view of the society:

'The whole expense of maintaining the fixed capital must evidently be excluded from the neat revenue of the society. Neither the materials necessary for supporting their useful machines and instruments of trade, their profitable buildings, etc., nor the produce of the labour necessary for fashioning those materials into the proper form, can ever make any part of it. The price of that labour may indeed make a part of it; as the workmen so employed may place the whole value of their wages in their stock reserved for immediate consumption. But in other sorts of labour, both the price and the produce go to this stock, the price to that of the workmen, the produce to that of other people whose subsistence, convenience and amusements are augmented by the labour of those workmen.'[14]

Here Smith comes up against the important distinction between workers who produce means of production and those who produce consumer goods. With regard to the former he remarks that they create the value—destined to replace their wages and to serve as their income—in the form of means of production such as raw materials and instruments which in their natural form cannot be consumed. With regard to the latter category of workers, Smith observes that conversely the total product, or better that part of value contained in it which replaces the wages, the income of the workers together with its other remaining value, appears here in the form of consumer goods. (The real meaning latent in this conclusion, though Smith does not say so explicitly, is that the part of the product which represents the fixed capital employed in its production appears likewise in this form.) In the further course of our investigation we shall see how close Smith has here come to the vantage point from which Marx tackled the problem. The general conclusion, however, maintained by Smith without any further examination of the fundamental question, is that, in any case, whatever is destined for the preservation and renewal of the fixed capital of society cannot be added to society's net income.

The position is different with regard to circulating capital. 'But though the whole expenses of maintaining the fixed capital is thus

[14] Smith, op. cit., vol. ii, pp. 19–20.

necessarily excluded from the neat revenue of the society, it is not the same case with that of maintaining the circulating capital. Of the four parts of which this latter capital is composed, money, provisions, materials and finished work, the three last, it has already been observed, are regularly withdrawn from it and placed either in the fixed capital of the society, or in their stock reserved for immediate consumption. Whatever portion of those consumable goods is not employed in maintaining the former, goes all to the latter, and makes a part of the neat revenue of the society, besides what is necessary for maintaining the fixed capital.'[15]

We see that Smith here simply includes in this category of circulating capital everything but the fixed capital already employed, that is to say, foodstuffs and raw materials and in part commodities which, according to their natural form, belong to the replacement of fixed capital. Thus he has made the concept of circulating capital vague and ambiguous. But a further and most important distinction crops up and cuts right through this conception: 'The circulating capital of a society is in this respect different from that of an individual. That of an individual is totally excluded from making any part of his neat revenue, which must consist altogether in his profits. But though the circulating capital of every individual makes a part of that of the society to which he belongs, it is not upon that account totally excluded from making a part likewise of their neat revenues.'[16]

In the following illustration Smith expounds what he means: 'Though the whole goods in a merchant's shop must by no means be placed in his own stock reserved for immediate consumption, they may in that of other people, who, from a revenue derived from other funds, may regularly replace their value to him, together with its profits, without occasioning any diminution either of his capital or theirs.'[17]

Here Smith has established fundamental categories with regard to the reproduction and movement of circulating social capital. Fixed and circulating capital, private and social capital, private and social revenue,

---

[15] Ibid., vol. i, pp. 21–2.
[16] Ibid., p. 22.
[17] Ibid.

means of production and consumer goods, are marked out as comprehensive categories, and their real, objective interrelation is partly indicated and partly drowned in the subjective and theoretical contradictions of Smith's analysis. The concise, strict, and classically clear scheme of the Physiocrat theory is dissolved here into a disorderly jumble of concepts and relations which at first glance appears an absolute chaos. But we may already perceive new connections within the social process of reproduction, understood by Smith in a deeper, more modern and vital way than was within Quesnay's grasp, though, like Michelangelo's slave in the unhewn block of marble, they are still inchoate.

This is the only illustration Smith gives of this problem. But at the same time he attacks it from another angle—by an analysis of value. This very same theory which represents an advance beyond the Physiocrats—the theory that it is an essential quality of all labour to create value; the strictly capitalist distinction between paid labour replacing wages, and unpaid labour creating surplus value; and, finally, the strict division of surplus value into its two main categories, of profit and rent—all this progress from the analysis of the Physiocrats leads Smith to the strange proposition that the price of every commodity consists of wages, plus profits, plus rent, or, in Marx's shorthand, of $v + s$. In consequence, the commodities annually produced by society as a whole can be resolved completely, as to value, into the two components: wages and surplus value. Here the category of capital has disappeared all of a sudden; society produces nothing but income, nothing but consumer goods, which it also consumes completely. Reproduction without capital becomes a paradox, and the treatment of the problem as a whole has taken an immense backward step against that of the Physiocrats.

The followers of Adam Smith have tackled this twofold theory from precisely the wrong approach. Before Marx nobody concerned himself with the important beginnings of an exact exposition of the problem in Smith's second book, while most of his followers jealously preserved Smith's radically wrong analysis of prices, accepting it, like Ricardo, without question, or else, like Say, elaborating it into a trite doctrine. Where Smith raised fruitful doubts and stimulating contradictions, Say flaunted the opinionated presumption of a commonplace mind.

Smith's observation that the capital of one person may be the revenue of another induced Say to proclaim every distinction between capital and income on the social scale to be absurd. The absurdity, however, that income should completely absorb the total value of annual production which is thus consumed completely, assumes in Say's treatment the character of an absolutely valid dogma. If society annually consumes its own total product completely, social reproduction without any means of production whatever must become an annual repetition of the Miracle of the Creation.

In this state the problem of reproduction remained up to the time of Karl Marx.

3

A CRITICISM OF SMITH'S
ANALYSIS

Let us recapitulate the conclusions to which Smith's analysis has brought us:

(1) There is a fixed capital of society, no part of which enters into its net revenue. This fixed capital consists in 'the materials necessary for supporting their useful machines and instruments of trade' and 'the produce of labour necessary for fashioning those materials into the proper form'.[1] By singling out the production of such fixed capital as of a special kind, and explicitly contrasting it with the production of consumer goods, Smith in effect transformed fixed capital into what Marx calls 'constant capital'—that part of capital which consists of all material means of production, as opposed to labour power.

(2) There is a circulating capital of society. After eliminating the part of fixed, or constant, capital, there remains only the category of consumer goods; these are not capital for society but net revenue, a fund of consumption.

(3) Capital and net revenue of an individual do not strictly correspond with capital and net revenue of society. What is nothing but

---

[1] *An Enquiry into the Nature and Causes of the Wealth of Nations*, vol. i, p. 19.

fixed, or constant capital for society as a whole cannot be capital for the individual; it must be revenue, too, a fund of consumption, comprising as it does those parts of fixed capital which represent the workers' wages and the capitalists' profits. On the other hand, the circulating capital of the individuals cannot be capital for society but must be revenue, especially in so far as it takes the form of provisions.

(4) As regards the value of the total annual social product, no trace of capital remains. It can be resolved completely into the three kinds of income: wages, profits of capital, and rents.

If we tried from this haphazard collection of odd ideas to build up a picture of the annual reproduction of total social capital, and of its mechanism, we should soon despair of our task. Indeed, all these observations leave us infinitely remote from the solution of the problem how social capital is annually renewed, how everybody's consumption is ensured by his income, while the individuals can nevertheless adhere to their own points of view on capital and income. Yet if we wish to appreciate fully Marx's contribution to the elucidation of this problem, we must be fully aware of all this confusion of ideas, the mass of conflicting points of view.

Let us begin with Adam Smith's last thesis which alone would suffice to wreck the treatment of the problem of reproduction in classical economics.

Smith's basic principle is that the total produce of society, when we consider its value, resolves itself completely into wages, profits and rents: this conception is deeply rooted in his scientific theory that value is nothing but the product of labour. All labour performed, however, is wage labour. This identification of human labour with capitalist wage labour is indeed the classical element in Smith's doctrine. The value of the aggregate product of society comprises both the recompense for wages advanced and a surplus from unpaid labour appearing as profit for the capitalist and rent for the landowner. What holds good for the individual commodity must hold good equally for the aggregate of commodities. The whole mass of commodities produced by society—taken as a quantity of value—is nothing but a product of labour, of paid as well as unpaid labour, and thus it is also to be completely resolved into wages, profits, and rents.

It is of course true that raw materials, instruments, and the like, must be taken into consideration in connection with all labour. Yet is it not true also that these raw materials and instruments in their turn are equally products of labour which again may have been paid or unpaid? We may go back as far as we choose, we may twist and turn the problem as much as we like, yet we shall find no element in the value of any commodity—and therefore none in the price—which cannot be resolved purely in terms of human labour. We can distinguish, however, two parts in all labour: one part repays the wages and the other accrues to the capitalist and landlord. There seems nothing left but wages and profits—and yet, there is capital, individual and social capital. How can we overcome this blatant contradiction? The fact that Marx himself stubbornly pursued this matter for a long time without getting anywhere at first as witness his *Theories of the Surplus Value*,[2] proves that this theoretical problem is indeed extremely hard to solve. Yet the solution he eventually hit on was strikingly successful, and it is based upon his theory of value. Adam Smith was perfectly right: nothing but labour constitutes the value of the individual commodity and of the aggregate of commodities. He was equally right in saying that from a capitalist point of view all labour is either paid labour which restores the wages, or unpaid labour which, as surplus value, accrues to the various classes owning the means of production. What he forgot, however, or rather overlooked, is the fact that, apart from being able to create new value, labour can also transfer to the new commodities the old values incorporated in the means of production employed. A baker's working day of ten hours is, from the capitalist point of view, divided into paid and unpaid hours, into $v+s$. But the commodity produced in these ten hours will represent a greater value than that of ten hours' labour, for it will also contain the value of the flour, of the oven which is used, of the premises, of the fuel and so on, in short the value of all the means of production necessary for baking. Under one condition alone could the value of any one commodity be strictly equal to $v+s$; if a man were to work in mid-air, without raw materials, without tools or workshop. But since all work on materials (material labour) presupposes means of production of some sort which themselves

[2] *Theorien über den Mehrwert* (Stuttgart, 1905), vol. i, pp. 179–252.

result from preceding labour, the value of this past labour is of necessity transferred to the new product.

The process in question does not only take place in capitalist production; it is the general foundation of human labour, quite independent of the historical form of society. The handling of man-made tools is a fundamental characteristic of human civilisation. The concept of past labour which precedes all new labour and prepares its basis, expresses the nexus between man and nature evolved in the history of civilisation. This is the eternal chain of closely interwoven labouring efforts of human society, the beginnings of which are lost in the grey dawn of the socialisation of mankind, and the termination of which would imply the end of the whole of civilised mankind. Therefore we have to picture all human labour as performed with the help of tools which themselves are already products of antecedent labour. Every new product thus contains not only the new labour whereby it is given its final form, but also past labour which had supplied the materials for it, the instruments of labour and so forth. In the production of value, that is commodity production into which capitalist production also enters, this phenomenon is not suspended, it only receives a particular expression. Here the labour which produces commodities assumes a twofold characteristic: it is on the one hand useful concrete labour of some kind or other, creating the useful object, the value-in-use. On the other hand, it is abstract, general, socially necessary labour and as such creates value. In its first aspect it does what labour has always done: it transfers to the new product past labour, incorporated in the means of production employed, with this distinction only, that this past labour, too, now appears as value, as old value. In its second aspect, labour creates new value which, in capitalist terms, can be reduced to paid and unpaid labour, to $v+s$. Thus the value of every commodity must contain old value which has been transferred by labour qua useful concrete labour from the means of production to the commodity, as well as the new value, created by the same labour qua socially necessary labour merely as this labour is expended hour by hour.

This distinction was beyond Smith: he did not differentiate the twofold character of value-creating labour. Marx once claimed to have discovered the ultimate source of Smith's strange dogma—that the aggregate of produced values can be completely resolved into $v+s$—in his fundamentally erroneous theory of value.[3] Failure to differentiate between the two aspects of commodity-producing labour as concrete and useful labour on the one hand, and abstract and socially necessary labour on the other, indeed forms one of the most important characteristics of the theory of value as conceived not only by Smith but by all members of the classical school.

Disregarding all social consequences, classical economics recognised that human labour alone is the factor which creates value, and it worked out this theory to that degree of clarity which we meet in Ricardo's formulation. There is a fundamental distinction, however, between Marx's theory of value and Ricardo's, a distinction which has been misunderstood not only by bourgeois economists but also in most cases by the popularisers of Marx's doctrine: Ricardo, conceiving as he did, of bourgeois economy in terms of natural law, believed also that the creation of value, too, is a natural property of human labour, of the specific and concrete labour of the individual human being.

This view is even more blatantly revealed in the writings of Adam Smith who for instance declares what he calls the 'propensity to exchange' to be a quality peculiar to human nature, having looked for it in vain in animals, particularly in dogs. And although he doubted the existence of the propensity to exchange in animals, Smith attributed to animal as well as human labour the faculty of creating value, especially when he occasionally relapses into the Physiocrat doctrine:

'No equal capital puts into motion a greater quantity of productive labour than that of the farmer. Not only his labouring servants, but his labouring cattle, are productive labourers . . .'[4]

'The labourers and labouring cattle, therefore, employed in agriculture, not only occasion, like the workmen in manufactures, the reproduction of a value equal to their own consumption, or to the capital which employs them, together with its owner's profits, but of a much greater value. Over and above the capital of the farmer and all its profits, they regularly occasion the reproduction of the rent of the landlord.'[5]

---

[3] *Capital*, vol. ii, p. 435.
[4] Smith, op. cit., vol. ii, p. 148.
[5] Ibid., p. 149.

Smith's belief that the creation of value is a direct physiological property of labour, a manifestation of the animal organism in man, finds its most vivid expression here. Just as the spider produces its web from its own body, so labouring man produces value—labouring man pure and simple, every man who produces useful objects—because labouring man is by birth a producer of commodities; in the same way human society is founded by nature on the exchange of commodities, and a commodity economy is the normal form of human economy.

It was left to Marx to recognise that a given value covers a definite social relationship which develops under definite historical conditions. Thus he came to discriminate between the two aspects of commodity-producing labour: concrete individual labour and socially necessary labour. When this distinction is made, the solution of the money problem becomes clear also, as though a spotlight had been turned on it.

Marx had to establish a dynamic distinction in the course of history between the commodity producer and the labouring man, in order to distinguish the twin aspects of labour which appear static in bourgeois economy. He had to discover that the production of commodities is a definite historical form of social production before he could decipher the hieroglyphics of capitalist economy. In a word, Marx had to approach the problem with methods of deduction diametrically opposed to those of the classical school, he had in his approach to renounce the latter's faith in the human and normal element in bourgeois production and to recognise their historical transience: he had to reverse the metaphysical deductions of the classics into their opposite, the dialectical.

On this showing Smith could not possibly have arrived at a clear distinction between the two aspects of value-creating labour, which on the one hand transfers the old value incorporated in the means of production to the new product, and on the other hand creates new value at the same time. Moreover, there seems to be yet another source of his dogma that total value can be completely resolved into $v+s$. We should be wrong to assume that Smith lost sight of the fact that every commodity produced contains not only the value created by its production, but also the values incorporated in all the means of production that had been spent upon it in the process of manufacturing it. By the very fact that he continually refers us from one stage of production to a former one—sending us, as Marx complains, from pillar to post, in order to show the complete divisibility of the aggregate value into $v+s$—Smith proves himself well aware of the point. What is strange in this connection is that he again and again resolves the old value of the means of production, too, into $v+s$, so as finally to cover the whole value contained in the commodity.

'In the price of corn, for example, one part pays the rent of the landlord, another pays the wages of maintenance of the labourers and labouring cattle employed in producing it, and the third pays the profit of the farmer. These three parts (wages, profit, and rent) seem either immediately or ultimately to make up the whole price of corn. A fourth part, it may perhaps be thought, is necessary for replacing the stock of the farmer, or for compensating the wear and tear of his labouring cattle and other instruments of husbandry. But it must be considered that the price of any instrument of husbandry, such as a labouring horse, is itself made up of the same three parts: the rent of the land upon which he is reared, the labour of tending and rearing him, and the profits of the farmer who advances both the rent of this land and the wages of this labour. Though the price of the corn, therefore, may pay the price as well as the maintenance of the horse, the whole price still resolves itself either immediately or ultimately into the same three parts of rent, of labour, and profit.'[6]

Apparently Smith's confusion arose from the following premises: first, that all labour is performed with the help of means of production of some kind or other—yet what are these means of production associated with any given labour (such as raw materials and tools) if not the product of previous labour? Flour is a means of production to which the baker adds new labour. Yet flour is the result of the miller's work, and in his hands it was not a means of production but the very product, in the same way as now the bread and pastries are the product of the baker. This product, flour, again presupposes grain as a means of production, and if we go one step further back, this corn is not a means of production in the hands of the farmer but the product. It is impossible to find any means of production in which value is embodied, without it being itself the product of some previous labour.

[6] Op. cit., vol. i, pp. 86–7.

Secondly, speaking in terms of capitalism, it follows further that all capital which has been completely used up in the manufacture of any commodity, can in the end be resolved into a certain quantity of performed labour.

Thirdly, the total value of the commodity, including all capital advances, can readily be resolved in this manner into a certain quantity of labour. What is true for every commodity, must go also for the aggregate of commodities produced by a society in the course of a year; its aggregate value can similarly be resolved into a quantity of performed labour.

Fourthly, all labour performed under capitalist conditions is divided into two parts: paid labour which restores the wages advanced, and unpaid labour which creates profit and rent, or surplus value. All labour carried out under capitalist conditions thus corresponds to our formula $v + s$.[7]

All the arguments outlined above are perfectly correct and unassailable. Smith handled them in a manner which proves his scientific analysis consistent and undeviating, and his conceptions of value and surplus value a distinct advance on the Physiocrat approach. Only occasionally, in his third thesis, he went astray in his final conclusion, saying that the aggregate value of the annually produced aggregate of commodities can be resolved into the labour of that very year, although he himself had been acute enough to admit elsewhere that the value of the commodities a nation produces in the course of one year necessarily includes the labour of former years as well, that is the labour embodied in the means of production which have been handed down.

But even if the four statements enumerated are perfectly correct in themselves, the conclusion Smith draws from them—that the total value of every commodity, and equally of the annual aggregate of commodities in a society, can be resolved entirely into $v + s$—is absolutely wrong. He has the right idea that the whole value of a

---

[7] In this connection, we have disregarded the contrary conception which also runs through the work of Smith. According to that, the *price* of the commodity cannot be resolved into $v + s$, though the *value* of commodities consists in $v + s$. This distinction, however, is more important with regard to Smith's theory of value than in the present context where we are mainly interested in his formula $v + s$.

commodity represents nothing but social labour, yet identifies it with a false principle, that all value is nothing but $v + s$. The formula $v + s$ expresses the function of living labour under capitalism, or rather its double function, first to restore the wages, or the variable capital, and secondly, to create surplus value for the capitalist. Wage labour fulfils this function whilst it is employed by the capitalists, in virtue of the fact that the value of the commodities is realised in cash. The capitalist takes back the variable capital he had advanced in form of wages, and he pockets the surplus value as well. $v + s$ therefore expresses the relation between wage labour and capitalist, a relationship that is terminated in every instance as soon as the process of commodity production is finished. Once the commodity is sold, and the relation $v + s$ is realised for the capitalist in cash, the whole relationship is wiped out and leaves no traces on the commodity. If we examine the commodity and its value, we cannot ascertain whether it has been produced by paid or by unpaid labour, nor in what proportion these have contributed. Only one fact is beyond doubt: the commodity contains a certain quantity of socially necessary labour which is expressed in its exchange. It is completely immaterial for the act of exchange as well as for the use of the commodity whether the labour which produced it could be resolved into $v + s$ or not. In the act of exchange all that matters is that the commodity represents value, and only its concrete qualities, its usefulness, are relevant to the use we make of it. Thus the formula $v + s$ only expresses, as it were, the intimate relationship between capital and labour, the social function of wage labour, and in the actual product this is completely wiped out. It is different with the constant capital which has been advanced and invested in means of production, because every activity of labour requires certain raw materials, tools, and buildings. The capitalist character of this state of affairs is expressed by the fact that these means of production appear as capital, as c, as the property of a person other than the labourer, divorced from labour, the property of those who themselves do not work. Secondly, the constant capital c, a mere advance laid out for the purpose of creating surplus value, appears here only as the foundation of $v + s$. Yet the concept of constant capital involves more than this: it expresses the function of the means of production in the process of human labour, quite independently of all its historical or social forms. Everybody must have raw materials and working tools, the means of production, be it the South Sea Islander for making his family canoe, the communist peasant community in India for the cultivation of their communal land, the Egyptian fellah for tilling his village lands or for building Pharaoh's pyramids, the Greek slave in the small workshops of Athens, the feudal serf, the master craftsman of the medieval guild, or the modern wage labourer. They all require means of production which, having resulted from human labour, express the link between human labour and natural matter, and constitute the eternal and universal prerequisites of the human process of production. c in the formula $c + v + s$ stands for a certain function of the means of production which is not wiped out in the succession of the labour process. Whereas it is completely immaterial, for both the exchange and the actual use made of a commodity, whether it has been produced by paid or by unpaid labour, by wage labour, slave labour, forced labour or any other kind of labour; on the other hand, it is of decisive importance, as for using it, whether the commodity is itself a means of production or a consumer good. Whether paid or unpaid labour has been employed in the production of a machine, matters to the machinery manufacturer and to his workers, but only to them; for society, when it acquires this machine by an act of exchange, only the quality of this machine as a means of production, only its function in the process of production is of importance. Just as every producing society, since time immemorial, has had to give due regard to the important function of the means of production by arranging, in each period of production, for the manufacture of the means of production requisite for the next period, so capitalist society, too, cannot achieve its annual production of value to accord with the formula $v + s$—which indicates the exploitation of wage labour— unless there exists, as the result of the preceding period, the quantity of means of production necessary to make up the constant capital. This specific connection of each past period of production with the period following forms the universal and eternal foundation of the social process of reproduction and consists in the fact that in every period parts of the produce are destined to become the means of production for the succeeding period: but this relation remained hidden from Smith's sight. He was not interested in means of production in respect of their specific function within the process to which they are applied;

he was only concerned with them in so far as they are like any other commodity, themselves the product of wage labour that has been employed in a capitalist manner. The specifically capitalist function of wage labour in the productive process completely obscured for him the eternal and universal function of the means of production within the labour process. His narrow bourgeois approach overlooked completely the general relations between man and nature underneath the specific social relations between capital and wage labour. Here, it seems, is the real source of Adam Smith's strange dogma, that the total value of the annual social product can be resolved into $v + s$. He overlooked the fact that c as the first link in the formula $c + v + s$ is the essential expression of the general social foundation of exploitation of wage labour by capital.

We conclude that the value of every commodity must be expressed by the formula $c + v + s$. The question now arises how far this formula applies to the aggregate of commodities within a society. Let us turn to the doubts expressed by Smith on this point, the statement that an individual's fixed and circulating capital and his revenue do not strictly correspond to the same categories from the point of view of society. (Cf. above, pp. 35–6, no. 3.) What is circulating capital for one person is not capital for another, but revenue, as for instance capital advances for wages. This statement is based upon an error. If the capitalist pays wages to the workers, he does not abandon his variable capital and let it stray into the workers' hands, to become their income. He only exchanges the value-form of his variable capital against its natural form, labour power. The variable capital remains always in the hand of the capitalist, first as money, and then as labour power, to revert to him later together with the surplus value as the cash proceeds from the commodities. The worker, on the other hand, never gains possession of the variable capital. His labour power is never capital to him, but it is his only asset, the power to work is the only thing he possesses. Again, if he has sold it and taken a money wage, this wage is for him not capital but the price of his commodity which he has sold. Finally, the fact that the worker buys provisions with the wages he has received, has no more connection with the function this money once fulfilled as variable capital in the hands of the capitalist, than has the private use a vendor of a commodity can make of the money he has obtained by a sale. It is not the capitalist's variable capital which becomes the workers' income, but the price of the worker's commodity 'labour power' which he has sold, while the variable capital, now as ever, remains in the hands of the capitalist and fulfils its specific function. Equally erroneous is the conception that the income of the capitalist (the surplus value) which is hidden in machines—in our example of a machinery manufacturer—which has not as yet been realised, is fixed capital for another person, the buyer of the machines. It is not the machines, or parts of them, which form the income of the machinery manufacturer, but the surplus value that is hidden in them—the unpaid labour of his wage labourers. After the machine has been sold, this income simply remains as before in the hand of the machinery manufacturer; it has only changed its outward shape: it has been changed from the 'machine-form' into the 'money-form'. Conversely, the buyer of this machine has not, by its purchase, newly obtained possession of his fixed capital, for he had this fixed capital in hand even before the purchase, in the form of a certain amount of cash. By buying this machine, he has only given to his capital the adequate material form for it to become productive. The income, or surplus value, remains in the hands of the machinery manufacturer before and after the sale of the machine, and the fixed capital remains in the hands of the other person, the capitalist buyer of the machine, just as the variable capital in the first example always remained in the hands of the capitalist and the income in the hands of the worker.

Smith and his followers have caused confusion because, in their investigation of capitalist exchange, they mixed up the use-form of the commodities with their relations of value. Further, they did not distinguish the individual circulations of capitals and commodities which are ever interlacing. One and the same act of exchange can be circulation of capital, when seen from one aspect, and at the same time simple commodity exchange for the purpose of consumption. The fallacy that whatever is capital for one person must be income for another, and *vice versa*, must be translated thus into the correct statement that what is circulation of capital for one person, may be simple commodity exchange for another, and *vice versa*. This only expresses the capacity of capital to undergo transformations of its character, and the interconnections of various spheres of interest in the social process of exchange. The sharply outlined existence of capital in contrast with income still stands in both its clearly defined forms of constant and variable capital. Even so, Smith comes very close to the truth when he states that capital and income of the individual are not strictly identical with the same categories from the point of view of the community. Only a few further connecting links are lacking for a clear revelation of the true relationship.

4

MARX'S SCHEME OF SIMPLE REPRODUCTION

Let us now consider the formula $c + v + s$ as the expression of the social product as a whole. Is it only a theoretical abstraction, or does it convey any real meaning when applied to social life—has the formula any objective existence in relation to society as a whole? It was left to Marx to establish the fundamental importance of c, the constant capital, in economic theory. Yet Adam Smith before him, working exclusively with the categories of fixed and circulating capital, in effect transformed this fixed capital into constant capital, though he was not aware of having achieved this result. This constant capital comprises not only those means of production which wear out in the course of years, but also those which are completely absorbed by production in any one year. His very dogma that the total value is resolved into $v + s$ and his arguments on this point lead Smith to distinguish between the two categories of production—living labour and inanimate means of production. On the other hand, when he tries to construe the social process of reproduction on the basis of the capitals and incomes of individuals, the fixed capital he conceives of as existing apart from these, is, in fact, constant capital.

Every individual capitalist uses for the production of his commodities certain material means of production such as premises, raw materials and instruments. In order to produce the aggregate of commodities in a given society, an aggregate of all material means of production used by the individual capitalists is an obvious requisite. The existence of these means of production within the society is a real fact, though they themselves exist in the form of purely private individual capitals. This is the universal absolute condition of social production in all its historical forms.[1]

The specific capitalist form manifests itself in the fact that the material means of production function as c, as constant capital, the property of those who do not work; it is the opposite pole to proletarianised labour power, the counterpart of wage labour. The variable capital, v, is the aggregate of wages actually paid in the society in the course of a year's production. This fact, too, has real objective existence, although it manifests itself in an innumerable mass of individual wages. In every society the amount of labour power actually engaged in production and the annual maintenance of the workers is a question of decisive importance. Where this factor takes the specific capitalist form of v, the variable capital, it follows that the means of subsistence first come to the workers in form of a wage which is the price of the labour power they have sold to another person, the owner of the material means of production who does not work himself; under this aspect, it is the latter's capitalist property. Further, v is an aggregate of money, that is to say it is the means of subsistence for the workers in a form of pure value. This concept of v implies that the workers are free in a double sense—free in person and free of all means of production. It also expresses the fact that in a given society the universal form of production is commodity production.

Finally, s, the surplus value, stands for the total of all surplus values gained by the individual capitalists. Every society performs surplus labour, and even a socialist society will have to do the same. It must perform surplus labour in a threefold sense: it has to provide a quantity of labour for the maintenance of non-workers (those who are unable

---

[1] For the sake of simplicity, we shall follow general usage and speak here and in the following of annual production, though this term, strictly speaking, applies in general to agriculture only. The periods of industrial production, or of the turnover of capitals, need not coincide with calendar years.

to work, such as children, old people, invalids, and also civil servants and the so-called liberal professions who do not take an immediate part in the satisfaction of material[2] wants), it has to provide a fund of social insurance against elementary disasters which may threaten the annual produce, such as bad harvests, forest fires and floods; and lastly it must provide a fund for the purpose of increasing production, either because of an increase in the population, or because higher standards of civilisation lead to additional wants. It is in two respects that the capitalist character manifests itself: surplus labour comes into being (1) as surplus value, i.e. in commodity-form, realisable in cash, and (2) as the property of non-workers, of those who own the means of production.

Similarly, if we consider $v + s$, these two amounts taken together, we see that they represent objective quantities of universal validity: the total of living labour that has been performed within a society in the course of one year. Every human society, whatever its historical form, must take note of this datum, with reference to both the results that have been achieved, and the existing and available labour power. The division into $v + s$ is a universal phenomenon, independent of the society's particular historical form. In its capitalist form, this division shows itself not only in the qualitative peculiarities of both v and s as already outlined, but also in their quantitative relationship: v tends to become depressed to a minimum level, just sufficient for the physiological and social existence of the worker, and s tends to increase continually at the cost of, and relative to, v.

The predominant feature of capitalist production is expressed in this last circumstance: it is the fact that the creation and appropriation of surplus value is the real purpose of, and the incentive to, production.

We have examined the relations upon which the capitalist formula of the aggregate product is based, and have found them universally valid. In every planned economy they are made the object of conscious

---

[2] The distinction between intellectual and material labour need not involve special categories of the population in a planned society, based on common ownership of the means of production. It will always find expression in the existence of a certain number of spiritual leaders who must be materially maintained. The same individuals may exercise these various functions at different times.

regulation on the part of society; in a communist society by the community of workers and their democratic organs, and in a society based upon class-rule by the nucleus of owners and their despotic power. In a system of capitalist production there is no such planned regulation. The aggregate of the society's capitals and the aggregate of its commodities alike consist in reality of innumerable fragments of individual capitals and individual items of merchandise, taken together.

Thus the question arises whether these sums themselves mean anything more in a capitalist society than a mere statistical enumeration which is, moreover, inexact and fluid. Applying the standards of society as a whole, we perceive that the completely independent and sovereign individual existence of private enterprises is only the historically conditioned form, whereas it is social interconnections that provide the foundation. Although individual capitals act in complete independence of one another, and a social regulation is completely lacking, the movement of capitals forms a homogeneous whole. This movement, too, appears in specifically capitalist forms. In every planned system of production it is, above all, the relation between all labour, past and present, and the means of production (between $v + s$ and c, according to our formula), or the relation between the aggregate of necessary consumer goods (again, in the terms of our formula, $v + s$) and c which are subjected to regulation. Under capitalist conditions, on the other hand, all social labour necessary for the maintenance of the inanimate means of production and also of living labour power is treated as one entity, as capital, in contrast with the surplus labour that has been performed, i.e. with the surplus value s. The relation between these two quantities c and $(v + s)$ is a palpably real, objective relationship of capitalist society: it is the average rate of profit; every capital is in fact treated only as part of a common whole, the whole of social capital, and assigned the profit to which it is entitled, according to its size, out of the surplus value wrested from society, regardless of the quantity which this particular capital has actually created. Thus social capital and its counterpart, the whole of social surplus value, are not merely real quantities, having an objective existence, but, what is more, the relation between them, the average profit, guides and directs the whole process of exchange. This it does in three ways: (1) by the mechanism of the law of value which establishes the quantitative relations of exchange between the individual kinds of commodities independently of their specific value relationship; (2) by the social division of labour, the assignment of certain portions of capital and labour to the individual spheres of production; (3) by the development of labour productivity which on the one hand stimulates individual capitals to engage in pioneering work for the purpose of securing a higher profit than the average, and on the other hand extends the progress that has been achieved by individuals over the whole field of production. By means of the average rate of profit, in a word, the total capital of society completely governs the seemingly independent motions of individual capitals.

The formula $c + v + s$ thus applies to the aggregate of commodities produced in a society under capitalism no less than to the value composition of every individual commodity. It is, however, only the value-composition for which this holds good—the analogy cannot be carried further.

The formula is indeed perfectly exact if we regard the total product of a capitalistically producing society as the output of one year's labour, and wish to analyse it into its respective components. The quantity c shows how much of the labour of former years has been taken over towards the product of the present year in the form of means of production. Quantities $v + s$ show the value components of the product created by new labour during the last year only; the relation between v and s finally shows us how the annual labour programme of society is apportioned to the two tasks of maintaining the workers and maintaining those who do not work. This analysis remains valid and correct also with regard to the reproduction of individual capital, no matter what may be the material form of the product this capital has created. All three, c, v, and s, appear alike to a capitalist of the machinery industry in the form of machinery and its parts; to the owner of a music hall they are represented by the charms of the dancers and the skill of the acrobats. So long as the product is left undifferentiated, c, v, and s differ from one another only in so far as they are *aliquot* components of value. This is quite sufficient for the reproduction of individual capital, as such reproduction begins with the value-form of capital, a certain amount of money that has been gained by the realisation of the manufactured product. The formula $c + v + s$ then is the given basis for the division of this amount of money; one part for the purchase of the material means of production, a second part for the purchase of labour power, and a third part—in the case of simple reproduction assumed in the first instance—for the capitalist's personal consumption. In the case of expanding reproduction part three is further subdivided, only a fraction of it being devoted to the capitalist's personal consumption, the remainder to increasing his capital. In order to reproduce his capital actually, the capitalist must, of course, turn again to the commodity market with the capital he has divided in this manner, so that he can acquire the material prerequisites of production such as raw materials, instruments, and so on. It seems a matter of course to the individual capitalist as well as to his scientific ideologist, the 'vulgar economist', that he should in fact find there just those means of production and labour power he needs for his business.

The position is different as regards the total production of a society. From the point of view of society as a whole, the exchange of commodities can only effect a shifting around, whereby the individual parts of the total product change hands. The material composition of the product, however, cannot be changed by this process. After this change of places, as well as before it, there can be reproduction of total capital, if, and only if, there is in the total product of the preceding period: first, a sufficient quantity of means of production, secondly, adequate provisions to maintain the same amount of labour as hitherto, and, last but not least, the goods necessary to maintain the capitalist class and its hangers-on in a manner suitable to their station. This brings us to a new plane: we are now concerned with material points of view instead of pure relations of value. It is the use-form of the total social product that matters now. What the individual capitalist considers nobody else's business becomes a matter of grave concern for the totality of capitalists. Whereas it does not make the slightest difference to the individual capitalist whether he produces machinery, sugar, artificial manure or a progressive newspaper—provided only that he can find a buyer for his commodity so that he can get back his capital plus surplus value—it matters infinitely to the 'total capitalist' that his total product should have a definite use-form. By that we mean that it must provide three essentials: the means of production to renew the labour process, simple provisions for the maintenance of the workers, and provisions of higher quality and luxury goods for the preservation of the 'total capitalist' himself. His desire in this respect is not general and vague, but determined precisely and quantitatively. If we ask what quantities of all three categories are required by the 'total capitalist', the value-composition of last year's total product gives us a definite estimate, as long, that is, as we confine ourselves to simple reproduction, which we have taken for our starting point. Hitherto we have conceived of the formula $c + v + s$ as a merely quantitative division of the total value, applicable alike to total capital and to individual capital, and representing the quantity of labour contained in the annual product of society. Now we see that the formula is also the basis of the material composition of the product. Obviously the 'total capitalist', if he is to take up reproduction to the same extent as before, must find in his new total product as many means of production as correspond to the size of c, as many simple provisions for the workers as correspond to the sum of wages v, and as many provisions of better quality for himself and his hangers-on as correspond to s. In this way our analysis of the value of the society's aggregate product is translated into a general recipe for this product as follows: the total c of society must be re-embodied in an equal quantity of means of production, the v in provision for the workers, and the s in provision for the capitalists, in order that simple reproduction may take place.

Here we come up against palpable differences between the individual capitalist and the total capitalist. The manner in which the former always reproduces his constant and variable capital as well as his surplus value is such that all three parts are contained in the same material form within his homogeneous product, that this material form, moreover, is completely irrelevant and may have different qualities in the case of each individual capitalist. The 'total capitalist', for his part, reproduces every component of the value of his annual product in a different material form, c as means of production, v as provisions for the workers, and s as provisions for the capitalist. In the case of the reproduction of individual capitals, there is no discrepancy between relations of value and material points of view. Besides, it is quite clear that individual capital may concentrate on aspects of value, accepting material conditions as a law from heaven, as self-evident phenomena of commodity-exchange, whereas the 'total capitalist' has to reckon with material points of view. If the total c of society were not reproduced annually in the form of an equal amount of means of production, every individual capitalist would be doomed to search the commodity market in vain with his c realised in cash, unable to find the requisite materials for his individual reproduction. From the point of view of reproducing the total capital, the formula $c + v + s$ is inadequate. This again is proof of the fact that the concept of total capital is something real and does not merely paraphrase the concept of production. We must, however, make general distinctions in our exposition of total capital: instead of showing it as a homogeneous whole, we must demonstrate its three main categories; and we shall not vitiate our theory if, for the sake of simplicity, we consider for the present only two departments of total capital: the production of producer goods, and that of consumer goods for workers and capitalists. We have to examine each department separately, adhering to the fundamental conditions of capitalist production in each case. At the same time, we must also emphasise the mutual connections between these two departments from the point of view of reproduction. For only if each is regarded in connection with the other, do they make up the basis of the social capital as a whole.

We made a start by investigating individual capital. But we must approach the demonstration of total capital and its total product in a somewhat different manner. Quantitatively, as a quantity of value, the c of society consists precisely in the total of individual constant capitals, and the same applies to the other amounts, v and s. But the outward shape of each has changed—the c of constant capitals re-emerges from the process of production as an element of value with infinitely varied facets, comprising a host of variegated objects for use, but in the total product it appears, as it were, contracted into a certain quantity of means of production. Similarly with v and s, which in the case of the individual capitalist re-emerge as items in a most colourful jumble of commodities, being provisions in adequate quantities for the workers and capitalists. Adam Smith came very close to recognising this fact when he observed that the categories of fixed and circulating capital and of revenue in relation to the individual capitalist do not coincide with these categories in the case of society.

We have come to the following conclusions:

(1) The formula $c + v + s$ serves to express the production of society viewed as a whole, as well as the production of individual capitalists.
(2) Social production is divided into two departments, engaged in the production of producer and consumer goods respectively.
(3) Both departments work according to capitalist methods, that is to say they both aim at the production of surplus value, and thus the formula $c + v + s$ will apply to each of them.
(4) The two departments are interdependent, and are therefore bound to display a certain quantitative relationship, namely the one department must produce all means of production, the other all provisions for the workers and capitalists of both departments.

Proceeding from this point of view, Marx devised the following diagram of capitalist reproduction:

   I. $4,000c + 1,000v + 1,000s = 6,000$ means of production
  II. $2,000c + \quad 500v + \quad 500s = 3,000$ articles of consumption.[3]

The figures in this diagram express quantities of value, amounts of money which are chosen arbitrarily, but their ratios are exact. Each department is characterised by the use-form of the commodities produced. Their mutual circulation takes place as follows: Department I supplies the means of production for the entire productive process, for itself as well as for Department II. From this alone it follows that for the undisturbed continuance of reproduction—for we still presume simple reproduction on the old scale—the total produce of Department I (I 6,000) must have the same value as the sum of constant capitals in both departments: (I 4,000c + II 2,000c). Similarly, Department II supplies provisions for the whole of society, for its own workers and capitalists as well as for the workers and capitalists of Department I. Hence it follows that for the undisturbed course of consumption and production and its renewal on the old scale it is necessary that the total

[3] *Capital*, vol. ii, p. 459.

quantity of provisions supplied by Department II should equal in value all the incomes of the employed workers and capitalists of society [here II $3,000 = I(1,000v + 1,000s) + II(500v + 500s)$].

Here we have indeed expressed relationships of value which are the foundation not only of capitalist reproduction but of reproduction in every society. In every producing society, whatever its social form, in the primitive small village community of the Bakairi of Brazil, in the *oikos* of a Timon of Athens with its slaves, or in the imperial *corvée* farm of Charlemagne, the labour power available for society must be distributed in such a way that means of production as well as provisions are produced in adequate quantities. The former must suffice for the immediate production of provisions as well as for the future renewal of the means of production themselves, and the provisions in their turn must suffice for the maintenance of the workers occupied in the production alike of these same provisions and of the means of production, and moreover for the maintenance of all those who do not work.

In its broad outline, Marx's scheme corresponds with the universal and absolute foundation of social reproduction, with only the following specifications: socially necessary labour appears here as value, the means of production as constant capital, the labour necessary for the maintenance of the workers as variable capital and that necessary for the maintenance of those who do not work as surplus value.

In capitalist society, however, the connections between these two great departments depend upon exchange of commodities, on the exchange of equivalents. The workers and capitalists of Department I can only obtain as many provisions from Department II as they can deliver of their own commodities, the means of production. The demand of Department II for means of production, on the other hand, is determined by the size of its constant capital. It follows therefore that the sum of the variable capital and of the surplus value in the production of producer goods [here $I(1,000v + 1,000s)$] must equal the constant capital in the production of provisions [here $II(2,000c)$].

An important proviso remains to be added to the above scheme. The constant capital which has been spent by the two departments is in reality only part of the constant capital used by society. This constant capital is divided into two parts; the first is fixed capital—premises, tools, labouring cattle—which functions in a number of periods of production, in every one of which, however, only part of its value is absorbed by the product, according to the amount of its wear and tear. The second is circulating capital such as raw materials, auxiliary semi-finished products, fuel and lighting—its whole value is completely absorbed by the new product in every period of production. Yet only that part of the means of production is relevant for reproduction which is actually absorbed by the production of value; without becoming less correct, an exact exposition of social circulation may disregard the remaining part of the fixed capital which has not been absorbed by the product, though it should not completely forget it. This is easy to prove.

Let us assume that the constant capital, 6,000c, in the two departments, which is in fact absorbed by the annual product of these departments, consists of 1,500c fixed and 4,500c circulating capital, the 1,500c of fixed capital representing here the annual wear and tear of the premises, machinery and labouring cattle. This annual wear and tear equals, say, 10 per cent of the total value of the fixed capital employed. Then the total social capital would really consist of 19,500c + 1,500v, the constant capital in both departments being 1,500c of fixed and 4,500c of circulating capital. Since the term of life of the aggregate fixed capital, with a 10 per cent wear and tear, is ten years *ex hypothesi*, the fixed capital needs renewal only after the lapse of ten years. Meanwhile one-tenth of its value enters into social production in every year. If all the fixed capital of a society, with the same rate of wear and tear, were of equal durability, it would, on our assumption, need complete renewal once within ten years. This, however, is not the case. Some of the various use-forms which are part of the fixed capital may last longer and others shorter, wear and tear and duration of life are quite different in the different kinds and individual representations of fixed capital. In consequence, fixed capital need not be renewed—reproduced in its concrete use-form—all at once, but parts of it are continually renewed at various stages of social production, while other parts still function in their older form. Our assumption of a fixed capital of 15,000c with a 10 per cent rate of wear and tear does not mean that this must be renewed all at once every ten years, but that an annual average renewal and replacement must be effected of a part of the total fixed social capital corresponding to one-tenth of its value; that is to say, Department I which has to satisfy the needs of society for means of production must reproduce, year by year, not only all its raw and partly finished materials, etc., its circulating capital to the value of 4,500, but must also reproduce the use-forms of its fixed capital—premises, machinery, and the like—to the extent of 1,500, corresponding with the annual wear and tear of fixed capital. If Department I continues in this manner to renew one-tenth of the fixed capital in its use-form every year, the result will be that every ten years the total fixed capital of society will have been replaced throughout by new items; thus it follows that the reproduction of those parts disregarded so far is also completely accounted for in the above scheme.

In practice, the procedure is that every capitalist sets aside from his annual production, from the realisation of his commodities, a certain amount for the redemption of his fixed capital. These individual annual deductions must amount to a certain quantity of capital, therefore the capitalist has in fact renewed his fixed capital, that is, he has replaced it by new and more efficient items. This alternating procedure of building up annual reserves of money for the renewal of fixed capital and of the periodical employment of the accumulated amounts for the actual renewal of fixed capital varies with the individual capitalist, so that some are accumulating reserves, while others have already started their renewals. Thus every year part of the fixed capital is actually renewed. The monetary procedure here only disguises the real process which characterises the reproduction of fixed capital.

On closer observation we see that this is as it should be. The whole of the fixed capital takes part in the process of production, for physically the mass of usable objects, premises, machinery, labouring cattle, are completely employed. It is their peculiarity as fixed capital, on the other hand, that only part of the value is absorbed in the production of value, since in the process of reproduction (again postulating simple reproduction), all that matters is to replace in their natural form the values which have been actually used up as means of subsistence and production during a year's production. Therefore, fixed capital need only be reproduced to the extent that it has in fact been used up in the production of commodities. The remaining portion of value, embodied in the total use-form of fixed capital, is of decisive importance for production as a labour process, but does not exist for the annual reproduction of society as a process of value-formation.

Besides, this process which is here expressed by relations of value applies equally to every society, even to a community which does not produce commodities. If once upon a time, for instance, say ten years' labour of 1,000 fellaheen was required for the construction of the famous Lake Moeris and the related Nile canals—that miraculous lake, which Herodotus tells us was made by hand—and if for the maintenance of this, the most magnificent drainage system of the world, the labour of a further 100 fellaheen was annually required (the figures, of course, are chosen at random), we might say that after every hundred years the Moeris dam and the canals were reproduced anew, although in fact the entire system was not constructed as a whole in every century. This is manifestly true. When, amid the stormy incidents of political history and alien conquests, the usual crude neglect of old monuments of culture set in—as displayed, e.g. by the English in India when the reproductional needs of ancient civilisations were understood no longer—then in the course of time the whole Lake Moeris, its water, dikes and canals, the two pyramids in its midst, the colossus upon it and other marvellous erections, disappeared without a trace, as though they had never been built. Only ten lines in Herodotus, a dot on Ptolemy's map of the world, traces of old cultures, and of villages and cities bear witness that at one time rich life sprang from this magnificent irrigation system, where to-day there are only stretches of arid desert in inner Lybia, and desolate swamps along the coast. There is only one point where Marx's scheme of simple reproduction may appear unsatisfactory or incomplete in relation to constant capital, and that is when we go back to that period of production, when the total fixed capital was first created. Indeed, society possesses transformed labour amounting to more than those parts of fixed capital which are absorbed into the value of the annual product and are in turn replaced by it. In the figures of our example the total social capital does not consist of $6,000c + 1,500v$, as in the diagram, but of $19,500c + 1,500v$. Though 1,500 of the fixed capital (which, on our assumption, amounts to 15,000) are annually reproduced in the form of appropriate means of production, an equal amount is also consumed by the same production each year, though the whole of the fixed capital as a use-form, an aggregate of objects, has been renewed. After ten years, society possesses in the eleventh, just as in any other year, a fixed capital of 15,000, whereas it has annually achieved only 1,500c; and its constant capital as a whole is 19,500, whereas it has created only 6,000. Obviously, since it must have created this surplus of 13,500 fixed capital by its labour, it possesses more accumulated past labour than our scheme of reproduction warrants. Even at this stage, the annual labour of society must be based on some previous annual labour that has been hoarded. This question of past labour, however, as the foundation of all present labour, brings us to the very first beginning which is as meaningless with regard to the economic development of mankind as it is for the natural development of matter. The scheme of reproduction grasps the social process as perpetually in motion, as a link in the endless chain of events, it neither wants to demonstrate its initial origin, nor should it do so. The social reproductive process is always based on past labour, we may trace it back as far as we like. Social labour has no beginning, just as it has no end. Like the historical origin of Herodotus' Lake Moeris, the beginnings of the reproductive process in the history of civilisation are lost in the twilight of legend. With the progress of techniques and with cultural development, the means of production change their form, crude paleoliths are replaced by sharpened tools, stone implements by elegant bronze and iron, the artisan's tool by steam-driven machinery. Yet, though the means of production and the social organisation of the productive process continually change their form, society already possesses for its labour process a certain amount of past labour serving as the basis for annual reproduction.

Under capitalist methods of production past labour of society preserved in the means of production takes the form of capital, and the question of the origin of this past labour which forms the foundation of the reproductive process becomes the question of the genesis of capital. This is much less legendary, indeed it is writ in letters of blood in modern history. The very fact, however, that we cannot think of simple reproduction unless we assume a hoard of past labour, surpassing in volume the labour annually performed for the maintenance of society, touches the sore spot of simple reproduction; and it shows that simple reproduction is a fiction not only for capitalist production but also for the progress of civilisation in general. If we merely wish to understand this fiction properly, and to reduce it to a scheme, we must presume, as its *sine qua non*, results of a past productive process which cannot possibly be restricted to simple reproduction but inexorably points towards enlarged reproduction. By way of illustration, we might compare the aggregate fixed capital of society with a railway. The durability and consequently the annual wear and tear of its various parts is very different. Parts such as viaducts and tunnels may last for centuries, steam engines for decades, but other rolling stock will be used up in a short time, in some instances in a few months. Yet it is possible to work out an average rate of wear and tear, say thirty years, so that the value of the whole is annually depreciated by one-thirtieth. This loss of value is now continually made good by partial reproduction of the railway (which may count as repairs), so that a coach is renewed to-day, part of the engine to-morrow, and a section of sleepers the day after. On our assumption then, the old railway is replaced by a new one after thirty years, a similar amount of labour being performed each year by the society so that simple reproduction takes place. But the railway can only be reproduced in this manner—it cannot be so produced. In order to make it fit for use and to make good its gradual wear and tear, the railway must have been completed in the first place. Though the railway can be repaired in parts, it cannot be made fit for use piecemeal, an axle to-day and a coach to-morrow. Indeed, the very essence of fixed capital is always to enter into the productive process in its entirety, as a material use-value. In order to get this use-form ready in the first place, society must apply a more concentrated amount of labour to its manufacture. In terms of our example, the labour of thirty years that is used for repairs, must be compressed into, say, two or three years. During this period of manufacture, society must therefore expend an amount of labour far greater than the average, that is to say it must have recourse to expanding reproduction; later, when the railway is finished, it may return to simple reproduction. Though we need not visualise the aggregate fixed capital as a single coherent use-object or a conglomeration of objects which must be produced all at once, the manufacture of all the more important means of production, such as buildings, transport facilities, and agricultural structures, requires a more concentrated application of labour, and this is true for the modern railway or steamship as much as it was for the rough stone-axe and the handmill.

Therefore it is only in theory that simple reproduction can be conceived as alternating with enlarged reproduction; the latter is not only a general condition of a progressive civilisation and an expanding population, but also the *sine qua non* for the economic form of fixed capital, or those means of production which in every society correspond to the fixed capital.

Marx deals with this conflict between the formation of fixed capital and simple reproduction but indirectly, in connection with fluctuations in the wear and tear of the fixed capital, more rapid in some years than in others. Here he emphasises the need for perpetual 'overproduction', i.e. enlarged reproduction, since a strict policy of simple reproduction would periodically lead to reproductive losses. In short, he regards enlarged reproduction under the aspect of an insurance fund for the fixed capital of the society, rather than in the light of the actual productive process.[4]

In quite a different context Marx appears to endorse the opinion expressed above. In *Theories on the Surplus Value*, vol. ii, part 2, analysing the conversion of revenue into capital, he speaks of the peculiar reproduction of the fixed capital, the replacement of which in itself already provides a fund for accumulation. He draws the following conclusion:

'The point we have in mind is as follows: even if the aggregate capital employed in machine manufacture were just large enough to make good the annual wear and tear of the machines, many more machines could be annually produced than are required, since the wear and tear is in parts merely *idealiter* and must be made good *realiter*, *in natura*, only after a certain number of years. Capital so employed supplies each year a mass of machinery which becomes available for, and anticipates new, capital investments. Let us suppose, for instance, a machine manufacturer who starts production this year. During this year, he supplies machines for £12,000. If he were merely to reproduce the machines he has manufactured, he would have to produce, during the subsequent eleven years, machines for £1,000 only, and even then, a year's production would not be consumed within the year. Still less could it be consumed, if he were to employ the whole of his capital. To keep this

---

[4] Ibid., pp. 544–7. Cf. also p. 202 on the necessity of enlarged reproduction under the aspect of a reserve fund.

capital working, to keep it reproducing itself every year, a new and continuous expansion of the branches of manufacture that require these machines, is indispensable. This applies even more, if the machine manufacturer himself accumulates. In consequence, even *if the capital invested in one particular branch of production is simply being reproduced*,[5] a continuous accumulation in the other branches of production must go with it.'[6]

We might take the machine manufacturer of Marx's example as illustrating the production of fixed capital. Then the inference is that if society maintains simple reproduction in this sphere, employing each year a similar amount of labour for the production of fixed capital (a procedure which is, of course, impossible in practical life), then annual production in all other spheres must expand. But if here, too, simple reproduction is to be maintained, then, if the fixed capital once created is to be merely renewed, only a small part of the labour employed in its creation can be expended. Or, to put it the other way round: if society is to provide for investment in fixed capital on a large scale, it must, even assuming simple reproduction to prevail on the whole, resort periodically to enlarged reproduction.

With the advance of civilisation, there are changes not only in the form of the means of production but also in the quantity of value they represent—or better, changes in the social labour stored up in them. Apart from the labour necessary for its immediate preservation, society has increasingly more labour time and labour power to spare, and it makes use of these for the manufacture of means of production on an ever increasing scale. How does this affect the process of reproduction? How, in terms of capitalism, does society create out of its annual labour a *greater* amount of capital than it formerly possessed? This question touches upon enlarged reproduction, and it is not yet time to deal with it.

---

[5] Marx's italics.
[6] *Theorien über den Mehrwert*, vol. ii, part 2, p. 248.

5

THE CIRCULATION OF MONEY

In our study of the reproductive process we have not so far considered
the circulation of money. Here we do not refer to money as a measur-
ing rod, an embodiment of value, because all relations of social labour
have been expressed, assumed and measured in terms of money. What
we have to do now is to test our diagram of simple reproduction under
the aspect of money as a means of exchange.

Quesnay already saw that we shall only understand the social reproductive process if we assume, side by side with the means of production and consumer goods, a certain quantity of money.[1]

Two questions now arise: (1) by whom should the money be
owned, and (2) how much of it should there be? The answer to the
first question, no doubt, is that the workers receive their wages in

[1] In his seventh note to the *Tableau Économique*, following up his arguments against the
mercantilist theory of money as identical with wealth, Quesnay says: 'The bulk of money
in a nation cannot increase unless this reproduction itself increases; otherwise, an
increase in the bulk of money would inevitably be prejudicial to the annual production of
wealth. . . . Therefore we must not judge the opulence of states on the basis of a greater
or smaller quantity of money: thus a stock of money, equal to the income of the landowners, is deemed much more than enough for an agricultural nation where the circulation proceeds in a regular manner, and where commerce takes place in confidence and
full liberty' (*Analyse du Tableau Économique*, ed. Oncken, pp. 324–5).

the form of money with which they buy consumer goods. From the point of view of society, this means merely that the workers are allocated a certain share of the fund for consumption: every society, whatever its historical form of production, makes such allocations to its workers. It is, however, an essential characteristic of the capitalist form of production that the workers do not obtain their share directly in the form of goods but by way of commodity exchange, just as it is an essential feature of the capitalist mode of production that their labour power is not applied directly, as a result of a relation of personal domination, but again by way of commodity exchange: the workers selling their labour power to the owners of the means of production, and purchasing freely their consumer goods. Variable capital in its money form is the expression and medium of both these transactions.

Money, then, comes first into circulation by the payment of wages. The capitalist class must therefore set a certain quantity of money circulating in the first place, and this must be equal to the amount they pay in wages. The capitalists of Department I need 1,000 units of money, and the capitalists of Department II need 500 to meet their wages bill. Thus, according to our diagram, two quantities of money are circulating: I(1,000v) and II(500v). The workers spend the total of 1,500 on consumer goods, i.e. on the products of Department II. In this way, labour power is maintained, that is to say the variable capital of society is reproduced in its natural form, as the foundation of all other reproductions of capital. At the same time, the capitalists of Department II dispose of their aggregate product (1,500) in the following manner: their own workers receive 500 and the workers of Department I receive 1,000. This exchange gives the capitalists of Department II possession of 1,500 money units: 500 are their own variable capital which has returned to them; these may start circulating again as variable capital but for the time being they have completed their course. The other 1,000 accrue to them year by year out of the realisation of one-third of their own products. The capitalists of Department II now buy means of production from the capitalists of Department I for these 1,000 money units in order to renew the part of their own constant capital that has been used up. By means of this purchase, Department II renews in its natural form half of the constant capital IIc it requires. Department I now has in return 1,000 money units which are nothing more than the money originally paid to its own workers. Now, after having changed hands twice, the money has returned to Department I, to become effective later as variable capital. This completes the circulation of this quantity of money for the moment, but the circulation within society has not yet come to an end. The capitalists of Department I have not yet realised their surplus value to buy consumer goods for themselves; it is still contained in their product in a form which is of no use to them. Moreover, the capitalists of Department II have not yet renewed the second half of their constant capital. These two acts of exchange are identical both in substance and in value, for the capitalists of Department I receive their goods from Department II in exchange for the I(1,000c) means of production needed by the capitalists of Department II. However, a new quantity of money is required to effect this exchange. It is true that the same money which has already completed its course, might be brought into circulation again for this purpose—in theory, there could be no objection to this. In practice, however, this solution is out of the question, for the needs of the capitalists, as consumers, must be satisfied just as constantly as the needs of the workers—they run parallel to the process of production and must be mediated by specific quantities of money. Hence it follows that the capitalists of both departments— that is to say all capitalists—must have a further cash reserve in hand, in addition to the money required as variable capital, in order to realise their own surplus value in the form of consumer goods. On the other hand, before the total product is realised and during the process of its production, certain parts of the constant capital must be bought continually. These are the circulating parts of the constant capital, such as raw and auxiliary materials, semi-finished goods, lighting and the like. Therefore, not only must the capitalists of Department I have certain quantities of money in hand to satisfy their needs as consumers, but the capitalists of Department II must also have money to meet the requirements of their constant capital. The exchange of 1,000s I (the surplus value of Department I contained in the means of production) against goods is thus effected by money which is advanced partly by the capitalists of Department I in order to satisfy their needs as consumers, and partly by the capitalists of Department II in order to satisfy their needs as producers.[2] Both lots of capitalists may each advance 500 units of the money necessary for the exchange, or possibly the two departments will contribute in different proportions. At any rate, two things are certain: (a) the money set aside for the purpose by both departments must suffice to effect the exchange between I(1,000s) and II(1,000c); (b) whatever the distribution of this money between the two departments may have been, the exchange transaction completed, each department of capitalist production must again possess the same amount of money it had earlier put into circulation. This latter maxim applies quite generally to social circulation as a whole: once the process of circulation is concluded, money will always have returned to its point of origin. Thus all capitalists, after universal exchange, have achieved a twofold result: first they have exchanged products which, in their natural form, were of no use to them, against other products which, in their natural form, the capitalists require either as means of production or for their own consumption. Secondly, they have regained possession of the money which they set in circulation so as to effect these acts of exchange.

This phenomenon is unintelligible from the point of view of simple commodity circulation, where commodity and money continually change places—possession of the commodity excluding the possession of money, as money constantly usurps the place which the commodity has given up, and *vice versa*. Indeed, this is perfectly true with regard to every individual act of commodity exchange which is the form of social circulation. Yet this social circulation itself is more than mere exchange of commodities: it is the circulation of capital. It is, however, an essential and characteristic feature of this kind of circulation, that it does not only return to the capitalist the value of his original capital plus an increase, the surplus value, but that it also assists social reproduction by providing the means of production and labour power in the natural form of productive capital, and by ensuring the maintenance of those who do not work. Possessing both the means of production and

---

[2] Marx (*Capital*, vol. ii, p. 482) takes the money spent directly by the capitalists of Department II as the starting point of this act of exchange. As Engels rightly says in his footnote, this does not affect the final result of circulation, but the assumption is not the correct condition of circulation within society. Marx himself has given a better exposition in *Capital*, vol. ii, pp. 461–2.

the money needed, the capitalists start the total social process of circulation; as soon as the social capital has completed its circuit, everything is again in their hands, apportioned to each department according to the investments made by it. The workers have only temporary possession of money during which time they convert the variable capital from its money form into its natural form. The variable capital in the capitalists' hands is nothing but the outward shape of part of their capital, and for this reason it must always revert to them.

So far, we have only considered circulation as it takes place between the two large departments of production. Yet 4,000 units of the first department's produce remain there in the form of means of production to renew its constant capital of 4,000c. Moreover 500 of the consumer goods produced in Department II [corresponding to the surplus value II(500s)] also remain in this department in the form of consumer goods for the capitalist class. Since in both departments the mode of production is capitalistic, that is unplanned, private production, each department can distribute its own products—means of production in Department I and consumer goods in Department II—amongst its own capitalists only by way of commodity exchange, i.e. by a large number of individual sale transactions between capitalists of the same department. Therefore the capitalists of both departments must have a reserve of money with which to perform these exchange transactions—to renew both the means of production in Department I and the consumer goods for the capitalist class in Department II. This part of circulation does not present any features of specific interest, as it is merely simple commodity circulation. Vendor and purchaser alike belong to the same category of agents of production, and circulation is concerned only with money and commodity changing hands within the same class and department. All the same, the money needed for this circulation must from the outset be in the hands of the capitalist class: it is part of their capital.

So far, the circulation of total social capital presents no peculiarities, even if we consider the circulation of money. From the very outset it is self-evident that society must possess a certain quantity of money to make this circulation possible, and this for two reasons: first, the general form of capitalist production is that of commodity production which implies the circulation of money; secondly, the circulation of capital is based upon the continuous alternation of the three forms of capital: money capital, productive capital, and commodity capital. And as it is this very money, finally, which operates as capital—our diagram referring to capitalist production exclusively—the capitalist class must have possession of this money, as it has possession of every other form of capital; it throws it into circulation in order to regain possession as soon as the process of circulation has been completed.

At first glance, only one detail might strike us: if the capitalists themselves have set in motion all the money which circulates in society, they must also advance the money needed for the realisation of their own surplus value. Thus it seems that the capitalists as a class ought to buy their own surplus value with their own money. As the capitalist class has possession of this money resulting from previous periods of production, even prior to the realisation of the product of each working period, the appropriation of surplus value at first sight does not seem to be based upon the unpaid labour of the wage labourer—as it in fact is—but merely the result of an exchange of commodities against an equivalent quantity of money both supplied by the capitalist class itself. A little reflection, however, dispels this illusion. After the general completion of circulation, the capitalists, now as before, possess their money funds which either reverted to them or remained in their hands. Further, they acquired consumer goods for the same amount which they have consumed. (Note that we are still confining ourselves to simple reproduction as the prime condition of our diagram of reproduction: the renewal of production on the old scale and the use of all surplus value produced for the personal consumption of the capitalist class.)

Moreover, the illusion vanishes completely if we do not confine ourselves to one period of production but observe a number of successive periods in their mutual interconnections. The value the capitalist puts into circulation to-day in the form of money for the purpose of realising his own surplus value, is in fact nothing but his surplus value resulting from the preceding period of production in form of money. The capitalist must advance money out of his own pocket in order to buy his goods for consumption. On the one hand, the surplus value which he produces each year either exists in a natural form which renders it unfit for consumption, or, if it takes a consumable form, it is temporarily in the hands of another person. On the other hand, he (the capitalist) has regained possession of the money, and he is now making his advances by realising his surplus value from the preceding period. As soon as he has realised his new surplus value, which is still embodied in the commodity-form, this money will return to him. Consequently, in the course of several periods of production, the capitalist class draws its consumer goods from the pool, as well as the other natural forms of its capital. The quantity of money originally in its possession, however, remains unaffected by this process.

Investigation of the circulation of money in society shows that the individual capitalist can never invest the whole of his money capital in production but must always keep a certain money reserve to be employed as variable capital, i.e. as wages. Further, he must keep a capital reserve for the purchase of means of production at any given period, and in addition, he must have a cash reserve for his personal consumption.

The process of reproducing the total social capital thus entails the necessity of producing and reproducing the substance of money. Money is also capital, for Marx's diagram which we have discussed before, conceives of no other than capitalist production. Thus the diagram seems incomplete. We ought to add a further department, that of production of the means of exchange, to the other two large departments of social production [those of means of production (I) and of consumer goods (II)]. It is, indeed, a characteristic feature of this third department that it serves neither the purposes of production nor those of consumption, merely representing social labour in an undifferentiated commodity that cannot be used. Though money and its production, like the exchange and production of commodities, are much older than the capitalist mode of production, it was only the latter which made the circulation of money a general form of social circulation, and thus the essential element of the social reproductive process. We can only obtain a comprehensive diagram of the essential points of capitalist production if we demonstrate the original relationship between the production and reproduction of money and the two other departments of social production.

Here, however, we deviate from Marx. He included the production of gold (we have reduced the total production of money to the production of gold for the sake of simplicity) in the first department of social production.

'The production of gold, like that of metals generally, belongs to Department I, which occupies itself with means of production.'[3]

This is correct only in so far as the production of gold is the production of metal for industrial purposes (jewellery, dental stoppings, etc.). But gold in its capacity as money is not a metal but rather an embodiment of social labour *in abstracto*. Thus it is no more a means of production than it is a consumer good. Besides, a mere glance at the diagram of reproduction itself shows what inconsistencies must result from confusing means of exchange with means of production. If we add a diagrammatic representation of the annual production of gold as the substance of money to the two departments of social production, we get the following three sets of figures:

$$\text{I.} \quad 4,000c + 1,000v + 1,000s = 6,000 \text{ means of production}$$
$$\text{II.} \quad 2,000c + 500v + 500s = 3,000 \text{ means of subsistence}$$
$$\text{III.} \quad 20c + 5v + 5s = 30 \text{ means of exchange}$$

This quantity of value of 30, chosen by Marx as an example, obviously does not represent the quantity of money which circulates annually in society; it only stands for that part which is annually reproduced, the annual wear and tear of the money substance which, on the average, remains constant so long as social reproduction remains on the same level. The turnover of capital goes on in a regular manner and the realisation of commodities proceeds at an equal pace. If we consider the third line as an integral part of the first one, as Marx wants us to do, the following difficulty arises: the constant capital of the third department consists of real and concrete means of production, premises, tools, auxiliary materials, vessels, and the like, just as it does in the two other departments. Its product, however, the 30g which represent money, cannot operate in its natural form as constant capital in any process of production. If we therefore include this 30g as an essential part of the product of Department I (6,000 means of production) the means of production will show a social deficit of this size which will

---

[3] Ibid., p. 548.

prevent Departments I and II from resuming their reproduction on the old scale. According to the previous assumption—which forms the foundation of Marx's whole diagram—reproduction as a whole starts from the product of each department in its actual use-form. The proportions of the diagram are based upon this assumption; without it, they dissolve in chaos. Thus the first fundamental relation of value is based upon the equation: $I(6,000)$ equals $I(4,000c) + II(2,000c)$. This cannot apply to the product $III(30g)$, since neither department can use gold as a means of production [say, in the proportion of $I(20c) + II(10c)$]. The second fundamental relation derived from this is based upon the equation $I(1,000v) + I(1,000s) = II(2,000c)$. This would mean, with regard to the production of gold, that as many consumer goods are taken from Department II as there are means of production supplied to it. But this is equally untrue. Though the production of gold removes concrete means of production from the total social product and uses them as its constant capital, though it takes concrete consumer goods for the use of its workers and capitalists, corresponding to its variable capital and surplus value, the product it supplies yet cannot operate in any branch of production as a means of production, nor is it a consumer good, fit for human consumption. To include the production of money in the activities of Department I, therefore, is to run counter to all the general proportions which express the relations of value in Marx's diagram, and to diminish the diagram's validity.

The attempt by Marx to find room for the production of gold within Department I (means of production) moreover leads to dubious results. The first act of circulation between this new sub-department (called by Marx Ig) and Department II (consumer goods) consists as usual in the workers' purchase of consumer goods from Department II with the money obtained as wages from the capitalists. This money is not yet a product of the new period of production. It has been reserved by the capitalists of Department Ig out of the money contained in their product of an earlier period. This, indeed, is the normal procedure. But now Marx allows the capitalists of Department II to buy gold from Ig with the money they have reserved, gold as a commodity material to the value of 2. This is a leap from the production of money into the industrial production of gold which is no more to do with the problem of the production of money than with the production of boot-polish.

Yet out of the 5 Ig v that have been reserved, 3 still remain, and as the capitalist, unable to use them as constant capital, does not know what to do with them, Marx arranges for him to add them on to his own reserve of money. Marx further finds the following way out to avoid a deficit in the constant capital of II which must be exchanged completely against the means of production (Iv + Is):

'Therefore, this money must be entirely transferred from IIc to IIs, no matter whether it exists in necessities of life or articles of luxury, and vice versa, a corresponding value of commodities must be transferred from IIs to IIc. Result: A portion of the surplus-value is accumulated as a hoard of money.'[4]

A strange result, in all conscience! We have achieved an increase in money, a surplus of the money substance, by simply confining ourselves to the annual wear and tear of the money fund. This surplus value comes into existence, for some unknown reason, at the expense of the capitalists in the consumer goods department. They practise abstinence, not because they may want to expand their production of surplus value, let us say, but in order to secure a sufficient quantity of consumer goods for the workers engaged in the production of gold.

The capitalists of Department II, however, get poor reward for this Christian virtue. In spite of their abstinence, they are not only unable to expand their reproduction, but they are no longer even in the position to resume their production on its former scale. Even if the corresponding 'commodity value' is transferred from IIg to IIc, it is not only the value but its actual and concrete form which matters. As the new part of the product of I now consists of money which cannot be used as a means of production, Department II, in spite of its abstinence, cannot renew its constant material capital on the old scale. As our diagram presupposes simple reproduction, its conditions are thus violated in two directions: surplus value is being hoarded, and the constant capital shows a deficit. Marx's own results, then, prove that the production of gold cannot possibly find a place in either of the two departments of his diagram; the whole diagram is upset as soon as the first act of exchange between Departments I and II has been completed. As Engels remarks, in his footnote, 'the analysis of the exchange of newly

[4] Ibid., p. 550.

produced gold within the constant capital of Department I is not contained in the MS.'[5] Besides, the inconsistency would then only have been greater. The point of view we advocate is confirmed by Marx himself when he gives an exhaustive answer to the question, as striking as it is brief: 'Money in itself is not an element of actual reproduction.'[6]

There is another important reason why we should put the production of money in a third and separate department of social production as a whole: Marx's diagram of simple reproduction is valid as the starting-point and foundation of the reproductive process not only for capitalism but also, *mutatis mutandis*, for every regulated and planned economic order, for instance a socialist one. However, the production of money, just like the commodity-form of the products, becomes obsolete when private ownership of the means of production is abolished. It constitutes the 'illegitimate' liabilities, the *faux frais* of the anarchic economy under capitalism, a peculiar burden for a society based upon private enterprise, which implies the annual expenditure of a considerable amount of labour on the manufacture of products which are neither means of production nor yet consumer goods. This peculiar expenditure of labour by a society producing under capitalism will vanish in a socially planned economy. It is most adequately demonstrated by means of a separate department within the process of reproducing social capital. It is quite immaterial in this connection whether we picture a country which produces its own gold or a country which imports gold from abroad. The same expenditure of social labour which in the first case is necessary for the direct production of gold, is required in the second case to effect the exchange transactions.

These observations show that the problem of the reproduction of total capital is not so crude as it often appears to those who approach it merely from the point of view of crises. The central problem might be formulated as follows: how is it possible that, in an unplanned economy, the aggregate production of innumerable individual capitalists can satisfy all the needs of society? One answer that suggests itself points to the continual fluctuations in the level of production in accordance with the fluctuating demand, i.e. the periodical changes in

[5] Ibid., p. 551.
[6] Ibid., p. 572.

the market. This point of view, which regards the aggregate product of society as an undifferentiated mass of commodities, and treats social demand in an equally absurd way, overlooks the most important element, the *differentia specifica* of the capitalist mode of production. We have seen that the problem of capitalist reproduction contains quite a number of precisely defined relations referring to specific capitalist categories and also, *mutatis mutandis*, to the general categories of human labour. The real problem consists in their inherent tendencies towards both conflict and harmony. Marx's diagram is the scientific formulation of the problem.

Inquiry must now be made into the implications of this diagram analytic of the process of production. Has it any real bearing on the problems of actual life? According to the diagram, circulation absorbs the entire social product; all consumers' needs are satisfied, and reproduction takes place without friction. The circulation of money succeeds the circulation of commodities, completing the cycle of social capital. But what is the position in real life? The relations outlined in the diagram lay down a precise first principle for the division of social labour in a planned production—always providing a system of simple reproduction, i.e. no changes in the volume of production. But no such planned organisation of the total process exists in a capitalist economy, and things do not run smoothly, along a mathematical formula, as suggested by the diagram. On the contrary, the course of reproduction shows continual deviations from the proportions of the diagram which become manifest (a) in the fluctuations of prices from day to day; (b) in the continual fluctuations of profits; (c) in the ceaseless flow of capital from one branch of production to another, and finally in the periodical and cyclical swings of reproduction between overproduction and crisis.

And yet, apart from all these deviations, the diagram presents a socially necessary average level in which all these movements must centre, to which they are always striving to return, once they have left it. That is why the fluctuating movements of the individual capitalists do not degenerate into chaos but are reduced to a certain order which ensures the prolonged existence of society in spite of its lack of a plan.

In comparison, the similarities and the profound discrepancies between Marx's diagram of reproduction and Quesnay's *Tableau*

Économique strike us at once. These two diagrams, the beginning and end of the period of classical economics, are the only attempts to describe an apparent chaos in precise terms, a chaos created by the interrelated movements of capitalist production and consumption, and by the disparity of innumerable private producers and consumers. Both writers reduce this chaotic jumble of individual capitals to a few broadly conceived rules which serve, as it were, as moorings for the development of capitalist society, in spite of its chaos. They both achieve a synthesis between the two aspects which are the basis of the whole movement of social capital: that circulation is at one and the same time a capitalist process of production and appropriating surplus value, and also a social process of producing and consuming material goods necessary to civilised human existence. Both show the circulation of commodities to act as a mediator for the social process as a whole, and both conceive of the circulation of money as a subsidiary phenomenon, an external and superficial expression of the various stages within the circulation of commodities.

It is socially necessary labour which creates value. This inspired fundamental law of Marx's theory of value which provided the solution of the money problem, amongst others, further led him first to distinguish and then to integrate those two aspects in the total reproductive process: the aspect of value and that of actual material connections. Secondly, Marx's diagram is based upon the precise distinction between constant and variable capital which alone reveals the internal mechanisms of the production of surplus value and brings it, as a value-relationship, into precise relation with the two material categories of production: that of producer and consumer goods.

After Quesnay, some classical economists, Adam Smith and Ricardo in particular, came fairly close to this point of view. Ricardo's contribution, his precise elaboration of the theory of value, has even been frequently confused with that of Marx. On the basis of his own theory of value, Ricardo saw that Smith's method of resolving the price of all commodities into $v + s$—a theory which wrought so much havoc in the analysis of reproduction—is wrong; but he was not much interested in Smith's mistake, nor indeed very enthusiastic about the problem of reproduction as a whole. His analysis, in fact, represents a certain decline after that of Adam Smith, just as Smith had partly retrogressed as against the Physiocrats. If Ricardo expounded the fundamental value categories of bourgeois economy—wages, surplus value and capital— much more precisely and consistently than his predecessors, he also treated them more rigidly. Adam Smith had shown infinitely more understanding for the living connections, the broad movements of the whole. In consequence he did not mind giving two, or, as in the case of the problem of value, even three or four different answers to the same question. Though he contradicts himself quite cheerfully in the various parts of his analysis, these very contradictions are ever stimulating him to renewed effort, they make him approach the problem as a whole from an ever different point of view, and so to grasp its dynamics. Ultimately, it was the limitation of their bourgeois mentalities which doomed both Smith and Ricardo to failure. A proper understanding of the fundamental categories of capitalist production, of value and surplus value as living dynamics of the social process demands the understanding of this process in its historical development and of the categories themselves as historically conditioned forms of the general relations of labour. This means that only a socialist can really solve the problem of the reproduction of capital. Between the *Tableau Économique* and the diagram of reproduction in the second volume of *Capital* there lies the prosperity and decline of bourgeois economics, both in time and in substance.

6

ENLARGED REPRODUCTION

The shortcomings of the diagram of simple reproduction are obvious: it explains the laws of a form of reproduction which is possible only as an occasional exception in a capitalist economy. It is not simple but enlarged reproduction which is the rule in every capitalist economic system, even more so than in any other.[1]

Nevertheless, this diagram is of real scientific importance in two respects. In practice, even under conditions of enlarged reproduction, the greater part of the social product can be looked on as simple reproduction, which forms the broad basis upon which production in every case expands beyond its former limits. In theory, the analysis of simple reproduction also provides the necessary starting point for all scientific exposition of enlarged reproduction. The diagram of simple reproduction of the aggregate social capital therefore inevitably

[1] 'The premise of simple reproduction, that $I(v + s)$ is equal to IIc, is irreconcilable with capitalist production, although this does not exclude the possibility that a certain year in an industrial cycle of ten or eleven years may not show a smaller total production than the preceding year, so that there would not have been even a simple reproduction, compared to the preceding year. Indeed, considering the natural growth of population per year, simple reproduction could take place only in so far as a correspondingly larger number of unproductive servants would partake of the 1,500 representing the aggregate surplus-product. But accumulation of capital, actual capitalist production, would be impossible under such circumstances' (*Capital*, vol. ii, p. 608).

introduces the further problem of the enlarged reproduction of the total capital.

We already know the historical peculiarity of enlarged reproduction on a capitalist basis. It must represent itself as accumulation of capital, which is both its specific form and its specific condition. That is to say, social production as a whole—which on a capitalist basis is the production of surplus value—can in every case be expanded only in so far as the social capital that has been previously active is now augmented by surplus value of its own creation. This use of part of the surplus value (and in particular the use of an increasing part of it) for the purpose of production instead of personal consumption by the capitalist class, or else the increase of reserves, is the basis of enlarged reproduction under capitalist conditions of production.

The characteristic feature of enlarged reproduction of the aggregate social capital—just as in our previous assumption of simple reproduction—is the reproduction of individual capitals, since production as a whole, whether regarded as simple or as enlarged production, can in fact only occur in the form of innumerable independent movements of reproduction performed by private individual capitals.

The first comprehensive analysis of the accumulation of individual capitals is given in volume i of Marx's *Capital*, section 7, chapters 22, 23. Here Marx treats of (a) the division of the surplus value into capital and revenue; (b) the circumstances which determine the accumulation of capital apart from this division, such as the degree of exploitation of labour power and labour productivity; (c) the growth of fixed capital relative to the circulating capital as a factor of accumulation; and (d) the increasing development of an industrial reserve army which is at the same time both a consequence and a prerequisite of the process of accumulation. In the course of this discussion, Marx deals with two inspired notions of bourgeois economists with regard to accumulation: the 'theory of abstinence' as held by the more vulgar economists, who proclaim that the division of surplus value into capital, and thus accumulation itself, is an ethical and heroic act of the capitalists; and the fallacy of the classical economists, their doctrine that the entire capitalised part of the surplus value is used solely for consumption by the productive workers, that is to say spent altogether on wages for the workers employed year by year. This erroneous assumption, which completely overlooks the fact that every increase of production must manifest itself not only in the increased number of employed workers but also in the increase of the material means of production (premises, tools, and, certainly, raw materials) is obviously rooted in that 'dogma' of Adam Smith which we have already discussed. Moreover, the assumption that the expenditure of a greater amount of capital on wages is sufficient to expand production, also results from the mistaken idea that the prices of all commodities are completely resolved into wages and surplus value, so that the constant capital is disregarded altogether. Strangely enough, even Ricardo who was, at any rate occasionally, aware of this element of error in Smith's doctrine, subscribes most emphatically to its ultimate inferences, mistaken though they were:

'It must be understood, that all the productions of a country are consumed; but it makes the greatest difference imaginable whether they are consumed by those who reproduce, or by those who do not reproduce another value. When we say that revenue is saved, and added to capital, what we mean is, that the portion of revenue, so said to be added to capital, is consumed by productive, instead of unproductive labourers.'[2]

If all the goods produced are thus swallowed up by human consumption, there can clearly be no room to spare in the total social product for such unconsumable means of production as tools and machinery, new materials and buildings, and consequently enlarged reproduction, too, will have to take a peculiar course. What happens—according to this odd conception—is simply that staple foodstuffs for new workers will be produced to the amount of the capitalised part of surplus value instead of the choice delicacies previously provided for the capitalist class. The classical theory of enlarged reproduction does not admit of any variations other than those connected with the production of consumer goods. After our previous observations it is not surprising that Marx could easily dispose of this elementary mistake of both Ricardo and Smith. Just as simple reproduction requires a regulated renewal of the constant capital, the material means of production,

---

[2] Ricardo, *Principles*, chap. viii, 'On Taxes'. MacCulloch's edition of Ricardo's Works, p. 87, note. (Reference not given in original.)

quite apart from the production of consumer goods in the necessary quantity for labourer and capitalist, equally so in the case of expanding production must part of the new additional capital be used to enlarge the constant capital, that is to add to the material means of production. Another law, Marx discovered, must also be applied here. The constant capital, continually overlooked by the classical economists, increases relative to the variable capital that is spent on wages. This is merely the capitalist expression of the general effects of increasing labour productivity. With technical progress, human labour is able to set in motion ever larger masses of means of production and to convert them into goods. In capitalist terms, this means a progressive decrease in expenses for living labour, in wages, relative to the expenses for inanimate means of production. Contrary to the assumption of Adam Smith and Ricardo, enlarged reproduction must not only start with the division of the capitalised part of the surplus value into constant and variable capital, but, as the technique of production advances, it is bound to allocate in this division ever increasing portions to the constant, and ever diminishing portions to the variable capital. This continuous qualitative change in the composition of capital is the specific manifestation of the accumulation of capital, that is to say of enlarged reproduction on the basis of capitalism.[3]

---

[3] 'The specifically capitalist mode of production, the development of the productive power of labour corresponding to it, and the change thence resulting in the organic composition of capital, do not merely keep pace with the advance of accumulation, or with the growth of social wealth. They develop at a much quicker rate, because mere accumulation, the absolute increase of the total social capital, is accompanied by the centralisation of the individual capitals of which that total is made up; and because the change in the technological composition of the additional capital goes hand in hand with a similar change in the technological composition of the original capital. With the advance of accumulation, therefore, the proportion of constant to variable capital changes. If it was originally say $1:1$, it now becomes successively $2:1$, $3:1$, $4:1$, $5:1$, $7:1$, etc., so that, as the capital increases, instead of $\frac{1}{2}$ of its total value, only $\frac{1}{3}$, $\frac{1}{4}$, $\frac{1}{5}$, $\frac{1}{6}$, $\frac{1}{8}$, etc., is transformed into labour-power, and, on the other hand, $\frac{2}{3}$, $\frac{3}{4}$, $\frac{4}{5}$, $\frac{5}{6}$, $\frac{7}{8}$ into means of production. Since the demand for labour is determined not by the amount of capital as a whole, but by its variable constituent alone, that demand falls progressively with the increase of the total capital, instead of, as previously assumed, rising in proportion to it. It falls relatively to the magnitude of the total capital, and at an accelerated rate, as this magnitude increases. With the growth of the total capital, its variable constituent or the labour incorporated in it, also does increase, but in a constantly diminishing proportion. The

The other side of this picture of continual changes in the relation between the portions of constant and variable capital is the formation of a relative surplus population, as Marx called it, that is to say that part of the working population which exceeds the average needs of capital, and thus becomes redundant. This reserve of unemployable industrial labour (taken here in a broader sense, and including a proletariat that is dominated by merchant capital) is always present. It forms a necessary prerequisite of the sudden expansion of production in times of boom, and is another specific condition of capitalist accumulation.[4]

From the accumulation of individual capitals we can therefore deduce the following four characteristic phenomena of enlarged reproduction:

(1) The volume of enlarged reproduction is independent, within certain limits, of the growth of capital, and can transcend it. The necessary methods for achieving this are: increased exploitation of labour and natural forces, and increased labour productivity (including increased efficiency of the fixed capital).

(2) All real accumulation starts with that part of the surplus value which is intended for capitalisation being divided into constant and variable capital.

(3) Accumulation as a social process is accompanied by continuous changes in the relation between constant and variable capital, whereby that portion of capital which is invested in inanimate

intermediate pauses are shortened, in which accumulation, works as simple extension of production, on a given technical basis. It is not merely that an accelerated accumulation of total capital, accelerated in a constantly growing progression, is needed to absorb an additional number of labourers, or even, on account of the constant metamorphosis of old capital, to keep employed those already functioning. In its turn, this increasing accumulation and centralisation becomes a source of new changes in the composition of capital, of a more accelerated diminution of its variable, as compared with its constant constituent' (*Capital*, vol. i, pp. 642–3).

[4] 'The course characteristic of modern industry, viz., a decennial cycle (interrupted by smaller oscillations), of periods of average activity, production at high pressure, crisis and stagnation, depends on the constant formation, the greater or less absorption, and the re-formation of the industrial reserve army or surplus population. In their turn, the varying phases of the industrial cycle recruit the surplus population, and become one of the most energetic agents of its reproduction' (ibid., pp. 646–7).

means of production continually increases as compared with that expended on wages.

(4) Concomitant with the accumulative process, and as a condition of the latter, there develops an industrial reserve army.

These characteristics, derived from the reproductive process as it is performed by the individual capitals, represent an enormous step forward as compared with the analyses of bourgeois economists. Now, however, our problem is to demonstrate the accumulation of the aggregate capital which originates from these movements of individual capitals, and on the basis of the diagram of simple reproduction to establish the precise relations between the aspects of value prevalent in the production of surplus value and the material considerations in the production of consumer and producer goods, with a view to accumulation.

The essential difference between enlarged reproduction and simple reproduction consists in the fact that in the latter the capitalist class and its hangers-on consume the entire surplus value, whereas in the former a part of the surplus value is set aside from the personal consumption of its owners, not for the purpose of hoarding, but in order to increase the active capital, i.e. for capitalisation. To make this possible, the new additional capital must also find the material prerequisites for its activity forthcoming. Here the concrete composition of the aggregate social product becomes important. Marx says already in volume i, when he considers the accumulation of individual capitals:

'The annual production must in the first place furnish all those objects (use-values) from which the material components of capital, used up in the course of the year, have to be replaced. Deducting these there remains the net or surplus-product, in which the surplus-value lies. And of what does this surplus-product consist? Only of things destined to satisfy the wants and desire of the capitalist class, things which, consequently, enter into the consumption fund of the capitalists? Were that the case, the cup of surplus-value would be drained to the very dregs, and nothing but simple reproduction would ever take place.—To accumulate it is necessary to convert a portion of the surplus-product into capital. But we cannot, except by a miracle, convert into capital anything but such articles as can be employed in the labour-process (i.e. means of production), and such further articles as are suitable for the sustenance of the labourer, (i.e. means of subsistence). Consequently, a part of the annual surplus-labour must have been applied to the production of additional means of production and subsistence, over and above the quantity of these things required to replace the capital advanced. In one word, surplus-value is convertible into capital solely because the surplus-product, whose value it is, already comprises the material elements of new capital.'[5]

Additional means of production, however, and additional consumer goods for the workers alone are not sufficient; to get enlarged reproduction really going, additional labour is also required. Marx now finds a specific difficulty in this last condition:

'For this the mechanism of capitalist production provides beforehand, by converting the working class into a class dependent on wages, a class whose ordinary wages suffice, not only for its maintenance, but for its increase. It is only necessary for capital to incorporate this additional labour-power, annually supplied by the working class in the shape of labourers of all ages, with the surplus means of production comprised in the annual produce, and the conversion of surplus-value into capital is complete.'[6]

This is the first solution which Marx gave to the problem of the accumulation of the aggregate capital. Having dwelt on this aspect of the question already in volume i of *Capital*, Marx returns to the problem at the end of the second volume of his main work whose concluding 21st chapter is devoted to accumulation and enlarged reproduction of the aggregate capital.

Let us examine Marx's diagrammatic exposition of accumulation more closely. On the model of the diagram of simple reproduction with which we are already familiar, he devised a diagram for enlarged reproduction, the difference appearing most clearly if we compare the two.

Assuming that society's annual aggregate product can be represented by an amount to the value of 9,000 (denoting millions of working hours, or, in capitalist monetary terms, any arbitrary amount of money), the aggregate product is to be distributed as follows:

[5] *Capital*, vol. i, pp. 593–4.
[6] Ibid., p. 594.

$$\begin{array}{llll}
\text{I.} & 4,000c + 1,000v + 1,000s = 6,000 \\
\text{II.} & 2,000s + 500v + 500s = \underline{3,000} \\
& & \text{Total:} & \overline{9,000}
\end{array}$$

Department I represents means of production, Department II consumer goods. One glance at the proportion of the figures shows that in this case simple reproduction alone is possible. The means of production made in Department I equal the total of the means of production actually used by the two departments. If these are merely renewed, production can be repeated only on its previous scale. On the other hand, the aggregate product of Department II equals the total of wages and surplus value in both departments. This shows that the consumer goods available permit only the employment of just as many workers as were previously employed, and that the entire surplus value is similarly spent on consumer goods, i.e. the personal consumption of the capitalist class.

Now let us take the same aggregate product of 9,000 in the following equation:

$$\begin{array}{llll}
\text{I.} & 4,000c + 1,000v + 1,000s = 6,000 \\
\text{II.} & 1,500c + 750v + 750s = \underline{3,000} \\
& & \text{Total:} & \overline{9,000}
\end{array}$$

Here a double disproportion confronts us: 6,000 means of production are created—more than those which are actually used by the society, i.e. $4,000c + 1,500c$, leaving a surplus of 500. Similarly, less consumer goods (3,000) are produced than the sum of what is paid out in wages (i.e. $1,000v + 750v$, the requirement of the workers), plus the aggregate of surplus value that has been produced ($1,000s + 750s$). This results in a deficit of 500. Since our premises do not allow us to decrease the number of workers employed, the consequence must be that the capitalist class cannot consume the entire surplus value it has pocketed. This proves fully consistent with the two material preconditions of enlarged reproduction on a capitalist basis: part of the appropriated surplus value is not to be consumed but is used for the purposes of production; and more means of production must be produced so as to ensure the use of the capitalised surplus value for the actual expansion of reproduction.

In considering the diagram of simple reproduction, we saw that its fundamental social conditions are contained in the following equation: the aggregate of means of production (the product of Department I) must be equivalent to the constant capital of both departments, but the aggregate of consumer goods (the product of Department II) must equal the sum of variable capitals and surplus values of the two departments. As regards enlarged reproduction, we must now infer a precise inverse double ratio. The general precondition of enlarged reproduction is that the product of Department I must be greater in value than the constant capital of both departments taken together, and that of Department II must be so much less than the sum total of both the variable capital and the surplus value in the two departments.

This, however, by no means completes the analysis of enlarged reproduction; rather has it led us merely to the threshold of the question. Having deduced the proportions of the diagram, we must now pursue their further activities, the flow of circulation and the continuity of reproduction. Just as simple reproduction may be compared to an unchanging circle, to be repeated time and again, so enlarged reproduction, to quote Sismondi, is comparable to a spiral with ever expanding loops. Let us begin by examining the loops of this spiral. The first general question arising in this connection is how actual accumulation proceeds in the two departments under the conditions now known to us, i.e. how the capitalists may capitalise part of their surplus value, and at the same time acquire the material prerequisites necessary for enlarged reproduction.

Marx expounds the question in the following way:

Let us assume that half the surplus value of Department I is being accumulated. The capitalists, then, use 500 for their consumption but augment their capital by another 500. In order to become active, this additional capital of 500 must be divided, as we now know, into constant and variable capital. Assuming the ratio of 4 to 1 remains what it was for the original capital, the capitalists of Department I will divide their additional capital of 500 thus: they will buy new means of production for 400 and new labour for 100. This does not present any difficulties, since we know that Department I has already produced a surplus of 500 means of production. Yet the corresponding enlargement of the variable capital by 100 units of money is not enough, since the new additional labour power must also find adequate consumer goods which can only be supplied by Department II. Now the circulation between the two large departments is shifting. Formerly, under conditions of simple reproduction, Department I acquired 1,000 consumer goods for its own workers, and now it must find another 100 for its new workers. Department I therefore engages in enlarged reproduction as follows:

$$4,400c + 1,100v.$$

Department II, in turn, after selling these consumer goods to the value of 100, is now in a position to acquire additional means of production to the same amount from Department I. And in fact, Department I still has precisely one hundred of its surplus product left over which now find their way into Department II, enabling the latter to expand its own reproduction as well. Yet here, too, the additional means of production alone are not much use; to make them operate, additional labour power is needed. Assuming again that the previous composition of capital has been maintained, with a ratio of 2 to 1 as regards constant and variable capital, additional labour to the tune of 50 is required to work the additional 100 means of production. This additional labour, however, needs additional consumer goods to the amount of its wages, which are in fact supplied by Department II itself. This department must therefore produce, in addition to the 100 additional consumer goods for the new workers of Department I and the goods for the consumption of its own workers, a further amount of consumer goods to the tune of 50 as part of its aggregate product. Department II therefore starts on enlarged reproduction at a rate of $1,600c + 800v$.

Now the aggregate product of Department I (6,000) has been absorbed completely. 5,500 were necessary for renewing the old and used-up means of production in both departments, and the remaining 500 for the expansion of production: 400 in Department I and 100 in Department II. As regards the aggregate product of Department II (3,000), 1,900 have been used for the increased labour force in the two departments, and the 1,100 consumer goods which remain serve the capitalists for their personal consumption, the consumption of their surplus value. 500 are consumed in Department I, and 600 in Department II where, out of a surplus value of 700, only 150 had been capitalised (100 being expended on means of production and 50 on wages).

Enlarged reproduction can now proceed on its course. If we maintain our rate of exploitation at 100 per cent, as in the case of the original capital, the next period will give the following results:

$$
\begin{array}{ll}
\text{I.} & 4{,}400c + 1{,}100v + 1{,}100s = 6{,}600 \\
\text{II.} & 1{,}600c + 800v + 800s = \underline{3{,}200} \\
& \text{Total: } 9{,}800
\end{array}
$$

The aggregate product of society has grown from 9,000 to 9,800, the surplus value of Department I from 1,000 to 1,100, and of Department II from 750 to 800. The object of the capitalist expansion of production, the increased production of surplus value, has been gained. At the same time, the material composition of the aggregate social product again shows a surplus of 600 as regards the means of production (6,600) over and above those which are actually needed (4,400 + 1,600), and also a deficit in consumer goods as against the sum total made up by the wages previously paid (1,100v + 800v) and the surplus value that has been created (1,100s + 800s). And thus we again have the material possibility as well as the necessity to use part of the surplus value, not for consumption by the capitalist class, but for a new expansion of production.

The second enlargement of production, and increased production of surplus value, thus follows from the first as a matter of course and with mathematical precision. The accumulation of capital, once it has started, automatically leads farther and farther beyond itself. The circle has become a spiral which winds itself higher and higher as if compelled by a natural law in the guise of mathematical terms. Assuming that in the following years there is always capitalisation of half the surplus value, while the composition of the capital and the rate of exploitation remain unchanged, the reproduction of capital will result in the following progression:

2nd year:
 I. $4,840c + 1,210v + 1,210s = 7,260$
 II. $1,760c + 880v + 880s = \underline{3,520}$
 Total: $\overline{10,780}$

3rd year:
 I. $5,324c + 1,331v + 1,331s = 7,986$
 II. $1,936c + 968v + 968s = \underline{3,872}$
 Total: $\overline{11,858}$

4th year:
 I. $5,856c + 1,464v + 1,464s = 8,784$
 II. $2,129c + 1,065v + 1,065s = \underline{4,259}$
 Total: $\overline{13,043}$

5th year:
 I. $6,442c + 1,610v + 1,610s = 9,662$
 II. $2,342c + 1,712v + 1,712s = \underline{4,686}$
 Total: $\overline{14,348}$

Thus, after five years of accumulation, the aggregate social product is found to have grown from 9,000 to 14,348, the social aggregate capital from $(5,500c + 1,750v = 7,250)$ to $(8,784c + 2,782v = 11,566)$ and the surplus value from $(1,000s + 500s = 1,500)$ to $(1,464s + 1,065s = 2,529)$, whereby the surplus value for personal consumption, being 1,500 at the beginning of accumulation, has grown to $732 + 958 = 1,690$ in the last year.[7] The capitalist class, then, has capitalised more, it has practised greater abstinence, and yet it has been able to live better. Society, in a material respect, has become richer, richer in means of production, richer in consumer goods, and it has equally become richer in the capitalist sense of the term since it produces more surplus value. The social product circulates in *toto* in society. Partly it serves to enlarge reproduction and partly it serves consumption. The requirements of capitalist accumulation correspond to the material composition of the aggregate social product. What Marx said in volume i of *Capital* is true: the increased surplus value can be added on to capital because the social surplus product comes into the world from the very first in the material form of means of production, in a form incapable of utilisation except in the productive process. At the same time reproduction expands in strict conformity with the laws of circulation: the mutual supply of the two departments of production with additional

[7] Op. cit., vol. ii, pp. 596–601.

means of production and consumer goods proceeds as an exchange of equivalents. It is an exchange of commodities in the course of which the very accumulation of one department is the condition of accumulation in the other and makes this possible. The complicated problem of accumulation is thus converted into a diagrammatic progression of surprising simplicity. We may continue the above chain of equations *ad infinitum* so long as we observe this simple principle: that a certain increase in the constant capital of Department I always necessitates a certain increase in its variable capital, which predetermines beforehand the extent of the increase in Department II, with which again a corresponding increase in the variable capital must be co-ordinated. Finally, it depends on the extent of increase in the variable capital in both departments, how much of the total may remain for personal consumption by the capitalist class. The extent of this increase will also show that this amount of consumer goods which remains for private consumption by the capitalist is exactly equivalent to that part of the surplus value which has not been capitalised in either department.

There are no limits to the continuation of this diagrammatic development of accumulation in accordance with the few easy rules we have demonstrated. But now it is time to take care lest we should only have achieved these surprisingly smooth results through simply working out certain fool-proof mathematical exercises in addition and subtraction, and we must further inquire whether it is not merely because mathematical equations are easily put on paper that accumulation will continue *ad infinitum* without any friction.

In other words: the time has come to look for the concrete social conditions of accumulation.

7

ANALYSIS OF MARX'S DIAGRAM OF ENLARGED REPRODUCTION

The first enlargement of reproduction gave the following picture:

$$
\begin{array}{ll}
\text{I.} & 4{,}400c + 1{,}100v + 1{,}100s = 6{,}600 \\
\text{II.} & 1{,}600c + 800v + 800s = \underline{3{,}200} \\
& \phantom{1{,}600c + 800v + 800s = } \text{Total: } 9{,}800
\end{array}
$$

This already clearly expresses the interdependence of the two departments—but it is a dependence of a peculiar kind. Accumulation here originates in Department I, and Department II merely follows suit. Thus it is Department I alone that determines the volume of accumulation. Marx effects accumulation here by allowing Department I to capitalise one-half of its surplus value; Department II, however, may capitalise only as much as is necessary to assure the production and accumulation of Department I. He makes the capitalists of Department II consume $600s$ as against the consumption of only $500s$ by the capitalists of Department I who have appropriated twice the amount of value and far more surplus value. In the next year, he assumes the capitalists of Department I again to capitalise half their surplus value, this time making the capitalists of Department II capitalise more than in the previous year—summarily fixing the amount to tally exactly with the needs of Department I. 500s now remain for the consumption of the capitalists of Department II—less than the year before—surely a rather queer result of accumulation on any showing. Marx now describes the process as follows:

'Then let Department I continue accumulation at the same ratio, so that 550s are spent as revenue, and 55s accumulated. In that case, 1,100 Iv are first replaced by 1,100 Ic, and 550 Is must be realised in an equal amount of commodities of II, making a total of 1,650 I(v + s). But the constant capital of II, which is to be replaced, amounts only to 1,600, and the remaining 50 must be made up out of 800 IIs. Leaving aside the money aspect of the matter, we have as a result of this transaction:

'I. 4,400c + 550s (to be capitalised); furthermore, realised in commodities of II for the fund for consumption of the capitalists and labourers of I, 1,650 (v + s).

'II. 1,650c + 825v + 725s.

'In Department I, 550s must be capitalised. If the former proportion is maintained, 440 of this amount form constant capital, and 110 variable capital. These 110 must be eventually taken out of 725 IIs, that is to say, articles of consumption to the value of 110 are consumed by the labourers of I instead of the capitalists of II, so that the latter are compelled to capitalise these 110s which they cannot consume. This leaves 615 IIs of the 725 IIs. But if II thus converts these 110 into additional constant capital, it requires an additional variable capital of 55. This again must be taken out of its surplus value. Subtracting this amount from 615 IIs, we find that only 560 IIs remain for the consumption of the capitalists of II, and we obtain the following values of capital after accomplishing all actual and potential transfers:

I. $(4,400c + 440c) + (1,100v + 110v) = 4,840c + 1,210v = 6,050$
II. $(1,600c + 50c + 110c) + (800v + 25v + 55v) =$
$$1,760c + 880v = \underline{2,640}$$
$$\text{Total: } \overline{8,690}\text{'}[1]$$

[1] *Capital*, vol. ii, pp. 598–9.

This quotation is given at length since it shows very clearly how Marx here effects accumulation in Department I at the expense of Department II. In the years that follow, the capitalists of the provisions department get just as rough a deal. Following the same rules, Marx allows them in the third year to accumulate 264s—a larger amount this time than in the two preceding years. In the fourth year they are allowed to capitalise 290s and to consume 678s, and in the fifth year they accumulate 320s and consume 745s. Marx even says: 'If things are to proceed normally, accumulation in II must take place more rapidly than in I, because that portion of $I(v + s)$ which must be converted into commodities of IIc, would otherwise grow more rapidly than IIc, for which it can alone be exchanged.'[2]

Yet the figures we have quoted fail to show a quicker accumulation in Department II, and in fact show it to fluctuate. Here the principle seems to be as follows: Marx enables accumulation to continue by broadening the basis of production in Department I. Accumulation in Department II appears only as a condition and consequence of accumulation in Department I: absorbing, in the first place, the other's surplus means of production and supplying it, secondly, with the necessary surplus of consumer goods for its additional labour. Department I retains the initiative all the time, Department II being merely a passive follower. Thus the capitalists of Department II are only allowed to accumulate just as much as, and are made to consume no less than, is needed for the accumulation of Department I. While in Department I half the surplus value is capitalised every time, and the other half consumed, so that there is an orderly expansion both of production and of personal consumption by the capitalists, the twofold process in Department II takes the following erratic course:

1st year:	150 are capitalised,	600 consumed
2nd	240	660
3rd	254	626
4th	290	678
5th	320	745

[2] Ibid., p. 599.

Here there is no rule in evidence for accumulation and consumption to follow; both are wholly subservient to the requirements of accumulation in Department I.

Needless to say, the absolute figures of the diagram are arbitrary in every equation, but that does not detract from their scientific value. It is the *quantitative ratios* which are relevant, since they are supposed to express strictly determinate relationships. Those precise logical rules that lay down the relations of accumulation in Department I, seem to have been gained at the cost of any kind of principle in construing these relations for Department II; and this circumstance calls for a revision of the immanent connections revealed by the analysis.

It might, however, be permissible to assume the defect to lie in a rather unhappy choice of example. Marx himself, dissatisfied with the diagram quoted above, proceeded forthwith to give a second example in order to elucidate the movements of accumulation, where the figures of the equation run in the following order:

$$
\begin{array}{llll}
\text{I.} & 5,000c + 1,000v + 1,000s = 7,000 \\
\text{II.} & 1,430c + 285v + 285s = \underline{2,000} \\
& & & \text{Total: } \underline{9,000}
\end{array}
$$

In contrast to the previous example, the capital of both departments is here seen to have the same composition, i.e. constant and variable capital are in a ratio of 5 to 1. This already presupposes a considerable development of capitalist production, and accordingly of social labour productivity—a considerable preliminary expansion of the scale of production, and finally, a development of all the circumstances which bring about a relatively redundant surplus population in the working class. We are no longer introduced to enlarged reproduction, as in the first example, at the stage of the original transition from simple to enlarged reproduction—the only point of that is in any case for the sake of abstract theory. This time, we are brought face to face with the process of accumulation as it goes on at a definite and rather advanced stage of development. It is perfectly legitimate to assume these conditions, and they in no way distort the principles we must employ in order to work out the individual loops of the reproductive spiral. Here again Marx takes for a starting point the capitalisation of half the surplus value in Department I.

'Now take it that the capitalist class of I consumes one-half of the surplus-value, or 500, and accumulates the other half. In that case $(1,000v + 500s)$ I, or 1,500, must be converted into 1,500 IIc. Since IIc amounts to only 1,430, it is necessary to take 70 from the surplus-value. Subtracting this sum from 285s leaves 215 IIs. Then we have:

'I. $5,000c + 500s$ (to be capitalised) $+ 1,500$ $(v + s)$ in the fund set aside for consumption by capitalists and labourers.

'II. $1,430c + 70s$ (to be capitalised) $+ 285v + 215s$. As 70 IIs are directly annexed by IIc, a variable capital of 70:5, or 14, is required to set this additional constant capital in motion. These 14 must come out of the 215s, so that only 201 remain, and we have:

'II $(1,430) + 70c + (285v + 14v) + 201s$.'[3]

After these preliminary arrangements, capitalisation can now proceed. This is done as follows:

In Department I the 500s which have been capitalised are divided into five-sixths ($417c$) + one-sixth ($83v$). These 83v withdraw a corresponding amount from IIs which serves to buy units of constant capital and thus accrues to IIc. An increase of IIc by 83 involves the necessity of an increase in IIv by 17 (one-fifth of 83). After the completion of this turnover we therefore have:

I. $(5,000c + 417s) + (1,000v + 83s)v = 5,417c + 1,083v = 6,500$
II. $(1,500c + 82s) \quad + \quad (299v + 17s) \ = 1,538c + \quad 316v = \underline{1,899}$
$$\text{Total } \underline{8,399}$$

The capital of Department I has grown from 6,000 to 6,500, i.e. by one-twelfth; in Department II it has grown from 1,715 to 1,899, i.e. by just over one-ninth.

At the end of the next year, the results of reproduction on this basis are:

I. $5,417c + 1,083v + 1,083s = 7,583$
II. $1,583c + \quad 316v + \quad 316s = \underline{2,215}$
$$\text{Total: } \underline{9,798}$$

[3] Ibid., pp. 600–1.

If the same ratio is maintained in the continuance of accumulation, the result at the end of the second year is as follows:

$$
\begin{array}{ll}
\text{I.} & 5,869c + 1,173v + 1,173s = 8,215 \\
\text{II.} & 1,715c + 342v + 342s = \underline{2,399} \\
& \text{Total: } \overline{10,614}
\end{array}
$$

And at the end of the third year:

$$
\begin{array}{ll}
\text{I.} & 6,358c + 1,271v + 1,271s = 8,900 \\
\text{II.} & 1,858c + 371v + 371s = \underline{2,600} \\
& \text{Total: } \overline{11,500}
\end{array}
$$

In the course of three years, the total social capital has increased from I.6,000 + II.1,715 = 7,715 to I.7,629 + II.2,229 = 9,858, and the total product from 9,000 to 11,500.

Accumulation in both departments here proceeds uniformly, in marked difference from the first example. From the second year onwards, both departments capitalise half their surplus value and consume the other half. A bad choice of figures in the first example thus seems to be responsible for its arbitrary appearance. But we must check up to make sure that it is not only a mathematical manipulation with cleverly chosen figures which this time ensures the smooth progress of accumulation.

In the first as well as in the second example, we are continually struck by a seemingly general rule of accumulation: to make any accumulation possible, Department II must always enlarge its constant capital by precisely the amount by which Department I increases (a) the proportion of surplus value for consumption and (b) its variable capital. If we take the example of the first year as an illustration, the constant capital of Department II must be increased by 70. And why? because this capital was only 1,430 before.

But if the capitalists of Department I wish to accumulate half their surplus value (1,000) and to consume the other half, they need consumer goods for themselves and for their workers to the tune of 1,500 units which they can obtain only from Department II in exchange for their own products—means of production. Since Department II has already satisfied its own demand for producer goods to the extent of its own constant capital (1,430), this exchange is only possible if Department II decides to enlarge its own constant capital by 70. This means that it must enlarge its own production—and it can do so only by capitalising a corresponding part of its surplus value. If this surplus value amounts of 285 in Department II, 70 of it must be added to the constant capital. The first step towards expansion of production in Department II is thus demonstrated to be at the same time the condition for, and the consequence of, increased consumption by the capitalists of Department I. But to proceed. Hitherto, the capitalists of Department I could only spend one-half of their surplus value (500) on personal consumption. To capitalise the other half, they must redistribute these 500s in such a way as to maintain at least the previous ratio of composition, i.e. they must increase the constant capital by 417 and the variable capital by 83. The first operation presents no difficulties: the surplus value of 500 belonging to the capitalists of Department I is contained in a natural form in their own product, the means of production, and is fit straightway to enter into the process of production; Department I can therefore enlarge its constant capital with the appropriate quantity of its own product. But the remaining 83 can only be used as variable capital if there is a corresponding quantity of consumer goods for the newly employed workers. Here it becomes evident for the second time that accumulation in Department I is dependent upon Department II: Department I must receive for its workers 83 more consumer goods than before from Department II. As this is again possible only by way of commodity exchange, Department I can satisfy its demands only on condition that Department II is prepared for its part to take up products of Department I, producer goods, to the tune of 83. Since Department II has no use for the means of production except to employ them in the process of production, it becomes not only possible but even necessary that Department II should increase its own constant capital by these very 83 which will now be used for capitalisation and are thus again withdrawn from the consumable surplus value of this department. The increase in the variable capital of Department I thus entails the second step in the enlargement of production in Department II. All material prerequisites of accumulation in Department I are now present and enlarged reproduction can proceed.

Department II, however, has so far made only two increases in its constant capital. The result of this enlargement is that if the newly acquired means of production are indeed to be used, the quantity of labour power must be increased correspondingly. Maintaining the previous ratio, the new constant capital of 153 requires a new variable capital of 31. This implies the necessity to capitalise a corresponding further amount of the surplus value. Thus the fund for the capitalists' personal consumption in Department II comes to be what remains of the surplus value (285s) after deduction of the amounts used for twice enlarging the constant capital (70 + 83) and a commensurate increase in the variable capital (31)—a fund of 101, after deducting a total of 184. Similar operations in the second year of accumulation result for Department II in its surplus value being divided into 158 for capitalisation and 158 for the consumption of its capitalists, and in the third year, the figures become 172 and 170 respectively.

We have studied this process so closely, tracing it step by step, because it shows clearly that the accumulation of Department II is completely determined and dominated by the accumulation of Department I. Though this dependence is no longer expressed, as in Marx's first example, by arbitrary changes in the distribution of the surplus value, it does not do away with the fact itself, even if now the surplus value is always neatly halved by each department, one-half for capitalisation and the other for personal consumption. Though there is nothing to choose between the capitalists of the two departments as far as the figures are concerned, it is quite obvious that Department I has taken the initiative and actively carries out the whole process of accumulation, while Department II is merely a passive appendage. This dependence is also expressed in the following precise rule: accumulation must proceed simultaneously in both departments, and it can do so only on condition that the provisions-department increases its constant capital by the precise amount by which the capitalists of the means-of-production-department increase both their variable capital and their fund for personal consumption. This equation (increase IIc = increase Iv + increase Is.c.)[4] is the mathematical cornerstone of Marx's diagram of accumulation, no matter what figures we may choose for its

---

[4] Surplus consumption.

concrete application. But now we must see whether capitalist accumulation does in actual fact conform to this hard and fast rule.

Let us first return to simple reproduction. Marx's diagram, it will be remembered, was as follows:

I. $4,000c + 1,000v + 1,000s = 6,000$ means of production
II. $2,000c + 500v + 500s = \underline{3,000}$ means of consumption
$9,000$ total production

Here, too, we established certain equations which form the foundation of simple reproduction; they were:

(a) The product of Department I equals in value the sum of the two constant capitals in Departments I and II.
(b) The constant capital of Department II equals the sum of variable capital and surplus value in Department I—a necessary consequence of (a).
(c) The product of Department II equals the sum of variable capital and surplus value in both departments—a necessary consequence of (a) and (b).

These equations correspond to the conditions of capitalist commodity production (at the restricted level of simple reproduction, however). Equation (b), for instance, is a result of the production of commodities, entailed by the fact, in other words, that the entrepreneurs of either department can only obtain the products of the other by an exchange of equivalents. Variable capital and surplus value in Department I together represent the demand of this department for consumer goods. The product of Department II must provide for the satisfaction of this demand, but consumer goods can only be obtained in exchange for an equivalent part of the product of Department I, the means of production. These equivalents, useless to Department II in their natural form if not employed as constant capital in the process of production, will thus determine how much constant capital there is to be in Department II. If this proportion were not adhered to, if, e.g., the constant capital of Department II (as a quantity of value) were larger than $I(v + s)$, then it could not be completely transformed into means of production, since the demand of Department I for consumer goods would be too small; if the constant capital (II) were smaller than I(v + s.c.), either the previous quantity of labour power could not be employed in this department, or the capitalists could not consume the whole of their surplus value. In all these cases, the premises of simple reproduction would be violated.

These equations, however, are not just an exercise in mathematics, nor do they merely result from the system of commodity production. To convince us of this fact, there is a simple means at hand. Let us imagine for a moment that, instead of a capitalist method of production, we have a socialist, i.e. a planned society in which the social division of labour has come to replace exchange. This society also will divide its labour power into producers of means of production and producers of means of consumption. Let us further imagine the technical development of labour to be such that two-thirds of social labour are employed in the manufacture of producer goods and one-third in the manufacture of consumer goods. Suppose that under these conditions 1,500 units (reckoned on a daily, monthly, or yearly basis) suffice to maintain the whole working population of the society, one thousand of these being employed, according to our premise, in Department soc. I (making means of production), and five hundred in Department soc. II (making consumer goods), and that the means of production dating from previous labour periods and used up during one year's labour, represent 3,000 labour units. This labour programme, however, would not be adequate for the society, since considerably more labour will be needed to maintain all those of its members who do not work in the material, the productive sense of the term: the child, the old and sick, the civil servant, the artist and the scientist. Moreover, every society needs certain reserves against a rainy day, as a protection against natural calamities. Taking it that precisely the same quantity of labour and, similarly, of means of production as that required for the workers' own maintenance is needed to maintain all the non-workers and to build up the reserves, then, from the figures previously assumed, we should get the following diagram for a regulated production:

I. $4,000c + 1,000v + 1,000s = 6,000$ means of production
II. $2,000c + 500v + 500s = 3,000$ means of consumption

Here c stands for the material means of production that have been used, expressed in terms of social labour time; v stands for the social labour time necessary to maintain the workers themselves and s for that needed to maintain those who do not work and to build up the reserves.

If we check up on the proportions of this diagram, we obtain the following result: there is neither commodity production nor exchange, but in truth a social division of labour. The products of Department I are assigned to the workers of Department II in the requisite quantities, and the products of Department II are apportioned to everyone, worker or no, in both departments, and also to the reserve-fund; all this being the outcome not of an exchange of equivalents but of a social organisation that plans and directs the process as a whole—because existing demands must be satisfied and production knows no other end but to satisfy the demands of society.

Yet all that does not detract from the validity of the equations. The product of Department I must equal $Ic + IIc$: this means simply that Department I must annually renew all the means of production which society has used up during one year's labour. The product of Department II must equal the sum of $I(v + s) + II(v + s)$: this means that society must each year produce as many consumer goods as are required by all its members, whether they work or not, plus a quota for the reserve fund. The proportions of the diagram are as natural and as inevitable for a planned economy as they are for a capitalist economy based upon anarchy and the exchange of commodities. This proves the diagram to have objective social validity, even if, just because it concerns *simple* reproduction, it has hardly more than theoretical interest for either a capitalist or a planned economy, finding practical application only in the rarest of cases.

The same sort of scrutiny must now be turned on the diagram of enlarged reproduction. Taking Marx's second example as the basis for our test, let us again imagine a socialist society. From the point of view of a regulated society we shall, of course, have to start with Department II, not with Department I. Assuming this society to grow rapidly, the result will be an increasing demand for provisions by its members, whether they work or not. This demand is growing so quickly that a constantly increasing quantity of labour—disregarding for the moment the progress of labour productivity—will be needed for the production of consumer goods. The quantities required, expressed in terms of social labour incorporated in them, increase from year to year in a progression of, say, 2,000:2,215:2,399:2,600 and so on. Let us further assume that technical conditions demand an increasing amount of means of production for producing this growing quantity of provisions, which, again measured in terms of social labour, mounts from year to year in the following progression: 7,000:7,583:8,215:8,900 and so on. To achieve this enlargement of production, we must further have a growth in the labour performed *per annum* according to the following progression: 2,570:2,798:3,030:3,284. [The figures correspond to the respective amounts of $I(v + s) + II(v + s)$.] Finally, the labour performed annually must be so distributed that one-half is always used for maintaining the workers themselves, a quarter for maintaining those who do not work, and the last quarter for the purpose of enlarging production in the following year. Thus we obtain the proportions of Marx's second diagram of enlarged reproduction for a socialist society. In fact, three conditions are indispensable if production is to be enlarged in any society, even in a planned economy: (1) the society must have an increasing quantity of labour power at its disposal; (2) in every working period, the immediate needs of society must not claim the whole of its working time, so that part of the time can be devoted to making provision for the future and its growing demands; (3) means of production must be turned out year after year in sufficiently growing quantities—without which production cannot be enlarged on a rising scale. In respect of all these general points, Marx's diagram of enlarged reproduction has objective validity—*mutatis mutandis*—for a planned society.

It remains to test whether it is also valid for a capitalist economy. Here we must ask first of all: what is the starting point of accumulation? That is the approach on which we have to investigate the mutual dependence of the accumulative process in the two departments of production. There can be no doubt that under capitalist conditions Department II is dependent upon Department I in so far as its accumulation is determined by the additional means of production available. Conversely, the accumulation in Department I depends upon a corresponding quantity of additional consumer goods being available for its additional labour power. It does not follow, however, that so long as both these conditions are observed, accumulation in both departments is bound, as Marx's diagram makes it appear, to go on automatically year after year. The conditions of accumulation we have enumerated are no more than those without which there can be no accumulation. There may even be a desire to accumulate in both departments, yet the desire to accumulate plus the technical prerequisites of accumulation is not enough in a capitalist economy of commodity production. A further condition is required to ensure that accumulation can in fact proceed and production expand: the effective demand for commodities must also increase. Where is this continually increasing demand to come from, which in Marx's diagram forms the basis of reproduction on an ever rising scale?

It cannot possibly come from the capitalists of Departments I and II themselves—so much is certain right away—it cannot arise out of their personal consumption. On the contrary, it is the very essence of accumulation that the capitalists refrain from consuming a part of their surplus value which must be ever increasing—at least as far as absolute figures are concerned—that they use it instead to make goods for the use of other people. It is true that with accumulation the personal consumption of the capitalist class will grow and that there may even be an increase in the total value consumed; nevertheless it will still be no more than a part of the surplus value that is used for the capitalists' consumption. That indeed is the foundation of accumulation: the capitalists' abstention from consuming the whole of their surplus value. But what of the remaining surplus value, the part that is accumulated? For whom can it be destined? According to Marx's diagram, Department I has the initiative: the process starts with the production of producer goods. And who requires these additional means of production? The diagram answers that Department II needs them in order to produce means of consumption in increased quantities. Well then, who requires these additional consumer goods? Department I, of course—replies the diagram—because it now employs a greater number of workers. We are plainly running in circles. From the capitalist point of view it is absurd to produce more consumer goods merely in order to maintain more workers, and to turn out more means of production merely to keep this surplus of workers occupied. Admittedly, as far as the individual capitalist is concerned, the worker is just as good a consumer, i.e. purchaser of his commodity, as another capitalist or anyone else, provided that he can pay. Every individual capitalist realises his surplus value in the price of his commodity, whether he sells it to the worker or to some other buyer. But this does not hold true from the point of view of the capitalist class as a whole. The working class in general receives from the capitalist class no more than an assignment to a determinate part of the social product, precisely to the extent of the variable capital. The workers buying consumer goods therefore merely refund to the capitalist class the amount of the wages they have received, their assignment to the extent of the variable capital. They cannot return a groat more than that; and if they are in a position to save in order to make themselves independent as small entrepreneurs, they may even return less, though this is the exception.

Part of the surplus value is consumed by the capitalist class itself in form of consumer goods, the money exchanged for these being retained in the capitalists' pockets. But who can buy the products incorporating the other, the capitalised part of the surplus value? Partly the capitalists themselves—the diagram answers—who need new means of production for the purpose of expanding production, and partly the new workers who will be needed to work these new means of production. But that implies a previous capitalist incentive to enlarge production; if new workers are set to work with new means of production, there must have been a new demand for the products which are to be turned out.

Perhaps the answer is that the natural increase of the population creates this growing demand. In fact, the growth of the population and its needs provided the starting point for our examination of enlarged reproduction in an hypothetical socialist society. There the requirements of society could serve as an adequate basis, since the only purpose of production was the satisfaction of wants. In a capitalist society, however, the matter is rather different. What kind of people are we thinking of when we speak of an increase in the population? There are only two classes of the population according to Marx's diagram, the capitalists and the workers. The natural increase of the former is already catered for by that part of the surplus value which is consumed inasmuch as it increases in absolute quantity. In any case, it cannot be the capitalists who consume the remainder, since capitalist consumption of the entire surplus value would mean a reversion to simple reproduction. That leaves the workers, their class also growing by natural increase. Yet a capitalist economy is not interested in this increase for its own sake, as a starting point of growing needs.

The production of consumer goods for Iv and IIv is not an end in itself, as it would be in a society where the economic system is shaped for the workers and the satisfaction of their wants. In a capitalist system, Department II does not produce means of consumption in large quantities simply to keep the workers of Departments I and II. Quite the contrary: a certain number of workers in Departments I and II can support themselves in every case because their labour power is useful under the obtaining conditions of supply and demand. This means that the starting point of capitalist production is not a given number of workers and their demands, but that these factors themselves are constantly fluctuating, 'dependent variables' of the capitalist expectations of profit. The question is therefore whether the natural increase of the working class also entails a growing effective demand over and above the variable capital. And that is quite impossible. The only source of money for the working class in our diagram is the variable capital which must therefore provide in advance for the natural increase of the workers. One way or the other: either the older generation must earn enough to keep their offspring—who cannot, then, count as additional consumers; or, failing that, the next generation, the young workers, must turn to work in order to obtain wages and means of subsistence for themselves—in which case the new working generation is already included in the number of workers employed. On this count, the process of accumulation in Marx's diagram cannot be explained by the natural increase of the population.

But wait! Even under the sway of capitalism, society does not consist exclusively of capitalists and wage labourers. Apart from these two classes, there are a host of other people: the landowners, the salaried employees, the liberal professions such as doctors, lawyers, artists and scientists. Moreover, there is the Church and its servants, the Clergy, and finally the State with its officials and armed forces. All these strata of the population can be counted, strictly speaking, neither among the capitalist nor among the working class. Yet society has to feed and support them. Perhaps it is they, these strata apart from the capitalists and wage labourers, who call forth enlarged reproduction by their demand. But this seeming solution cannot stand up to a closer scrutiny. The landowners must as consumers of rent, i.e. of part of the surplus value, quite obviously be numbered among the capitalist class; since we are here concerned with the surplus value in its undivided, primary form, their consumption is already allowed for in the consumption of the capitalist class. The liberal professions in most cases obtain their money, i.e. the assignment to part of the social product, directly or indirectly from the capitalist class who pay them with bits of their own surplus value. And the same applies to the Clergy, with the difference only that its members also obtain their purchasing power in part from the workers, i.e. from wages. The upkeep of the State, lastly, with its officers and armed forces is borne by the rates and taxes, which are in their turn levied upon either the surplus value or the wages. Within the limits of Marx's diagram there are in fact only the two sources of income in a society: the labourers' wages and the surplus value. All the strata of the population we have mentioned as apart from the capitalists and the workers, are thus to be taken only for joint consumers of these two kinds of income. Marx himself rejects any suggestion that these 'third persons' are more than a subterfuge:

'All members of society not directly engaged in reproduction, with or without labour, can obtain their share of the annual produce of commodities—in other words, their articles of consumption . . . only out of the hands of those classes who are the first to handle the product, that is to say, productive labourers, industrial capitalists, and real estate owners. To that extent their revenues are substantially derived from wages (of the productive labourers), profit and ground rent, and appear as indirect derivations when compared to these primary sources of revenue. But, on the other hand, the recipients of these revenues, thus indirectly derived, draw them by grace of their social functions, for instance that of a king, priest, professor, prostitute, soldier, etc., and they may regard these functions as the primary sources of their revenue.'[5]

And about the consumers of interest and ground rent as buyers,

[5] Ibid., p. 429.

Marx says: 'Now, if that portion of the surplus-value of commodities, which the industrial capitalist yields in the form of ground rent or interest to other shareholders in the surplus-value, cannot be in the long run converted into money by the sale of the commodities, then there is an end to the payment of rent and interest, and the landowners or recipients of interest can no longer serve in the role of miraculous interlopers, who convert aliquot portions of the annual reproduction into money by spending their revenue. The same is true of the expenditure of all so-called unproductive labourers, State officials, physicians, lawyers, etc., and others who serve economists as an excuse for explaining inexplicable things, in the role of the 'general public'.[6]

Seeing that we cannot discover within capitalist society any buyers whatever for the commodities in which the accumulated part of the surplus value is embodied, only one thing is left: foreign trade. But there are a great many objections to a method that conceives of foreign trade as a convenient dumping ground for commodities which cannot be found any proper place in the reproductive process. Recourse to foreign trade really begs the question: the difficulties implicit in the analysis are simply shifted—quite unresolved—from one country to another. Yet if the analysis of the reproductive process actually intends not any single capitalist country but the capitalist world market, there can be no foreign trade: all countries are 'home'. This point is made by Marx already in the first volume of *Capital*, in connection with accumulation:

'We here take no account of export trade, by means of which a nation can change articles of luxury either into means of production or means of subsistence, and *vice versa*. In order to examine the object of our investigation in its integrity, free from all disturbing subsidiary circumstances, we must treat the whole world as one nation and assume that capitalist production is everywhere established and has possessed itself of every branch of industry.'[7]

The same difficulty presents itself if we consider the matter from yet another aspect. In Marx's diagram of accumulation we assumed that the portion of the social surplus value intended for accumulation exists

---

[6] Ibid., pp. 531–2.
[7] Op. cit., vol. i, p. 594, note 1.

from the first in a natural form which demands it to be used for capitalisation.

'In one word, surplus-value is convertible into capital solely because the surplus-product, whose value it is, already comprises the material elements of new capital.'[8]

In the figures of our diagram:

I. $5,000c + 1,000v + 1,000s = 7,000$ means of production
II. $1,430c + 285v + 285s = 2,000$ means of consumption

Here, a surplus value of 570s can be capitalised because from the very outset it consists in means of production. To this quantity of producer goods there correspond besides additional consumer goods to the amount of 114s so that 684s can be capitalised in all. But the process here assumed of simply transferring means of production to constant capital on the one hand, consumer goods to variable capital on the other, in commensurate quantities, is in contradiction with the very structure of capitalist commodity production. Whatever natural form the surplus value may have, there can be no immediate transfer to the place of production for the purpose of accumulation. It must first be realised, it must be turned into hard cash.[9]

Of the surplus value in Department I, 500 are fit to be capitalised, but not until they have first been realised; the surplus value has to shed its natural form and assume the form of pure value before it can be added to productive capital. This is true for each individual capitalist and also for the 'aggregate capitalist' of society, it being a prime condition for capitalist production that the surplus value must be realised in the form of pure value. Accordingly, regarding reproduction from the point of view of society as a whole—

'We must not follow the manner copied by Proudhon from bourgeois economy, which looks upon this matter as though a society with a capitalist mode of production would lose its specific historical and

---

[8] Ibid., p. 594.
[9] Here we can leave out of account instances of products capable in part of entering the process of production without any exchange, such as coal in the mines. Within capitalist production as a whole such cases are rare (cf. Marx, *Theorien* . . ., vol. ii, part 2, pp. 255 ff.).

economic characteristics by being taken as a unit. Not at all. We have, in that case, to deal with the aggregate capitalist.'[10]

The surplus value must therefore shed its form as surplus product before it can re-assume it for the purpose of accumulation; by some means or other it must first pass through the money stage. So the surplus product of Departments I and II must be bought—by whom? On the above showing, there will have to be an effective demand outside I and II, merely in order to realise the surplus value of the two departments, just so that the surplus product can be turned to cash. Even then, we should only have got to the stage where the surplus value has become money. If this realised surplus value is further to be employed in the process of enlarging reproduction, in accumulation, an even larger demand must be expected for the future, a demand which is again to come from outside the two departments. Either the demand for the surplus product will therefore have to increase annually in accordance with the rate of increase of the accumulated surplus value, or—*vice versa*—accumulation can only proceed precisely in so far as the demand outside I and II is rising.

---

[10] *Capital*, vol. ii, p. 503.

8

MARX'S ATTEMPT TO RESOLVE THE DIFFICULTY

Complete abstraction from the circulation of money, though making the process of accumulation so smooth and simple in the diagram of enlarged reproduction, has great disadvantages of its own, we see. There was much to be said for this method in the analysis of simple reproduction, where consumption is the be-all and end-all of production. Money there had an ephemeral part, mediating the distribution of the social product among the various groups of consumers—the agent for the renewal of capital. In the process of accumulation, however, the money form has an essential function: it no longer serves as a mere agent in the circulation of commodities—here it has come to be a feature of capital itself, an element in the circulation of capital. Even if the transformation of the surplus value is not essential to real reproduction, it is the economic *sine qua non* of capitalist accumulation. In the transition from production to reproduction, the surplus product is thus subjected to two metamorphoses: first it casts off its use-form and then it assumes a natural form which is fit for the purpose of accumulation. The point here is not that the different cycles of production are counted off in units of years. It would be just as well to take the month; for that matter, the successive transformation of individual portions of the surplus value in Departments I and II may even intersect in time. Series of years here do not mean units of time but really intend the sequence of economic transformations. What matters is that this sequence must be observed if accumulation is to keep its capitalist character, whether it extends over a longer or a shorter period of time. This brings us back to the old question: How, and by whom, is the accumulated surplus value to be realised?

Marx was well aware that his seemingly water-tight scheme of accumulation did not cover this point adequately, and he himself kept reviewing the problem from various angles. What he says is this:

'It has been shown in volume i, how accumulation works in the case of the individual capitalist. By the conversion of the commodity-capital into money, the surplus-product, in which the surplus-value is incorporated, is also monetised. The capitalist reconverts the surplus-value thus monetised into additional natural elements of his productive capital. In the next cycle of production the increased capital furnishes an increased product. But what happens in the case of the individual capital, must also show in the annual reproduction of society as a whole, just as we have seen it does in the case of reproduction on a simple scale, where the successive precipitation of the depreciated elements of fixed capital in the form of money, accumulated as a hoard, also makes itself felt in the annual reproduction of society.'[1]

He examines the mechanism of accumulation further from this very point of view, focusing on the fact that surplus value must pass through the money stage before it is accumulated.

'For instance, capitalist A, who sells during one year, or during a number of successive years, certain quantities of commodities produced by him, thereby converts that portion of the commodities, which bears surplus-value, the surplus-product, or, in other words, the surplus-value produced by himself, successively into money, accumulates it gradually, and thus makes for himself a new potential money-capital. It is potential money-capital on account of its capacity and destination of being converted into the elements of productive capital. But practically he merely accumulates a simple hoard, which is not an element of actual production. His activity for the time being consists

[1] Capital, vol. ii, p. 571.

only in withdrawing circulating money out of circulation. Of course, it is not impossible that the circulating money thus laid away by him was itself, before it entered into circulation, a portion of some other hoard.'[2] 'Money is withdrawn from circulation and accumulated as a hoard by the sale of commodities without a subsequent purchase. If this operation is conceived as one taking place universally, then it seems inexplicable where the buyers are to come from, since in that case everybody would want to sell in order to hoard, and no one would want to buy. And it must be so conceived, since every individual capital may be in process of accumulation.

'If we were to conceive of the process of circulation as one taking place in a straight line between the various divisions of annual reproduction—which would be incorrect as it consists with a few exceptions of mutually retroactive movements—then we should have to start out from the producer of gold (or silver) who buys without selling, and to assume that all others sell to him. In that case, the entire social surplus-product of the current year would pass into his hands, representing the entire surplus-value of the year, and all the other capitalists would distribute among themselves their relative shares in his surplus-product, which consists naturally of money, gold being the natural form of his surplus-value. For that portion of the product of the gold producer, which has to make good his active capital, is already tied up and disposed of. The surplus-value of the gold producer, in the form of gold, would then be the only fund from which all other capitalists would have to derive the material for the conversion of their annual surplus-product into gold. The magnitude of its value would then have to be equal to the entire annual surplus-value of society, which must first assume the guise of a hoard. Absurd as this assumption would be, it would accomplish nothing more than to explain the possibility of a universal formation of a hoard at the same period. It would not further reproduction itself, except on the part of the gold producer, one single step.

'Before we solve this *seeming* difficulty, we must distinguish . . .'[3]

The obstacle in the way of realising the surplus value which Marx

---

[2] Ibid., p. 572.
[3] Ibid., pp. 573–4.

here calls a 'seeming difficulty' nevertheless is important enough for the whole further discussion in *Capital*, volume ii, to be concentrated on overcoming it. As a first attempt, Marx proffers the solution of a hoard which, owing to the separation of the different individual constant capitals in the process of circulation, will inevitably be formed in a capitalist system of production. Inasmuch as different capital investments have different spans of life, and there is always an interval before the parts of a plant are due for renewal, at any given moment we may find that one individual capitalist is already busy renewing his plant, while another is still building up reserves from the proceeds yielded by the sale of his commodities against the day when he will have enough to renew his fixed capital.

'For instance, let A sell 600, representing $400c + 100v + 100s$ to B, who may represent more than one buyer. A sells 600 in commodities for 600 in money, of which 100 are surplus-value which he withdraws from circulation and hoards in the form of money. But these 100 in money are but the money-form of the surplus-product in which a value of 100 was incorporated.'[4]

In order to comprehend the problem in complete purity, Marx here assumes the whole of the surplus value to be capitalised, for which reason he ignores altogether that part of the surplus value is used for the capitalists' personal consumption; in addition, A', A" and A''' as well as B', B" and B''' here belong to Department I.

'The formation of a hoard, then, is not a production, nor is it an increment of production. The action of the capitalist consists merely in withdrawing from circulation 100 obtained by the sale of his surplus-product, in holding and hoarding this amount. This operation is carried on, not alone on the part of A, but at numerous points of the periphery of circulation by other capitalists named A', A", A''' . . . However, A accomplishes the formation of a hoard only to the extent that he acts as a seller, so far as his surplus-product is concerned, not as a buyer. His successive production of surplus-products, the bearers of his surplus-value convertible into money, is therefore a premise for the formation of his hoard. In the present case, where we are dealing only with the circulation within Department I, the natural form of the

---

[4] Ibid., p. 375.

surplus-product, and of the total product of I, which it is a part, is that of an element of constant capital of I, that is to say it belongs to the category of a means of production creating means of production. We shall see presently what becomes of it, what function it performs, in the hands of the buyers such as B, B', B'', etc.

'It must particularly be noted at this point that A, while withdrawing money from circulation and hoarding it, on the other hand throws commodities into it without withdrawing other commodities in return. The capitalists, B, B', B'', etc., are thereby enabled to throw only money into it and withdraw only commodities from it. In the present case, these commodities, according to their natural form and destination, become a fixed or circulating element of the constant capital of B, B', etc.'[5]

There is nothing new about this whole process. Marx had already described it extensively in connection with simple reproduction, since it alone can explain how a society is able to renew constant capital under conditions of capitalist reproduction. How this process can lay the besetting problem of our analysis of enlarged reproduction is far from self-evident. The difficulty had been that for the purpose of accumulation, part of the surplus value is not consumed by the capitalists but added to capital in order to expand production, giving rise to the question of buyers for this additional product. The capitalists do not want to consume it and the workers are not able to do so, their entire consumption being covered in every case by the available variable capital. Whence the demand for the accumulated surplus value? or, as Marx would have it: Whence the money to pay for the accumulated surplus value?

If, by way of answer, we are referred to the process of hoarding attendant upon the gradual renewal of the constant capital by the individual capitalists at various times, the connection between these two points remains obscure. As long as B, B' and B'', etc., buy producer goods from their colleagues A, A' and A'' in order to renew their constant capital that has in fact been used up, the limits of simple reproduction are not transcended, and the whole thing has nothing to do with our problem. The moment the producer goods purchased by

[5] Ibid., pp. 575–6.

B, B′, B″, etc., serve to increase their constant capital, however, for purposes of accumulation, a number of new questions clamour for attention. First and foremost where do the B's get the cash to buy an additional product from the A's? The only way they could have made their money is by sale of their own surplus product. Before they can acquire new means of production for expanding their enterprises, before they appear as buyers, that is to say, of the surplus product that is to be accumulated, they must first have disposed of their own surplus product—in a word, B, B′, B″, etc., must have been vendors themselves. But who could have bought their surplus product? It is obvious that the difficulty is simply shifted from the A's to the B's without having been mastered.

At one stage of the analysis it really does seem for a time as if a solution were found at last. After a short digression, Marx returns to the main line of his investigation in the following words:

'In the present case, this surplus-product consists at the outset of means of production used in the creation of means of production. It is not until it reaches the hands of B, B′, B″, etc., (I), that this surplus-product serves as an additional constant capital. But it is virtually that even in the hands of the accumulators of hoards, the capitalists A, A′, A″, (I), before it is sold. If we consider merely the volume of values of the reproduction on the part of I, then we are still moving within the limits of simple reproduction, for no additional capital has been set in motion for the purpose of creating this virtual additional capital (the surplus-product), nor has any greater amount of surplus-labour been performed than that done on the basis of simple reproduction. The difference is here only one of the form of the surplus-labour per-formed, of the concrete nature of its particularly useful service. It is expended in means of production for Department Ic instead of IIc, in means of production of means of production instead of means of production of articles of consumption. In the case of simple reproduc-tion it had been assumed that the entire surplus-value was spent as revenue in the commodities of II. Hence it consisted only of such means of production as restore the constant capital of IIc in its natural form. In order that the transition from simple to expanded reproduc-tion may take place, the production in Department I must be enabled to create fewer elements for the constant capital of II and more for that of

I. . . . Considering the matter merely from the point of view of the volume of values, it follows, then, that the material requirements of expanded reproduction are produced within simple reproduction. It is simply a question of the expenditure of the surplus-labour of the working class of I for the production of means of production, the creation of virtual additional capital of I. The virtual additional money-capital, created on the part of A, A′, A″, by the successive sale of their surplus-product, which was formed without any capitalist expenditure of money, is in this case simply the money-form of the additional means of production made by I.'[6]

On this interpretation, the difficulty seems to dissolve into thin air at our touch. Accumulation requires no new sources of money at all. Before, when the capitalists themselves consumed their surplus value, they had to have a corresponding money reserve in hand, the analysis of simple reproduction already having proved that the capitalist class must itself put into circulation the money needed for the realisation of their surplus value. Now, instead of consumer goods, the capitalist class, or rather B, B′, and B″, buy an equivalent amount of means of production in order to expand their production. In this way, money to the same value is accumulated in the hands of the other capitalist group, viz. A, A′, A″, etc.

'This hoarding . . . does not in any way imply an addition to the wealth in precious metals, but only a change of function on the part of money previously circulating. A while ago it served as a medium of circulation, now it serves as a hoard, as a virtual additional money-capital in process of formation.'[7]

And that is that! Yet this way out of the difficulty is open to us only on one condition, and that is not far to seek: Marx here takes accumulation in its first rudiments, in statu nascendi, as it begins to evolve from simple reproduction. In respect of the amount of value, production is not yet enlarged, it has only been rearranged so that its material elements are grouped in a different way. That the sources of money also seem adequate is therefore not surprising. This solution, however, is only true for one specific moment, the period of transition from

[6] Ibid., pp. 579–81.
[7] Ibid., p. 581.

simple reproduction to enlarged reproduction—in short, a moment that has no reference to reality and can only be conceived speculatively. Once accumulation has been established for some time, when increasing amounts of value are thrown upon the market in every period of production, buyers for these additional values cannot fail to become a problem. And on this point the proffered solution breaks down. For that matter, it was never more than a seeming solution, *not a real one*. On closer scrutiny, it fails us even at the precise instant it appears to have smoothed the way for us. For if we take accumulation just at the very moment of its emergence from simple reproduction, the prime condition it demands is a decrease in the consumption of the capitalist class. No sooner have we discovered a way to expand reproduction with the means of circulation already at hand, than we find previous consumers trickling away at the same rate. What, then, is the good of expanding production; who is there able to buy from B, B′ and B″ this increased amount of products which they could turn out only by denying themselves the money they need for buying new means of production from A, A′ and A″?

That solution, we see, was a mere illusion—the difficulty still persists. Marx himself at once re-opens the question where B, B′ and B″ get the money to buy the surplus product of A, A′ and A″.

'To the extent that the products created by B, B′, B″, etc., (I) re-enter in their natural form into their own process, it goes without saying that a corresponding portion of their own surplus-product is transferred directly (without any intervention of circulation) to their productive capital and becomes an element of additional constant capital. To the same extent they do not help to convert any surplus-product of A, A′, A″, etc., (I) into money. Aside from this, where does the money come from? We know that they have formed their hoard in the same way as A, A′, etc., by the sale of their respective surplus-products. Now they have arrived at the point where their accumulated hoard of virtual money-capital is to enter effectually upon its function as additional money-capital. But this is merely turning around in a circle. The question still remains: Where does the money come from, which the various B's (I) withdrew from the circulation and accumulated?'[8]

[8] Ibid., pp. 583–4.

His prompt reply again seems surprisingly simple: 'Now we know from the analysis of simple reproduction, that the capitalists of I and II must have a certain amount of ready money in their hands, in order to be able to dispose of their surplus-products. In that case, the money which served only for the spending of revenue in articles of consumption returned to the capitalists in the same measure in which they advanced it for the purpose of disposing of their commodities. Here the same money reappears, but in a different function. The A's and B's supply one another alternately with the money for converting their surplus-product into virtual additional capital, and throw the newly formed money-capital alternately into circulation as a medium of purchase.'[9]

That is harking back to simple reproduction all over again. It is quite true, of course, that the capitalists A and the capitalists B are constantly accumulating a hoard of money bit by bit so as to be able to renew their constant (fixed) capital from time to time, and in this way they really are assisting one another in realising their products. Yet this accumulating hoard does not drop from the clouds—it is simply a natural precipitation of the fixed capital that is (in terms of value) continually being transferred in instalments to the products which are then one by one realised in the process of sale. Owing to its very nature, the accumulated hoard can only cover the renewal of the old capital; there cannot possibly be enough to serve further for purchasing additional constant capital. That means that we are still within the limits of simple reproduction. Perhaps, though, that part of the medium of circulation which hitherto served the capitalists for their personal consumption, and is now to be capitalised, becomes a new source of additional money? For that to be true, however, we should have to be back at the unique and fleeting moment that has no more than theoretical existence—the period of transition from simple to enlarged reproduction. Beyond this gap accumulation cannot proceed—we are in truth going round in circles.

So the capitalist hoarding will not do as a way out of our difficulties. This conclusion should not come as a surprise, since the very exposition of the difficulty was misleading. It is not the source of money that

[9] Ibid., p. 584.

constitutes the problem of accumulation, but the source of the demand for the additional goods produced by the capitalised surplus value; not a technical hitch in the circulation of money but an economic problem pertaining to the reproduction of the total social capital. Quite apart from the question which had claimed Marx's entire attention so far, namely where B, B', etc., (I), get the money to buy additional means of production from A, A', etc., (I), successful accumulation will inevitably have to face a far more serious problem: to whom can B, B', etc., now sell their increased surplus product? Marx finally makes them sell their products to one another:

'It may be that the different B, B', B'', etc., (I), whose virtual new capital enters upon its active function, are compelled to buy from one another their product (portions of their surplus-product) or to sell it to one another. In that case, the money advanced by them for the circulation of their surplus-product flows back under normal conditions to the different B's in the same proportion in which they advanced it for the circulation of their respective commodities.'[10]

'In that case'—the problem simply has not been solved, for after all B, B', and B'' have not cut down on their consumption and expanded their production just so as to buy each other's increased product, i.e. means of production. Even that, incidentally, would only be possible to a very limited extent. Marx assumes a certain division of labour in Department I itself: the A's turn out means of production for making producer goods and the B's means of production for making consumer goods, which is as much as to say that, though the product of A, A', etc., need never leave Department I, the product of B, B', etc., is by its natural form predestined from the first for Department II. Already the accumulation of B, B', etc., it follows, must lead us to circulation between Departments I and II. Thus Marx's analysis itself confirms that, if Department I is to accumulate, the department for means of consumption must, in the last resort, increase its immediate or mediate demand for means of production, and so it is to Department II and its capitalists that we must look for buyers for the additional product turned out by Department I.

Sure enough, Marx's second attack on the problem takes up from

[10] Ibid., p. 585.

there: the demand of capitalists in Department II for additional means of production. Such a demand inevitably implies that the constant capital IIc is in process of expanding. This is where the difficulty becomes truly formidable:

'Take it now that A(I) converts his surplus-product into gold by selling it to a capitalist B in Department II. This can be done only by the sale of means of production on the part of A(I) to B(II) without a subsequent purchase of articles of consumption, in other words, only by a one-sided sale on A's part. Now we have seen that IIc cannot be converted into the natural form of productive constant capital unless not only Iv but also at least a portion of Is, is exchanged for a portion of IIc, which IIc exists in the form of articles of consumption. But now that A has converted his Is into gold by making this exchange impossible and withdrawing the money obtained from IIc out of circulation, instead of spending it for articles of consumption of IIc, there is indeed on the part of A(I) a formation of additional virtual money-capital, but on the other hand there is a corresponding portion of the value of the constant capital B(II) held in the form of commodity-capital, unable to transform itself into natural productive constant capital. In other words, a portion of the commodities of B(II), and at that a portion which must be sold if he wishes to reconvert his entire constant capital into its productive form, has become unsaleable. To that extent, there is an overproduction which clogs reproduction, even on the same scale.'[11]

Department I's efforts to accumulate by selling its additional product to Department II have met with an unlooked-for result: a deficit for the capitalists of Department II serious enough to prevent even simple reproduction on the old scale.

Having got to this crucial point, Marx seeks to lay bare the root of the problem by a careful and detailed exposition:

'Let us now take a closer look at the accumulation in Department II. The first difficulty with reference to IIc, that is to say the conversion of an element of the commodity-capital of II into the natural form of constant capital of II, concerns simple reproduction. Let us take the formula previously used. $(1,000v + 1,000s)$ I are exchanged for 2,000

[11] Ibid., pp. 586–7.

IIc. Now, if one half of the surplus-product of I, or 500s, is reincorpor-
ated in Department I as constant capital, then this portion, being
detained in Department I, cannot take the place of any portion of IIc.
Instead of being converted into articles of consumption, it is made to
serve as an additional means of production in Department I itself. . . . It
cannot perform this function simultaneously in I and II. The capitalist
cannot spend the value of his surplus-product for articles of consumption, and at the same time consume the surplus-product itself productively, by incorporating it in his productive capital. Instead of 2,000 I
$(v+s)$, only 1,500 are exchangeable for 2,000 IIc, namely $1,000v+500s$
of I. But 500 Ic cannot be reconverted from the form of commodities
into productive constant capital of II.'[12]

By now, hardly anybody could fail to be convinced that the difficulty
is real, but we have not taken a single step nearer a solution. This,
incidentally, is where Marx has to do penance for his ill-advised continual recourse in an earlier over-simplification, to a fictitious moment
of transition—in order to elucidate the problem of accumulation—
from simple reproduction to enlarged reproduction, making his major
premise accumulation at its very inception, in its feeble infancy instead
of its vigorous stride. There was something to be said, at least, for this
fiction, so long as it was just a question of accumulation within
Department I. The capitalists of Department I, who denied themselves
part of what they had been wont to consume, at once had a new hoard
of money in hand with which they could start capitalisation. But when
it comes to Department II, the same fiction only piles on the difficulties.
The 'abstinence' of the capitalists in Department I here finds expression
in a painful loss of consumers for whose expected demand production
had largely been calculated. Since the capitalists of Department II,
on whom we tried the experiment whether they might not possibly be
the long-sought buyers of the additional product of accumulation in
Department I, are themselves in sore straits—not knowing as yet where
to go with their own unsold product—they are even less likely to be of
any help to us. There is no shutting our eyes to the fact that an attempt
to make one group of capitalists accumulate at the expense of the other
is bound to get involved in glaring inconsistencies.

[12] Ibid., pp. 588–9.

Yet another attempt to get round the difficulty is subsequently mentioned by Marx who at once rejects it as a subterfuge. The unmarketable surplus value in Department II that is the result of accumulation in Department I might be considered a reserve of commodities the society is going to need in the course of the following year. This interpretation Marx counters with his usual thoroughness:

'(1) . . . the forming of such supplies and the necessity for it applies to all capitalists, those of I as well as of II. Considering them in their capacity as sellers of commodities, they differ only by the fact that they sell different kinds of commodities. A supply of commodities of II implies a previous supply of commodities of I. If we neglect this supply on the one side, we must also do so on the other. But if we count them in on both sides, the problem is not altered in any way. (2) Just as this year closes on the side of II with a supply of commodities for the next year, so it was opened by a supply of commodities on the same side, taken over from last year. In the analysis of annual reproduction, reduced to its abstract form, we must therefore strike it out at both ends. By leaving this year in possession of its entire production, including the supply held for next year, we take from it the supply of commodities transferred from last year, and thus we have actually to deal with the aggregate product of an average year as the object of our analysis. (3) The simple circumstance that the difficulty which must be overcome did not show itself in the analysis of simple reproduction proves that it is a specific phenomenon due merely to the different arrangement of the elements of Department I with a view to reproduction, an arrangement without which reproduction on an expanded scale cannot take place at all.'[13]

The last remark, be it noted, is equally damaging to his own earlier attempt at resolving the specific difficulties of accumulation by moments pertaining to simple reproduction, viz. the formation of a hoard consequent upon the gradual turnover of the fixed capital in the hands of the capitalists which was previously adduced as the explanation of accumulation in Department I.

Marx then proceeds to set out enlarged reproduction in the form of diagrams. But no sooner does he begin to analyse his diagram, than the

[13] Ibid., pp. 590–1.

same difficulty crops up anew in a slightly different guise. Assuming that the capitalists of Department II must for their part convert 140s into constant capital so as to make accumulation possible for the others, he asks:

'Therefore Department II must buy 140s for cash without recovering this money by a subsequent sale of its commodities to I. And this is a process which is continually repeated in every new annual production, so far as it is reproduction on an enlarged scale. Where does II get the money for this?'[14]

In the following, Marx tries out various approaches in order to discover this source. First the expenditure on variable capital by the capitalists in Department II is closely scrutinised. True, it exists in the form of money; but its proper function is the purchase of labour power, and it cannot possibly be withdrawn and made to serve, maybe, for purchasing additional means of production.

'This continually repeated departure from and return to the starting point, the pocket of the capitalist, does not add in any way to the money moving in this cycle. This, then, is not a source of the accumulation of money.'[15]

Marx then considers all conceivable dodges, only to show them up as evading the issue.

'But stop!' he exclaims. 'Isn't there a chance to make a little profit?'[15]

He considers whether the capitalists could not manage to save a little of the variable capital by depressing the wages of the workers below the normal average and thus to tap a new source of money for accumulation. A mere flick of his fingers, of course, disposes of this notion:

'But it must not be forgotten that the wages actually paid (which determine the magnitude of the variable capital under normal conditions) do not depend on the benevolence of the capitalists, but must be paid under certain conditions. This does away with this expedient as a source of additional money.'[15]

He even explores what hidden methods there may be of 'saving' on the variable capital, such as the truck system, frauds, etc., only to comment finally: 'This is the same operation as under (1), only disguised

[14] Ibid., p. 593.
[15] Ibid., p. 594.

and carried out by a detour. Therefore it must likewise be rejected as an explanation of the present problem.'[16]

All efforts to make the variable capital yield a new source of money for the purpose of accumulation are thus unrewarded: 'In short, we cannot accomplish anything with 376 IIv for the solution of this question.'[16]

Marx next turns to the cash reserves which the capitalists in Department II keep for the circulation of their own consumption and investigates whether none of this money can be diverted to the purposes of capitalisation. Yet this, he allows, is 'still more impossible'.

'Here the capitalists of the same department are standing face to face, heavily buying and selling their articles of consumption. The money required for these transactions serves only as a medium of circulation and must flow back to the interested parties in the normal course of things, to the extent that they have advanced it to the circulation, in order to pass again and again over the same course.'[17]

The next attempt to follow belongs, as was to have been expected, to the category of those 'subterfuges' which Marx ruthlessly refutes: the attempt to explain that money-capital can be formed in the hands of one capitalist group in Department II by defrauding the other capitalists within the same department—viz. in the process of the mutual selling of consumer goods. No time need be wasted on this little effort.

Then comes a more sober proposition: 'Or, a certain portion of IIs, represented by necessities of life, might be directly converted into new variable capital of Department II.'[18]

It is not quite clear how this can help us over the hurdle, help to get accumulation going. For one thing, the formation of additional variable capital in Department II is not much use if we have no additional constant capital for this department, being in fact engaged on the task of finding it. For another thing, our present concern is to see if we can find in Department II a source of money for the purchase of additional means of production from I, and Department II's problem how to place its own additional product in some way or other in the process of

---

[16] Ibid., p. 595.
[17] Ibid., p. 595.
[18] Ibid., p. 596.

production is beside the point. Further, is the implication that the respective consumer goods should be used 'direct', i.e. without the mediation of money, in the production of Department II, so that the corresponding amount of money can be diverted from variable capital to the purpose of accumulation? If so, we could not accept the solution. Under normal conditions of capitalist production, the remuneration of the workers by consumer goods direct is precluded, one of the corner-stones of capitalist economy being the money-form of the variable capital, the independent transaction between the worker as buyer of commodities and producer of consumer goods. Marx himself stresses this point in another context:

'We know that the actual variable capital consists of labour-power, and therefore the additional must consist of the same thing. It is not the capitalist of I who among other things buys from II a supply of necessities of life for his labourers, or accumulates them for this purpose, as the slave holder had to do. It is the labourers themselves who trade with II.'[19]

And that goes for the capitalists of Department II just as much as for those of Department I, thus disposing of Marx's last effort.

Marx ends up by referring us to the last part of *Capital*, volume ii, chapter 21, the 'Concluding Remarks *sub iv*', as Engels has called them. Here we find the curt explanation:

'The original source for the money of II is $v + s$ of the gold producers in Department I, exchanged for a portion of IIc. Only to the extent that the gold producer accumulates surplus-value or converts it into means of production of I, in other words, to the extent that he expands his production, does his $v+s$ stay out of Department II. On the other hand, to the extent that the accumulation of gold on the part of the gold producer himself leads ultimately to an expansion of production, a portion of the surplus-value of gold production not spent as revenue passes into Department II as additional variable capital of the gold producers, promotes the accumulation of new hoards in II and supplies it with means by which to buy from I without having to sell to it immediately.'[20]

[19] Ibid., p. 601.
[20] Ibid., p. 610.

After the breakdown of all conceivable attempts at explaining accumulation, therefore, after chasing from pillar to post, from A I to B I, and from B I to A II, we are made to fall back in the end on the very gold producer, recourse to whom Marx had at the outset of his analysis branded as 'absurd'. The analysis of the reproductive process, and the second volume of *Capital*, finally comes to a close without having provided the long sought-for solution to our difficulty.

9

THE DIFFICULTY VIEWED FROM THE ANGLE OF THE PROCESS OF CIRCULATION

The flaw in Marx's analysis is, in our opinion, the misguided formulation of the problem as a mere question of 'the sources of money', whereas the real issue is the effective demand, the use made of goods, not the source of the money which is paid for them. As to money as a means of circulation: when considering the reproductive process as a whole, we must assume that capitalist society must always dispose of money, or a substitute, in just that quantity that is needed for its process of circulation. What has to be explained is the great social transaction of exchange, caused by real economic needs. While it is important to remember that capitalist surplus value must invariably pass through the money stage before it can be accumulated, we must nevertheless try to track down the economic demand for the surplus product, quite apart from the puzzle where the money comes from. As Marx himself says in another passage:

'The money on one side in that case calls forth expanded reproduction on the other, because the possibility for it exists without the money. For money in itself is not an element of actual reproduction.'[1]

[1] Capital, vol. ii, p. 572.

And in a different context, Marx actually shows the question about the 'sources of money' to be a completely barren formulation of the problem of accumulation.

In fact, he had come up against this difficulty once before when examining the process of circulation. Still dealing with simple reproduction, he had asked, in connection with the circulation of the surplus value:

'But the commodity capital must be monetised before its conversion into productive capital, or before the surplus-value contained in it can be spent. Where does the money for this purpose come from? This question seems difficult at the first glance, and neither Tooke nor anyone else has answered it so far.'[2]

And he was then quite uncompromising about getting to the root of the matter: 'The circulating capital of 500 p.st. advanced in the form of money-capital, whatever may be its period of turn-over, may now stand for the total capital of society, that is to say, of the capitalist class. Let the surplus-value be 100 p.st. How can the entire capitalist class manage to draw continually 600 p.st. out of the circulation, when they continually throw only 500 p.st. into it?'[3]

All that, mind you, refers to simple reproduction, where the entire surplus value is used for the personal consumption of the capitalist class. The question should therefore from the outset have been put more precisely in this form: how can the capitalists secure for themselves consumer goods to the amount of £100 surplus value on top of putting £500 into circulation for constant and variable capital? It is immediately obvious that those £500 which, in form of capital, always serve to buy means of production and to pay the workers, cannot simultaneously defray the expense of the capitalists' personal consumption. Where, then, does the additional money come from?—the £100 the capitalists need to realise their own surplus value? Thus all theoretical dodges one might devise for this point are summarily disposed of by Marx right away:

'It should not be attempted to avoid this difficulty by plausible subterfuges.

[2] Ibid., pp. 380–1.
[3] Ibid., p. 381.

'For instance: So far as the constant circulating capital is concerned, it is obvious that not all invest it simultaneously. While the capitalist A sells his commodities so that his advanced capital assumes the form of money, there is on the other hand, the available money-capital of the buyer B which assumes the form of his means of production which A is just producing. The same transaction, which restores that of B to its productive form, transforms it from money into materials of production and labour-power; the same amount of money serves in the two-sided process as in every simple purchase C-M. On the other hand, when A reconverts his money into means of production, he buys from C, and this man pays B with it, etc., and thus the transaction would be explained.

'But none of the laws referring to the quantity of the circulating money, which have been analysed in the circulation of commodities (vol. i, chap. iii), are in any way changed by the capitalist character of the process of production.

'Hence, when we have said that the circulating capital of society, to be advanced in the form of money, amounts to 500 p.st., we have already accounted for the fact that this is on the one hand the sum simultaneously advanced, and that, on the other hand, it sets in motion more productive capital than 500 p.st., because it serves alternately as the money fund of different productive capitals. This mode of explanation, then, assumes that money as existing whose existence it is called upon to explain.

'It may be furthermore said: Capitalist A produces articles which capitalist B consumes unproductively, individually. The money of B therefore monetises the commodity-capital of A, and thus the same amount serves for the monetisation of the surplus-value of B and the circulating constant capital of A. But in that case, the solution of the question to be solved is still more directly assumed, the question: Whence does B get the money for the payment of his revenue? How does he himself monetise this surplus-portion of his product?

'It might also be answered that that portion of the circulating variable capital, which A continually advances to his labourers, flows back to him continually from the circulation, and only an alternating part stays continually tied up for the payment of wages. But a certain time elapses between the expenditure and the reflux, and meanwhile the money paid out for wages might, among other uses, serve for the monetisation of surplus-value. But we know, in the first place, that, the greater the time, the greater must be the supply of money which the capitalist A must keep continually in reserve. In the second place, the labourer spends the money, buys commodities for it, and thus monetises to that extent the surplus-value contained in them. Without penetrating any further into the question at this point, it is sufficient to say that the consumption of the entire capitalist class, and of the unproductive persons dependent upon it, keeps step with that of the labouring class; so that, simultaneously with the money thrown into circulation by the labouring class, the capitalists must throw money into it, in order to spend their surplus-value as revenue. Hence money must be withdrawn from circulation for it. This explanation would merely reduce the quantity of money required, but not do away with it.

'Finally it might be said: A large amount of money is continually thrown into circulation when fixed capital is first invested, and it is not recovered from the circulation until after the lapse of years, by him who threw it into circulation. May not this sum suffice to monetise the surplus-value? The answer to this is that the employment as fixed capital, if not by him who threw it into circulation, then by some one else, is probably implied in the sum of 500 p.st. (which includes the formation of a hoard for needed reserve funds). Besides, it is already assumed in the amount expended for the purchase of products serving as fixed capital, that the surplus-value contained in them is also paid, and the question is precisely, where the money for this purpose came from.'[4]

This parting shot, by the way, is particularly noteworthy in that Marx here expressly repudiates the attempt to explain realisation of the surplus value, even in the case of simple reproduction, by means of a hoard formed for the periodical renewal of fixed capital. Later on, with a view to realising the surplus value under the much more difficult conditions of accumulation, he makes more than one tentative effort to substantiate an explanation of this type which he himself dismissed as a 'plausible subterfuge'.

Then follows a solution which has a somewhat disconcerting ring: 'The general reply has already been given: When a mass of commodities

[4] Ibid., pp. 381–3.

valued at x times 1,000 p.st. has to circulate, it changes absolutely noth-ing in the quantity of the money required for this circulation, whether this mass of commodities contains any surplus-value or not, and whether this mass of commodities has been produced capitalistically or not. In other words, *the problem itself does not exist*. All other conditions being given, such as velocity of circulation of money, etc., a definite sum of money is required in order to circulate the value of commod-ities worth x times 1,000 p.st., quite independently of the fact how much or how little of this value falls to the share of the direct producers of these commodities. So far as any problem exists here, it coincides with the general problem: Where does all the money required for the circulation of the commodities of a certain country come from?'[5]

The argument is quite sound. The answer to the general question about the origin of the money for putting a certain quantity of com-modities into circulation within a country will also tell us where the money for circulating the surplus value comes from. The division of the bulk of value contained in these commodities into constant and variable capital, and surplus value, does not exist from the angle of the circulation of money—in this connection, it is quite meaningless. But it is only from the angle of the circulation of money, or of a simple commodity circulation, that the problem has no existence. Under the aspect of social reproduction as a whole, it is very real indeed; but it should not, of course, be put in that misleading form that brings us back to simple commodity circulation, where it has no meaning. We should not ask, accordingly: Where does the money required for realis-ing the surplus value come from? but: Where are the consumers for this surplus value? It is they, for sure, who must have this money in hand in order to throw it into circulation. Thus, Marx himself, although he just now denied the problem to exist, keeps coming back to it time and again:

'Now, there are only two points of departure: The capitalist and the labourer. All third classes of persons must either receive money for their services from these two classes, or, to the extent that they receive it without any equivalent services, they are joint owners of the surplus-value in the form of rent, interest, etc. The fact that the surplus-value

---

[5] Ibid., p. 383.

does not all stay in the pocket of the industrial capitalist, but must be shared by him with other persons, has nothing to do with the present question. The question is: How does he maintain his surplus-value, not, how does he divide the money later after he has secured it? For the present case, the capitalist may as well be regarded as the sole owner of his surplus-value. As for the labourer it has already been said that he is but the secondary point of departure, while the capitalist is the primary starting point of the money thrown by the labourer into circulation. The money first advanced as variable capital is going through its second circulation, when the labourer spends it for the payment of means of subsistence.

'The capitalist class, then, remains the sole point of departure of the circulation of money. If they need 400 p.st. for the payment of means of production, and 100 p.st. for the payment of labour-power, they throw 500 p.st. into circulation. But the surplus-value incorporated in the product, with a rate of surplus-value of 100 per cent, is equal to the value of 100 p.st. How can they continually draw 600 p.st. out of circulation, when they continually throw only 500 p.st. into it? From nothing comes nothing. The capitalist class as a whole cannot draw out of circulation what was not previously in it.'[6]

Marx further explodes another device which might conceivably be thought adequate to the problem, i.e. a more rapid turnover of money enabling a larger amount of value to circulate by means of a smaller amount of money. The dodge will not work, of course, since the velocity of money in circulation is already taken into account by equating the aggregate bulk of commodities with a certain number of pounds sterling. But then at last we seem in sight of a proper solution:

'Indeed, paradoxical as it may appear at first sight, it is the capitalist class itself that throws the money into circulation which serves for the realisation of the surplus-value incorporated in the commodities. But, mark well, it is not thrown into circulation as advanced money, not as capital. The capitalist class spends it for their individual consumption. The money is not advanced by them, although they are the point of departure of its circulation.'[7]

[6] Ibid., pp. 384–5.
[7] Ibid., p. 385.

This lucid and comprehensive account is the best evidence that the problem is not just imaginary but very real. It provides a solution, not by disclosing a new 'source of money' for the realisation of the surplus value, but by pointing out at last the consumers of this surplus value. We are still, on Marx's assumption, within the bounds of simple reproduction; the capitalist class, that is to say, use the whole of their surplus value for personal consumption. Since the capitalists are the consumers of surplus value, it is not so much a paradox as a truism that they must, in the nature of things, possess the money for appropriating the objects of consumption, the natural form of this surplus value. The circulatory transaction of exchange is the necessary consequence of the fact that the individual capitalist cannot immediately consume his individual surplus value, and accordingly the individual surplus product, as could, for instance, the employer of slave labour. As a rule the natural material form of the surplus product tends to preclude such use. The aggregate surplus value of the capitalists in general is, however, contained in the total social product—as long as there is simple reproduction—as expressed by a corresponding quantity of consumer goods for the capitalist class, just as the sum total of variable capital has its corresponding equivalent in the quantity of consumer goods for the working class, and as the constant capital of all individual capitalists taken together is represented by material means of production in an equivalent quantity. In order to exchange the unconsumable individual surplus values for a corresponding amount of consumer goods, a double transaction of commodity exchange is needed: first, the sale of one's own surplus product and then the purchase of consumer goods out of the surplus product of society. These two transactions can only take place among members of the capitalist class, among individual capitalists, which means that their agent, the money, thereby merely changes hands as between one capitalist and another without ever being alienated from the capitalist class in general. Since simple reproduction inevitably implies the exchange of equivalents, one and the same amount of money can serve year by year for the circulation of the surplus value, and only an excess of zeal will inspire the further query: where does the money which mediates the capitalists' own consumption come from in the first place? This question, however, reduces to a more general one: how did money capital initially come into the hands of the capitalists, that money capital of which they always retain a certain part for their personal consumption, apart from what they use for productive investment? Put in this way, however, the question belongs in the chapter of so-called 'primitive accumulation', i.e. the historical genesis of capital, going beyond the framework of an analysis of the process of circulation as well as of reproduction.

Thus the fact is clear and unequivocal—so long as we remain within the bounds of simple reproduction. Here the problem is solved by the premises themselves; in fact, the solution is already anticipated by the very concept of simple reproduction which indeed is based on the entire surplus value being consumed by the capitalist class. This implies that it must also be the latter who buy it, that is to say, individual capitalists must buy it from each other.

'In the present case', Marx says himself, 'we had assumed, that the sum of money which the capitalist throws into circulation until the first surplus-value flows back to him, is exactly equal to the surplus-value which he is going to produce and monetise. This is obviously an arbitrary assumption, so far as the individual capitalist is concerned. But it must be correct when applied to the entire capitalist class, when simple reproduction is assumed. It expresses the same thing that this assumption does, namely, that the entire surplus-value is consumed unproductively, but it only, not any portion of the original capital stock.'[8]

But simple reproduction on a capitalist basis is after all an imaginary quantity in economic theory: no more and no less legitimate, and quite as unavoidable as $\sqrt{-1}$ in mathematics. What is worse, it cannot offer any help at all with the problem of realising the surplus value in real life, i.e. with regard to enlarged reproduction or accumulation. Marx himself says so for a second time in the further development of his analysis.

Where does the money for realising the surplus value come from if there is accumulation, i.e. not consumption but capitalisation of part of the surplus value? Marx's first answer is as follows:

---

[8] Ibid., p. 387.

'In the first place, the additional money-capital required for the function of the increasing productive capital is supplied by that portion of the realised surplus-value which is thrown into circulation by the capitalists as money-capital, not as the money form of their revenue. The money is already present in the hands of the capitalists. Only its employment is different.'[9]

Our investigation of the reproductive process has already made us familiar with this explanation, and we are equally familiar with its defects; for one thing, the answer rests on the moment of the first transition from simple reproduction to accumulation. The capitalists only yesterday consumed their entire surplus value, and thus had in hand an appropriate amount of money for their circulation. To-day they decide to 'save' part of the surplus value and to invest it productively instead of squandering it. Provided that material means of production were manufactured instead of luxury goods, they need only put part of their personal money fund to a different use. But the transition from simple reproduction to expanded reproduction is no less a theoretical fiction than simple reproduction of capital itself, for which reason Marx immediately goes on to say:

'Now, by means of the additional productive capital, its product, an additional quantity of commodities, is thrown into circulation. Together with this additional quantity of commodities, a portion of the additional money required for its circulation is thrown into circulation, so far as the value of this mass of commodities is equal to that of the productive capital consumed in their production. This additional quantity of money has precisely been advanced as an additional money-capital, and therefore it flows back to the capitalist through the turn-over of his capital. Here the same question reappears, which we met previously. Where does the additional money come from, by which the additional surplus-value now contained in the form of commodities is to be realised?'[10]

The problem could not be put more precisely. But instead of a solution, there follows the surprising conclusion:

'The general reply is again the same. The sum total of the prices of

[9] Ibid., p. 397.
[10] Ibid., p. 397.

the commodities has been increased, not because the prices of a given quantity of commodities have risen, but because the mass of the commodities now circulating is greater than that of the previously circulating commodities, and because this increase has not been offset by a fall in prices. The additional money required for the circulation of this greater quantity of commodities of greater value must be secured, either by greater economy in the circulating quantity of money—whether by means of balancing payments, etc., or by some measure which accelerates the circulation of the same coins,—or by the transformation of money from the form of a hoard into that of a circulating medium.'[11]

All this amounts to an exposition along these lines: under conditions of developing and growing accumulation, capitalist reproduction dumps ever larger masses of commodity values on the market. To put this commodity mass of a continually increasing value into circulation requires an ever larger amount of money. This increasing amount of money must be found somehow or other. All this is, no doubt, plausible and correct as far as it goes, but our problem is not solved, it is merely wished away.

One thing or the other! Either we regard the aggregate social product in a capitalist economy simply as a mass, a conglomeration of commodities of a certain value, seeing under conditions of accumulation, a mere increase in this undifferentiated mass of commodities and in the bulk of its value. Then all we need say is that a corresponding quantity of money is required for circulating this bulk of value, that with an increasing bulk of value the quantity of money must also increase, unless this growth of value is offset by acceleration of, and economy in, the traffic. And the final question, where does all money originally come from, could then be answered on Marx's recipe: from the gold mines. This, of course, is one way of looking at things, that of simple commodity circulation. But in that case there is no need to drag in concepts such as constant and variable capital, or surplus value, which have no place in simple commodity circulation, belonging essentially to the circulation of capitals and to social reproduction; nor is there need to inquire for sources

[11] Ibid., pp. 397–8.

of money for the realisation of the social surplus value under conditions of first simple, and then enlarged, reproduction. Under the aspect of simple commodity circulation puzzles of this kind are without meaning or content. But once these questions have been raised, once the course has been set for an investigation into the circulation of capitals and social reproduction, there can be no appealing to the sphere of simple commodity circulation, where there is no such problem at all, and consequently no solution to it. There can be no looking for the answer there, and then saying triumphantly that the problem has long been solved and in fact never really existed.

All this time, it appears, Marx has been tackling the problem from a wrong approach. No intelligent purpose can be served by asking for the source of the money needed to realise the surplus value. The question is rather where the demand can arise—to find an effective demand for the surplus value. If the problem had been put in this way at the start, no such long-winded detours would have been needed to show whether it can be solved or not. On the basis of simple reproduction, the matter is easy enough: since all surplus value is consumed by the capitalists, they themselves are the buyers and provide the full demand for the social surplus value, and by the same token they must also have the requisite cash in hand for circulation of the surplus value. But on this showing it is quite evident that under conditions of accumulation, i.e. of capitalisation of part of the surplus value, it cannot, *ex hypothesi*, be the capitalists themselves who buy the entire surplus value, that they cannot possibly realise it. True, if the capitalised surplus value is to be realised at all, money must be forthcoming in adequate quantities for its realisation. But it is quite impossible that this money should come from the purse of the capitalist class itself. Just because accumulation is postulated, the capitalists cannot buy their surplus value themselves, even though they might, *in abstracto*, have the money to do so. But who else could provide the demand for the commodities incorporating the capitalised surplus value?

'Apart from this class (the capitalists), there is, according to our assumption—the general and exclusive domination of capitalist production—no other class but the working class. All that the working class buys is equal to the sum total of its wages, equal to the sum total of the variable capital advanced by the entire capitalist class.'[12]

The workers, then, are even less able than the capitalist class to realise the capitalised surplus value. Somebody must buy it, if the capitalists are still to be able to recover the capital they have accumulated and advanced; and yet—we cannot think of any buyers other than capitalists and workers. 'How can the entire capitalist class accumulate money under such circumstances?'[12]

Realisation of the surplus value outside the only two existing classes of society appears as indispensable as it looks impossible. The accumulation of capital has been caught in a vicious circle. At any rate, the second volume of *Capital* offers no way out.

If we should now ask why Marx's *Capital* affords no solution to this important problem of the accumulation of capital, we must bear in mind above all that this second volume is not a finished whole but a manuscript that stops short half way through.

The external form of its last chapters in particular proves them to be in the nature of notes, intended to clear the author's own mind, rather than final conclusions ready for the reader's enlightenment. This fact is amply authenticated by the man best in the position to know: Friedrich Engels, who edited the second volume. In his introduction to the second volume he reports in detail on the conditions of the preliminary studies and the manuscripts Marx had left, which were to form the basis of this volume:

'The mere enumeration of the manuscripts left by Marx as a basis for Volume II proves the unparalleled conscientiousness and strict self-criticism which he practised in his endeavour to fully elaborate his great economic discoveries before he published them. This self-criticism rarely permitted him to adapt his presentation of the subject, in content as well as in form, to his ever widening horizon, which he enlarged by incessant study.

'The material . . . consists of the following parts: First, a manuscript entitled "A Contribution to the Critique of Political Economy", containing 1,472 quarto pages in 23 divisions, written in the time from August, 1861, to June, 1863. It is a continuation of the work of the

---

[12] Ibid., p. 401.

same title, the first volume of which appeared in Berlin, in 1859. . . . This manuscript, valuable though it is, could not be used in the present edition of Volume II.

'The manuscript next following in the order of time is that of Volume III . . .

'The period after the publication of Volume I, which is next in order, is represented by a collection of four manuscripts for Volume II, marked I–IV by Marx himself. Manuscript I (150 pages) presumably written in 1865 or 1867, is the first independent, but more or less fragmentary, elaboration of the questions now contained in Volume II. This manuscript is likewise unsuited for this edition. Manuscript III is partly a compilation of quotations and references to the manuscripts containing Marx's extracts and comments, most of them relating to the first section of Volume II, partly an elaboration of special points, particularly a critique of Adam Smith's statements as to fixed and circulating capital and the source of profits; furthermore, a discussion of the relations of the rate of surplus-value to the rate of profit, which belongs in Volume III. The references furnished little that was new, while the elaborations for Volumes II and III were rendered valueless through subsequent revisions and had to be ruled out for the greater part. Manuscript IV is an elaboration, ready for printing, of the first section and the first chapters of the second section of Volume II, and has been used in its proper place. Although it was found that this manuscript had been written earlier than Manuscript II, yet it was far more finished in form and could be used with advantage for the corresponding part of this volume. I had to add only a few supplementary parts of Manuscript II. This last manuscript is the only fairly completed elaboration of Volume II and dates from the year 1870. The notes for the final revision, which I shall mention immediately, say explicitly: "The second elaboration must be used as a basis."

'There is another interruption after 1870, due mainly to ill health. Marx employed this time in his customary way, that is to say he studied agronomics, agricultural conditions in America and especially Russia, the money market and banking institutions, and finally natural sciences, such as geology and physiology. Independent mathematical studies also form a large part of the numerous manuscripts of this period. In the beginning of 1877, Marx had recovered sufficiently to resume once more his chosen life's work. The beginning of 1877 is marked by references and notes from the above named four manuscripts intended for a new elaboration of Volume II, the beginning of which is represented by Manuscript V (56 pages in folio). It comprises the first four chapters and is not very fully worked out. Essential points are treated in footnotes. The material is rather collected than sifted, but it is the last complete presentation of this most important first section. A preliminary attempt to prepare this part for the printer was made in Manuscript VI (after October, 1877, and before July, 1878), embracing 17 quarto pages, the greater part of the first chapter. A second and last attempt was made in Manuscript VII, dated July 2, 1878, and consisting of 7 pages in folio.

'About this time Marx seems to have realised that he would never be able to complete the second and third volume in a manner satisfactory to himself, unless a complete revolution in his health took place. Manuscripts V–VIII show traces of hard struggles against depressing physical conditions far too frequently to be ignored. The most difficult part of the first section had been worked over in Manuscript V. The remainder of the first, and the entire second section, with the exception of Chapter 17, presented no great theoretical difficulties. But the third section, dealing with the reproduction and circulation of social capital, seemed to be very much in need of revision. Manuscript II, it must be pointed out, had first treated of this reproduction without regard to the circulation which is instrumental in effecting it, and then taken up the same question with regard to circulation. It was the intention of Marx to eliminate this section and to reconstruct it in such a way that it would conform to his wider grasp of the subject. This gave rise to Manuscript VIII, containing only 70 pages in quarto. A comparison with Section III, as printed after deducting the paragraphs inserted out of Manuscript II, shows the amount of matter compressed by Marx into this space.

'Manuscript VIII is likewise merely a preliminary presentation of the subject, and its main object was to ascertain and develop the new points of view not set forth in Manuscript II, while those points were ignored about which there was nothing new to say. An essential part of Chapter 17, Section II, which is more or less relevant to Section III, was at the same time drawn into this discussion and expanded. The logical sequence was frequently interrupted, the treatment of the subject was incomplete in various places, and especially the conclusion was very fragmentary. But Marx expressed as nearly as possible what he intended to say on the subject.

'This is the material for Volume II, out of which I was supposed "to make something", as Marx said to his daughter Eleanor shortly before his death.'[13]

We cannot but admire this 'something' which Engels managed to 'make' from material of such a kind. As far as our present problem is concerned, however, this detailed report makes it clear that no more than the first two of the three sections that make up volume ii were anything like ready for print in the manuscripts Marx left: the section 'On the Circulation of Money and Commodity Capital' and on 'The Causes of Circulation and the Turnover of Capital'. The third section which treats of the reproduction of total capital is merely a collection of fragments which Marx himself considered to be 'very much in need of revision'. Yet it is the last part of this section, i.e. chapter 21, 'On Accumulation and Enlarged Reproduction', which is of primary importance in the present context, and of the whole book this is the most incomplete. It comprises thirty-five pages of print in all and breaks off right in the middle of the analysis.

Besides this extraneous circumstance, we would suggest another point of great influence. Marx's investigation of the social reproductive process starts off, as we have seen, from the analysis of Adam Smith which came to grief, among other reasons, because of the erroneous doctrine that the price of all commodities is composed of $v+s$. Polemics against this dogma dominated Marx's entire analysis of the reproductive process. He devoted all his attention to proving that the total capital of society must serve, not only for consumption to the full amount of the various sources of revenue, but also for renewal of the constant capital. And inasmuch as the purest theoretical form for this line of reasoning is given, not by enlarged reproduction, but by simple reproduction, Marx tends to consider reproduction mainly from a point of view that is the very opposite of accumulation, from the assumption that the entire surplus value is consumed by the capitalists.

---

[13] Ibid., pp. 8 ff.

How greatly these polemics influenced his analysis is proved by his returning time and again in the course of his work to the attack on Adam Smith from the most various angles. So already in volume i, the following pages are devoted to it: vol. i, sect. 7, chap. 24, (2), pp. 588–602, and in vol. ii, pp. 417–56, p. 473, pp. 504–8, and pp. 554 f.

Marx again takes up the question of total reproduction in volume iii but from the start becomes once more involved with the problem set by Smith to which he devotes the whole of his 49th chapter and most of chapter 50 (pp. 968–92 and 992–1022). Finally, in *Theorien ueber den Mehrwert*, we again find detailed polemics against Smith's dogma: pp. 164–253 in vol. i, and pp. 92, 95, 126, 233, and 262 in vol. ii, part 2. Marx repeatedly stressed and emphasised the fact that he considered replacement of the constant capital from the aggregate social product the most difficult and important problem of reproduction.[14] The other problem, that of accumulation, i.e. realisation of the surplus value for the purpose of capitalisation, was thus pushed into the background, so that in the end Marx hardly touched upon it.

This problem being of such paramount importance for capitalist economy, it is not surprising that bourgeois economists have dealt with it again and again. Attempts to grapple with this vital question for capitalist economy, with the question whether capital accumulation is possible in practice, come up time and again in the history of economic theory. To these historical attempts, before and after Marx, at solving this problem we shall now turn.

[14] Cf. e.g. ibid., pp. 430, 522, and 529.

Section II

Historical Exposition of
the Problem

First Round
Sismondi–Malthus *v.*
Say–Ricardo–MacCulloch

10

SISMONDI'S THEORY OF REPRODUCTION

The first grave doubts as to the divine character of the capitalist order came to bourgeois economists under the immediate impact of the first crises of 1815 and 1818–19 in England. Even then it had still been external circumstances which led up to these crises, and they appeared to be ephemeral. Napoleon's blockade of the Continent which for a time had cut off England from her European markets and had favoured a considerable development of home industries in some of the continental countries, was partly responsible; for the rest the material exhaustion of the Continent, owing to the long period of war, made for a smaller demand for English products than had been expected when the blockade was lifted. Still, these early crises were enough to reveal to the contemporary world the sinister aspects of this best of all social orders. Glutted markets, shops filled with goods nobody could buy, frequent bankruptcies—and on the other hand the glaring poverty of the toiling masses—for the first time all this starkly met the eyes of theorists who had preached the gospel of the beautiful harmonies of bourgeois *laissez-faire* and had sung its praises in all keys. All contemporary trade reports, periodicals and travellers' notes told of the losses sustained by English merchants. In Italy, Germany, Russia, and Brazil, the English disposed of their commodity stocks at a loss of anything between 25 per cent and 33⅓ per cent. People at the Cape of Good Hope in 1818 complained that all the shops were flooded with European goods offered at lower prices than in Europe and still unmarketable. From Calcutta there came similar complaints. From New Holland whole cargoes returned to England. In the United States, a contemporary traveller reports, 'there was no town nor hamlet from one end of the other of this immense and prosperous continent where the amount of commodities displayed for sale did not considerably exceed the means of the purchasers, although the vendors tried to attract custom by long-term credits, all sorts of facilities for payment, payment by instalments and acceptance of payment in kind'.

At the same time, England was hearing the desperate outcry of her workers. The *Edinburgh Review* of 1820[1] quotes an address by the Nottingham frame-work knitters which contained the following statements:

'After working from 14 to 16 hours a day, we only earn from 4s. to 7s. a week, to maintain our wives and families upon; and we farther state, that although we have substituted bread and water, or potatoes and salt, for that more wholesome food an Englishman's table used to abound with, we have repeatedly retired, after a heavy day's labour, and have been under the necessity of putting our children supperless to bed, to stifle the cries of hunger. We can most solemnly declare, that for

---

[1] In the review of an essay on *Observations on the injurious Consequences of the Restrictions upon Foreign Commerce, by a Member of the late Parliament, London, 1820* (*Edinburgh Review*, vol. lxvi, pp. 331 ff.). This interesting document, from which the following extracts are taken, an essay with a Free Trade bias, paints the general position of the workers in England in the most dismal colours. It gives the facts as follows: 'The manufacturing classes in Great Britain . . . have been suddenly reduced from affluence and prosperity to the extreme of poverty and misery. In one of the debates in the late Session of Parliament, it was stated that the wages of weavers of Glasgow and its vicinity which, when highest, had averaged about 25s. or 27s. a week, had been reduced in 1816 to 10s.; and in 1819 to the wretched pittance of 5–6s. or 6s. They have not since been materially augmented.' In Lancashire, according to the same evidence, the direct weekly wage of the weavers was from 6s. to 12s. a week for 15 hours' labour a day, whilst half-starved children worked 12 to 16 hours a day for 2s. or 3s. a week. Distress in Yorkshire was, if possible, even greater. As to the address by the frame-work knitters of Nottingham, the author says that he himself investigated conditions and had come to the conclusion that the declarations of the workers 'were not in the slightest degree exaggerated'.

the last eighteen months we have scarcely known what it was to be free from the pangs of hunger.'[2]

Then Owen in England, and Sismondi in France, almost simultaneously raised their voices in a weighty indictment of capitalist society. Owen, as a hard-headed Englishman and citizen of the leading industrial state, constituted himself spokesman for a generous social reform, whereas the petty-bourgeois Swiss rather lost himself in sweeping denunciations of the imperfections of the existing social order and of classical economics. And yet, by so doing, Sismondi gave bourgeois economics a much harder nut to crack than Owen, whose fertile practical activities were directly applied to the proletariat.

Sismondi explained in some detail that the impetus for his social criticism came from England, and especially her first crisis. In the second edition of his *Nouveaux Principes d'Economie Politique Ou De La Richesse Dans Ses Rapports Avec La Population,*[3] eight years after the publication of the first edition in 1819, he writes as follows:

'It was in England that I performed the task of preparing the new edition. England has given birth to the most celebrated Political Economists: the science is cultivated even at this time with increased ardour. . . . Universal competition or the effort always to produce more and always cheaper, has long been the system in England, a system which I have attacked as dangerous. This system has used production by manufacture to advance with gigantic steps, but it has from time to time precipitated the manufacturers into frightful distress. It was in presence of these convulsions of wealth that I thought I ought to place myself, to review my reasonings and compare them with facts.—The study of England has confirmed me in my "New Principles". In this astonishing country, which seems to be subject to a great experiment for the instruction of the rest of the world, I have seen production increasing, whilst enjoyments were diminishing. The mass of the nation here, no less than philosophers, seems to forget that the increase of wealth is not the end in political economy, but its instrument in procuring the happiness of all. I sought for this happiness in every class, and I could nowhere find it. The high English aristocracy has indeed arrived to a degree of wealth

[2] Ibid., p. 334.
[3] Paris, 1827.

and luxury which surpasses all that can be seen in other nations; nevertheless it does not itself enjoy the opulence which it seems to have acquired at the expense of the other classes; security is wanting and in every family most of the individuals experience privation rather than abundance. . . . Below this titled and not titled aristocracy, I see commerce occupy a distinguished rank; its enterprises embrace the whole world, its agents brave the ices of the poles, and the heats of the equator, whilst every one of its leading men, meeting on Exchange, can dispose of thousands. At the same time, in the streets of London, and in those of the other great towns of England, the shops display goods sufficient for the consumption of the world.—But have riches secured to the English merchant the kind of happiness which they ought to secure him? No: in no country are failures so frequent, nowhere are those colossal fortunes, sufficient in themselves to supply a public loan to uphold an Empire, or a republic, overthrown with as much rapidity. All complain that business is scarce, difficult, not remunerative. Twice, within an interval of a few years, a terrible crisis has ruined part of the bankers, and spread desolation among all the English manufacturers. At the same time another crisis has ruined the farmers, and been felt in its rebound by retail dealers. On the other hand, commerce, in spite of its immense extent, has ceased to call for young men who have their fortunes to make; every place is occupied, in the superior ranks of society no less than in the inferior; the greater number offer their labour in vain, without being able to obtain remuneration.—Has, then, this national opulence, whose material progress strikes every eye, nevertheless tended to the advantage of the poor? Not so. The people of England are destitute of comfort now, and of security for the future. There are no longer yeomen, they have been obliged to become day labourers. In the towns there are scarcely any longer artisans, or independent heads of a small business, but only manufacturers. The operative, to employ a word which the system has created, does not know what it is to have a station; he only gains wages, and as these wages cannot suffice for all seasons, he is almost every year reduced to ask alms from the poor-rates.—This opulent nation has found it more economical to sell all the gold and silver which she possessed, to do without coin, and to depend entirely on a paper circulation; she has thus voluntarily deprived herself of the most valuable of all the advantages of coin: stability of value.

The holders of the notes of the provincial banks run the risk every day of being ruined by frequent and, as it were, epidemic failures of the bankers; and the whole state is exposed to a convulsion in the fortune of every individual, if an invasion or a revolution should shake the credit of the national bank. The English nation has found it more economical to give up those modes of cultivation which require much hand-labour, and she has dismissed half the cultivators who lived in the fields. She has found it more economical to supersede workmen by steam-engines; she has dismissed . . . the operatives in towns, and weavers giving place to power-looms, are now sinking under famine; she has found it more economical to reduce all working people to the lowest possible wages on which they can subsist, and these working people being no longer anything but a rabble, have not feared plunging into still deeper misery by the addition of an increasing family. She has found it more economical to feed the Irish with potatoes, and clothe them in rags; and now every packet brings legions of Irish, who, working for less than the English, drive them from every employment. What is the fruit of this immense accumulation of wealth? Have they had any other effect than to make every class partake of care, privation and the danger of complete ruin? Has not England, by forgetting men for things, sacrificed the end to the means?'[4]

This mirror, held up to capitalist society almost a century before the time of writing, is clear and comprehensive enough in all conscience. Sismondi put his finger on every one of the sore spots of bourgeois economics: the ruin of small enterprise; the drift from the country; the proletarisation of the middle classes; the impoverishment of the workers; the displacement of the worker by the machine; unemployment; the dangers of the credit system; social antagonisms; the insecurity of existence; crises and anarchy. His harsh, emphatic scepticism struck a specially shrill discord with the complacent optimism, the idle worship of harmony as preached by vulgar economics which, in the person of MacCulloch in England and of Say in France, was becoming the fashion in both countries. It is easy to imagine what a deep and painful impression remarks like the following were bound to make:

[4] Preface to the second edition. Translation by M. Mignet, in *Political Economy and the Philosophy of Government* (London, 1847), pp. 114 ff.

'There can only be luxury if it is bought with another's labour; only those will work hard and untiringly who have to do so in order to get not the frills but the very necessities of life.'[5]

'Although the invention of the machine which increases man's capacity, is a blessing for mankind, it is made into a scourge for the poor by the unjust distribution we make of its benefits.'[6]

'The gain of an employer of labour is sometimes nothing if not despoiling the worker he employs; he does not benefit because his enterprise produces much more than it costs, but because he does not pay all the costs, because he does not accord the labourer a remuneration equal to his work. Such an industry is a social evil, for it reduces those who perform the work to utmost poverty, assuring to those who direct it but the ordinary profits on capital.'[7]

'Amongst those who share in the national income, one group acquires new rights each year by new labours, the other have previously acquired permanent rights by reason of a primary effort which makes a year's labour more advantageous.'[8]

'Nothing can prevent that every new discovery in applied mechanics should diminish the working population by that much. To this danger it is constantly exposed, and society provides no remedy for it.'[9]

'A time will come, no doubt, when our descendants will condemn us as barbarians because we have left the working classes without security, just as we already condemn, as they also will, as barbarian the nations who reduced those same classes to slavery.'[10]

Sismondi's criticism thus goes right to the root of the matter; for him there can be no compromise or evasion which might try to gloss over the dark aspects of capitalist enrichment he exposed, as merely temporary shortcomings of a transition period. He concludes his investigation with the following rejoinder to Say:

'For seven years I have indicated this malady of the social organism, and for seven years it has continuously increased. I cannot regard such

---

[5] *Nouveaux Principes* . . . (2nd ed.), vol. i, p. 79.

[6] Ibid., p. xv.

[7] Ibid., p. 92.

[8] Ibid., pp. 111–12.

[9] Ibid., p. 335.

[10] Op. cit., vol. ii, p. 435.

prolonged suffering as the mere frictions which always accompany a change. Going back to the origin of income, I believe to have shown the ills we experience to be the consequence of a flaw in our organisation, to have shown that they are not likely to come to an end.'[11]

The disproportion between capitalist production and the distribution of incomes determined by the former appears to him the source of all evil. This is the point from which he comes to the problem of accumulation with which we are now concerned.

The main thread of his criticism against classical economics is this: capitalist production is encouraged to expand indefinitely without any regard to consumption; consumption, however, is determined by income.

'All the modern economists, in fact, have allowed that the fortune of the public, being only the aggregation of private fortunes, has its origin, is augmented, distributed and destroyed by the same means as the fortune of each individual. They all know perfectly well, that in a private fortune, the most important fact to consider is the income, and that by the income must be regulated consumption or expenditure, or the capital will be destroyed. But as, in the fortune of the public, the capital of one becomes the income of another, they have been perplexed to decide what was capital, and what income, and they have therefore found it more simple to leave the latter entirely out of their calculations. By neglecting a quality so essential to be determined, Say and Ricardo have arrived at the conclusion, that consumption is an unlimited power, or at least having no limits but those of production, whilst it is in fact limited by income. . . . They announced that whatever abundance might be produced, it would always find consumers, and they have encouraged the producers to cause that glut in the markets, which at this time occasions the distress of the civilised world; whereas they should have forewarned the producers that they could only reckon on those consumers who possessed income.'[12]

Sismondi thus grounds his views in a theory of income. What is income, and what is capital? He pays the greatest attention to this distinction which he calls 'the most abstract and difficult question of

[11] Ibid., p. 463.
[12] Op. cit., vol. i, p. xiii (pp. 120–1 of Mignet's translation).

political economics'. The fourth chapter of his second book is devoted to this problem. As usual, Sismondi starts his investigation with Robinson Crusoe. For such a one, the distinction between capital and income was still 'confused'; it becomes 'essential' only in society. Yet in society, too, this distinction is very difficult, largely on account of the already familiar myth of bourgeois economics, according to which 'the capital of one becomes the income of another', and *vice versa*. Adam Smith was responsible for this confusion which was then elevated to an axiom by Say in justification of mental inertia and superficiality. It was loyally accepted by Sismondi.

'The nature of capital and of income are always confused by the mind; we see that what is income for one becomes capital for another, and the same object, in passing from hand to hand, successively acquires different denominations; the value which becomes detached from an object that has been consumed, appears as a metaphysical quantity which one expends and the other exchanges, which for one perishes together with the object itself and which for the other renews itself and lasts for the time of circulation.'[13]

After this promising introduction, Sismondi dives right into the difficult problem and declares: all wealth is a product of labour; income is part of wealth, and must therefore have the same origin. However, it is 'customary' to recognise three kinds of income, called rent, profit and wage respectively, which spring from the three sources of 'land, accumulated capital and labour'. As to the first thesis, he is obviously on the wrong tack. As the wealth of a society, i.e. as the aggregate of useful objects, of use-values, wealth is not merely a product of labour but also of nature who both supplies raw materials and provides the means to support human labour. Income, on the other hand, is a concept of value. It indicates the amount to which an individual or individuals can dispose over part of the wealth of society or of the aggregate social product. In view of Sismondi's insistence that social income is part of social wealth, we might assume him to understand by social income the actual annual fund for consumption. The remaining part of wealth that has not been consumed, then, is the capital of society. Thus we obtain at least a vague outline of the required distinction

[13] Ibid., p. 84.

between capital and income on a social basis. At the very next moment, however, Sismondi accepts the 'customary' distinction between three kinds of income, only one of which derives exclusively from 'accumulated capital' while in the other two 'land' or 'labour' are conjoined with capital. The concept of capital thus at once becomes hazy again. However, let us see what Sismondi has to say about the origin of these three kinds of income which betray a rift in the foundations of society. He is right to take a certain development of labour productivity as his point of departure.

'By reason of the advances both in industry and science, by which man has subjugated the forces of nature, every worker can produce more, far more, in a day than he needs to consume.'[14]

Sismondi thus rightly stresses the fact that the productivity of labour is an indispensable condition for the historical foundation of exploitation. Yet he goes on to explain the actual origin of exploitation in a way typical of bourgeois economics: 'But even though his labour produces wealth, this wealth, if he is called upon to enjoy it, will make him less and less fit for work. Besides, wealth hardly ever remains in the possession of the man who must live by the work of his hands.'[14]

Thus he makes exploitation and class antagonism the necessary spur to production, quite in accord with the followers of Ricardo and Malthus. But now he comes to the real cause of exploitation, the divorce of labour power from the means of production.

'The worker cannot, as a rule, keep the land as his own; land, however, has a productive capacity which human labour but directs to the uses of man. The master of the land on which labour is performed, reserves a share in the fruits of labour to which his land has contributed, as his remuneration for the benefits afforded by this productive capacity.'[15]

This is called rent. And further: 'In our state of civilisation, the worker can no longer call his own an adequate fund of objects for his consumption, enough to live while he performs the labours he has undertaken—until he has found a buyer. He no longer owns the raw materials, often coming from far away, on which he must exercise his

[14] Ibid., p. 85.
[15] Ibid., p. 86.

industry. Even less does he possess that complicated and costly machinery which facilitates his work and makes it infinitely more productive. The rich man who possesses his consumption goods, his raw materials and his machines, need not work himself, for by supplying the worker with all these, he becomes in a sense the master of his work. As reward for the advantages he has put at the worker's disposal, he takes outright the greater part of the fruits of his labour.'[16]

This is called capital profits. What remains of wealth, after the cream has been taken off twice, by landlord and capitalist, is the wage of labour, the income of the worker. And Sismondi adds: 'He can consume it without reproduction.'[17]

Thus, Sismondi makes the fact of non-reproduction the criterion of income as distinct from capital for wages as well as for rent. In this, however, he is only right with regard to rent and the consumed part of capital profits; as for the part of the social product which is consumed in form of wages, it certainly does reproduce itself; it becomes the labour power of the wage labourer, for him a commodity by whose sale he lives, which he can bring to market again and again; for society it becomes the material form of variable capital which must reappear time and again in the aggregate reproduction of a year, if there is to be no loss.

So far so good. Hitherto we have only learned two facts: the productivity of labour permits of the exploitation of the workers by those who do not work themselves, and exploitation becomes the actual foundation of the distribution of income owing to the divorce of the worker from his means of production. But we still do not know what is capital and what income, and Sismondi proceeds to clarify this point, starting as usual with Robinson Crusoe:

'In the eyes of the individual all wealth was nothing but a provision prepared beforehand for the time of need. Even so, he already distinguished two elements in this provision ... one part which he budgets to have at hand for immediate or almost immediate use, and the other which he will not need until it is to afford him new production. Thus one part of his corn must feed him until the next harvest,

[16] Ibid., pp. 86–7.
[17] Ibid., p. 87.

another part, reserved for sowing, is to bear fruit the following year. The formation of society and the introduction of exchange, permit to increase this seed, this fertile part of accumulated wealth, almost indefinitely, and this is what is called capital.'[18]

Balderdash would be a better name for all this. In using the analogy of seed, Sismondi here identifies means of production and capital, and this is wrong for two reasons. First, means of production are capital not intrinsically, but only under quite definite historical conditions; secondly, the concept of capital covers more than just the means of production. In capitalist society—with all the conditions Sismondi ignores—the means of production are only a part of capital, i.e. they are constant capital.

Sismondi here lost his thread plainly because he tried to establish a connection between the capital concept and the material aspects of social reproduction. Earlier, so long as he was concerned with the individual capitalist, he listed means of subsistence for the workers together with means of production as component parts of capital—again a mistake in view of the material aspects of the reproduction of individual capitals. Yet as soon as he tries to focus the material foundations of social reproduction and sets out to make the correct distinction between consumer goods and means of production, the concept of capital dissolves in his hands.

However, Sismondi well knows that the means of production are not the sole requisites for production and exploitation; indeed, he has the proper instinct that the core of the relation of exploitation is the very fact of exchange with living labour. Having just reduced capital to constant capital, he now immediately reduces it exclusively to variable capital:

'When the farmer has put in reserve all the corn he expects to need till the next harvest, he will find a good use for the surplus corn: he will feed what he has left over to other people who are going to work for him, till his land, spin and weave his hemp and wool, etc. . . . By this procedure, the farmer converts a part of his income into capital, and in fact, this is the way in which new capital is always formed. . . . The corn he has reaped over and above what he must eat while

---

[18] Ibid., pp. 87–8.

he is working, and over and above what he will have to sow in order to maintain the same level of exploitation, is wealth which he can give away, squander and consume in idleness without becoming any poorer; it was income, but as soon as he uses it to feed producers, as soon as he exchanges it for labour, or for the fruits to come from the work of his labourers, his weavers, his miners, it is a permanent value that multiplies and will no longer perish; it is capital.'[19]

Here there is some grain mixed up with quite a lot of chaff. Constant capital seems still required to maintain production on the old scale, although it is strangely reduced to circulating capital, and although the reproduction of fixed capital is completely ignored. Circulating capital apparently is also superfluous for the expansion of reproduction, for accumulation: the whole capitalised part of the surplus value is converted into wages for new workers who evidently labour in mid-air, without material means of production. The same view is expressed even more clearly elsewhere:

'When the rich man cuts down his income in order to add to his capital, he is thus conferring a benefit on the poor, because he himself shares out the annual product; and whatever he calls income, he will keep for his own consumption; whatever he calls capital, he gives to the poor man to constitute an income for him.'[20]

Yet at the same time Sismondi gives due weight to the 'secret of profit-making' and the origin of capital. Surplus value arises from the exchange of capital for labour, from variable capital, and capital arises from the accumulation of surplus value.

With all this, however, we have not made much progress towards a distinction between capital and income. Sismondi now attempts to represent the various elements of production and income in terms of the appropriate parts of the aggregate social product.

'The employer of labour, as also the labourer, does not use all his productive wealth for the sowing; he devotes part of it to buildings, mills and tools which render the work easier and more productive, just as a share of the labourer's wealth had been devoted to the permanent

[19] Ibid., pp. 88–9.
[20] Ibid., pp. 108–9.

work of making the soil more fertile. Thus we see how the different kinds of wealth successively come into being and become distinct. One part of the wealth accumulated by society is devoted by every one who possesses it to render labour more profitable by slow consumption, and make the blind forces of nature execute the work of man; this part is called *fixed capital* and comprises reclaiming, irrigation, factories, the tools of trade, and mechanical contrivances of every description. A second part of wealth is destined for immediate consumption, to reproduce itself in the work it gets done, to change its form, though not its value, without cease. This part is called *circulating capital* and it comprises seed, raw materials for manufacture, and wages. Finally, a third part of wealth becomes distinguishable from the second: it is the value by which the finished job exceeds the advances which had to be made: this part is called *income* on capitals and is destined to be consumed without reproduction.'[21]

After this laborious attempt to achieve a division of the aggregate social production according to incommensurable categories, fixed capital, circulating capital, and surplus value, Sismondi soon shows unmistakable signs that he means constant capital when he speaks of fixed capital, and variable capital when he speaks of circulating capital. For 'all that is created', is destined for human consumption, though fixed capital is consumed 'mediately' while the circulating capital 'passes into the consumption fund of the worker whose wage it forms'.[22] Thus we are a little nearer to the division of the social product into constant capital (means of production), variable capital (provisions for the workers) and surplus value (provisions for the capitalists). But so far Sismondi's explanations are not particularly illuminating on the subject which he himself describes as 'fundamental'. In this welter of confusion, at any rate, we cannot see any progress beyond Adam Smith's 'massive thought'.

Sismondi feels this himself and would clarify the problem 'by the simplest of all methods', sighing that 'this movement of wealth is so abstract and requires such great power of concentration to grasp it properly'.[22] Thus again we put on blinkers with a focus on Robinson

---

[21] Ibid., pp. 93–4.
[22] Ibid., p. 95.

[Crusoe], who in the meantime has changed to the extent that he has produced a family and is now a pioneer of colonial policy:

'A solitary farmer in a distant colony on the border of the desert has reaped 100 sacks of corn this year; there is no market where to bring them; this corn, in any case, must be consumed within the year, else it will be of no value to the farmer; yet the farmer and his family eat only 30 sacks of it; this will be his expenditure, constituting the exchange of his income; it is not reproduced for anybody whatever. Then he will call for workers, he will make them clear woods, and drain swamps in his neighbourhood and put part of the desert under the plough. These workers will eat another 30 sacks of corn: this will be their expenditure; they will be in a position to afford this expenditure at the price of their revenue, that is to say their labour; for the farmer it will be an exchange: he will have converted his 30 sacks into fixed capital. In the end, he is left with 40 sacks. He will sow them that year, instead of the 20 he had sown the previous year; this constitutes his circulating capital which he will have doubled. Thus the 100 sacks will have been consumed, but of these 100 sacks 70 are a real investment for him, which will reappear with great increase, some of them at the very next harvest, and the others in all subsequent harvests.—The very isolation of the farmer we have just assumed gives us a better feeling for the limitations of such an operation. If he has only found consumers for 60 of the 100 sacks harvested in that year, who is going to eat the 200 sacks produced the following year by the increase in his sowing? His family, you might say, which will increase. No doubt; but human generations do not multiply as quickly as subsistence. If our farmer had hands available to repeat this assumed process each year, his corn harvest will be doubled every year, and his family could at the most be doubled once in 25 years.'[23]

Though the example is naïve, the vital question stands out clearly in the end: where are the buyers for the surplus value that has been capitalised? The accumulation of capital can indefinitely increase the production of the society. But what about the consumption of society? This is determined by the various kinds of income. Sismondi explains this important subject in chapter v of book ii, 'The Distribution of the

[23] Ibid., pp. 95–6.

National Income Among the Various Classes of Citizens', in a resumed effort to describe the components of the social product.

'Under this aspect, the national income is composed of two parts and no more; the one consists in annual production ... the profit arising from wealth. The second is the capacity for work which springs from life. This time we understand by wealth both territorial possessions and capital, and by profit the net income accruing to the owners as well as the profit of the capitalist.'[24]

Thus all the means of production are separated from the national income as 'wealth', and this income is divided into surplus value and labour power, or better, its equivalent, the variable capital. This, then, though still far too vague, is our division into constant capital, variable capital and surplus value. But 'national income', it soon transpires, means for Sismondi the annual aggregate product of society:

'Similarly, annual production, or the result of all the nation's work in the course of a year, is composed of two parts: one we have just discussed—the profit resulting from wealth; the other is the capacity for work, which is assumed to equal the part of wealth for which it is exchanged, or the subsistence of the workers.'[25]

The aggregate social product is thus resolved, in terms of value, into two parts: variable capital and surplus value—constant capital has disappeared. We have arrived at Smith's dogma that the commodity price is resolved into $v+s$ (or is composed of $v+s$)—in other words, the aggregate product consists solely of consumer goods for workers and capitalists.

Sismondi then goes on to the problem of realising the aggregate product. On the one hand, the sum total of incomes in a society consists of wages, capital profits and rents, and is thus represented by $v+s$; on the other hand, the aggregate social product, in terms of value, is equally resolved into $v+s$ 'so that national income and annual production balance each other (and appear as equal quantities)', i.e. so that they must be equal in value.

'Annual production is consumed altogether during the year, but in part by the workers who, by exchanging their labour for it, convert it

[24] Ibid., pp. 104–5.
[25] Ibid., p. 105.

into capital and reproduce it; in part by the capitalists who, exchanging their income for it, annihilate it. The whole of the annual income is destined to be exchanged for the whole of annual production.'[26]

This is the basis on which, in the sixth chapter of book ii, 'On Reciprocal Determination of Production and Consumption', Sismondi finally sets up the following precise law of reproduction: 'It is the income of the past year which must pay for the production of the present year.'[27]

If this is true, how can there be any accumulation of capital? If the aggregate product must be completely consumed by the workers and capitalists, we obviously remain within the bounds of simple reproduction, and there can be no solution to the problem of accumulation. Sismondi's theory in fact amounts to a denial of the possibility of accumulation. The aggregate social demand being the bulk of wages given to the workers and the previous consumption of the capitalists, who will be left to buy the surplus product if reproduction expands? On this count, Sismondi argues that accumulation is objectively impossible, as follows:

'What happens after all is always that we exchange the whole of production for the whole production of the previous year. Besides, if production gradually increases, the exchange, at the same time as it improves future conditions, must entail a small loss every year.'[28]

In other words, when the aggregate product is realised, accumulation is bound each year to create a surplus that cannot be sold. Sismondi, however, is afraid of drawing this final conclusion, and prefers a 'middle course', necessitating a somewhat obscure subterfuge: 'If this loss is not heavy, and evenly distributed, everyone will bear with it without complaining about his income. This is what constitutes the national economy, and the series of such small sacrifices increase capital and common wealth.'[28]

If, on the other hand, there is ruthless accumulation, this surplus residue becomes a public calamity, and the result is a crisis. Thus a petty-bourgeois subterfuge becomes the solution of Sismondi: putting

[26] Ibid., pp. 105–6.
[27] Ibid., pp. 113, 120.
[28] Ibid., p. 121.

the dampers on accumulation. He constantly polemises against the classical school which advocates unrestricted development of the productive forces and expansion of production; and his whole work is a warning against the fatal consequences of giving full rein to the desire to accumulate.

Sismondi's exposition proves that he was unable to grasp the reproductive process as a whole. Quite apart from his unsuccessful attempt to distinguish between the categories of capital and income from the point of view of society, his theory of reproduction suffers from the fundamental error he took over from Adam Smith: the idea that personal consumption absorbs the entire annual product, without leaving any part of the value for the renewal of society's constant capital, and also, that accumulation consists merely of the transformation of capitalised surplus value into variable capital. Yet, if later critics of Sismondi, e.g. the Russian Marxist Ilyin,[29] think that pointing out this fundamental error in the analysis of the aggregate product can justify a cavalier dismissal of Sismondi's entire theory of accumulation as inadequate, as 'nonsense', they merely demonstrate their own obtuseness in respect of Sismondi's real concern, his ultimate problem. The analysis of Marx at a later date, showing up the crude mistakes of Adam Smith for the first time, is the best proof that the problem of accumulation is far from solved just by attending to the equivalent of the constant capital in the aggregate product. This is proved even more strikingly in the actual development of Sismondi's theory: his views involved him in bitter controversy with the exponents and popularisers of the classical school, with Ricardo, Say and MacCulloch. The two parties to the conflict represent diametrically opposed points of view: Sismondi stands for the sheer impossibility, the others for the unrestricted possibility, of accumulation. Sismondi and his opponents alike disregard constant capital in their exposition of reproduction, and it was Say in particular who presumed to perpetuate Adam Smith's confused concept of the aggregate product as $v+s$ as an unassailable dogma.

The knowledge we owe to Marx that the aggregate product must, apart from consumer goods for the workers and capitalists ($v+s$), also

[29] Vladimir Ilyich [Lenin], *Economic Studies and Essays*, St. Petersburg, 1899.

contain means of production to renew what has been used, that accumulation accordingly consists not merely in the enlargement of variable but also of constant capital, is not enough, as amply demonstrated by this entertaining turn of events, to solve the problem of accumulation. Later we shall see how this stress on the share of constant capital in the reproductive process gave rise to new fallacies in the theory of accumulation. At present it will suffice to put on record that the deference to Smith's error about the reproduction of aggregate capital is not a weakness unique to Sismondi's position but is rather the common ground on which the first controversy about the problem of accumulation was fought out. Scientific research, not only in this sphere, proceeds in devious ways; it often tackles the upper storeys of the edifice, as it were, without making sure of the foundations; and so this conflict only resulted in that bourgeois economics took on the further complicated problem of accumulation without even having assimilated the elementary problem of simple reproduction. At all events, Sismondi, in his critique of accumulation, had indubitably given bourgeois economics a hard nut to crack—seeing that in spite of his transparently feeble and awkward deductions, Sismondi's opponents were still unable to get the better of him.

11

MacCULLOCH *v.* SISMONDI

Sismondi's emphatic warnings against the ruthless ascendancy of capital in Europe called forth severe opposition on three sides: in England the school of Ricardo, in France J. B. Say, the commonplace vulgariser of Adam Smith; and the St. Simonians. While Owen in England, profoundly aware of the dark aspects of the industrial system and of the crises in particular, saw eye to eye with Sismondi in many respects, the school of that other great European, St. Simon, who had stressed the world-embracing conception of large industrial expansion, the unlimited unfolding of the productive forces of human labour, felt perturbed by Sismondi's alarms. Here, however, we are interested in the controversy between Sismondi and the Ricardians which proved the most fruitful from the theoretical point of view. In the name of Ricardo, and, it seemed, with Ricardo's personal approval, MacCulloch anonymously published a polemical article[1] against Sismondi in the

---

[1] The article in the *Edinburgh Review* was really directed against Owen, sharply attacking on 24 pages of print the latter's four treatises: (1) 'A New View of Society, or Essays on the formation of Human Character', (2) 'Observations on the Effects of the Manufacturing System', (3) 'Two Memorials on Behalf of the Working Classes, Presented to the Governments of America and Europe', and finally (4) 'Three Tracts' and 'An Account of Public Proceedings relative to the Employment of the Poor'. 'Anonymous' here attempts a detailed proof that Owen's reformist ideas by no means get down to the real causes of

Edinburgh Review in October 1819, i.e. immediately after the publication of the *Nouveaux Principes*.

In 1820, Sismondi replied in Rossi's *Annales de Jurisprudence* with an essay entitled: 'Does the Power of Consuming Necessarily Increase with the Power to Produce? An Enquiry.'[2]

In his reply Sismondi[3] himself states that his polemics were conceived under the impact of the commercial crisis: 'This truth we are both looking for, is of utmost importance under present conditions. It may be considered as fundamental for economics. Universal distress is in evidence in the trade, in industry and, in many countries certainly, even in agriculture. Such prolonged and extraordinary suffering has brought misfortune to countless families and insecurity and despondency to all, until it threatens the very bases of the social order. Two contrasting explanations have been advanced for the distress that has caused such a stir. Some say: we have produced too much, and others: we have not produced enough. "There will be no equilibrium," say the

the misery of the English proletariat, these causes being: the transition to the cultivation of barren land (Ricardo's theory of ground rent!), the corn laws and high taxation pressing upon farmer and manufacturer alike. Free trade and *laissez-faire* thus is his alpha and omega. Given unrestricted accumulation, all increase in production will create for itself an increase in demand. Owen is accused of 'profound ignorance' as regards Say and James Mill.—'In his reasonings, as well as in his plans, Mr. Owen shows himself profoundly ignorant of all the laws which regulate the production and distribution of wealth.'—From Owen, the author proceeds to Sismondi and formulates the point of contention as follows: 'He [Owen] conceives that when competition is unchecked by any artificial regulations, and industry permitted to flow in its natural channels, the use of machinery may increase the supply of the several articles of wealth beyond the demand for them, and by creating an excess of all commodities, throw the working classes out of employment. This is the position which we hold to be fundamentally erroneous; and as it is strongly insisted on by the celebrated M. de Sismondi in his *Nouveaux Principes d'Economic Politique*, we must entreat the indulgence of our readers while we endeavour to point out its fallacy, and to demonstrate, that the power of consuming necessarily increases with every increase in the power of producing' (*Edinburgh Review*, Oct. 1819, p. 470).

[2] The original title is: *Examen de cette question: Le pouvoir de consommer s'accroît-il toujours dans la société avec le pouvoir de produire?* We have not been able to obtain a copy of Rossi's *Annales*, but the essay as a whole was incorporated by Sismondi in the second edition of his *Nouveaux Principes*.

[3] At the time of writing, Sismondi was still in the dark as to the identity of 'Anonymous' in the *Edinburgh Review*.

former, "no peace and no prosperity until we consume the entire commodity surplus which remains unsold on the market, until we organise production for the future in accordance with the buyers' demand."—"There will be a new equilibrium," say the latter, "if only we double our efforts to accumulate as well as to produce. It is a mistake to believe that there is a glut on the market; no more than half our warehouses are full; let us fill the other half, too, and the mutual exchange of these new riches will revive our trade." '[4]

In this supremely lucid way, Sismondi sets out and underlines the real crux of the dispute. MacCulloch's whole position in truth stands or falls with the statement that exchange is actually an interchange of commodities; every commodity accordingly represents not only supply but demand. The dialogue then continues as follows:

'Demand and supply are truly correlative and convertible terms. The supply of one set of commodities constitutes the demand for another. Thus, there is a demand for a given quantity of agricultural produce, when a quantity of wrought goods equal thereto in productive cost is offered in exchange for it; and conversely, there is an effectual demand for this quantity of wrought goods, when the supply of agricultural produce which it required the same expense to raise, is presented as its equivalent.'[5]

The Ricardian's dodge is obvious: he has chosen to ignore the circulation of money and to pretend that commodities are immediately bought and paid for by commodities.

From the conditions of highly developed capitalist production, we are thus suddenly taken to a stage of primitive barter such as we might find still flourishing at present in Central Africa. There is a distant element of truth in this trick since money, in a simple circulation of commodities, plays merely the part of an agent. But of course, it is just the intervention of an agent which separates the two transactions of circulation, sale and purchase, and makes them independent of one another in respect of both time and place. That is why a further purchase need not follow hard upon a sale for one thing; and secondly, sale and purchase are by no means bound up with the same people: in

---

[4] Sismondi, op. cit., vol. ii, pp. 376–8.
[5] MacCulloch, loc. cit., p. 470.

fact, they will involve the same performers only in rare and exceptional cases. MacCulloch, however, makes just this baseless assumption by confronting, as buyer and seller, industry on the one hand and agriculture on the other. The universality of these categories, *qua* total categories of exchange, obscures the actual splitting up of this social division of labour which results in innumerable private exchange transactions where the sale and purchase of two commodities rarely come to the same thing. MacCulloch's simplified conception of commodity exchange in general which immediately turns the commodity into money and pretends that it can be directly exchanged, makes it impossible to understand the economic significance of money, its historical appearance.

Sismondi's answer to this is regrettably clumsy. In order to show that MacCulloch's explanation of commodity exchange has no application for capitalist production, he takes recourse to the Leipsic Book Fair.[6]

'At the Book Fair of Leipsic, booksellers from all over Germany arrive, each with four or five publications of his own in some 40 or 50 dozen copies; these are exchanged for others and every seller takes home 200 dozen books, just as he has brought 200 dozen, with the sole difference, that he brought four different works and takes home 200. This is the demand and the production which, according to M. Ricardo's disciple, are correlative and convertible; one buys the other, one pays for the other, one is the consequence of the other. But as far as we are concerned, for the bookseller and for the general public, demand and consumption have not even begun. For all that it has changed hands at Leipsic, a bad book will still be just as unsold (a bad mistake of Sismondi's, this!), it will still clutter up the merchants' shops, either because nobody wants it, or because everyone has a copy already. The books exchanged at Leipsic will only sell if the booksellers can find individuals who not only want them but are also prepared to

---

[6] Incidentally, Sismondi's Leipsic Book Fair, as a microcosm of the capitalist world, has staged a come-back after 55 years—in Eugen Duehring's 'system'. Engels, in his devastating criticism of that unfortunate 'universal genius' adduces this idea as proof that Duehring, by attempting to elucidate a real industrial crisis by means of an imaginary one on the Leipsic Book Fair, a storm at sea by a storm in a teacup, has shown himself a 'real German *literatus*'. But, as in many other instances exposed by Engels, the great thinker has simply borrowed here from someone else on the sly.

make sacrifices in order to withdraw them for circulation. They alone constitute an effective demand.'[7]

Although this example is rather crude, it shows clearly that Sismondi was not side-tracked by his opponent's trick, that he knows after all what he is talking about.

MacCulloch then attempts to turn the examination from abstract commodity exchange to concrete social conditions: 'Supposing, for the sake of illustration, that a cultivator advanced food and clothing for 100 labourers, who raised for him food for 200; while a master-manufacturer also advanced food and clothing for 100, who fabricated for him clothing for 200. Then the farmer, besides replacing the food of his own labourers, would have food for 100 to dispose of; while the manufacturer, after replacing the clothing of his own labourers, would have clothing for 100 to bring to market. In this case, the two articles would be exchanged against each other, the supply of food constituting the demand for the clothing, and that of the clothing the demand for the food.'[8]

What are we to admire more in this hypothesis: the absurdity of the set-up which reverses all actual relations, or the effrontery which simply takes for granted in the premises all that is later claimed proven? In order to prove that it is always possible to create an unlimited demand for all kinds of goods, MacCulloch chooses for his example two commodities which pertain to the most urgent and elementary wants of every human being: food and clothing. In order to prove that commodities may be exchanged at any time, and without regard to the needs of society, he chooses for his example two products in quantities which are right from the start in strict conformity with these needs, and which therefore contain no surplus as far as society is concerned. And yet he calls this quantity needed by society a surplus—viz. as measured against the producer's personal requirements for his own product, and is consequently able to demonstrate brilliantly that any amount of commodity 'surplus' can be exchanged for a corresponding 'surplus' of other commodities. Finally, in order to prove that different privately produced commodities can yet be exchanged, although their quantity,

[7] Sismondi, op. cit., vol. ii, pp. 381–2.
[8] MacCulloch, loc. cit., p. 470.

production costs and social importance must of course be different, he chooses for his example commodities whose quantity, production cost and general social necessity are precisely the same right from the start. In short, MacCulloch posits a planned, strictly regulated production without any over-production in order to prove that no crisis is possible in an unplanned private economy.

The principal joke of canny Mac, however, lies elsewhere. What is at issue is the problem of accumulation. Sismondi was worried by, and worried Ricardo and his followers with, the following question: if part of the surplus value is capitalised, i.e. used to expand production over and above the income of society, instead of being privately consumed by the capitalists, where are we to find buyers for the commodity surplus? What will become of the capitalised surplus value? Who will buy the commodities in which it is hidden? Thus Sismondi. And the flower of Ricardo's school, its official representative on the Chair of London University, the authority for the then English Ministers of the Liberal Party and for the City of London, the great Mr. MacCulloch replies—by constructing an example in which no surplus value whatever is produced. His 'capitalists' slave away in agriculture and industry in the name of charity, and all the time the entire social product, including the 'surplus', is only enough for the needs of the workers, for the wages, while the 'farmer' and 'manufacturer' see to production and exchange without food and clothing.

Sismondi, justly impatient, now exclaims: 'The moment we want to find out what is to constitute the surplus of production over consumption of the workers, it will not do to abstract from that surplus which forms the due profit of labour and the due share of the master.'[9]

MacCulloch's only reaction is to multiply his silly argument by a thousand. He asks the reader to assume '1,000 farmers', and 'also 1,000 master-manufacturers' all acting as ingenuously as the individuals. The exchange, then, proceeds as smoothly as can be desired. Finally, he exactly doubles labour productivity 'in consequence of more skilful application of labour and of the introduction of machinery—thus that every one of the 1,000 farmers, by advancing food and clothing for 100 labourers, obtains a return consisting of

[9] Sismondi, op. cit., vol. ii, p. 384.

ordinary food for 200 together with sugar, grapes and tobacco equal in production cost to that food', while every manufacturer obtains, by an analogous procedure, in addition to the previous quantity of clothing for all workers, 'ribbands, cambrics and lace, equal in productive cost, and therefore in exchangeable value, to that clothing'.[10] After such complete reversal of the chronological order, the assumption, that is, of first the existence of private property with wage labour, and then, at a later stage, such level of labour productivity as makes exploitation possible at all, he now assumes labour productivity to progress with equal speed in all spheres, the surplus product to contain precisely the same amount of value in all branches of industry, and to be divided among precisely the same number of people. When these various surplus products are then exchanged against one another, is it any wonder that the exchange proceeds smoothly and completely to everybody's satisfaction? It is only another of his many absurdities that MacCulloch makes the capitalists who had hitherto lived on air and exercised their profession in their birthday suits, now live exclusively on sugar, tobacco and wine, and array themselves only in ribbons, cambrics and lace.

The most ridiculous performance, however, is the *volte-face* by which he evades the real problem. The question had been what happens to the capitalist surplus, that surplus which is used not for the capitalist's own consumption but for the expansion of production. MacCulloch solves it on the one hand by ignoring the production of surplus value altogether, and on the other, by using all surplus value in the production of luxury goods. What buyers, then, does he advance for this new luxury production? The capitalists, evidently; the farmers and manufacturers, since, apart from these, there are only workers in Mac-Culloch's model. Thus the entire surplus value is consumed for the personal satisfaction of the capitalists, that is to say, simple reproduction takes place. The answer to the problem of the capitalisation of surplus value is, according to MacCulloch, either to ignore surplus value altogether, or to assume simple reproduction instead of accumulation as soon as surplus value comes into being. He still *pretends* to speak of expanding reproduction, but again, as before when he pretended to

---

[10] MacCulloch, loc. cit., p. 471.

deal with the 'surplus', he uses a trick, viz. first setting out an impossible species of capitalist production without any surplus value, and then persuading the reader that the subsequent *début* of the surplus value constitutes an expansion of production.

Sismondi is not quite up to these Scottish acrobatics. He had up to now succeeded in pinning his Mac down, proving him to be 'obviously absurd'. But now he himself becomes confused with regard to the crucial point at issue. On the above rantings of his opponent, he should have declared coldly: Sir, with all respect for the flexibility of your mind, you are dodging the issue. I keep on asking, who will buy the surplus product, if the capitalists use it for the purpose of accumulation, i.e. to expand production, instead of squandering it altogether? And you reply: Oh well, they will expand their production of luxury goods, which they will, of course, eat up themselves. But this is a conjuring trick, seeing that the capitalists consume the surplus value in so far as they spend it on their luxuries—they do not accumulate at all. My question is about the possibility of accumulation, not whether the personal luxuries of the capitalists are possible. Answer this clearly, if you can, or else go play with your wine and tobacco, or go to blazes for all I care.

But Sismondi, instead of putting the screws on the vulgariser, suddenly begins to moralise with pathos and social conscience. He exclaims: 'Whose demand? Whose satisfaction? The masters or the workers in town or country? On this new conception [of Mac's] there is a surplus of products, an advantage from labour—to whom will it accrue?'[11] and gives his own answer in the following impassioned words: 'But we know full well, and the history of the commercial world teaches us all too thoroughly, that it is not the worker who profits from the increase in products and labour; his pay is not in the least swelled by it. M. Ricardo himself said formerly that it ought not to be, unless you want the social wealth to stop growing. On the contrary, sorry experience teaches us that wages nearly always contract by very reason of this increase. Where, then, does the accumulation of wealth make itself felt as a public benefit? Our author assumes 1,000 farmers who profit, while 100,000 workers toil; 1,000 entrepreneurs who wax

[11] Sismondi, op. cit., vol. ii, pp. 394–5.

rich, while 100,000 artisans are kept under their orders. Whatever good may result from the accumulation of the frivolous enjoyment of luxuries is only felt by a 100th part of the nation. And will this 100th part, called upon to consume the entire surplus product of the whole working class, be adequate to a production that may grow without let or hindrance, owing to progress of machinery and capitals? In the assumption made by the author, every time the national product is doubled, the master of the farm or of the factory must increase his consumption a hundredfold; if the national wealth to-day, thanks to the invention of so many machines, is a hundred times what it was when it only covered the cost of production, every employer would to-day have to consume enough products to support 10,000 workers.'[12]

At this point Sismondi again believes himself to have a firm grasp on how crises begin to arise: 'We might imagine, if put to it, that a rich man can consume the goods manufactured by 10,000 workers, this being the fate of the ribbons, lace and cambrics whose origin the author has shown us. But a single individual would not know how to consume agricultural products to the same tune, the wines, sugar and spices which M. Ricardo [whom Sismondi evidently suspected of having written the article since he only got to know 'Anonymous' of the *Edinburgh Review* at a later date] conjures up in exchange, are too much for the table of one man. They will not sell, or else the strict proportion between agricultural and industrial products, apparently the basis of his whole system, cannot be maintained.'[13]

Sismondi, we see, has thus fallen into MacCulloch's trap. Instead of waiving an answer to the problem of accumulation which refers to the production of luxuries, he pursues his opponent into this field without noticing that the ground under his feet has shifted. Here he finds two causes for complaint. For one thing, he has moral objections to Mac-Culloch's allowing the capitalists instead of the workers to benefit by the surplus value, and is side-tracked into polemising against distribution under capitalism. From this digression, he unexpectedly reverts to the original problem which he now formulates as follows: the capitalists, then, consume the entire surplus value in luxuries. Let it be so. But

[12] Ibid., pp. 396–7.
[13] Ibid., pp. 397–8.

could anyone increase his consumption as rapidly and indefinitely as the progress of labour productivity makes the surplus value increase? And in this second instance, Sismondi himself abandons his own problem. Instead of perceiving that it is the lack of consumers other than workers and capitalists which accounts for the difficulty in capitalist accumulation, he discovers a snag in simple reproduction because the capitalists' capacity to consume has physical limits. Since the absorptive capacity of the capitalists for luxuries cannot keep up with labour productivity, that is to say with the increase in surplus value, there must be crises and over-production. We have encountered this line of thought once before in the *Nouveaux Principes*—so Sismondi himself was manifestly not quite clear about the problem at all times. And that is hardly surprising, since one can really come to grips with the whole problem of accumulation only when one has fully grasped the problem of simple reproduction, and we have seen how much Sismondi was at fault in this respect.

Yet in spite of all this, the first time that Sismondi crossed swords with the heirs of the classical school, he proved himself by no means the weaker party. On the contrary, in the end he routed his opponent. If Sismondi misunderstood the most elementary principles of social reproduction and ignored constant capital, quite in keeping with Adam Smith's dogma, he was in this respect no worse at any rate than his opponent. Constant capital does not exist for MacCulloch either, his farmers and manufacturers 'advance' merely food and clothing to their workers, and food and clothing between them make up the aggregate product of society. If there is, then, nothing to choose between the two as far as this elementary blunder is concerned, Sismondi towers heads above Mac because of his intuitive understanding of the contradictions in the capitalist mode of production. In the end, the Ricardian was at a loss to answer Sismondi's scepticism concerning the possibility of realising the surplus value. Sismondi also shows himself more penetrating in that he throws the Nottingham proletarians' cry of distress in the teeth of the apostles and apologists of harmony with their smug complacency, of those who deny 'any surplus of production over demand, any congestion of the market, any suffering', when he proves that the introduction of the machine must of necessity create a 'super-abundant population', and particularly in the end, when he underlines the tendency of the capitalist world market in general with its inherent contradictions. MacCulloch denies outright that general over-production is possible. He has a specific for every partial over-production up his sleeve:

'It may be objected, perhaps, that on the principle that the demand for commodities increases in the same ratio as their supply, there is no accounting for the gluts and stagnation produced by overtrading. We answer very easily—A glut is an increase in the supply of a particular class of commodities, unaccompanied by a corresponding increase in the supply of those other commodities which should serve as their equivalents. While our 1,000 farmers and 1,000 master-manufacturers are exchanging their respective surplus products, and reciprocally affording a market to each other, if 1,000 new capitalists were to join their society, employing each 100 labourers in tillage, there would be an immediate glut in agricultural produce . . . because in this case there would be no contemporaneous increase in the supply of the manufactured articles which should purchase it. But let one half of the new capitalists become manufacturers, and equivalents in the form of wrought goods will be created for the new produce raised by the other half: the equilibrium will be restored, and the 1,500 farmers and 1,500 master-manufacturers will exchange their respective surplus products with exactly the same facility with which the 1,000 farmers and 1,000 manufacturers formerly exchanged theirs.'[14]

Sismondi answers this buffoonery which 'very easily' pokes about in a fog, by pointing to the real changes and revolutions which take place before his own eyes. 'It was possible to put barbarous countries under the plough, and political revolutions, changes in the financial system, and peace, at once brought cargoes to the ports of the old agricultural countries which almost equalled their entire harvest. The recent Russian conquest of the vast provinces on the Black Sea, the change in the system of government in Egypt, and the outlawing of piracy in High Barbary, have suddenly poured the granaries of Odessa, Alexandria and Tunis into the Italian ports and have put such an abundance of corn on the markets that all along the coasts the farmer's trade is fighting a losing battle. Nor is the remainder of Europe safe from a similar

---

[14] MacCulloch, loc. cit., pp. 471–2.

revolution, caused by the simultaneous ploughing under of immense expanses of new land on the banks of the Mississippi, which export all their agricultural produce. Even the influence of New Holland may one day be the ruin of English industry, if not in the price of foodstuffs, which are too expensive to transport, at least in respect of wool and other agricultural products which are easier to transport.'[15]

What would MacCulloch have to advise in view of such an agrarian crisis in Southern Europe? That half the new farmers should turn manufacturer. Whereupon Sismondi counters: 'Such counsel cannot seriously apply to the Tartars of the Crimea or to the fellaheen of Egypt.' And he adds: 'The time is not yet ripe to set up new industries in the regions overseas or in New Holland.'[16]

Sismondi's acuity recognised that industrialisation of the lands overseas was only a matter of time. He was equally aware of the fact that the expansion of the world market would not bring with it the solution to the difficulty but would only reproduce it in a higher degree, in yet more potent crises. His prediction for the expansive tendency of capitalism is that it will reveal an aspect of fiercer and fiercer competition, of mounting anarchy within production itself. Indeed, he puts his finger on the fundamental causes of crises in a passage where he states the trend of capitalist production precisely as surpassing all limits of the market. At the end of his reply to MacCulloch he says: 'Time and again it has been proclaimed that the equilibrium will re-establish itself, that work will start again, but a single demand each time provides an impetus in excess of the real needs of trade, and this new activity must soon be followed by a yet more painful glut.'[17]

To such a profound grasp of the real contradictions in the movements of capital, the *vulgarus* on the Chair of London University with his harmony cant and his country-dance of 1,000 beribboned farmers and 1,000 bibulous manufacturers could find no effective answer.

---

[15] Sismondi, op. cit., vol. ii, pp. 400–1.
[16] Ibid., p. 401.
[17] Ibid., pp. 405–6.

12

RICARDO *v.* SISMONDI

MacCulloch's reply to Sismondi's theoretical objections evidently did not settle the matter to Ricardo's own satisfaction. Unlike that shrewd 'Scottish arch-humbug', as Marx calls him, Ricardo really wanted to discover the truth and throughout retained the genuine modesty of a great mind.[1] That Sismondi's polemics against him and his pupil had made a deep impression is proved by Ricardo's revised approach to the question of the effects of the machine, that being the point on which Sismondi, to his eternal credit, had confronted the classical school of harmony with the sinister aspects of capitalism. Ricardo's followers had enlarged upon the doctrine that the machine can always create as many or even more opportunities for the wage labourers as it takes away by displacing living labour. This so-called theory of compensation was subjected to a stern attack by Sismondi in the chapter 'On the Division of Labour and Machinery'[2] and in another chapter

[1] It is typical that on his election to Parliament in 1819, when he already enjoyed the highest reputation on account of his economic writings, Ricardo wrote to a friend: 'You will have seen that I have taken my seat in the House of Commons. I fear I shall be of little use there. I have twice attempted to speak but I proceeded in the most embarrassed manner, and I have no hope of conquering the alarm with which I am assailed the moment I hear the sound of my own voice' (*Letters of D. Ricardo to J. R. MacCulloch*, N.Y., 1895, pp. 23–4). Such diffidence was quite unknown to the gasbag MacCulloch.
[2] *Nouveaux Principes* . . ., book iv, chap. vii.

significantly entitled: 'Machinery Creates a Surplus Population',[3] both published in the Nouveaux Principes of 1819, two years later than Ricardo's main work. In 1821, after the MacCulloch–Sismondi controversy, Ricardo inserted a new chapter in the third edition of his Principles, where he frankly confesses to his error and says in the strain of Sismondi: 'That the opinion entertained by the labouring classes, that the employment of machinery is frequently detrimental to their interests, is not founded on prejudice and error, but is conformable to the correct principles of political economy.'[4]

He, like Sismondi, had to defend himself against the suspicion that he is opposing technical progress, but, less ruthless, he compromises with the evasion that the evil emerges only gradually. 'To elucidate the principle, I have been supposing, that improved machinery is suddenly discovered, and extensively used; but the truth is, that these discoveries are gradual, and rather operate in determining the employment of the capital which is saved and accumulated, than in diverting capital from its actual employment.'[5]

Yet the problem of crises and accumulation continued to worry Ricardo also. In 1823, the last year of his life, he spent some days in Geneva in order to talk the problem over face to face with Sismondi. The result of these talks is Sismondi's essay 'On the Balance Between Consumption and Production', published in the Revue Encyclopédique of May 1824.[6]

In his Principles, Ricardo had at the crucial points completely accepted Say's trite doctrine of harmony in the relations between production

[3] Ibid., book vii, chap. vii.
[4] D. Ricardo, On the Principles of Political Economy and Taxation (3rd edition, London, 1821), p. 474.
[5] Ibid., p. 478.
[6] This essay, Sur la Balance des Consommations avec les Productions, is reprinted in the second edition of Nouveaux Principes, vol. ii, pp. 408 ff. Sismondi tells us about this discussion: 'M. Ricardo, whose recent death has been a profound bereavement not only to his friends and family but to all those whom he enlightened by his brilliance, all those whom he inspired by his lofty sentiments, stayed for some days in Geneva in the last year of his life. We discussed in two or three sessions this fundamental question on which we disagreed. To this enquiry he brought the urbanity, the good faith, the love of truth which distinguished him, and a clarity which his disciples themselves had not heard, accustomed as they were to the efforts of abstract thought he demanded in the lecture room.'

and consumption. In chapter xxi he had declared: 'M. Say has, however, most satisfactorily shown, that there is no amount of capital which may not be employed in a country, because demand is only limited by production. No man produces, but with a view to consume or sell, and he never sells, but with an intention to purchase some other commodity, which may be immediately useful to him, or which may contribute to future production. By producing, then, he necessarily becomes either the consumer of his own goods, or the purchaser and consumer of the goods of some other person.'[7]

To this conception of Ricardo's, Sismondi's *Nouveaux Principes* were a powerful challenge, and the dispute as a whole turned also on this point. Ricardo could not deny the fact of crises which had but recently passed over England and other countries. What was at issue was the explanation for them. Right at the outset of their debate, Sismondi and Ricardo had agreed on a remarkably lucid and precise formulation of the problem, excluding the question of foreign commerce altogether. Sismondi grasped the significance and necessity of foreign trade for capitalist production, its need for expansion, well enough; in this line he was quite in step with Ricardo's Free Traders, whom he considerably excelled in his dialectical conception of the expansionist needs of capital. He fully admitted that industry 'is increasingly led to look for its vents on foreign markets where it is threatened by greater revolutions'.[8] He forecast, as we have seen, the rise of a dangerous competition for European industry in the overseas countries. This was after all a creditable achievement in the year 1820, and one which reveals Sismondi's deep insight into the relations of capitalist world economy. But even so, Sismondi was in fact far from conceiving the problem of realising the surplus value, the problem of accumulation, to depend on foreign commerce as its only means of salvation, a view attributed to him by later critics. On the contrary, Sismondi was quite explicit in the sixth chapter of volume i:[9] 'In order to make these calculations with greater certainty and to simplify these questions, we have hitherto

---

[7] Ricardo, op. cit., p. 339.

[8] Sismondi, op. cit., vol. ii, p. 361.

[9] *Nouveaux Principes* . . ., book iv, chap. iv: 'Comment la Richese commerciale suit l'Accroissement du Revenu' (vol. i, p. 115).

made complete abstraction from foreign trade and supposed an isolated nation; this isolated nation is human society itself, and what is true for a nation without foreign commerce, is equally true for mankind.'

In other words: in considering the entire world market as one society producing exclusively by capitalist methods, Sismondi grounds his problem in the same premises as Marx was to do after him. That was also the basis on which he came to terms with Ricardo. 'From the question that troubled us, we had each of us dismissed the instance of a nation that sold more abroad than it needed to buy there, that could command a growing external market for its growing internal production. In any case, it is not for us to decide whether fortunes of war or politics could perhaps bring forth new consumers for a nation—what is needed is proof that a nation can create these for itself simply by increasing its production.'[10]

This is how Sismondi formulated the problem of realising the surplus value in all precision, just as it confronts us throughout the ensuing era in economics, in contrast with Ricardo who actually maintains along with Say, as we are already aware and shall show in further detail, that production creates its own demand.

Ricardo's thesis in the controversy with Sismondi takes the following form: 'Supposing that 100 workers produce 1,000 sacks of corn, and 100 weavers 1,000 yards woollen fabric. Let us disregard all other products useful to man and all intermediaries between them, and consider them alone in the world. They exchange their 1,000 yards against the 1,000 sacks. Supposing that the productive power of labour has increased by a tenth owing to a successive progress of industry, the same people will exchange 1,100 yards against 1,100 sacks, and each will be better clothed and fed; new progress will make them exchange 1,200 yards for 1,200 sacks, and so on. The increase in products always only increases the enjoyment of those who produce.'[11]

The great Ricardo's standards of reasoning, it must regretfully be stated, are if anything even lower than those of the Scottish arch-humbug, MacCulloch. Once again we are invited to witness a harmonious and graceful country-dance of sacks and yards—the very

[10] Sismondi, op. cit., vol. ii, p. 412.
[11] Ibid., p. 416.

proportion which is to be proved, is again taken for granted. What is more, all relevant premises for the problem are simply left out. The real problem—you will recollect—the object of the controversy had been the question: who are the buyers and consumers of the surplus product that comes into being if the capitalists produce more goods than are needed for their own and their workers' consumption; if, that is to say, they capitalise part of their surplus value and use it to expand production, to increase their capital? Ricardo answers it by completely ignoring the capital increase. The picture he paints of the various stages of production is merely that of a gradually increasing productivity of labour. According to his assumptions, the same amount of labour first produces 1,000 sacks and 1,000 yards textiles, then 1,100 sacks and 1,100 yards, further 1,200 sacks and 1,200 yards, and so on, in a gracefully ascending curve. Not only that the image of a marshalled uniform progression on both sides, of conformity even in the number of objects brought to exchange, is wearisome, the expansion of capital is nowhere as much as mentioned in the model. Here we have no enlarged but simple reproduction with a greater bulk of use-values indeed, but without any increase in the value of the aggregate social product. Since only the amount of value, not the number of use-values is relevant to the exchange transaction, and this amount remains constant in the example, Ricardo makes no real advances, even though he seems to analyse the progressive expansion of production. Finally, he is quite oblivious of the relevant categories of reproduction. MacCulloch had begun by making the capitalists produce without any surplus value and live on air, but at least he recognised the existence of the workers, making provision for their consumption. Ricardo, however, does not even mention the workers; for him the distinction between variable capital and surplus value does not exist at all. Besides this major omission, it is of small account that he, just like his disciple, takes no notice of constant capital. He wants to solve the problem of realising the surplus value and expanding capital without positing more than the existence of a certain quantity of commodities which are mutually exchanged.

Sismondi was blind to the fact that the venue has been changed altogether. Yet he tried faithfully to bring the fantasies of his famous guest and opponent down to earth and to analyse their invisible contradictions, plaintively saying that these assumptions, 'just like German metaphysics, abstract from time and space'.[12] He grafts Ricardo's hypothesis on to 'society in its real organisation, with unpropertied workers whose wage is fixed by competition and who can be dismissed the moment their master has no further need of their work . . . for'—remarks Sismondi, as acute as he is modest—'it is just this social organisation to which our objection refers'.[13]

He lays bare the many difficulties and conflicts bound up with the progress of labour productivity under capitalism, and shows that Ricardo's postulated changes in the technique of labour, from the point of view of society, lead to the following alternative: Either a number of workers corresponding to the increase in labour productivity will have to be dismissed outright—then there will be a surplus of products on the one hand, and on the other unemployment and misery—a faithful picture of present-day society. Or the surplus product will be used for the maintenance of the workers in a new field of production, the production of luxury goods. Here Sismondi undoubtedly proves himself superior: he suddenly remembers the existence of the constant capital, and now it is he who subjects the English classic to a frontal attack:

'For setting up a new industry for manufacturing luxuries, new capital is also needed; machines will have to be built, raw materials procured, and distant commerce brought into activity; for the wealthy are rarely content with enjoying what is immediately in front of them. Where, then, could we find this new capital which may perhaps be much more considerable than that required by agriculture? . . . Our luxury workers are still a long way from eating our labourers' grain, from wearing the clothes from our common factories; they are not yet made into workers, they may not even have been born yet, their trade does not exist, the materials on which they are to work have not arrived from India. All those among whom the former should distribute their bread, wait for it in vain.'[14]

Sismondi now takes constant capital into account, not only in the

---

[12] Ibid., p. 424.
[13] Ibid., p. 417.
[14] Ibid., pp. 425–6.

production of luxuries, but also in agriculture, and further raises the following objection against Ricardo: 'We must abstract from time, if we make the assumption that the cultivator, whom a mechanical discovery or an invention of rural industry enables to treble the productive power of his workers, will also find sufficient capital to treble his exploitation, his agricultural implements, his equipment, his livestock, his granaries: to treble the circulating capital which must serve him while waiting for his harvest.'[15]

In this way Sismondi breaks with the superstition of the classical school that with capital expanding all additional capital would be exclusively spent on wages, on the variable capital. He clearly dissents from Ricardo's doctrine—which did not, however, prevent his allowing all the errors arising out of this doctrine three years later again to creep into the second edition of his *Nouveaux Principes*. In opposition to Ricardo's facile doctrine of harmony, Sismondi underlines two decisive points: on the one hand, the objective difficulties of the process of enlarged reproduction which works by no means so smoothly in capitalist reality as it does in Ricardo's absurd hypothesis; on the other hand, the fact that all technical progress in social labour productivity is always achieved under capitalism at the expense of the working class, bought with their suffering. Sismondi shows himself superior to Ricardo in yet a third point: he represents the broad horizon of the dialectical approach as against Ricardo's blunt narrow-mindedness with its incapacity to conceive of any forms of society other than those of bourgeois economics:

'Our eyes,' he exclaims, 'are so accustomed to this new organisation of society, this universal competition, degenerating into hostility between the rich and the working class, that we no longer conceive of any mode of existence other than that whose ruins surround us on all sides. They believe to prove me absurd by confronting me with the vices of preceding systems. Indeed, as regards the organisation of the lower classes, two or three systems have succeeded one another; yet, since they are not to be regretted, since, after first doing some good, they then imposed terrible disasters on mankind, may we conclude from this that we have now entered the true one? May we conclude that

[15] Ibid., p. 429.

we shall not discover the besetting vice of the system of wage labour as we have discovered that of slavery, of vassalage, and of the guilds? A time will come, no doubt, when our descendants will condemn us as barbarians because we have left the working classes without security, just as we already condemn, as they also will, as barbarian the nations who have reduced those same classes to slavery.'[16]

Sismondi's statement, putting in a nutshell the vital differences between the parts played by the proletariat in a modern society and in the society of ancient Rome, shows his profound insight into historical connections. He shows no less discernment, in his polemics against Ricardo, when analysing the specific economic character of the slave-system and of feudal economy as well as their relative historical significance, and finally when emphasising, as the dominant universal tendency of bourgeois economy, 'that it severs completely all kind of property from every kind of labour'.

The second round, no more than the first, between Sismondi and the classical school, brought little glory for Sismondi's opponents.[17]

---

[16] Ibid., pp. 434–5.

[17] Thus, if Tugan-Baranovski, championing Say–Ricardo's views, tells us about the controversy between Sismondi and Ricardo (*Studies on the Theory and History of Commercial Crises in England*, p. 176), that Sismondi was compelled 'to acknowledge as correct the doctrine he had attacked and to concede his opponent all that is necessary'; that Sismondi himself 'had abandoned his own theory which still finds so many adherents', and that 'the victory in this controversy lies with Ricardo', this shows a lack of discrimination—to put it mildly—such as is practically unheard-of in a work of serious scientific pretensions.

13

SAY *v*. SISMONDI

Sismondi's essay against Ricardo in the *Revue Encyclopédique* of May 1824, was the final challenge for J. B. Say, at that time the acknowledged 'prince of economic science' (*prince de la science économique*), the so-called representative, heir and populariser of the school of Adam Smith on the Continent. Say, who had already advanced some arguments against Sismondi in his letters to Malthus, countered the following July with an essay on 'The Balance Between Consumption and Production' in the *Revue Encyclopédique*, to which Sismondi in turn published a short reply. The chronology of Sismondi's polemical engagements was thus inverse to the sequence of the opposing theories, for it had been Say who first communicated his doctrine of a divinely established balance between production and consumption to Ricardo who had in turn handed it down to MacCulloch. In fact, as early as 1803, Say, in his *Traité d'Économie Politique*, book i, chapter xii, had coined the following peremptory statement: 'Products are paid for with other products. It follows that if a nation has too many goods of one kind, the means of selling them would be to create goods of a different kind.'[1]

---

[1] 'L'argent ne remplit qu'un office passager dans ce double échange. Les échanges terminés, il se trouve qu'on a payé des produits avec des produits. En conséquence, quand une nation a trop de produits dans un genre, le moyen de les écouler est d'en créer d'un autre genre' (J. B. Say, *Traité d'Économie Politique*, Paris, 1803, vol. i, p. 154).

Here we meet again the all too familiar conjuring recipe which was accepted alike by Ricardo's school and by the 'vulgar economists' as the corner-stone of the doctrine of harmony.[2]

Essentially, Sismondi's principal work constitutes a sustained polemic against this thesis. At this stage Say charges to the attack in the *Revue Encyclopédique* with a complete *volte-face*, as follows:

'Objection may be made that, because of man's intelligence, because of the advantage he can draw from the means provided by nature and artifice, every human society can produce *all* the things fit to satisfy its needs and increase its enjoyment in far larger quantities than it can itself consume. But there I would ask how it is possible that we know of no nation that is supplied with everything. Even in what rank as prospering nations seven-eighths of the population are lacking in a multitude of things considered necessities in . . . I will not say a wealthy family, but in a modest establishment. The village I live in at present lies in one of the richest parts of France; yet in 19 out of 20 houses I enter here, I see but the coarsest fare and nothing that makes for the well-being of the people, none of the things the English call comforts.'[3]

There is something to admire about the effrontery of the excellent Say. It was he who had maintained that in a capitalist economy there could be no difficulties, no surplus, no crises and no misery; since goods can be bought one for the other, we need only go on producing more and more and everything in the garden will be lovely. It was in

---

[2] In fact, here again, Say's only achievement lies in having given a pompous and dogmatic form to an idea that others had expressed before him. As Bergmann points out, in his *Theory of Crises* (Stuttgart, 1895), the work of Josiah Tucker (1752), Turgot's annotations to the French pamphlets, the writings of Quesnay, Dupont de Nemours, and of others contain quite similar observations on a natural balance, or even identity, between demand and supply. Yet the miserable Say, as Marx once called him, claims credit as the evangelist of harmony for the great discovery of the 'théorie des débouchés', modestly comparing his own work to the discovery of the principles of thermo-dynamics, of the lever, and of the inclined plane. In the preface and table of contents, e.g. to the 6th edition of his *Traité* (1841, pp. 51, 616) he says: 'The theory of exchange and of vents, such as it is developed in this work, will transform world politics.' The same point of view is also expounded by James Mill in his 'Commerce Defended' of 1808, and it is he whom Marx calls the real father of the doctrine of a natural equilibrium between production and demand.

[3] Say in *Revue Encyclopédique*, vol. 23, July 1824, pp. 20 f.

Say's hands that this postulate had become a tenet of the doctrine of harmony, that doctrine so typical of vulgar economics, which had evoked a sharp protest from Sismondi who proved this view untenable. The latter had shown that goods cannot be sold in any quantity you like, but that a limit is set to the realisation of goods by the income of society in each case, by $v+s$; inasmuch as the wages of the workers are depressed to a mere subsistence level, and inasmuch as there is also a natural limit to the consumptive capacity of the capitalist class, an expansion of production, Sismondi says, must inevitably lead to slumps, crises and ever greater misery for the great masses. Say's comeback to this is masterly in its ingenuity: If you will insist that overproduction is possible, how can it happen that there are so many people in our society who are naked, hungry and in want? Pray, explain this contradiction if you can. Say, whose own position excels by contriving blithely to shrug off the circulation of money altogether by operating with a system of barter, now censures his critic for speaking of an over-abundance of products in relation not only to purchasing power but to the real needs of society, and that although Sismondi had left no doubt at all about this very salient point of his deductions. 'Even if there is a very great number of badly fed, badly clothed and badly housed people in a society, the society can only sell what it buys, and, as we have seen, it can only buy with its income.'[4]

A little further on, Say concedes this point but alleges that his opponent has made a new mistake: 'It is not consumers, then, in which the nation is lacking,' he says, 'but purchasing power. Sismondi believes that this will be more extensive, when the products are rare, when consequently they are dearer and their production procures ampler pay for the workers.'[5]

That is how Say attempts to degrade, in his own trite method of thought, or better, method of canting, Sismondi's theory which attacked the very foundations of capitalist organisation and its mode of distribution. He burlesques the *Nouveaux Principes*, turning them into a plea for 'rare' goods and high prices, and holds up to them the mirror of an artfully flattered capitalist accumulation at its peak. If production

---

[4] *Noveaux Principes* . . ., vol. i, p. 117.

[5] Say, loc. cit., p. 21.

becomes more vigorous, he argues, labour grows in numbers and the volume of production expands, the nations will be better and more universally provided for, and he extols the conditions in countries where industrial development is at its highest, as against the misery of the Middle Ages. Sismondi's maxims he declares subversive to capitalist society: 'Why does he call for an inquiry into the laws which might oblige the entrepreneur to guarantee a living for the worker he employs? Such an inquiry would paralyse the spirit of enterprise. Merely the fear that the authorities might interfere with private contracts is a scourge and harmful to the wealth of a nation.'[6]

Not to be diverted from his purpose by this indiscriminate apologia of Say's, Sismondi once more turns the discussion on the fundamental issue:

'Surely I have never denied that since the time of Louis XIV France has been able to double her population and to quadruple her consumption, as he contends. I have only claimed that the increase of products is a good if it is desired, paid for and consumed; that, on the other hand, it is an evil if, there being no demand, the only hope of the producer is to entice the consumers of a rival industry's products. I have tried to show that the natural course of the nations is progressive increase of their property, an increase consequent upon their demand for new products and their means to pay for them, but that in consequence of our institutions, of our legislation having robbed the working class of all property and every security, they have also been spurred to a disorderly labour quite out of touch with the demand and with purchasing power, which accordingly only aggravates poverty.'[7]

And he winds up the debate by inviting the preacher of harmony to reflect upon the circumstance that, though a nation may be rich, public

---

[6] Say, loc. cit., p. 29. Say indicts Sismondi as the arch-enemy of bourgeois society in the following ranting peroration: 'It is against the modern organisation of society, an organisation which, by despoiling the working man of all property save his hands, gives him no security in the face of a competition directed towards his detriment. What! Society despoils the working man because it ensures to every kind of entrepreneur free disposition over his capital, that is to say his property! I repeat: there is nothing more dangerous than views conducive to a regulation of the employment of property' for 'hands and faculties . . . are also property' (ibid., p. 30).

[7] Sismondi, op. cit., pp. 462–3.

misery no less than material wealth is constantly on the increase, the class which produces everything being daily brought nearer to a position where it may consume nothing. On this shrill discordant note of capitalist contradictions closes the first clash about the problem of accumulation.

Summing up the general direction of this first battle of wits, we must note two points:

(1) In spite of all the confusion in Sismondi's analysis, his superiority to both Ricardo and his followers and to the self-styled heir to the mantle of Adam Smith is quite unmistakable. Sismondi, in taking things from the angle of reproduction, looks for concepts of value (capital and income) and for factual elements (producer and consumer goods) as best he can, in order to grasp how they are interrelated within the total social process. In this he is nearest to Adam Smith, with the difference only that the contradictions there appearing as merely subjective and speculative, are deliberately stressed as the keynote of Sismondi's analysis where the problem of capital accumulation is treated as the crucial point and principal difficulty.

Sismondi has therefore made obvious advances on Adam Smith, while Ricardo and his followers as well as Say throughout the debate think solely in terms of simple commodity production. They only see the formula C—M—C, even reducing everything to barter, and believe that such barren wisdom can cover all the problems specific to the process of reproduction and accumulation. This is a regress even on Smith, and over such myopic vision, Sismondi scores most decisively. He, the social critic, evinces much more understanding for the categories of bourgeois economics than their staunchest champions—just as, at a later date, the socialist Marx was to grasp infinitely more keenly than all bourgeois economists together the *differentia specifica* of the mechanism of capitalist economy. If Sismondi exclaims in the face of Ricardo's doctrine: 'What, is wealth to be all, and man a mere nothing?'[8] it is indicative not only of the vulnerable moral strain in his petty-bourgeois approach compared to the stern, classical impartiality of Ricardo, but also of a critical perception, sharpened by social sensibilities for the living social connections of economy; an eye, that is, for

[8] Ibid., p. 331.

intrinsic contradictions and difficulties as against the rigid, hidebound and abstract views of Ricardo and his school. The controversy had only shown up the fact that Ricardo, just like the followers of Adam Smith, was not even able to grasp, let alone solve the puzzle of accumulation put by Sismondi.

(2) The clue to the problem, however, was already impossible of discovery, because the whole argument had been side-tracked and concentrated upon the problem of crises. It is only natural that the outbreak of the first crisis should dominate the discussion, but no less natural that this effectively prevented either side from recognising that crises are far from constituting the problem of accumulation, being no more than its characteristic phenomenon: one element in the cyclical form of capitalist reproduction. Consequently, the debate could only result in a twofold quid pro quo: one party deducing from crises that accumulation is impossible, and the other from barter that crises are impossible. Subsequent developments of capitalism were to give the lie to both conclusions alike.

And yet, Sismondi's criticism sounds the first alarm of economic theory at the domination of capital, and for this reason its historical importance is both great and lasting. It paves the way for the disintegration of a classical economics unable to cope with the problem of its own making. But for all Sismondi's terror of the consequences attendant upon capitalism triumphant, he was certainly no reactionary in the sense of yearning for pre-capitalistic conditions, even if on occasion he delights in extolling the patriarchal forms of production in agriculture and handicrafts in comparison with the domination of capital. He repeatedly and most vigorously protests against such an interpretation as e.g. in his polemic against Ricardo in the *Revue Encyclopédique*:

'I can already hear the outcry that I jib at improvements in agriculture and craftsmanship and at every progress man could make; that I doubtless prefer a state of barbarism to a state of civilisation, since the plough is a tool, the spade an even older one, and that, according to my system, man ought no doubt to work the soil with his bare hands.

'I never said anything of the kind, and I crave indulgence to protest once for all against all conclusions imputed to my system such as I myself have never drawn. Neither those who attack me nor those who defend me have really understood me, and more than once I have been put to shame by my allies as much as by my opponents.'—'I beg you to realise that it is not the machine, new discoveries and inventions, not civilisation to which I object, but the modern organisation of society, an organisation which despoils the man who works of all property other than his arms, and denies him the least security in a reckless over-bidding that makes for his harm and to which he is bound to fall a prey.'[9]

There can be no question that the interests of the proletariat were at the core of Sismondi's criticism, and he is making no false claims when he formulates his main tendency as follows:

'I am only working for means to secure the fruits of labour to those who do the work, to make the machine benefit the man who puts it in motion.'[10]

When pressed for a closer definition of the social organisation towards which he aspires, it is true he hedges and confesses himself unable to do so:

'But what remains to be done is of infinite difficulty, and I certainly do not intend to deal with it to-day. I should like to convince the economists as completely as I am convinced myself that their science is going off on a wrong tack. But I cannot trust myself to be able to show them the true course; it is a supreme effort—the most my mind will run to—to form a conception even of the actual organisation of society. Yet who would have the power to conceive of an organisation that does not even exist so far, to see the future, since we are already hard put to it to see the present?'[11]

Surely it was no disgrace to admit oneself frankly powerless to envisage a future beyond capitalism in the year 1820—at a time when capitalism had only just begun to establish its domination over the big industries, and when the idea of socialism was only possible in a most Utopian form. But, as Sismondi could neither advance beyond capitalism nor go back to a previous stage, the only course open to his criticism was a petty-bourgeois compromise. Sceptical of the possibility of

---

[9] Ibid., pp. 432–3.
[10] Ibid., p. 449.
[11] Ibid., p. 448.

developing fully both capitalism and the productive forces, he found himself under necessity to clamour for some moderation of accumulation, for some slowing down of the triumphant march of capitalism. That is the reactionary aspect of his criticism.[12]

---

[12] Marx, in his history of the opposition to Ricardo's school and its dissolution, makes only brief mention of Sismondi, explaining: 'I leave Sismondi out of this historical account, because the criticism of his views belongs to a part with which I can deal only after this treatise, the actual movement of capital (competition and credit)' (*Theorien über den Mehrwert*, vol. iii, p. 52). Later on, however, in connection with Malthus, he also deals with Sismondi in a passage that, on the whole, is comprehensive: 'Sismondi is profoundly aware of the self-contradiction of capitalist production; he feels that its forms, its productive conditions, spur on an untrammelled development of the productive forces and of wealth on the one hand, yet that these conditions, on the other, are only relative; that their contradictions of value-in-use and value-in-exchange, of commodity and money, of sale and purchase, of production and consumption, of capital and wage-labour, and so on, take on ever larger dimensions, along with the forward strides of the productive forces. In particular, he feels the fundamental conflict: here the untrammelled development of productive power and of a wealth which, at the same time, consists in commodities, must be monetised; and there the basis—restriction of the mass of producers to the necessary means of subsistence. He therefore does not, like Ricardo, conceive of the crises as merely incidental, but as essential, as eruptions of the immanent conflicts on ever grander scale and at determinate periods. Which faces him with the dilemma: is the state to put restrictions on the *productive forces* to adapt them to the productive conditions, or upon the *productive conditions* to adapt them to the *productive forces*? Frequently he has recourse to the past, becomes *laudator temporis acti*, and seeks to master the contradictions by a different regulation of income relative to capital, or of distribution relative to production, quite failing to grasp that the relations of distribution are nothing but the relations of production *sub alia specie*. He has a perfect picture of the contradictions immanent in bourgeois production, yet he does not understand them, and therefore fails also to understand the process of their disintegration. (And indeed, how could he, seeing this production was still in the making?—R.L.) And yet, his view is in fact grounded in the premonition that *new* forms of appropriating wealth must answer to the productive forces, developed in the womb of capitalist production, to the material and social conditions of creating this wealth; that the bourgeois forms of appropriation are but transitory and contradictory, wealth existing always with contrary aspects and presenting itself at once as its opposite. Wealth is ever based on the premises of poverty, and can develop only by developing poverty' (ibid., p. 55).

In *The Poverty of Philosophy*, Marx opposes Sismondi to Proudhon in sundry passages, yet about the man himself he only remarks tersely: 'Those, who, like Sismondi, wish to return to the true proportions of production, while preserving the present basis of society, are reactionary, since, to be consistent, they must also wish to bring back all the other conditions of industry of former times' (*The Poverty of Philosophy*, London, 1936,

p. 57). Two short references to Sismondi are in *On the Critique of Political Economy*: once he is ranked, as the last classic of bourgeois economics in France, with Ricardo in England; in another passage emphasis is laid on the fact that Sismondi, contrary to Ricardo, underlined the specifically social character of labour that creates value.—In the *Communist Manifesto*, finally, Sismondi is mentioned as the head of the petty-bourgeois school.

14

MALTHUS

At the same time as Sismondi, Malthus also waged war against some of the teachings of Ricardo. Sismondi, in the second edition of his work as well as in his polemics, repeatedly referred to Malthus as an authority on his side. Thus he formulated the common aims of his campaign against Ricardo in the *Revue Encyclopédique*:

'Mr. Malthus, on the other hand, has maintained in England, as I have tried to do on the Continent, that consumption is not the necessary consequence of production, that the needs and desires of man, though they are truly without limits, are only satisfied by consumption in so far as means of exchange go with them. We have affirmed that it is not enough to create these means of exchange, to make them circulate among those who have these desires and wants; that it can even happen frequently that the means of exchange increase in society together with a decrease in the demand for labour, or wages, so that the desires and wants of one part of the population cannot be satisfied and consumption also decreases. Finally, we have claimed that the unmistakable sign of prosperity in a society is not an increasing production of wealth, but an increasing demand for labour, or the offer of more and more wages in compensation for this labour. Messrs. Ricardo and Say, though not denying that an increasing demand for labour is a symptom of prosperity, maintained that it inevitably results from an increase of production.

As for Mr. Malthus and myself, we regard these two increases as result-ing from independent causes which may at times even be in oppos-ition. According to our view, if the demand for labour has not preceded and determined production, the market will be flooded, and then new production becomes a cause of ruin, not of enjoyment.'[1]

These remarks suggest far-reaching agreement, a brotherhood in arms of Sismondi and Malthus, at least in their opposition against Ricardo and his school. Marx considers the *Principles of Political Economy*, which Malthus published in 1820, an outright plagiarism of the *Nou-veaux Principes* which had been published the year before. Yet Sismondi and Malthus are frequently at odds regarding the problem with which we are here concerned.

Sismondi is critical of capitalist production, he attacks it sharply, even denounces it, while Malthus stands for the defence. This does not mean that he denies its inherent contradictions, as Say or MacCulloch had done. On the contrary he raises them quite unmercifully to the status of a natural law and asserts their absolute sanctity. Sismondi's guiding principle is the interests of the workers. He aspires, though rather generally and vaguely, towards a thoroughgoing reform of dis-tribution in favour of the proletariat. Malthus provides the ideology for those strata who are the parasites of capitalist exploitation, who live on ground rent and draw upon the common wealth, and advocates the allocation of the greatest possible portion of the surplus value to these 'unproductive consumers'. Sismondi's general approach is predomin-antly ethical, it is the approach of the social reformer. Improving upon the classics, he stresses, in opposition to them, that 'consumption is the only end of accumulation', and pleads for restricted accumulation. Malthus, on the contrary, bluntly declares that production has no other purpose than accumulation and advocates unlimited accumulation by the capitalists, to be supplemented and assured by the unlimited con-sumption of their parasites. Finally, Sismondi starts off with a critical analysis of the reproductive process, of the relation between capital and income from the point of view of society; while Malthus, opposing Ricardo, begins with an absurd theory of value from which he de-rives an equally absurd theory of surplus value, attempting to explain

[1] *Nouveaux Principes* . . ., vol. ii, p. 409.

capitalist profits as an addition to the price over and above the value of commodities.[2]

Malthus opposes the postulate that supply and demand are identical with a detailed critique in chapter vi of his *Definitions in Political Economy*.[3] In his *Elements of Political Economy*, James Mill had declared:

'What is it that is necessarily meant, when we say that the supply and the demand are accommodated to one another? It is this: that goods which have been produced by a certain quantity of labour, exchange for goods which have been produced by an equal quantity of labour. Let this proposition be duly attended to, and all the rest is clear.—Thus, if a pair of shoes is produced with an equal quantity of labour as a hat, so long as a hat exchanges for a pair of shoes, so long the supply and demand are accommodated to one another. If it should so happen, that shoes fell in value, as compared with hats, which is the same thing as hats rising in value compared with shoes, this would simply imply that more shoes had been brought to market, as compared with hats. Shoes would then be in more than the due abundance. Why? Because in them the produce of a certain quantity of labour would not exchange for the produce of an equal quantity. But for the very same reason hats would be in less than the due abundance, because the produce of a certain quantity of labour in them would exchange for the produce of more than an equal quantity in shoes.'[4]

Against such trite tautologies, Malthus marshals a twofold argument. He first draws Mill's attention to the fact that he is building without solid foundations. In fact, he argues, even without an alteration in the ratio of exchange between hats and shoes, there may yet be too great a quantity of *both* in relation to the demand. This will result in both being sold at less than the cost of production plus an appropriate profit.

'But can it be said on this account', he asks, 'that the supply of hats is suited to the demand for hats, or the supply of shoes suited to the demand for shoes, when they are both so abundant that neither of

---

[2] Cf. Marx, *Theorien über den Mehrwert*, vol. iii, pp. 1–29, which give a detailed analysis of Malthus' theory of value and profits.

[3] Dedicated to James Mill and published in 1827.

[4] James Mill, *Elements of Political Economy* (3rd edition, London, 1826), pp. 239–40.

them will exchange for what will fulfil the conditions of their continued supply?'[5]

In other words, Malthus confronts Mill with the possibility of general over-production: '. . . when they are compared with the costs of production . . . it is evident that . . . they may all fall or rise at the same time'.[6]

Secondly, he protests against the way in which Mill, Ricardo and company are wont to model their postulates on a system of barter: 'The hop planter who takes a hundred bags of hops to Weyhill fair, thinks little more about the supply of hats and shoes than he does about the spots in the sun. What does he think about, then? and what does he want to exchange his hops for? Mr. Mill seems to be of opinion that it would show great ignorance of political economy, to say that what he wants is money; yet, notwithstanding the probable imputation of this great ignorance, I have no hesitation in distinctly asserting, that it really is money which he wants . . .'[7]

For the rest, Malthus is content to describe the machinery by which an excessive supply can depress prices below the cost of production and so automatically bring about a restriction of production, and *vice versa*.

'But this tendency, in the natural course of things, to cure a glut or a scarcity, is no . . . proof that such evils have never existed.'[8]

It is clear that in spite of his contrary views on the question of crises, Malthus thinks along the same lines as Ricardo, Mill, Say, and MacCulloch. For him, too, everything can be reduced to barter. The social reproductive process with its large categories and interrelations which claimed the whole of Sismondi's attention, is here completely ignored.

In view of so many contradictions within the fundamental approach, the criticism of Sismondi and Malthus have only a few points in common: (1) Contrary to Say and the followers of Ricardo, they both deny the hypothesis of a pre-established balance of consumption and

---

[5] Malthus, *Definitions in Political Economy* (London, 1827), p. 51.

[6] Ibid., p. 64.

[7] Ibid., pp. 53–4.

[8] Ibid., pp. 62–3.

production. (2) They both maintain that not only partial but also universal crises are possible.

But here their agreement ends. If Sismondi seeks the cause of crises in the low level of wages and the capitalists' limited capacity for consumption, Malthus, on the other hand, transforms the fact of low wages into a natural law of population movements; for the capitalists' limited capacity for consumption, however, he finds a substitute in the consumption of the parasites on surplus value such as the landed gentry and the clergy with their unlimited capacity for wealth and luxury. 'The church with a capacious maw is blest.'

Both Malthus and Sismondi look for a category of consumers who buy without selling, in order to redeem capitalist accumulation and save it from a precarious position. But Sismondi needs them to get rid of the surplus product of society over and above the consumption of the workers and capitalists, that is to say, to get rid of the capitalised part of the surplus value. Malthus wants them as 'producers' of profit in general. It remains entirely his secret, of course, how the *rentiers* and the incumbents of the state can assist the capitalists in appropriating their profits by buying commodities at an increased price, since they themselves obtain their purchasing power mainly from these capitalists. In view of these profound contrasts, the alliance between Malthus and Sismondi does not go very deep. And if Malthus, as Marx has it, distorts Sismondi's *Nouveaux Principes* into a Malthusian caricature, Sismondi in turn stresses only what is common to them both and quotes Malthus in support, giving the latter's critique of Ricardo a somewhat Sismondian cast. On occasion, no doubt, Sismondi actually succumbs to the influence of Malthus; for instance, he takes over the latter's theory of reckless state expenditure as an emergency measure in aid of accumulation and so becomes involved in contradictions with his own initial assumptions.

On the whole, Malthus neither rendered an original contribution to the problem of reproduction, nor even grasped it fully. In his controversy with the followers of Ricardo, he operated with the concepts of simple commodity circulation, just as they did in their controversy with Sismondi. His quarrel with that school turns on the 'unproductive consumption' by the parasites of the surplus value; it is not a quarrel about the social foundations of capitalist reproduction. Malthus' edifice tumbles to the ground as soon as the absurd mistakes in his theory of profits are uncovered. Sismondi's criticism remains valid, and his problems remain unsolved even if we accept Ricardo's theory of value with all its consequences.

Section II

Historical Exposition of
the Problem

Second Round
The Controversy between
Rodbertus and von Kirchmann

15

v. KIRCHMANN'S THEORY OF REPRODUCTION

The second theoretical polemics about the problem of accumulation was also started by current events. If the first English crisis and its attendant misery of the working class had stimulated Sismondi's opposition against the classical school, it was the revolutionary working-class movement arisen since which, almost twenty-five years later, provided the incentive for Rodbertus' critique of capitalist production. The risings of the Lyons silk weavers and the Chartist movement in England were vastly different from the shadowy spectres raised by the first crisis, and the ears of the bourgeoisie were made to ring with their criticism of the most wonderful of all forms of society. The first socio-economic work of Rodbertus, probably written for the *Augsburger Allgemeine Zeitung* in the late thirties but not published by that paper, bears the significant title, *The Demands of the Working Classes*,[1] and begins as follows:

'What do the working classes want? Will the others be able to keep it from them? Will what they want be the grave of modern civilisation? Thoughtful people have long realised that a time must come when history would put this question with great urgency. Now, the man

[1] *Die Forderungen der arbeitenden Klassen.*

in the street has learned it too, from the Chartist meetings and the Birmingham scenes.'

During the forties, the leaven of revolutionary ideas was most vigorously at work in France in the formation of the various secret societies and socialist schools of the followers of Proudhon, Blanqui, Cabet, Louis Blanc, etc. The February revolution and the June proclamation of the 'right to work' led to a first head-on clash between the two worlds of capitalist society—an epoch-making eruption of the contradictions latent in capitalism. As regards the other, visible form of those contradictions—the crises—the available data for observation at the time of the second controversy were far more comprehensive than in the early twenties of the century. The dispute between Rodbertus and v. Kirchmann took place under the immediate impact of the crises in 1837, 1839, 1847, and even of the first world crisis in 1857— Rodbertus writing his interesting pamphlet *On Commercial Crises and the Mortgage Problem of the Landowners*[2] in 1858. Thus the inherent contradictions of capitalist society meeting his eyes were in strident discord with the doctrine of harmony held by the English classics and their vulgarisers both in England and on the Continent, quite unlike any critique in the times when Sismondi had raised his voice in warning.

Incidentally, a quotation from Sismondi in Rodbertus' first writing proves that the former's strictures immediately influenced Rodbertus. He was thus familiar with contemporary French writings against the classical school, though perhaps less so with the far more numerous English literature. There is no more than this flimsy support for the myth of the German professors about the so-called 'priority' of Rodbertus over Marx in the 'foundation of socialism'. Accordingly, Professor Diehl writes in his article on Rodbertus in *Handwörterbuch der Staatswissenschaften*: 'Rodbertus must be considered the real founder of scientific socialism in Germany, since in his writings between 1839 and 1842, even before Marx and Lassalle, he provided a comprehensive socialist system, a critique of Adam Smith's doctrine, new theoretical foundations and proposals for social reform.'

This piece of god-fearing, pious righteousness comes from the second edition of 1901, after all that had been written by Engels, Kautsky

---

[2] *Die Handelskrisen und die Hypothekennot der Grundbesitzer.*

and Mehring to destroy this learned legend, and in spite of it. Quite inevitably, of course, and proof against any evidence to the contrary, however weighty, it was only right in the eyes of all the learned German economists that the palm of 'priority' should be wrested from Marx, the revolutionary anarchist, by Rodbertus, the 'socialist' with monarchist, Prussian and nationalist leanings, the man who believed in communism five hundred years from now, but for the present supported a steady exploitation rate of 200 per cent. However, we are interested in another aspect of Rodbertus' analysis. The same Professor Diehl continues his eulogy as follows: 'Rodbertus was not only a pioneer of socialism; political economy as a whole owes much stimulation and furtherance to him; economic theory in particular is indebted to him for the critique of classical economics, for the new theory of the distribution of income, for the distinction between the logical and historical categories of capital, and so on.'

Here we shall deal with these latter achievements of Rodbertus, especially with the 'and so on'.

Rodbertus' decisive treatise, *Towards the Understanding of Our Politico-Economic Conditions*[3] of 1842, set the ball rolling. v. Kirchmann replied in *Demokratische Blätter* with two essays—*On the Social Aspects of Ground Rent*[4] and *The Society of Barter*[5]—and Rodbertus parried in 1850 with his *Letters on Social Problems.*[6] Thus the discussion entered the same theoretical arena where Malthus–Sismondi and Say–Ricardo–MacCulloch had fought out their differences thirty years earlier. In his earliest writings, Rodbertus had already expressed the thought that the wages of labour present an ever diminishing part of the national product in modern society where the productivity of labour is increasing. He claimed this to be an original idea, and from that moment until his death thirty years later he did nothing but reiterate it and formulate it in various ways. This 'declining wage rate' is for him the root of all evils to be found in modern society, in particular of pauperism and the crises, whose combination he calls 'the social problem of our times'.

---

[3] *Zur Erkenntnis unserer staatswirtschaftlichen Zustände.*
[4] *Über die Grundrente in socialer Beziehung.*
[5] *Die Tauschgesellschaft.*
[6] *Soziale Briefe.*

v. Kirchmann does not agree with this explanation. He traces pauperism back to the effects of a rising ground rent; crises, on the other hand, to a lack of markets. About the latter especially he says: 'The greatest part of social ills is caused not by defects of production but by a lack of markets for the products . . . the more a country can produce, the more means it has for satisfying every need, the more it is exposed to the danger of misery and want.'—The labour-problem is here included as well, for 'the notorious right to work ultimately reduces to the question of markets'. 'We see', he concludes, 'that the social problem is almost identical with the problem of markets. Even the ills of much-abused competition will vanish, once markets are secure; its advantages alone will remain. There will remain a spirit of rivalry to supply good and cheap commodities, but the life-and-death struggle will disappear which is caused only by insufficient markets.'[7]

The difference between the points of view of Rodbertus and v. Kirchmann is evident. Rodbertus sees the root of the evil in a faulty distribution of the national product, and v. Kirchmann in the limitations of the markets for capitalist production. Notwithstanding all the confusion in his expositions, especially in his idealist vision of a capitalist competition content with a laudable rivalry for better and cheaper commodities, and also in his conception of the 'notorious right to work' as a problem of markets, v. Kirchmann up to a point still shows more understanding for the sore spot of capitalist production, i.e. the limitations of its market, than Rodbertus who clings to distribution. Thus it is v. Kirchmann who now takes up the problem which Sismondi had originally put on the agenda. Nevertheless, he by no means agrees with Sismondi's elucidation and solution of the problem, siding rather with the opponents of the latter. Not only does he accept Ricardo's theory of ground rent, and Adam Smith's dogma that 'the price of the commodity is composed of two parts only, of the interests on capital and the wages of labour' (v. Kirchmann transforms the surplus value into 'interest on capital'); he also subscribes to the thesis of Say and Ricardo that products are only bought with other products and that

---

[7] Rodbertus quotes v. Kirchmann's arguments explicitly and in great detail. But according to his editors, no complete copy of *Demokratische Blätter* with the original essay is obtainable.

production creates its own demand, so that if one side appears to have produced too much, it only means there was not enough production on the other. v. Kirchmann, we see, faithfully follows the classics, if in a somewhat 'German edition'. He begins by arguing, e.g., that Say's law of a natural balance between production and demand 'still does not give a comprehensive picture of reality', and adds:

'Commerce involves yet further hidden laws which prevent this postulated order from obtaining in complete purity. They must be discovered if we are to explain the present flooding of the market, and their discovery might perhaps also show us the way to avoid this great evil. We believe that there are three relations in the modern system of society which cause these conflicts between Say's indubitable law and reality.'

These relations are (1) 'too inequitable a distribution of the products'—here, as we see, v. Kirchmann somewhat approximates to Sismondi's point of view; (2) the difficulties which nature puts in the way of human labour engaged in production; and (3) finally, the defects of commerce as a mediator between production and consumption. Disregarding the last two obstacles to Say's law, we shall now consider v. Kirchmann's reasoning of his first point.

'The first relation', he explains, 'can be put more briefly as too low a wage of labour, which is thus the cause of a slump. Those who know that the price of commodities is composed of two parts only, of the interest on capital and the wage of labour, might consider this a startling statement; if the wage of labour is low, prices are low as well, and if one is high, so is the other.'

(We see v. Kirchmann accepts Smith's dogma even in its most misleading form: the price is not *resolved* into wage of labour and surplus value, but is *composed* of them as a mere sum—a view in which Adam Smith strayed furthest from his own theory of the value of labour.)

'Wage and price thus are directly related, they balance each other. England only abolished her corn laws, her tariffs on meat and other victuals, in order to cause wages to fall and thus to enable her manufacturers to oust all other competitors from the world markets by means of still cheaper commodities. This, however, only holds good up to a point and does not affect the ratio in which the product is distributed among the workers and the capitalists. Too inequitable a distribution among these two is the primary and most important cause why Say's law is not fulfilled in real life, why the markets are flooded although there is production in all branches.'

v. Kirchmann gives a detailed illustration of this statement. Using the classical method, he takes us, of course, to an imaginary isolated society which makes an unresisting, if thankless, object for the experiments of political economy. v. Kirchmann suggests we should imagine a place (Ort) which comprises 903 inhabitants, no more, no less, viz. three entrepreneurs with 300 workers each. Ort is to be able to satisfy all needs by its own production—in three establishments, that is to say, one for clothing, a second for food, lighting, fuel and raw materials, and a third for housing, furniture and tools. In each of these three departments, the 'capital together with the raw materials' is to be provided by the entrepreneur, and the remuneration of the workers is to be so arranged that the workers obtain as their wage one half of the annual produce, the entrepreneurs retaining the other half 'as interest on capital and profits of the enterprise'. Every business is to produce just enough to satisfy all the needs of the 903 inhabitants. Ort accordingly has 'all the conditions necessary for general well-being', and everybody can therefore tackle his work with courage and vigour. After a few days, however, joy and delight turn into a universal misery and gnashing of teeth: something has happened on v. Kirchmann's Island of the Blessed which was no more to be expected than for the skies to fall: an industrial and commercial crisis according to all modern specifications has broken out! Only the most essential clothing, food and housing for the 900 workers has been produced, yet the warehouses of the three entrepreneurs are full of clothes and raw materials, and their houses stand empty: they complain of a lack of demand, while the workers in turn complain that their wants are not fully satisfied. What has gone wrong? Could it be that there is too much of one kind of produce and too little of another, as Say and Ricardo would have it? Not at all, answers v. Kirchmann. Everything is available in Ort in well-balanced quantities, just enough to satisfy all the wants of the community. What, then, has thrown a spanner into the works, why the crisis? The obstruction is caused by distribution alone—but this must be savoured in v. Kirchmann's own words:

'The obstacle, why nevertheless no smooth exchange takes place, lies solely and exclusively in the distribution of these products. They are not distributed equitably among all, but the entrepreneurs retain half of them for themselves as interest and profit, and only give half to the workers. It is clear that the worker in the clothing department can exchange, against half of his product, only half of the food, lodging, etc., that has been produced, and it is clear that the entrepreneur cannot get rid of the other half since no worker has any more products to give in exchange. The entrepreneurs do not know what to do with their stocks, the workers do not know what to do for hunger and nakedness.'

Nor does the reader, we might add, know what to do with v. Kirchmann's constructions. His model is so childish that every advance leads deeper into the maze.

First of all, there seems to be no reason whatever why, and to what purpose, v. Kirchmann should devise this splitting-up of production into three parts. If analogous examples by Ricardo and MacCulloch usually confront tenant farmers and manufacturers, that is presumably only inspired by the antiquated Physiocrat conception of social reproduction which Ricardo had adopted, although his own theory of value as against the Physiocrats deprived it of all meaning, and although Adam Smith had already made a good start in considering the real material foundations of the social reproductive process. Still, we have seen that the tradition of distinguishing between agriculture and industry as the foundation of reproduction was kept up in economic theory until Marx introduced his epoch-making distinction of the two productive departments in society for producer and consumer goods. v. Kirchmann's three departments, however, have no real significance at all. Obviously, no material consideration of reproduction can have been responsible for this supremely arbitrary division which jumbles up tools and furniture, raw materials and food, but makes clothing a department in its own right. One might as well postulate one department for food, clothing and housing, another for medicines and a third for tooth brushes. v. Kirchmann's primary concern, no doubt, is with the social division of labour; hence the assumption of as nearly equal quantities of products as possible in the transactions of exchange. Yet this exchange, on which the argument turns, plays no part at all in v. Kirchmann's example since it is not the value which is distributed but the quantities of products, the bulk of use-values as such. In this intriguing Ort of v. Kirchmann's imagining, again, the products are distributed first, and only afterwards, when the distribution is accomplished, is there to be universal exchange, whereas on the solid ground of capitalist production it is, as we know, the exchange which inaugurates the distribution of the product and serves as its agent. Besides, the queerest things happen in v. Kirchmann's distributive system: 'As we all know', the prices of the products, i.e. the price of the aggregate product of society, consist of $v + s$, of wage and capital interest alone— so that the aggregate product must be distributed entirely among workers and entrepreneurs; but then unhappily v. Kirchmann dimly remembers the fact that production needs things like raw materials and tools. So Ort is provided with raw materials furtively introduced among the food, and with tools among the furniture. But now the question arises: who is to get these indigestible items in the course of general distribution? the workers as wages, or the capitalists as profits of enterprise? They could hardly expect a warm welcome from either. And on such feeble premises the star turn of the performance is to take place: the exchange between workers and entrepreneurs. The fundamental transaction of exchange in capitalist production, the exchange between workers and capitalists, is transformed by v. Kirchmann from an exchange between living labour and capital into an exchange of products. Not the first act, that of exchanging labour power for variable capital, but the second, the realisation of the wage received from the variable capital is put at the centre of the whole machinery, the entire commodity exchange of capitalist society being in turn reduced to this realisation of the labour-wage. And the crowning glory is that this exchange between workers and entrepreneurs, the king-pin of all economic life, dissolves into nothing on a closer scrutiny—it does not take place at all. For as soon as all workers have received their natural wages in the form of half their product, an exchange will be possible only among the workers themselves; every worker will only keep one-third of his wage consisting exclusively of either clothing, food or furniture, as the case may be, and realise the remainder to equal parts in the two other product-groups. The entrepreneurs no longer come into this at all; the three of them are left high and dry with their surplus value: half the clothing, furniture and food that has been produced by the society;

and they have no idea what to do with the stuff. In this calamity of v. Kirchmann's creation, even the most generous distribution of the product would be of no use. On the contrary, if larger quantities of the social product were allotted to the workers, they would have even less to do with the entrepreneurs in this transaction: all that would happen is that the exchange of the workers among themselves would increase in volume. The surplus product which the entrepreneurs have on their hands would then contract, it is true, though not indeed because the exchange of the surplus product would be facilitated, but merely because there would be less surplus value altogether. Now as before, an exchange of the social product between workers and entrepreneurs is out of the question. One must confess that the puerile and absurd economics here crammed into comparatively little space exceed the bounds even of what might be put up with from a Prussian Public Prosecutor—such having been v. Kirchmann's profession, though he must be credited with having incurred disciplinary censure on two occasions. Nevertheless, after these unpromising preliminaries, v. Kirchmann goes right to the root of the matter. He admits that his assuming the surplus product in a concrete use-form is the reason why the surplus value cannot be usefully employed. As a remedy he now allows the entrepreneurs to devote half of the social labour appropriated as surplus value to the production not of common goods but of luxuries. The 'essence of luxury-goods being that they enable the consumer to use up more capital and labour power than in the case of ordinary goods', the three entrepreneurs manage to consume by themselves in the form of laces, fashionable carriages and the like, their entire half-share in all the labour performed by the society. Now nothing unsaleable is left, and the crisis is happily avoided; over-production is made impossible once and for all, capitalists and workers alike are safe; the name of v. Kirchmann's magic cure which has brought all these benefits to pass, and which re-establishes the balance between production and consumption, being: luxury. In other words, the capitalists who do not know what to do with their surplus value which they cannot realise, are advised by the dear fellow—to eat it up! As it happens, luxury is in fact an old familiar invention of capitalist society, and still there are recurrent crises. Why is this? v. Kirchmann enlightens us: 'The answer can only be that in real life sluggish markets are entirely due to the fact that there are still *not enough* luxuries, or, in other words, that the capitalists, i.e. those who can afford to consume, still consume too little.'

This misguided abstinence of the capitalists, however, results from a bad habit which political economists have been ill-advised to encourage: the desire to save for purposes of 'productive consumption'. In other words: crises are caused by accumulation. This is v. Kirchmann's principal thesis. He proves it again by means of a touchingly simple example: 'Let us assume conditions which economists praise as more favourable,' he says, 'where the entrepreneurs say: we do not want to spend our income to the last penny in splendour and luxury, but will re-invest it productively. What does this mean? Nothing but the setting-up of all sorts of productive enterprises for delivering new goods of such a kind that their sale can yield interest (v. Kirchmann means profits) on a capital saved and invested by the three entrepreneurs from their unconsumed revenues. Accordingly, the three entrepreneurs decide to consume only the produce of a hundred workers, that is to say to restrict their luxury considerably, and to employ the labour power of the remaining 350 workers together with the capital they use for setting up new productive enterprises. The question now arises in what kind of productive enterprises these funds are to be used.'

Since, according to v. Kirchmann's assumption, constant capital is not reproduced, and the entire social product consists entirely of consumer goods, 'the three entrepreneurs can only choose again between enterprises for the manufacture of ordinary goods or for that of luxuries'.

In this way, however, the three entrepreneurs will be faced with the already familiar dilemma: if they turn out 'common goods', there will be a crisis, since the workers lack means to purchase these additional provisions, having been bought off with half the value of their produce. If they go in for luxuries, they will have to consume them alone. There is no other possibility. The dilemma is not even affected by foreign trade which would 'only increase the range of commodities on the home market' or increase productivity.

'These foreign commodities are therefore either common goods— then the capitalist will not, and the worker, lacking the means, cannot buy them, or they are luxuries, in which case the worker, of course, is even less able to buy them, and the capitalist will not want them either because of his efforts to save.'

This argument, however primitive, yet shows quite nicely and clearly the fundamental conception of v. Kirchmann and the nightmare of all economic theory: in a society consisting exclusively of workers and capitalists, accumulation will be impossible. v. Kirchmann is therefore frankly hostile to accumulation, 'saving', 'productive consumption' of the surplus value, and strongly attacks these errors advocated by classical economics. His gospel is increasing luxury together with the productivity of labour as the specific against crises. We see that v. Kirchmann, if he grotesquely aped Ricardo and Say in his theoretical assumptions, is a caricature of Sismondi in his final conclusions. Yet it is imperative to get v. Kirchmann's approach to the problem perfectly clear, if we are to understand the import of Rodbertus' criticism and the outcome of the whole controversy.

16

RODBERTUS' CRITICISM OF THE CLASSICAL SCHOOL

Rodbertus digs deeper than v. Kirchmann. He looks for the roots of evil in the very foundations of social organisation and declares bitter war on the predominant Free Trade school—not against a system of unrestricted commodity circulation or the freedom of trade which he fully accepts, but against the Manchester doctrine of *laissez-faire* within the internal social relations of economy. At that time, after the period of storm and stress of classical economics, a system of unscrupulous apologetics was already in full sway which found its most perfect expression in the 'doctrine of harmony' of M. Frédéric Bastiat, the famous vulgarian and idol of all Philistines, and quite soon the various Schultzes were to flourish as common-place, German imitations of the French prophet of harmony. Rodbertus' strictures are aimed at these unscrupulous 'peddlers of free trade'. In his first *Letter on Social Problems*[1] he exclaims:

'Because of their paltry incomes, five-sixths of the population are not only deprived of most of the benefits of civilisation, but are in constant danger of the most terrible outbreaks of real distress to which they sometimes succumb. Yet they are the creators of all the wealth of

[1] To v. Kirchmann, in 1880.

the society. Their labours begin at dawn and end at dusk, continuing even after night has fallen—but no exertion can change this fate; they cannot raise their income, and only lose that little leisure which ought to remain nowadays for the improvement of their minds. Hitherto it might have seemed as if all this suffering were necessary to the progress of civilisation, but now that a series of the most wonderful discoveries and inventions have increased human labour power more than a hundredfold, new prospects of changing these grim conditions are suddenly revealed. As a result, the wealth and assets of a nation increase at a growing rate as compared with the population. Could anything be more natural, I ask, or more justly demanded, than that this increase should also somehow benefit the creators of this old and new wealth? that their incomes should be raised or their working-hours shortened, or that they might join in increasing numbers the ranks of the lucky ones, privileged to reap the fruits of labour? Yet state economy, or better, national economy has only achieved the opposite result. Increasing poverty of these classes goes together with increasing wealth of the nation, there is even need of special legislation, lest the working day become longer, and finally, the working classes swell in number out of proportion with the others. Even that is not enough! The hundredfold increase of labour efficiency which was powerless to relieve five-sixths of the population, even threatens periodically the remaining sixth of the nation and thus society as a whole.'

'What contradictions in the economic sphere in particular! And what contradictions in the social sphere in general! The wealth of society is growing, and this growth is accompanied by a growth of poverty.—The creative efficiency of the means of production is increasing, and the consequence is that they are scrapped. Social conditions demand that the material position of the working classes should be raised to the level of their political status, and economic conditions, by way of answer, depress them further. Society needs the unrestricted growth of wealth, and contemporary leaders of production must create restrictions, in order to discourage poverty. In a single respect alone is there harmony: just as wrong as the conditions is the authoritative section of the society with its inclination to look for the root of the evil everywhere except in the right place. This egotism, which only too often dons the scholar's gown, also accuses the vices of the workers of being the cause of poverty. The responsibility for the crimes committed against them by all-powerful facts is ascribed to their alleged discontent and shiftlessness, and where even such egotism cannot close its eyes to their innocence, it makes an elaborate dogma of the "necessity of poverty". Unremittingly, it exhorts the workers only to work and to pray, impresses upon them the duty of abstinence and economy, and at best infringes upon their rights by the institution of compulsory saving, adding to the misery of the workers. It does not see that a blind force of commerce has transformed the prayer for work into the curse of enforced unemployment, that . . . abstinence is impossible or cruel, and that, lastly, morals always remain ineffective if commended by those of whom the poet says that they drink wine in secret but preach water in public.'[2]

Thirty years after Sismondi and Owen, twenty years after the indictment made by the English socialists, the followers of Ricardo, and last but not least, after the publication of the Communist Manifesto, such bold words alone cannot claim to break new ground. What matters above all now is the theoretical foundation of this indictment. Rodbertus here proposed a complete system which can be reduced to the following simple statements.

Owing to the laws of an economy left to its own devices, the high level of labour productivity achieved by history, together with the institutions of positive law, that is to say the right of private ownership, a whole series of wrong and unethical phenomena had emerged:

(1) In the place of 'normal', 'constituted' value we have exchange value, and accordingly coined money instead of a proper 'paper' or 'labour' currency which would genuinely correspond to the concept of money. The first principle is that all economic goods are products of labour, or, as we might put it, that labour alone is creative. This statement, however, does not imply that the value of the product must always equal the cost of labour, or that, in other words, value is even now measured in terms of labour. The truth is rather 'that this still has not become a *fact*, but is only an *idea* of political economy'.[3]

'If the value could be constituted in accordance with the labour

[2] Dr. Carl Rodbertus-Jagetzow, *Schriften* (Berlin, 1899), vol. iii, pp. 172–4, 184.
[3] Op. cit., vol. ii, pp. 104 f.

expended on the product, we might imagine a kind of money which would be, as it were, a leaf torn from the public account-book, a receipt written on the most rubbishy material, or rags, which everyone would receive for the value he has produced, and which he would realise as a voucher for an equivalent part of the national product subsequently under distribution. . . . If, however, for some reason or another, it is *impossible* or *not yet possible* to establish this value, money as such must still retain the value it is designed to liquidate; made of an intrinsically valuable commodity like gold or silver, it has to represent a pledge or pawn of the same value.'[4] 'As soon as capitalist commodity production has come into existence, everything is turned upside down: there can no longer be a constituted value, since it can only be exchange value',[5] and, 'since the value cannot be constituted, money cannot be *purely* money, it cannot fully conform to its concept'.[6] In an equitable exchange, the exchange value of the products would have to equal the quantity of labour needed for producing them, and an exchange of products would always mean an exchange of equal quantities of labour. Even assuming, however, that everybody produced just those use-values which another person requires, yet, 'since we are here concerned with human discernment and human volition, there must always be for a start a correct calculation, adjustment and allocation of the labour quantities contained in the products for exchange, there must be a *law* to which the facts will conform'.[7]

It is well-known that Rodbertus, in his discovery of 'constituted value', laid great stress on his priority to Proudhon which we shall gladly concede him. Marx, in his *Poverty of Philosophy*, and Engels in his preface to it, have comprehensively shown that this 'concept' is a mere phantom, still used in theory but in practice buried already in England well before Rodbertus' time, that it is but a Utopian distortion of Ricardo's doctrine of value. We therefore need not deal further with this 'music of the future, performed on a toy trumpet'.

(2) The 'economy of exchange' resulted in the 'degradation' of

---

[4] Op. cit., vol. i, p. 99.
[5] Ibid., p. 173.
[6] Ibid., p. 176.
[7] Op. cit., vol. ii, p. 65.

labour to a commodity, the labour wage being determined as an item of expenditure (*Kostenwert der Arbeit*) instead of representing a fixed rate of the national product. By a daring jump in history, Rodbertus derives his wages law indirectly from slavery and regards the specific traits which a capitalist production of commodities imposes on exploitation as no more than a lying deception against which he fulminates from a moral point of view.

'So long as the producers themselves remained the property of those who were not producing, so long as slavery was in existence, it was the advantage of the "masters" alone which unilaterally determined the volume of this share (of the workers). With the producers attaining full liberty of person, if nothing more as yet, both parties agree on the wage in advance. The wage, in modern terminology, is the object of a "free contract", that is to say, an object of competition. Labour is therefore as a matter of course subjected to the same laws of exchange as its products: labour itself acquires exchange value; the size of the wage depends on the effects of supply and demand.'

Rodbertus, after having thus turned everything upside down, after deriving the exchange value of labour from competition, now immediately derives its value from its exchange value.

'Under the laws of exchange value, labour, like produced goods, comes to have a kind of "cost value" which exercises some magnetic effects upon its exchange value, the amount of the labour wage. It is that particular amount of payment which is necessary for the "main-tenance" of labour, in other words, which enables labour to continue, if only in the persons of its progeny—it is the so-called "minimum of subsistence".'

For Rodbertus, however, this is not a statement of objective eco-nomic laws, but merely an object for moral indignation. He calls the thesis of the classical school, that labour is worth no more than the wages it can command, a 'cynical' statement, and he is determined to expose the 'string of lies' leading to this 'crude and unethical' conclusion.[8]

'It was a degrading view to estimate the wages of labour in accord-ance with the "necessary subsistence", like so many machines to be

[8] *Schriften*, vol. i, pp. 182–4.

kept in repair. Now that labour, the fountain-head of all commodities, has itself become a commodity of exchange, it is no less degrading to speak of its "natural price", of its "costs", just as we speak of the natural price and costs of its product, and to include this natural price, these costs, in the amount of goods that is necessary to call forth a continuous flow of labour on the market.'

This commodity character of labour power, however, and the corresponding determination of its value, are nothing but a malicious misrepresentation of the Free Trade school. Like the good Prussian he was, Rodbertus put capitalist commodity production as a whole in the dock, as offending against the obtaining constitutional law, instead of pointing out its inherent contradiction, the conflict between determining the value of labour and determining the value *created by* labour, as the English disciples of Ricardo had done.

'Stupid beyond words', he exclaims, 'is the dualist conception of those economists who would have the workers, as far as their legal status is concerned, join in deciding the fate of society, and would for all that, have these same workers from an economic point of view, always treated as mere commodities!'[9]

Now it only remains to find out why the workers put up with such stupid and blatant injustice—an objection which Hermann for instance raised against Ricardo's theory of value. Rodbertus is ready with this answer:

'What were the workers to do after their emancipation other than to agree to these regulations? Imagine their position: when the workers were freed, they were naked or in rags, they had nothing but their labour power. The abolition of slavery or serfdom, moreover, rescinded the master's legal or moral obligation to feed them and care for their needs. Yet these needs remained, they still had to live. How, then, could their labour power provide them with a living? Were they simply to grab some of the capital existing in the society for their maintenance? The capital of society was already in the hands of other people, and the organs of the "law" would not have tolerated such a step. What, then, could the workers have done? Only these alternatives were before them: either to overthrow the law of

[9] Ibid., pp. 182–4.

society or to return, under roughly the same conditions as before, to their former masters, the owners of the land and of capital, and to receive as wages what was formerly doled out to them to keep them fed.'[10]

It was fortunate for mankind and the Prussian state that the workers were 'wise' enough not to overthrow civilisation and preferred to submit to the 'base demands' of their 'former masters'. This, then, is the origin of the capitalist wage system, of the wages law as 'a kind of slavery' resulting from an abuse of power on the part of the capitalists, and from the precarious position and the meek acquiescence on the part of the proletariat—if we are to believe the highly original explanations of that very Rodbertus whose theories Marx is reputed to have 'plagiarised'. Let Rodbertus claim 'priority' in this particular theory of value without challenge, seeing that English socialists and other social critics had already given far less crude and primitive analyses of the wage-system. The singular point about it all is that Rodbertus' display of moral indignation about the origin and the economic laws of the wages system does not lead up to the demand for doing away with this abominable injustice, the 'dualism stupid beyond words'. Far from it! He frequently reassures his fellow-men that he does not really mean anything very serious by roaring—he is no lion fell, only one Snug the joiner. Indeed, an ethical theory of the wages law is necessary only to achieve a further conclusion:

(3) Since the 'laws of exchange value' determine the wage, an advance in labour productivity must bring about an ever declining share in the product for the workers. Here we have arrived at the Archimedean fulcrum of Rodbertus' system. This 'declining wage rate' is his most important 'original' discovery on which he harps from his first writings on social problems (probably in 1839) until his death, and which he 'claims' as his very own. This conception, for all that, was but a simple corollary of Ricardo's theory of value and is contained implicit in the wages fund theory which dominated bourgeois economics up to the publication of Marx's *Capital*. Rodbertus nevertheless believed that this 'discovery' made him a kind of Galileo in economics, and he refers to his 'declining wage rate' as explaining every

[10] Ibid., p. 72.

evil and contradiction in capitalist economy. Above all, he derives from the declining wage rate the phenomenon of pauperism which, together with the crises, in his opinion constitutes the social question. It would be as well to draw the attention of contemporaries, 'out for Marx's blood', to the fact that it was not Marx but Rodbertus, a man much nearer their own heart, who set up a whole theory of progressive poverty in a very crude form, and that he, unlike Marx, made it the very pivot, not just a symptom, of the entire social problem. Compare for instance his argument in his first *Letter on Social Problems* to v. Kirchmann on the absolute impoverishment of the working class. The 'declining wage rate' must serve in addition to explain the other fundamental phenomena of the social problem—the crises. In this connection Rodbertus tackles the problem of balancing consumption with production, touching upon the whole lot of cognate controversial issues which had already been fought out between the schools of Sismondi and Ricardo.

Rodbertus' knowledge of crises was of course based upon far more material evidence than that of Sismondi. In his first *Letter on Social Problems* he already gives a detailed description of the four crises in 1818–19, 1825, 1837–9 and 1847. Since his observations covered a much longer period, Rodbertus could by and large gain a much deeper insight into the essential character of crises than his predecessors. As early as 1850 he formulated the periodical character of the crises which recur at ever shorter intervals and at the same time with ever increasing severity:

'Time after time, these crises have become more terrible in proportion with the increase in wealth, engulfing an ever greater number of victims. The crisis of 1818–19, although even this caused panic in commerce and inspired misgivings in economics, was of small importance compared to that of 1825–6. The first crisis had made such inroads on the capital assets of England that the most famous economists doubted whether complete recovery could ever be made. Yet it was eclipsed by the crisis of 1836–7. The crises of 1839–40 and 1846–7 wrought even greater havoc than previous ones.'—'According to recent experiences, however, the crises recur at ever shorter intervals. There was a lapse of 18 years between the first and the third crisis, of 14 years between the second and the fourth, and of only 12 years between the third and the fifth. Already the signs are multiplying that a new disaster is imminent, though no doubt the events of 1848 put off the catastrophe.'[11]

Rodbertus remarks that an extraordinary boom in production and great progress in industrial technique always are the heralds of a crisis. 'Every one of them [of the crises] followed upon a period of outstanding industrial prosperity.'[12]

From the crises in history he demonstrates that 'they occur only after a considerable increase of productivity'.[13] Rodbertus opposes what he terms the vulgar view which conceives of crises as mere disturbances in the monetary and credit system, and he criticises the whole of Peel's currency legislation as an error of judgment, arguing the point in detail in his essay *On Commercial Crises and the Mortgage Problem*. There he makes the following comment among others: 'We would therefore deceive ourselves if we were to regard commercial crises merely as crises of the monetary, banking, or credit system. This is only their outer semblance when they first emerge.'[14]

Rodbertus also shows a remarkably acute grasp of the part played by foreign trade in the problem of crises. Just like Sismondi, he states the necessity of expansion for capitalist production, but he simultaneously emphasises the fact that the periodical crises are bound to grow in volume.

'Foreign trade', he says, 'is related to slumps only as charity is related to poverty. They ultimately only enhance one another.'[15] And further: 'The only possible means of warding off further outbreaks of crises is the application of the two-edged knife of expanding foreign markets. The violent urge towards such expansion is largely no more but a morbid irritation caused by a sickly organ. Since one factor on the home market, productivity, is ever increasing, and the other factor, purchasing power, remains constant for the overwhelming majority of the population, commerce must endeavour to conjure up a similarly

---

[11] Op. cit., vol. iii, pp. 110–11.
[12] Ibid., p. 108.
[13] Op. cit., vol. i, p. 62.
[14] Op. cit., vol. iv, p. 226.
[15] In *Towards the Understanding of Our Politico-Economic Conditions*, part ii, n. 1.

unlimited amount of purchasing power on the foreign market.'[16] In this way, the irritation may be soothed to some extent so that at least there will not be a new outbreak of the calamity right away. Every foreign market opened defers the social problem in a like manner. Colonisation of primitive countries would have similar effects: Europe rears a market for herself in places where none had been before. Yet such a medicine would essentially do no more than appease the ill. As soon as the new markets are supplied, the problem will revert to its former state—a conflict between the two factors: limited purchasing power versus unlimited productivity. The new attack would be warded off the small market only to re-appear, in even wider dimensions and with even more violent incidents, on a larger one. And since the earth is finite and the acquisition of new markets must some time come to an end, the time will come when the question can no longer be simply adjourned. Sooner or later, a definite solution will have to be found.'[17]

---

[16] In *On Commercial Crises and the Mortgage Problem of the Landowners*, quoted above (op. cit., vol. iii, p. 186).

[17] Op. cit., vol. iv. p. 233. It is interesting to note in this connection how Rodbertus appears in practice as an extremely sober and realistically-minded prophet of capitalist colonial policy, in the manner of the present-day 'Pan-Germans', his moral ranting about the unhappy fate of the working classes notwithstanding. In a footnote to the above quotation, he writes: 'We can go on to glance briefly at the importance of the opening up of Asia, in particular of China and Japan, the richest markets in the world, and also of the maintenance of English rule in India. It is to defer the solution of the social problem.' (The eloquent avenger of the exploited ingenuously discloses the means by which the profiteering exploiters can continue 'their stupid and criminal error', their 'flagrant injustice' for as long as possible.) 'For the solution of this problem, the present lacks in unselfishness and moral resolution no less than in intelligence.' (Rodbertus' philosophical resignation is unparalleled!) 'Economic advantage cannot, admittedly, constitute a legal title to intervention by force, but on the other hand, a strict application of modern natural and international law to all the nations of the world, whatever their state of civilisation, is quite impracticable.' (A comparison with Dorine's words in Molière's *Tartuffe* is irresistible: 'Le ciel défend, de vraie, certains contentements, mais il y a avec lui des accommodements.')—'Our international law has grown from a civilisation of Christian ethics, and since all law is based upon reciprocity, it can only provide the standard for relations between nations of the same civilisation. If it is applied beyond these limits, it is sentiment rather than natural and international law and the Indian atrocities should have cured us of it. Christian Europe should rather partake of the spirit which made the Greeks and the Romans regard all the other peoples of the world as barbarians. The younger European nations might then regain the drive for making world history which impelled

Rodbertus also recognises the anarchical character of capitalist private enterprise to be conducive to crises, but only as one factor among many, seeing it as the source of a particular type of crises, not as the real cause of crises in general. About the crises at v. Kirchmann's *Ort*, e.g., he says: 'I maintain that a slump of this kind does not occur in real life. The market of to-day is large, there are countless wants and many branches of production, productivity is considerable and the data of commerce are obscure and misleading. The individual entrepreneur does not know how much others are producing, and so it may easily happen that he over-estimates the demand for a certain commodity with which he will then overstock the market.'

Rodbertus says outright that the only remedy for these crises is the

---

the Ancients to spread their native civilisation over the countries of the globe. They would reconquer Asia for world history by joint action. Such common purpose and action would in turn stimulate the greatest social progress, a firm foundation of peace in Europe, a reduction of armies, a colonisation of Asia in the ancient Roman style—in other words, a genuine solidarity of interests in all walks of social life.' The vision of capitalist colonial expansion inspires the prophet of the exploited and oppressed to almost poetical flights, all the more remarkable for coming at a time when a civilisation of Christian ethics accomplished such glorious exploits as the Opium Wars against China and the Indian atrocities—that is to say, the atrocities committed by the British in their bloody suppression of the Indian Mutiny.—In his second *Letter on Social Problems*, in 1850, Rodbertus had expressed the conviction that if society lacks the 'moral resolution' necessary to solve the social question, in other words, to change the distribution of wealth, history would be forced to 'use the whip of revolution against it' (op. cit., vol. ii, p. 83). Eight years later, however, the stalwart Prussian prefers to crack the whip of a colonial policy of Christian ethics over the natives of the colonial countries. It is, of course, what one might expect of the 'original founder of scientific socialism in Germany' that he should also be a warm supporter of militarism, and his phrase about the 'reduction of armies' is but poetic licence in his verbal fireworks. In his essay *On the Understanding of the Social Question* he explains that the 'entire national tax burden is perpetually gravitating towards the bottom, sometimes in form of higher prices for wage goods, and sometimes in form of lower money wages'. In this connection, he considers conscription 'under the aspect of a charge on the state', explaining that 'as far as the working classes are concerned, it is nothing like a tax but rather a confiscation of their entire income for many years'. He adds immediately: 'To avoid misunderstanding I would point out that I am a staunch supporter of our present military constitution (i.e. the military constitution of counter-revolutionary Prussia)—although it may be oppressive to the working classes and demand great financial sacrifices from the propertied classes' (op. cit., vol. iii, p. 34). That does not even sound like a lion's roar!

'complete reversal' of contemporary property-relations or a planned economy, concentrating all means of production 'in the hands of a single social authority'. To set troubled minds at rest, however, he is quick to add that he reserves judgment as to whether there can actually be such a state of affairs—'yet this would be the only possible way to prevent slumps of this kind'. Thus he expressly regards anarchy in the modern mode of production as responsible for only a specific and partial manifestation of crises.

Rodbertus scornfully rejects Say–Ricardo's axiom of a natural equilibrium between consumption and production; just like Sismondi, he emphasises that everything turns on the purchasing power of society, and also takes it to be dependent upon the distribution of income. All the same, he does not endorse Sismondi's theory of crises and disagrees sharply with the conclusions drawn from it. If Sismondi saw the source of all evil in the unlimited expansion of production without regard to the limitations of incomes, and advocated a restriction of production, Rodbertus, quite on the contrary, champions the most powerful and unrestricted expansion of production, of wealth and of the productive forces, believing this to be a social necessity. Whoever rejects the wealth of society, rejects at the same time its power, its progress, and, with its progress, its virtues. Whoever stands in the way of growing wealth, stands in the way of all social progress whatever. Every increase in knowledge, resolve and capacity is conceived as bound up with an increase in wealth.[18] From this point of view, Rodbertus is strongly in favour of issuing houses which he regards as the indispensable foundations for a rapid and unrestricted expansion of company promoting. Both his essay of 1859 on the mortgage problem and the treatise on the *Financial Crisis in Prussia*[19] are devoted to this plea. He even polemises outright against the Sismondian type of *caveat*, as usual broaching the matter first from his peculiar Utopian ethics.

'The entrepreneurs', he holds forth, 'are essentially civil servants of economy. By the institution of property, they are once and for all entrusted with the nation's means of production. If they set them to work and strain all their energies in the process, they do but their duty,

---

[18] *Schriften*, vol. iii, p. 182.
[19] Published already in 1845.

since capital—let me repeat—exists entirely for the sake of production.' And a further, factual argument: 'Or would you have them (the entrepreneurs) turn acute attacks of suffering into a chronic state by working persistently and from the first with fewer forces than are given by the means of production; are they to pay for a less severe form of the evil with its permanent duration? Even if we were silly enough to give them this advice, they would not be able to follow it. How could the entrepreneurs of the world recognise the limits beyond which the market would cease to be healthy? They engage in production without knowing the one of the other, they are producing in the most distant corners of the earth for a market hundreds of miles away, they produce with such vast forces that a month's production may already overstep the limit. How could production—so divided and yet so powerful—conceivably estimate in good time what will be enough? Where, for instance, are the organisations, the up-to-date statistical bureaux and the like to help them in this task? What is worse, the price alone, its rise and fall, indicates the position of the market, and this is not like a barometer which predicts the temperature of the market, but more like a thermometer which only registers it. If the price falls, the limit has been passed already, and the evil is with us.'[20]

These thrusts, obviously aimed at Sismondi, exhibit quite fundamental differences between the two opponents. If Engels then says in his *Anti-Duehring* that Sismondi first explained the crises as resulting from under-consumption, and that Rodbertus borrowed this view from him, he is not strictly accurate. All that Rodbertus and Sismondi have in common is their opposition against the classical school and the general explanation of crises as the result of the distribution of incomes. Even in this connection Rodbertus mounts his own particular hobby horse: over-production is not caused by the low level of working class incomes, nor yet, as Sismondi maintains, by the capitalists' limited capacity for consumption, but solely by the fact that with a growing productivity of labour, the workers' income, in terms of value, represents an ever smaller share of the product. Rodbertus takes pains to convince the opposition that it is not the small volume of the workers' share which causes the crises.

[20] *Schriften*, vol. iv, p. 231.

'Just imagine', he goes on to lecture v. Kirchmann, 'these shares to be so small as to ensure only a bare subsistence for those who are entitled to them. As long as you establish them as representing a proportion of the national product, you will have a constant "vessel for value" which can absorb ever increasing contents, and an ever increasing prosperity of the working classes as well. . . . And now imagine on the contrary as large a share for the working classes as you please, and let it become an ever smaller fraction of the national product that grows with increasing productivity. Then, provided it is not reduced to the present pittance, this share will still protect the workers from undue privations since the amount of products it represents will still be considerably greater than it is to-day. Once this share begins to decline, however, there will be spreading discontent, culminating in a commercial crisis for which the capitalists are not to blame inasmuch as they did not more than their duty in laying down the volume of production according to the given magnitude of these shares.'

That is why the 'declining wage rate' is the real cause of crises. It can only be counteracted by legal measures to ensure that the workers' share represents a stable and unchanging rate of the national product. This grotesque notion takes some understanding if we are to do justice to its economic implications.

17

RODBERTUS' ANALYSIS OF REPRODUCTION

To begin with, what does it mean that a decrease in the workers' share is bound immediately to engender over-production and commercial crises? Such a view can only make sense provided Rodbertus takes the 'national product' to consist of two parts, *vide* the shares of the workers and of the capitalists, in short of $v+s$, one share being exchangeable for the other. And that is more or less what he actually seems to say on occasions, e.g. in his first *Letter on Social Problems*:

'The poverty of the working classes precludes their income from giving scope to increasing production. The additional amount of products from the entrepreneurs' point of view lowers the value of the aggregate product so far as to bar production on the former scale, leaving the workers at best to their accustomed straits, though, if it could be made available to the workers, it would not only improve their lot but would further act as a counterweight by increasing the value of what is retained by the capitalists (and so enable the latter to keep their enterprises at the same level).'[1]

The 'counterweight' which in the hand of the workers increases the

---

[1] *Schriften*, vol. iii, p. 176.

'value' of 'what is retained' by the entrepreneurs, can in this context only be the demand. Once again, we have landed happily at the familiar Ort of v. Kirchmann's where workers and capitalists exchange their incomes for the surplus product, and where the crises arise because variable capital is small and the surplus value large. This peculiar notion has already been dealt with above. There are other occasions, however, when Rodbertus advances a somewhat different conception. The interpretation of his theory in the fourth *Letter on Social Problems* is that the continual shifts in the relations of demand, evident in the share of the working class and caused by the share of the capitalist class, must result in a chronic disproportion between production and consumption.

'What if the entrepreneurs endeavour to keep always within the limits of those shares, yet the shares themselves are all the time on the decline for the great majority of the society, the workers, decreasing gradually, unnoticeably, but with relentless force?—What if the share of these classes is continually decreasing to the same extent as their productivity is increasing?'—'Is it not really the fact that the capitalists of necessity organise production in accordance with the present volume of shares in order to make wealth universal, and that yet they always produce over and above this volume (of previous shares), thereby perpetuating dissatisfaction which culminates in this stagnation of trade?'[2]

On this showing, the explanation of crises should be as follows: the national product consists of a number of 'common goods', as v. Kirchmann puts it, for the workers, and of superior goods for the capitalists. The wages represent the quantity of the former, and aggregate surplus value that of the latter. If the capitalists organise their production on this footing, and if at the same time there is progressive productivity, a lack of proportion will immediately ensue. For the share of the workers to-day is no longer that of yesterday, but less. If the demand for 'common goods' had involved, say, six-sevenths of the national product yesterday, then to-day it involves only five-sevenths, and the entrepreneurs, having provided for six-sevenths of 'common goods', will find to their painful surprise that they over-produced by one-seventh. Now, wiser by this experience, they try to organise

[2] Op. cit., vol. i, pp. 53, 57.

tomorrow's output of 'common goods' to a mere five-sevenths of the total value of the national product, but they have a new disappointment coming to them, since the share of the national product falling to wages to-morrow is bound to be only four-sevenths, and so on.

In this ingenious theory there are quite a few points to make us wonder. If our commercial crises are entirely due to the fact that the workers' 'wage rate', the variable capital, represents a constantly diminishing portion of the total value of the national product, then this unfortunate law brings with it the cure for the evil it has caused, since it must be an ever smaller part of the aggregate product for which there is over-production. Although Rodbertus delights in such terms as 'an overwhelming majority', 'the large popular masses' of consumers, it is not the number of heads that make up the demand, but the value they represent which is relevant. This value, if Rodbertus is to be believed, forms a more and more trifling part of the aggregate product. Crises are thus made to rest on an ever narrowing economic basis, and all that remains to discover is how in spite of it all it can still happen that the crises are universal and increasingly severe besides, as Rodbertus is fully aware. The purchasing power lost by the working classes should be gained by the capitalist class; if v decreases, s must grow larger to make up for it. On this crude scheme, the purchasing power of society as a whole cannot change, as Rodbertus says in so many words: 'I know very well that what is taken from the workers' share goes ultimately to swell that of the "rentiers" (rent and surplus value are used as synonyms, R.L.), and that purchasing power remains constant on the whole and in the long run. But as far as the product on the market is concerned, the crisis always sets in before this increase can make itself felt.'[3]

In short, the most it can amount to is that there is 'too much' of 'common goods' and 'too little' of superior goods for the capitalists. Quite unawares, and by devious ways, Rodbertus here falls in with the Say–Ricardian theory he so ardently contested, the theory that over-production on one side always corresponds to under-production on the other. Seeing that the ratio of the two shares is persistently shifting to the advantage of the capitalists, our commercial crises might be

---

[3] Ibid., p. 206.

expected on the whole to take on increasingly the character of periodical under- instead of over-production! Enough of this exercise in logic.
The upshot of it all is that Rodbertus conceives the national product in
respect of its value as made up of two parts only, of s and v, thus wholly
subscribing to the views and traditions of the classical school he is
fighting tooth and nail, and even adding his own flourish that the
capitalists consume the entire surplus value. That is why he repeatedly
says without mincing his words, as in the fourth *Letter on Social Problems*:

'Accordingly, we must abstract from the reasons which cause the
division of rent in general into rent proper and capital rent, to find the
basic principle underlying the division of rent (surplus value) in general, the principle underlying *the division of the labour product into wage and
rent.*'[4] And, in the third *Letter*: 'Ground rent, capital profit and the wage
of labour are, let me repeat, revenue. By this means landlords, capitalists
and workers must live, must satisfy, that is to say, their immediate
human necessities. They must therefore draw their income in the form
of goods suitable for this purpose.'[5]

The misrepresentation of capitalist economy has never been formulated more crudely, and there is no doubt that Rodbertus claims the
palm of 'priority'—not so much over Marx as over all popular
economists—with full justification. To leave the reader in no doubt
about the utter muddle he has made, he goes on, in the same letter, to
rank capitalist surplus value as an economic category on the same level
as the revenue of the ancient slave-owner:

'The first state (that of slavery) goes with the most primitive natural
economy: that portion of the labour product which is withheld from
the income of workers or slaves and forms the master's or owner's
property, will undividedly accrue to the one man who owns the land,
the capital, the worker and the labour product; there is not even a
distinction of thought between rent and capital profits.—The second
state entails the most complicated money economy: that portion of the
labour product, withheld from the income of the now emancipated
workers, and accruing to the respective owners of land, and capital,
will be further divided among the owners of the raw material and the

---

[4] Ibid., vol. i, p. 19.
[5] Op. cit., vol. ii, p. 110.

manufactured product respectively; the one rent of the former state will be split up into ground rent and capital profits, and will have to be differentiated accordingly.'[6]

Rodbertus regards the splitting-up of the surplus value 'withheld' from the workers' 'income' as the most striking difference between exploitation by slavery and modern capitalist exploitation. It is not the specific historical form of sharing out newly created value among labour and capital, but the distribution of the surplus value among the various people it benefits, which, irelevant to the productive process, is yet the decisive fact in the capitalist mode of production. In all other respects, capitalist surplus value remains just the same as the old 'single rent' of the slave-owner: a private fund for the exploiter's own consumption!

Yet Rodbertus again contradicts himself in other places, remembering all of a sudden the constant capital and the necessity for its renewal in the reproductive process. Thus, instead of bisecting the aggregate product into v and s, he posits a triple division: c, v, and s. In his third *Letter on Social Problems* he argues on the forms of reproduction in a slave-economy:

'Since the master will see to it that part of the slave labour is employed in maintaining or even improving the fields, herds, agricultural and manufacturing tools, there will be "capital replacement", to use a modern term, in which part of the national economic product is immediately used for the upkeep of the estate, without any mediation by exchange or even by exchange value.'[7] And, passing on to capitalist reproduction, he continues: 'Now, in terms of value, one portion of the labour product, is used or set aside for the maintenance of the estate, for "capital replacement", another, for the workers' subsistence as their money wage; and the owners of the land, of capital, and of the labour product retain the last as their revenue or rent.'[8]

This, then, is an explicit expression of the triple division into constant capital, variable capital, and surplus value. Again, in this third *Letter*, he formulates the peculiarity of his 'new' theory with equal

[6] Ibid., p. 144.
[7] Ibid., p. 146.
[8] Ibid., p. 155.

precision: 'On this theory, then, and under conditions of adequate labour productivity, the portion of the product which remains for wages after the replacement of capital, will be distributed among workers and owners as wages and rent, on the basis of the ownership in land and capital.'[9]

It does seem now as if Rodbertus' analysis of the value of the aggregate product represents a distinct advance over the classical school. Even Adam Smith's 'dogma' is openly criticised a little further on, and it is really surprising that Rodbertus' learned admirers, Messrs. Wagner, Dietzel, Diehl & Co. failed to claim their white-headed boy's 'priority' over Marx on such an important point of economic theory. As a matter of fact, in this respect no less than in the general theory of value, Rodbertus' priority is of a somewhat dubious character. If he seems on occasion to gain true insight, it immediately turns out to be a misunderstanding, or at best a wrong approach. His criticism of Adam Smith's dogma affords a supreme example of his failure to cope with the triple division of the national product towards which he had groped his way. He says literally:

'You know that all economists since Adam Smith already divided the value of the product into wage of labour, rent, and capital profit, that it is therefore not a new idea to ground the incomes of the various classes, and especially the various items of the rent, in a division of the product. But the economists at once go off the track. All of them, not even excepting Ricardo's school, make the mistake, first, not to recognise that the aggregate product, the finished good, the national product as a whole, is an entity in which workers, landowners, and capitalists all share, but conceiving the division of the unfinished product to be of one kind shared among three partners, and that of the manufactured product as of another kind again, shared between only two partners. For these theories both the unfinished product and the manufactured product constitute as such separate items of revenue. Secondly,—though both Sismondi and Ricardo are free from this particular error—they regard the natural fact that labour cannot produce goods without material help, i.e. without the land, as an economic fact, and take the social fact for a primary datum that capital as

---

[9] Ibid., p. 223.

understood to-day is required by the division of labour. Thus they set up the fiction of a fundamental economic relationship on which they base also for the shares of the various owners, ground rent springing from the contribution of the land lent by the owner to production, capital profits from the contribution of capital employed by the capitalist to this end, and the wages finally from labour's contribution, seeing that there are separate owners of land, capital, and labour in the society. Say's school, elaborating on this mistake with much ingenuity, even invented the concept of productive service of land, capital, and labour in conformity with the shares in the product of their respective owners, so as to explain these shares as the result of productive service.—Thirdly, they are caught up in the ultimate folly of deriving the wage of labour and the items of rent from the value of the product, the value of the product in turn being derived from the wage of labour and the items of rent, so that the one is made to depend on the other and *vice versa*. This absurdity is quite unmistakable when some of these authors attempt to expound "The Influence of Rent Upon Production Prices" and "The Influence of Production Prices Upon Rent" in two consecutive chapters.'[10]

Yet for all these excellent critical comments—the last, particularly acute, actually does to some extent anticipate Marx's criticism of this point in *Capital*, volume ii—Rodbertus calmly falls in with the fundamental blunder of the classical school and its vulgar followers: to ignore altogether that part of the value of the aggregate product which is needed to replace the constant capital of the society. This way it was easier for him to keep up the singular fight against the 'declining wage rate'.

Under capitalist forms of production, the value of the aggregate social product is divided into three parts: one corresponding to the value of the constant capital, the second to the wage total, i.e. the variable capital, and the third to the aggregate surplus value of the capitalist class. In this composition, the portion corresponding to the variable capital is relatively on the decline, and this for two reasons. To begin with, the relation of c to $(v+s)$ within $c+v+s$ changes all the time in the direction of a relative increase of c and a relative decrease

[10] Ibid., p. 226.

of $v+s$. This is the simple law for a progressive efficiency of human labour, valid for all societies of economic progress, independently of their historical forms, a formula which only states that living labour is increasingly able to convert more means of production into objects for use in an ever shorter time. And if $(v+s)$ decreases as a whole, so must v, as its part, decrease in relation to the total value of the product. To kick against this, to try and stop the decrease, would be tantamount to contending against the general effects of a growing labour productivity. Further, there is within $(v+s)$ as well a change in the direction of a relative decrease in v and a relative increase in s, that is to say, an ever smaller part of the newly created value is spent on wages and an ever greater part is appropriated as surplus value. This is the specifically capitalist formula of progressive labour productivity which, under capitalist conditions of production, is no less valid than the general law. To use the power of the state to prevent a decrease of v as against s would mean that the fundamental commodity of labour power is debarred from this progress which decreases production costs for all commodities; it would mean the exemption of this one commodity from the economic effects of technical progress. More than that: the 'declining wage rate' is only another expression of the rising rate of surplus value which forms the most powerful and effective means of checking a decline of the profit rate, and which therefore represents the prime incentive for capitalist production in general, and for technical progress within this system of production in particular. Doing away with the 'declining wage rate' by way of legislation would be as much as to do away with the *raison d'être* of capitalist society, to deal a crippling blow to its entire system. Let us face the facts: the individual capitalist, just like capitalist society as a whole, has no glimmering that the value of the product is made up from the sum total of labour necessary in the society, and this is actually beyond his grasp. Value, as the capitalist understands it, is the derivative form, reversed by competition as production costs. While in truth the value of the product is broken down into the values of its component fragments c, v and s, the capitalist mind conceives of it as the summation of c, v and s. These, in addition, also appear to him from a distorted perspective and in a secondary form, as (1) the wear and tear of his fixed capital, (2) his advances on circulating capital, including workers' wages, and (3) the current profits, i.e. the average rate of profit on his entire capital. How, then, is the capitalist to be compelled by a law, say of the kind envisaged by Rodbertus, to maintain a 'fixed wage rate' in the face of the aggregate value of the product? It would be quite as brilliant to stipulate by law for exactly one-third, no more, no less, of the total price of the product to be payable for the raw materials employed in the manufacture of any commodity. Obviously, Rodbertus' supreme notion, of which he was so proud, on which he built as if it were a new Archimedean discovery, which was to be the specific for all the ills of capitalist production, is arrant nonsense from all aspects of the capitalist mode of production. It could only result from the muddle in the theory of value which is brought to a head in Rodbertus' inimitable phrase: that 'now, in a capitalist society, the product must have value-in-exchange just as it had to have value-in-use in ancient economy'.[11] People in ancient society had to eat bread and meat in order to live, but we of to-day are already satisfied with knowing the price of bread and of meat. The most obvious inference from Rodbertus' monomania about a 'fixed wage rate' is that he is quite incapable of understanding capitalist accumulation.

Previous quotations have already shown that Rodbertus thinks solely of simple commodity production, quite in keeping with his mistaken doctrine that the purpose of capitalist production is the manufacture of consumer goods for the satisfaction of 'human wants'. For he always talks of 'capital replacements', of the need to enable the capitalists to 'continue their enterprise on the previous scale'. His principal argument, however, is directly opposed to the accumulation of capital. To fix the rate of the surplus value, to prevent its growth, is tantamount to paralysing the accumulation of capital. Both Sismondi and v. Kirchmann had recognised the problem of balancing production and consumption to be indeed a problem of accumulation, that is to say of enlarged capitalist reproduction. Both traced the disturbances in the equilibrium of reproduction to accumulative tendencies denying the possibility of accumulation, with the only difference that the one recommended a damper on the productive forces as a remedy, while

[11] Ibid., p. 156.

the other favoured their increasing employment to produce luxuries, the entire surplus value to be consumed. In this field, too, Rodbertus follows his own solitary path. The others might try with more or less success to comprehend the fact of capitalist accumulation, but Rodbertus prefers to fight the very concept. 'Economists since Adam Smith have one after the other echoed the principle, setting it up as a universal and absolute truth, that capital could only come about by saving and accumulating.'[12]

Rodbertus is up in arms against this 'deluded judgment'. Over sixty pages of print he sets out in detail that (a) it is not saving which is the source of capital but labour, that (b) the economists' 'delusion' about 'saving' hails from the extravagant view that capital is itself productive, and that (c) this delusion is ultimately due to another: the error that capital is—capital.

v. Kirchmann for his part understood quite well what is at the bottom of capitalist 'savings'. He had the pretty argument: 'Everyone knows that the accumulation of capital is not a mere hoarding of reserves, an amassing of metal and monies to remain idle in the owners' vaults. Those who want to save do it for the sake of re-employing their savings either personally or through the agency of others as capital, in order to yield them revenue. That is only possible if these capitals are used in new enterprises which can produce so as to provide the required interest. One may build a ship, another a barn, a third may reclaim a desolate swamp, a fourth may order a new spinning frame, while a fifth, in order to enlarge his shoe-making business, would buy more leather and employ more hands—and so on. Only if the capital that has been saved is employed in this way, can it yield interest (meaning profit), and the latter is the ultimate object of all saving.'[13]

That is how v. Kirchmann described somewhat clumsily, but on the whole correctly, what is in fact the capitalisation of surplus value, the process of capitalist accumulation, which constitutes the whole significance of saving, advocated by classical economists 'since Adam Smith' with unerring instinct. Declaring war on saving and accumulation was quite in keeping with v. Kirchmann's premises, considering

[12] Op. cit., vol. i, p. 40.
[13] Op. cit., vol. ii, p. 25.

that he, like Sismondi, saw the immediate cause of the crises in accumulation. Here, too, Rodbertus is more 'thorough'. Having learned from Ricardo's theory of value that labour is the source of all value, and consequently of capital, too, he is completely blinded by this elementary piece of knowledge to the entire complexity of capitalist production and capital movements. Since capital is generated by labour, both the accumulation of capital, i.e. 'saving', and the capitalisation of the surplus value are nothing but eyewash.

In order to untangle this intricate network of errors by 'economists since Adam Smith', he takes, as we might expect, the example of the 'isolated husbandman' and proves all that he needs by a long-drawn vivisection of the unhappy creature. Here already he discovers 'capital', that is to say, of course, that famous 'original stick' with which 'economists since Adam Smith' have hooked the fruits of a theory of capital from the tree of knowledge. 'Would saving be able to produce this stick?' is his query. And since every normal person will understand that 'saving' cannot produce any stick, that Robinson [Crusoe] must have made it of wood, we have already proved that the 'savings' theory is quite mistaken. Presently, the 'isolated husbandman' hooks a fruit from the tree with the stick, and this fruit is his 'income'.

'If capital were the source of income, already this most elementary and primitive event would have to give evidence of this relation. Would it be true to say, then, without doing violence to facts and concepts, that the stick is a *source* of income or of part of the income consisting in the fruit brought down? can we trace income, wholly or in part, back to the stick as its *cause*, may we consider it, wholly or in parts, as a *product* of the stick?'[14]

Surely not. And since the fruit is the product, not of the stick which brought it down, but of the tree which grew it, Rodbertus has already proved that all 'economists since Adam Smith' are grossly mistaken if they maintain that income derives from capital. After a clear exposition of all fundamental concepts of economics on the example of Robinson [Crusoe]'s 'economy', Rodbertus transfers the knowledge thus acquired first to a fictitious society 'without ownership in capital or land', that is to say to a society with a communist mode of possession,

---

[14] Op. cit., vol. i, p. 250.

and then to a society 'with ownership in capital and land', that is to say contemporary society, and, lo and behold—all the laws of Robinson [Crusoe]'s economy apply point for point to these two forms of society as well. Rodbertus contrives here a theory of capital and income which is the very crown of his Utopian imagination. Since he has discovered that Robinson [Crusoe]'s 'capital' is the means of production pure and simple, he identifies capital with the means of production in capitalist economy as well. Thus reducing capital, with a wave of his hand, to constant capital, he protests in the name of justice and morality against the fact that the wages, the workers' means of subsistence, are also considered capital. He contends furiously against the *concept* of variable capital, seeing in it the cause of every disaster. 'If only', he grieves, 'economists would pay attention to what I say, if only they would examine without prejudice whether they are right or I. This is the focal point of all errors about capital in the ruling system, this is the ultimate source of injustice against the working classes, in theory and practice alike.'[15]

For 'justice' demands that the goods constituting the 'real wages' of the workers be counted, not as part of capital, but as belonging to the category of income. Though Rodbertus knows very well that the capitalist must regard the wages he has 'advanced' as part of his capital, just like the other part laid out on immediate means of production, yet in his opinion this applies only to individual capitals. As soon as it is a question of the social aggregate product, of reproduction as a whole, he declares the capitalist categories of production an illusion, a malicious lie and a 'wrong'. 'Capital *per se* (properly so-called), the items which make up capital, capital from the nation's point of view, is something quite different from private capital, capital *assets*, capital

---

[15] Ibid., p. 295. Rodbertus reiterates during a lifetime the ideas he had evolved as early as 1842 in his *Towards the Understanding of Our Politico-Economic Conditions*. 'Under present conditions, we have, however, gone so far as to consider not only the wage of labour part of the costs of the goods, but also rents and capital profits. We must therefore refute this opinion in detail. It has a twofold foundation: (*a*) a wrong conception of capital which counts the wage of labour as part of the capital just like materials and tools, while it is on the same level as rent and profit; (*b*) a confusion of the costs of the commodity and the advances of the entrepreneur or the costs of the enterprise' (*Towards the Understanding of Our Politico-Economic Conditions*, Neubrandenburg & Friedland, G. Barnovitz, 1842, p. 14).

property, all that "capital" in the modern use of the term usually stands for.'[16]

An individual capitalist produces by capitalist methods, but society as a whole must produce like Robinson [Crusoe], as a collective owner employing communist methods.

'It makes no difference from this general and national point of view that greater or smaller parts of the aggregate national product are now owned in all the various phases of production by private persons who must not be numbered among the producers proper, and that the latter always manufacture this national aggregate product as servants— without sharing in the ownership of their own product—of these few owners.'

Certain peculiarities of the relations within the society as a whole no doubt result from this, namely (1) the institution of 'exchange' as an intermediary, and (2) the inequality in the distribution of the product.

'Yet all these consequences do not affect the movements of national production and the shaping of the national product which are always the same, now as ever (under the rule of communism), no more than they alter in any respect, as far as the *national point of view* is concerned, the contrast between capital and income so far established.'

Sismondi had laboured in the sweat of his brow, as had Smith and many others, to disentangle the concepts of capital and income from the contradictions of capitalist production. Rodbertus has a simpler method and abstracts from the specific forms determined by capitalist production for society as a whole; he simply calls the means of production 'capital' and the article of consumption 'revenue' and leaves it at that.

'The essential influence of ownership in land and capital applies only to individuals having traffic with one another. If the nation is taken as a

---

[16] *Schriften*, vol. i, p. 304. Just so already in *Towards the Understanding of Our Politico-Economic Conditions*, 'We must distinguish between capital in its narrow or proper sense, and the fund of enterprise, or capital in a wider sense. The former comprises the actual reserves in tools and materials, the latter the fund necessary for running an enterprise under present conditions of division of labour. The former is capital absolutely necessary to production, and the latter achieves such relative necessity only by force of present conditions. Hence only the former is capital in the strict and proper meaning of the term; this alone is completely congruent with the concept of national capital' (ibid., pp. 23–4).

unit, the effects of such ownership upon the individuals completely disappear.'[17]

We see that as soon as Rodbertus comes up against the real problem, the capitalist aggregate product and its movements, he exhibits the Utopian's characteristic obtuseness in respect of the historical peculiarities of production. Marx's comment on Proudhon, that 'speaking of society as a whole, he pretends that this society is no longer capitalist' therefore fits him like a glove. The case of Rodbertus again exemplifies how every economist before Marx had been at a loss when it came to harmonising the concrete aspects of the labour process with the perspective of capitalist production which regards everything in terms of value, to mediating between the forms of movement performed by individual capitals and the movement of social capital. Such efforts as a rule vacillate from one extreme to another: the shallow approach of Say and MacCulloch, recognising only the conceptions of individual capital, and the Utopian approach of Proudhon and Rodbertus who recognise only those of the process of labour. That is the context in which Marx's penetration appears in its true light. His diagram of simple reproduction illuminates the entire problem by gathering up all these perspectives in their harmony and their contradictions, and so resolves the hopeless obscurities of innumerable tomes into two rows of figures of striking simplicity.

On the strength of such views on capital and income as these, capitalist appropriation is clearly quite impossible to understand. Indeed, Rodbertus simply brands it as 'robbery' and indicts it before the forum of the rights of property it so blatantly violates.

'This personal freedom of the workers which ought legally to involve ownership in the value of the labour product, leads in practice to their renunciation of the proprietary claims extorted under pressure of ownership in land and capital; but the owners do not admit to this great and universal wrong, almost as though they were instinctively afraid that history might follow its own stern and inexorable logic.'[18]

Rodbertus' 'theory in all its details is therefore conclusive proof that those who praise present-day relations of ownership without being

---

[17] *Schriften*, vol. i, p. 292.
[18] Op. cit., vol. ii, p. 136.

able at the same time to ground ownership in anything but labour, completely contradict their own principle. It proves that the property relations of to-day are in fact founded on a universal violation of this principle, that the great individual fortunes being amassed in society nowadays are the result of cumulative robbery mounting up in society with every newborn worker since time immemorial.'[19]

Since surplus value is thus branded as 'robbery', an increasing rate of surplus value must appear 'as a strange error of present-day economic organisation'. Brissot's crude paradox with its revolutionary ring— 'property is theft'—had been the starting point for Proudhon's first pamphlet, but Rodbertus' thesis is quite another matter, arguing that capital is theft perpetrated on property. It need only be set side by side with Marx's chapter on the transformation of the laws of ownership into the laws of capitalist appropriation—this triumph of historical dialectics in vol. i of Marx's *Capital*—in order to show up Rodbertus' 'priority'. By ranting against capitalist appropriation under the aspect of the 'right of property', Rodbertus closed his mind to capital as the source of surplus value just as effectively as he had previously been prevented by his tirades against 'saving' from seeing the surplus value as a source of capital. He is thus in an even worse position than v. Kirchmann, lacking all qualifications for understanding capitalist accumulation.

What it amounts to is that Rodbertus wants unrestricted expansion of production without saving, that is to say without capitalist accumulation! He wants an unlimited growth of the productive forces, and at the same time a rate of surplus value stabilised by an act of law. In short, he shows himself quite unable to grasp the real foundations of capitalist production he wishes to reform, and to understand the most important results of the classical economics he criticises so adversely.

It is no more than to be expected, therefore, that Prof. Diehl should declare Rodbertus a pioneer of economic theory on the strength of his 'new theory of income' and of the distinction between the logical and the historical categories of capital (capital properly so-called in contrast to individual capital), that Prof. Adolf Wagner should call him the 'Ricardo of economic socialism', proving himself ignorant at once of

[19] Ibid., p. 225.

Ricardo, Rodbertus and socialism alike. Lexis even judges that Rodbertus is at least the equal of 'his British rival' in power of abstract thinking, and by far his superior in 'virtuosity to lay bare the phenomena in their ultimate connections', in 'imaginative vitality', and above all in his 'ethical approach to economic life'. Rodbertus' real achievements in economic theory however, other than his critique of Ricardo's ground rent, his at times quite clear-cut distinction between surplus value and profit, his treatment of the surplus value as a whole in deliberate contrast with its partial manifestations, his critique of Smith's dogma concerning the analysis of commodities in terms of value, his precise formulation of the periodical character of the crises and his analysis of their manifestations—all these attempts to carry the investigation beyond Smith, Ricardo and Say, promising as such, though doomed to failure because of the confused basic concepts, are rather above the heads of Rodbertus' official admirers. As Franz Mehring already pointed out, it was Rodbertus' strange fortune to be lauded to heaven for his alleged prowess in economics by the same people who called him to task for his real merits in politics. This contrast between economic and political achievements, however, does not concern us here: in the realm of economic theory, his admirers built him a grand memorial on the barren field he had dug with the hopeless zeal of the visionary, while the modest beds where he had sown a few fertile seeds, were allowed to be smothered with weeds and forgotten.[20]

---

[20] A memorial of the worst kind, by the way, was that of the editors who published his works after his death. These learned gentlemen, Messrs. Wagner, Kozak, Moritz Wuertz & Co., quarrelled in the prefaces to his posthumous writings like a rough crowd of ill-mannered servants in an antechamber, fighting out publicly their petty personal feuds and jealousies, and slanging one another. They did not even bother in common decency to establish the dates for the individual manuscripts they had found. To take an instance, it needed Mehring to observe that the oldest manuscript of Rodbertus that had been found was not published in 1837, as laid down autocratically by Prof. Wagner, but in 1839 at the earliest, since it refers in its opening paragraphs to historical events connected with the Chartist movement belonging, as a professor of economics really ought to know, in the year 1839. In Professor Wagner's introduction to Rodbertus we are constantly bored by his pomposity, his harping on the 'excessive demands on his time'; in any case Wagner addresses himself solely to his learned colleagues and talks above the heads of the common crowd; he passes over in silence, as befits a great man, Mehring's elegant correction before the assembled experts. Just as silently, Professor Diehl altered

It cannot be said that the problem of accumulation had on the whole been much advanced beyond the first controversy by this Prusso-Pomeranian treatment. If in the interim the economic theory of harmony had dropped from the level of Ricardo to that of a Bastiat–Schultze, social criticism had correspondingly declined from Sismondi to Rodbertus. Sismondi's critique of 1819 had been an historical event, but Rodbertus' ideas of reform, even on their first appearance, were a miserable regression—still more so on their subsequent reiteration.

In the controversy between Sismondi on the one hand and Say and Ricardo on the other, one party proved that accumulation was impossible because of the crises, and therefore warned against full development of the productive forces. The other party proved that crises were impossible and advocated an unlimited development of accumulation. Though all argued from wrong premises, each was logically consistent.

v. Kirchmann and Rodbertus both started, were bound to start, from the fact of crises. Here the problem of enlarged reproduction of aggregate capital, the problem of accumulation, was completely identified with the problem of crises and side-tracked in an attempt to find a remedy for the crises, although the historical experience of fifty years had shown all too clearly that crises, as witnessed by their periodical

---

the date of 1837 to 1839 in the *Handwörterbuch der Staatswissenschaften*, without a word to say when and by whom he had been thus enlightened.

But the final touch is provided by the 'popular', 'new and inexpensive' edition of Puttkamer and Muehlbrecht (1899). Some of the quarrelling editors collaborated on it but still continue their disputes in the introductions. Wagner's former vol. ii has become vol. i in this edition, yet Wagner still refers to vol. ii in the introduction to vol. i. The first *Letter on Social Problems* is placed in vol. iii, the second and third in vol. ii and the fourth in vol. i. The order of the *Letters on Social Problems*, of the *Controversies*, of the parts of *Towards the Understanding* . . ., chronological and logical sequence, the dates of publication and of writing are hopelessly mixed up, making a chaos more impenetrable than the stratification of the soil after repeated volcanic eruptions. 1837 is maintained as the date of Rodbertus' earliest MS., probably out of respect to Professor Wagner—and this in 1899, although Mehring's rectification had been made in 1894. If we compare this with Marx's literary heritage in Mehring's and Kautsky's edition, published by Dietz, we see how such apparently superficial matters but reflect deeper connections: one kind of care for the scientific heritage of the authority of the class-conscious proletariat, and quite another in which the official experts of the bourgeoisie squander the heritage of a man who, in their own self-interested legends, had been a first-rate genius. *Suum cuique*—had this not been the motto of Rodbertus?

recurrence, are a necessary phase in capitalist reproduction. One side now sees the remedy in the complete consumption of the surplus value by the capitalist, that is to say in refraining from accumulation, the other in stabilisation of the rate of surplus value by legislative measures which comes to the same thing, i.e. renouncing accumulation altogether. This special fad of Rodbertus' sprang from his fervent and explicit belief in an unlimited capitalist expansion of the productive forces and of wealth, without accumulation of capital. At a time when capitalist production was developed to a degree which was soon to enable Marx to make his fundamental analysis, the last attempt of bourgeois economics to cope with the problem of reproduction degenerated into absurd and puerile Utopianism.

Section II

Historical Exposition of
the Problem

Third Round
Struve–Bulgakov–Tugan Baranovski
v. Vorontsov–Nikolayon

18

A NEW VERSION OF THE PROBLEM

The third controversy about capitalist accumulation takes place in an historical setting quite different from that of the two earlier ones. The time now is the period from the beginning of the eighties to the middle of the nineties, the scene Russia. In Western Europe, capitalism had already attained maturity. The rose-coloured classical view of Smith and Ricardo in a budding bourgeois economy had long since vanished . . . the self-interested optimism of the vulgarian Manchester doctrine of harmony had been silenced by the devastating impact of the world collapse in the seventies, and under the heavy blows of a violent class struggle that blazed up in all capitalist countries after the sixties. Even that harmony patched up with social reformism which had its hey-day after the early eighties, especially in Germany, soon ended in a hangover. The trial of twelve years' special legislation against the Social Democratic Party had brought about bitter disillusionment, and ultimately destroyed all the veils of harmony, revealing the cruel capitalist contradictions in their naked reality. Since then, optimism had only been possible in the camp of the rising working class and its theorists. This was admittedly not optimism about a natural, or artificially established equilibrium of capitalist economy, or about the eternal duration of capitalism, but rather the conviction that capitalism, by mightily furthering the development of the productive forces, and in virtue of its inherent contradictions, would provide an excellent soil for the historical progress of society towards new economic and social forms. The negative, depressing tendency of the first stage of capitalism, at the time realised by Sismondi alone and still observed by Rodbertus as late as the forties and fifties, is compensated by a tendency towards elation: the hopeful and victorious striving of the workers for ascendancy in their trade-union movement and by political action.

Such was the setting in Western Europe. In the Russia of that time, however, the picture was different indeed. Here, the seventies and eighties represent in every respect a period of transition, a period of internal crises with all its agonies. Big industry only now staged its real entry, fostered by the period of high protective tariffs. In particular, the introduction of a tariff on gold at the Western frontier in 1877 was a special landmark in the absolutist government's new policy of forcing the growth of capitalism. 'Primitive accumulation' of capital flourished splendidly in Russia, encouraged by all kinds of state subsidies, guarantees, premiums and government orders. It earned profits which would already seem legendary to the West. Yet the picture of internal conditions in contemporary Russia was anything but attractive and auspicious. On the plains, the decline and disintegration of rural economy under the pressure of exploitation by the Exchequer and the monetary system caused terrible conditions, periodical famines and peasant risings. In the towns, again the factory proletariat had not yet been consolidated, either socially or mentally, into a modern working class. For the greater part, it was still closely connected with agriculture, and remained semi-rural, particularly in the large industrial parts of Moscow-Vladimir, the most important centre of the Russian textile industry. Accordingly, primitive forms of exploitation were countered by primitive measures of defence. Not until the early eighties did the spontaneous factory revolts in the Moscow district with their smashing up of machines provide the impetus for the first rudiments of factory legislation in the Czarist Empire.

If the economic aspect of Russian public life showed at every step the harsh discords of a period of transition, there was a corresponding crisis in intellectual life. 'Populism', the indigenous brand of Russian socialism, theoretically grounded in the peculiarities of the Russian agrarian constitution, was politically finished with the failure of the terrorist party of 'Narodnaya Volya', its extreme revolutionary exponent. The first writings of George Plekhanov, on the other hand, which were to pave the way in Russia for Marxist trains of thought, had only been published in 1883 and 1885, and for about a decade they seemed to have little influence. During the eighties and up to the nineties the mental life of the Russian, and in particular of the socialist intelligentsia with their tendency towards opposition, was dominated by a peculiar mixture of 'indigenous' 'populist' remnants and random elements of theoretical Marxism. The most remarkable feature of this mixture was scepticism as to the possibility of capitalist development in Russia.

At an early date, the Russian intelligentsia had been preoccupied with the question whether Russia should follow the example of Western Europe and embark on capitalist development. At first, they noticed only the bleak aspects of capitalism in the West, its disintegrating effects upon the traditional patriarchal forms of production and upon the prosperity and assured livelihood for the broad masses of the population. As against that, the Russian rural communal ownership in land, the famous *obshchina*, seemed to offer a short-cut to the blessed land of socialism, a lead direct to a higher social development of Russia, without the capitalist phase and its attendant misery as experienced in Western Europe. Would it be right to fling away this fortunate and exceptional position, this unique historical opportunity, and forcibly transplant capitalist production to Russia with the help of the state? Would it be right to destroy the system of rural holdings and production, and open the doors wide to proletarisation, to misery and insecurity of existence for the toiling masses?

The Russian intelligentsia was preoccupied with this fundamental problem ever since the Agrarian Reform, and even earlier, since Hertzen, and especially since Chernishevski. This was the wholly unique world view of 'populism' in a nutshell. An enormous literature was created in Russia by this intellectual tendency ranging from the avowedly reactionary doctrines of the Slavophiles to the revolutionary theory of the terrorist party. On the one hand, it encouraged the collection of vast material by separate inquiries into the economic forms of Russian life, into 'national production' and its singular aspects, into agriculture as practised by the peasant communes, into the domestic industries of the peasants, the *artel*, and also into the mental life of the peasants, the sects and similar phenomena. On the other hand, a peculiar type of *belles lettres* sprang up as the artistic reflection of the contradictory social conditions, the struggle between old and new ways which beset the mind at every step with difficult problems. Finally, in the seventies and eighties, a peculiarly stuffy philosophy of history sprang up from the same root and found its champions in Peter Lavrov, Nicolai Mikhailovski, Professor Kareyev and V. Vorontsov. It was the 'subjective method in sociology' which declared 'critical thought' to be the decisive factor in social development, or which, more precisely, sought to make a down-at-heel intelligentsia the agent of historical progress.

Here we are interested only in one aspect of this wide field with its many ramifications, *viz.*: the struggle of opinions regarding the chances of capitalist development, and even then only in so far as these were based upon general reflections on the social conditions of the capitalist mode of production, since these latter were also to play a big part in the Russian controversial literature of the eighties and nineties.

The point at issue was to begin with Russian capitalism and its prospects, but this, of course, led further afield to the whole problem of capitalist development. The example and the experiences of the West were adduced as vital evidence in this debate.

One fact was of decisive importance for the theoretical content of the discussion that followed; not only was Marx's analysis of capitalist production as laid down in the first volume of *Capital* already common property of educated Russia, but the second volume, too, with its analysis of the reproduction of capital as a whole had already been published in 1885. This gave a fundamentally new twist to the discussion. No more did the problem of crises obscure the real crux of the problem: for the first time, the argument centred purely in the reproduction of capital as a whole, in accumulation. Nor was the analysis bogged any longer by an aimless fumbling for the concepts of income and of individual and aggregate capital. Marx's diagram of social reproduction had provided a firm foothold. Finally, the issue was no longer between *laissez-faire* and social reform, but between two varieties of socialism. The petty-bourgeois and somewhat muddled 'populist' brand of Russian socialists stood for scepticism regarding the possibility of capitalist development, much in the spirit of Sismondi and, in part, of Rodbertus, though they themselves frequently cited Marx as their authority. Optimism, on the other hand, was represented by the Marxist school in Russia. Thus the setting of the stage had been shifted completely.

One of the two champions of the 'populist' movement. Vorontsov, known in Russia mainly under the *nom de plume* V. V. (his initials), was an odd customer. His economics were completely muddled, and as an expert on theory he cannot be taken seriously at all. The other, Nikolayon (Danielson), however, was a man of wide education, and thoroughly conversant with Marxism. He had edited the Russian translation of the first volume of *Capital* and was a personal friend of Marx and Engels, with both of whom he kept up a lively correspondence (published in the Russian language in 1908). Nevertheless it was Vorontsov who influenced public opinion among the Russian intelligentsia in the eighties, and Marxists in Russia had to fight him above all. As for our problem: the general prospects of capitalist development, a new generation of Russian Marxists, who had learned from the historical experience and knowledge of Western Europe, joined forces with George Plekhanov in opposition to the above-mentioned two representatives of scepticism in the nineties. They were amongst others Professor Kablukov, Professor Manuilov, Professor Issayev, Professor Skvortsov, Vladimir Ilyin, Peter v. Struve, Bulgakov, and Professor Tugan Baranovski. In the further course of our investigation we shall, however, confine ourselves to the last three of these, since every one of them furnished a more or less finished critique of this theory on the point with which we are here concerned. This battle of wits, brilliant in parts, which kept the socialist intelligentsia spellbound in the nineties and was only brought to an end by the walkover of the Marxist school, officially inaugurated the infiltration into Russian thought of Marxism as an economico-historical theory. 'Legalist' Marxism at that time publicly took possession of the Universities, the Reviews and the economic book market in Russia—with all the disadvantages of such a position. Ten years later, when the revolutionary risings of the proletariat demonstrated in the streets the darker side of this optimism about capitalist development, none of this Pleïad of Marxist optimists, with but a single exception, was to be found in the camp of the proletariat.

19

VORONTSOV AND HIS 'SURPLUS'

The representatives of Russian 'populism' were convinced that capitalism had no future in Russia, and this conviction brought them to the problem of capitalist reproduction. V. V. laid down his theories on this point in a series of articles in the review *Patriotic Memoirs* and in other periodicals which were collected and published in 1882 under the title *The Destiny of Capitalism in Russia*. He further dealt with the problem in 'The Commodity Surplus in the Supply of the Market',[1] 'Militarism and Capitalism',[2] *Our Trends*,[3] and finally in *Outlines of Economic Theory*.[4] It is not easy to determine Vorontsov's attitude towards capitalist development in Russia. He sided neither with the purely slavophil theory which deduced the perversity and perniciousness of capitalism for Russia from the 'peculiarities' of the Russian economic structure and a specifically Russian 'national character', nor with the Marxists who saw in capitalist development an unavoidable historical stage which is needed to clear the way towards social progress for Russian society, too.

---

[1] An essay in *Patriotic Memoirs*, May 1883.
[2] An essay in the review *Russian Thought*, September 1889.
[3] A book published in 1893.
[4] A book published in 1895.

Vorontsov for his part simply asserts that denunciation and acclamation of capitalism are equally futile because, having no roots in Russia, capitalism is just impossible there and can have no future. The essential conditions of capitalist development are lacking in Russia, and love's labour's lost if the state tries to promote it artificially—one might as well spare these efforts together with the heavy sacrifices they entail. But if we look into the matter more closely, Vorontsov's thesis is not nearly so uncompromising. For if we pay attention to the fact that capitalism does not mean only the accumulation of capital wealth but also that the small producer is reduced to the proletarian level, that the labourer's livelihood is not assured and that there are periodical crises, then Vorontsov would by no means deny that all these phenomena exist in Russia. On the contrary, he explicitly says in his preface to *The Destiny of Capitalism in Russia*: 'Whilst I dispute the possibility of capitalism as a form of production in Russia, I do not intend to commit myself in any way as to its future as a form or degree of exploiting the national resources.'

Vorontsov consequently is of the opinion that capitalism in Russia merely cannot attain the same degree of maturity as in the West, whereas the severance of the immediate producer from the means of production might well be expected under Russian conditions. Vorontsov goes even further: he does not dispute at all that a development of the capitalist mode of production is quite possible in various branches of production, and even allows for capitalist exports from Russia to foreign markets. Indeed he says in his essay on 'The Commodity Surplus in the Supply of the Market' that 'in several branches of industry, capitalist production develops very quickly'[5] [in the Russian meaning of the term, of course—R. L.].

'It is most probable that Russia, just like any other country, enjoys certain natural advantages which enable her to act as a supplier of certain kinds of commodities on foreign markets. It is extremely possible that capital can profit by this fact and lay hands upon the branches of production concerned—that is to say the (inter)national division of labour will make it easy for our capitalists to gain a foothold in certain branches. This, however, is not the point. We do not speak of a merely

---

[5] *Patriotic Memoirs*, vol. v: 'A Contemporary Survey', p. 4.

incidental participation of capital in the industrial organisation of the country, but ask whether it is likely that the entire production of Russia can be put on a capitalist basis.'[6]

Put in this form, Vorontsov's scepticism looks quite different from what might have been expected at first. He doubts whether the capitalist mode of production could ever gain possession of the entire production in Russia; but then, capitalism has not so far accomplished this feat in any country of the world, not even in England. Such a brand of scepticism as to the future of capitalism appears at a glance quite international in outlook. And indeed, Vorontsov's theory here amounts to a quite general reflection on the nature and the essential conditions of capitalism; it is based upon a general theoretical approach to the reproductive process of social capital as a whole. Vorontsov gives the following very clear formulation of the specific relations between the capitalist mode of production and the problem of markets:

'The (inter)national division of labour, the distribution of all branches of industry among the countries taking part in international commerce, is quite independent of capitalism.

'The market which thus comes into being, the demand for the products of different countries resulting from such a division of labour among the nations, has intrinsically nothing in common with the market required by the capitalist mode of production. . . . The products of capitalist industry come on the market for another purpose; the question whether all the needs of the country are satisfied is irrelevant to them, and the entrepreneur does not necessarily receive in their stead another material product which may be consumed. Their main purpose is to realise the surplus value they contain. What, then, is this surplus value that it should interest the capitalist for its own sake? From our point of view, it is the surplus of production over consumption inside the country. Every worker produces more than he himself can consume, and all these surplus items accumulate in a few hands; their owners themselves consume them, exchanging them for the purpose against the most variegated kinds of necessities and luxuries. Yet eat, drink and dance as much as they like—they will not be able to squander the whole of the surplus value: a considerable remnant will be left

[6] Ibid., p. 10.

over, of which they have to dispose somehow even though they cannot exchange it for other products. They must convert it into money, since it would otherwise just go bad. Since there is no one inside the country on whom the capitalists could foist this remnant, it must be exported abroad, and that is why foreign markets are indispensable to countries embarking on the capitalist venture.'[7]

The above is a literal translation, showing all the peculiarities of Vorontsov's diction, so that the reader may have a taste of this brilliant Russian theorist with whom one can spend moments of sheer delight.

Later, in 1895, Vorontsov summarised the same views in his book *Outlines of Economic Theory* now claiming our attention. Here he takes a stand against the views of Say and Ricardo, and in particular also against John Stuart Mill who denied the possibility of general over-production. In the course of his argument he discovers something no one had known before: he has laid bare the source of all errors the classical school made about the problem of crises. This mistake lies in a falla-cious theory of the costs of production to which bourgeois economists are addicted. No doubt, from the aspect of the costs of production (which according to Vorontsov's equally unheard-of assumption do not comprise profits), both profit and crises are unthinkable and inexplicable. But we can only appreciate this original thought to the full in the author's own words:

'According to the doctrine of bourgeois economists, the value of a product is determined by the labour employed in its manufacture. Yet bourgeois economists, once they have given this determination of value, immediately forget it and base their subsequent explanation of the exchange phenomena upon a different theory which substitutes "costs of production" for labour. Thus two products are mutually exchanged in such quantities that the costs of production are equal on both sides. Such a view of the process of exchange indeed leaves no room for a commodity surplus inside the country. Any product of a worker's annual labour must, from this point of view, represent a cer-tain quantity of material of which it is made, of tools which have been used in its manufacture, and of the products which served to maintain the workers during the period of production. It [presumably the

[7] Ibid., p. 14.

product—R. L.] appears on the market in order to change its use-form, to reconvert itself into objects, into products for the workers and the value necessary for renewing the tools. As soon as it is split up into its component parts, the process of reassembling, the productive process, will begin, in the course of which all the values listed above will be consumed. In their stead, a new product will come into being which is the connecting link between past and future consumption.'

From this perfectly unique attempt to demonstrate social reproduction as a continuous process in the light of the costs of production, the following conclusion is promptly drawn: 'Considering thus the aggregate bulk of a country's products, we shall find no commodity surplus at all over and above the demand of society; an unmarketable surplus is therefore impossible from the point of view of a bourgeois economic theory of value.'

Yet, after having eliminated capitalist profit from the costs of production by an extremely autocratic manhandling of the bourgeois theory of value, Vorontsov immediately presents this deficiency as a great discovery: 'The above analysis, however, reveals yet another feature in the theory of value prevalent of late: it becomes evident that this theory leaves no room for capitalist profits.'

The argument that follows is striking in its brevity and simplicity: 'Indeed, if I exchange my own product, representing a cost of production of 5 roubles, for another product of equal value, I receive only so much as will be sufficient to cover my expense, but for my abstinence [literally so—R. L.] I shall get nothing.'

And now Vorontsov really comes to grips with the root of the problem:

'Thus it is proved on a strictly logical development of the ideas held by bourgeois economists that the destiny of the commodity surplus on the market and that of capitalist profit is identical. This circumstance justifies the conclusion that both phenomena are interdependent, that the existence of one is a condition of the other, and indeed, so long as there is no profit, there is no commodity surplus. . . . It is different if the profit comes into being inside the country. Such profit is not originally related to production; it is a phenomenon which is connected with the latter not by technical and natural conditions but by an extraneous social form. Production requires for its continuation . . .

only material, tools, and means of subsistence for the workers, therefore as such it consumes only the corresponding part of the products: other consumers must be found for the surplus which makes up the profit, and for which there is no room in the permanent structure of industrial life, in production—consumers, namely, who are not organically connected with production, who are fortuitous to a certain extent. The necessary number of such consumers may or may not be forthcoming, and in the latter case there will be a commodity surplus on the market.'[8]

Well content with the 'simple' enlightenment, by which he has turned the surplus product into an invention of capital and the capitalist into a 'fortuitous' consumer who is 'not organically connected with capitalist production', Vorontsov now turns to the crises. On the basis of Marx's 'logical' theory of the value of labour which he claims to 'employ' in his later works, he expounds them as an immediate result of the surplus value, as follows:

'If the working part of the population consumes what enters into the costs of production in form of the wages for labour, the capitalists themselves must destroy [literally so—R. L.] the surplus value, excepting that part of it which the market requires for expansion. If the capitalists are in a position to do so and act accordingly, there can be no commodity surplus; if not, over-production, industrial crises, displacement of the workers from the factories and other evils will result.'

According to Vorontsov, however, it is 'the inadequate elasticity of the human organism which cannot enlarge its capacity to consume as rapidly as the surplus value is increasing', which is in the end responsible for these evils. He repeatedly expresses this ingenious thought as follows: 'The Achilles heel of capitalist industrial organisation thus lies in the incapacity of the entrepreneurs to consume the whole of their income.'

Having thus 'employed' Marx's 'logical' version of Ricardo's theory of value, Vorontsov arrives at Sismondi's theory of crises which he adopts in as crude and simplified a form as possible. He believes, of course, that he is adopting the views of Rodbertus in reproducing those of Sismondi. 'The inductive method of research', he declares

---

[8] *Outlines of Economic Theory* (St. Petersburg, 1895), pp. 157 ff.

triumphantly, 'has resulted in the very same theory of crises and of pauperism which had been objectively stated by Rodbertus.'[9]

It is not quite clear what Vorontsov means by an 'inductive method of research' which he contrasts with the objective method—since all things are possible to Vorontsov, he may conceivably mean Marx's theory. Yet Rodbertus, too, was not to emerge unimproved from the hands of the original Russian thinker. Vorontsov corrects Rodbertus' theory merely in so far as he eliminates the stabilisation of the wage rate in accordance with the value of the aggregate product which, to Rodbertus, had been the pivot of his whole system. According to Vorontsov, this measure against crises is a mere palliative, since 'the immediate cause of the above phenomena (over-production, unemployment, etc.) is not that the working classes receive too small a share of the national income, but that the capitalist class cannot possibly consume all the products which every year fall to their share.'[10]

Yet, as soon as he has refuted Rodbertus' reform of the distribution of incomes, Vorontsov, with that 'strictly logical' consistency so peculiar to him, ultimately arrives at the following forecast for the future destiny of capitalism: 'If industrial organisation which prevails in W. Europe is to prosper and flourish further still, it can only do so provided that some means will be found to destroy [verbatim—R. L.] that portion of the national income which falls to the capitalists' share over and above their capacity to consume. The simplest solution of this problem will be an appropriate change in the distribution of the aggregate income among those who take part in production. If the entrepreneurs would retain for themselves only so much of all increase of the national income as they need to satisfy all their whims and fancies, leaving the remainder to the working class, the mass of the people, then the régime of capitalism would be assured for a long time to come.'[11]

The hash of Ricardo, Marx, Sismondi and Rodbertus thus is topped with the discovery that capitalist production could be radically cured of over-production, that it could 'prosper and flourish' in all eternity, if

[9] 'Militarism and Capitalism' in *Russian Thought* (1889), vol. ix, p. 78.
[10] Ibid., p. 80.
[11] Ibid., p. 83. Cf. *Outlines*, p. 196.

the capitalists would refrain from capitalising their surplus value and would make a free gift to the working class of the corresponding part of the surplus value. Meanwhile the capitalists, until they have become sensible enough to accept Vorontsov's good advice, employ other means for the annual destruction of a part of their surplus value. Modern militarism, amongst others, is one of these appropriate measures— and this precisely to the extent to which the bills of militarism are footed by the capitalists' income—for Vorontsov can be counted upon to turn things upside down—and not by the working masses. A primary remedy for capitalism, however, is foreign trade which again is a sore spot in Russian capitalism. As the last to arrive at the table of the world market, Russian capitalism fares worst in the competition with older capitalist countries and thus lacks both prospects as to foreign markets and the most vital conditions of existence. Russia remains the 'country of peasants', a country of 'populist' production.

'If all this is correct,' Vorontsov concludes his essay on 'The Commodity Surplus in the Supply of the Market', 'then capitalism can play only a limited part in Russia. It must resign from the direction of agriculture, and its development in the industrial sphere must not inflict too many injuries upon the domestic industries which under our economic conditions are indispensable to the welfare of the majority of the population. If the reader would comment that capitalism might not accept such a compromise, our answer will be: so much the worse for capitalism.'

Thus Vorontsov ultimately washes his hands of the whole thing, declining for his part all responsibility for the further fortunes of economic development in Russia.

20

NIKOLAYON

The second theorist of populist criticism, Nikolayon, brings quite a different economic training and knowledge to his work. One of the best-informed experts on Russian economic relations, he had already in 1880 attracted attention by his treatise on the capitalisation of agricultural incomes, which was published in the review *Slovo*. Thirteen years later, spurred on by the great Russian famine of 1891, he pursued his inquiries further in a book entitled *Outlines of Our Social Economy Since the Reform*. Here he gives a detailed exposition, fully documented by facts and figures, of how capitalism developed in Russia, and on this evidence proceeds to show that this development is the source of all evil, and so of the famine, also, so far as the Russian people are concerned. His views about the destiny of capitalism in Russia are grounded in a definite theory about the conditions of the development of capitalist production in general, and it is this with which we must now deal.

Since the market is of decisive importance for the capitalist mode of economy, every capitalist nation tries to make sure of as large a market as possible. In the first place, of course, it relies on its home market. But at a certain level of development, the home market is no longer sufficient for a capitalist nation, and this for the following reasons: all that social labour newly produces in one year can be divided into two parts—the share received by the workers in the form of wages, and that which is appropriated by the capitalists. Of the first part, only so many means of subsistence as correspond, in value, to the sum total of the wages paid within the country can be withdrawn from circulation. Yet capitalist economy decidedly tends to depress this part more and more. Its methods are a longer working day, stepping up the intensity of labour, and increasing output by technical improvements which enable the substitution of female and juvenile for male labour and in some cases displace adult labour altogether. Even if the wages of the workers still employed are rising, such increase can never equal the savings of the capitalists resulting from these changes. The result of all this is that the working class must play an ever smaller part as buyers on the home market. At the same time, there is a further change: capitalist production gradually takes over even the trades which provided additional employment to an agricultural people; thus it deprives the peasants of their resources by degrees, so that the rural population can afford to buy fewer and fewer industrial products. This is a further reason for the continual contraction of the home market. As for the capitalist class, we see that this latter is also unable to realise the entire newly created product, though for the opposite reason. However large the requirements of this class, the capitalists will not be able to consume the entire surplus product in person. First, because part of it is needed to enlarge production, for technical improvements which, to the individual entrepreneur, will be a necessary condition of existence in a competitive society. Secondly, because an expanding capitalist production implies an expansion in those branches of industry which produce means of production (e.g. the mining industry, the machine industry and so forth) and whose products from the very beginning take a use-form that is incapable of personal consumption and can only function as capital. Thirdly and lastly, the higher labour productivity and capital savings that can be achieved by mass production of cheap commodities increasingly impel society towards mass production of commodities which cannot all be consumed by a mere handful of capitalists.

Although one capitalist can realise his surplus value in the surplus product of another capitalist and *vice versa*, this is only true for products of a certain branch, for consumer goods. However, the incentive of capitalist production is not the satisfaction of personal wants, and this is further shown by the progressive decline in the production of consumer as compared to that of producer goods.

'Thus we see that the aggregate product of a capitalist nation must greatly exceed the requirements of the whole industrial population employed, in the same way as each individual factory produces vastly in excess of the requirements of both its workers and the entrepreneur, and this is entirely due to the fact that the nation is a capitalist nation, because the distribution of resources within the society does not aim to satisfy the real wants of the population but only the effective demand. Just as an individual factory-owner could not maintain himself as a capitalist even for a day if his market were confined to the requirements of his workers and his own, so the home market of a developed capitalist nation must also be insufficient.'

At a certain level, capitalist development thus has the tendency to impede its own progress. These obstacles are ultimately due to the fact that progressive labour productivity, involving the severance of the immediate producer from the means of production, does not benefit society as a whole, but only the individual entrepreneur; and the mass of labour power and men-hours which has been 'set free' by this process becomes redundant and thus is not only lost to society but will become a burden to it. The real wants of the masses can only be satisfied more fully in so far as there can be an ascendancy of a 'populist' mode of production based upon the union between the producer and his means of production. It is the aim of capitalism, however, to gain possession of just these spheres of production, and to destroy in the process the main factor which makes for its own prosperity. The periodical famines in India, for instance, recurring at intervals of ten or eleven years, were thus among the causes of periodical industrial crises in England. Any nation that sets out on capitalist development will sooner or later come up against these contradictions inherent in this mode of production. And the later a nation embarks on the capitalist venture, the more strongly will these contradictions make themselves felt, since, once the home market has been saturated, no substitute can be found, the outside market having already been conquered by the older competing countries.

The upshot of it all is that the limits of capitalism are set by the increasing poverty born of its own development, by the increasing number of redundant workers deficient in all purchasing power. Increasing labour productivity which can rapidly satisfy every effective demand of society corresponds to the increasing incapacity of ever broader masses of the population to satisfy their most vital needs; on the one hand, a glut of goods that cannot be sold—and on the other, large masses who lack the bare necessities.

These are Nikolayon's general views.[1] He knows his Marx, we see, and has turned the two first volumes of *Capital* to excellent use. And still, the whole trend of his argument is genuinely Sismondian. It is capitalism itself which brings about a shrinking home market since it impoverishes the masses; every calamity of modern society is due to the destruction of the 'populist' mode of production, that is to say the destruction of small-scale enterprise. That is his main theme. More openly even than Sismondi, Nikolayon sets the tenor of his critique by an apotheosis of small-scale enterprise, this sole approach to grace.[2] The aggregate capitalist product cannot, in the end, be realised within the society, this can only be done with recourse to outside markets. Nikolayon here comes to the same conclusion as Vorontsov, in spite of a quite different theoretical point of departure. Applied to Russia, it is the economic scientific ground for a sceptical attitude towards capitalism. Capitalist development in Russia has been without access to foreign markets from the first, it could only show its worst aspects—it has impoverished the masses of the people. In consequence, it was a 'fatal mistake' to promote capitalism in Russia.

On this point, Nikolayon fulminates like a prophet of the Old Testament: 'Instead of keeping to the tradition of centuries, instead of developing our old inherited principle of a close connection between the immediate producer and his means of production, instead of usefully applying the scientific achievements of W. Europe to their forms of production based on the peasants' ownership of their means of production, instead of increasing their productivity by concentrating the means of production in their hands, instead of benefiting, not by

[1] Cf. *Outlines of Our Social Economy*, in particular pp. 202–5, 338–41.
[2] Vladimir Ilyich [Lenin] has given detailed proof of the striking similarity between the position of the Russian 'populists' and the views of Sismondi in his essay *On the Characteristics of Economic Romanticism* (1897).

the forms of production in W. Europe, but by its organisation, its powerful co-operation, its division of labour, its machinery, etc., etc.— instead of developing the fundamental principle of a landowning peasantry and applying it to the cultivation of the land by the peasants, instead of making science and its application widely accessible to the peasants—instead of all this, we have taken the opposite turning. We have failed to prevent the development of capitalist forms of production, although they are based on the expropriation of the peasants; on the contrary, we have promoted with all our might the upsetting of our entire economic life which resulted in the famine of 1891.'

Though the evil is much advanced, it is not too late even now to retrace our steps. On the contrary, a complete reform of economic policy is just as urgently needed for Russia in view of the threatening proletarisation and collapse, as Alexander's reforms after the Crimean war were necessary in their time.

Now a social reform as advocated by Nikolayon is completely Utopian. His attitude exhibits an even more blatant petty-bourgeois and reactionary bias than Sismondi's ever did, considering that the Russian 'populist' writes after a lapse of seventy years. For in his opinion, the old *obshchina*, the rural community founded on the communal ownership of the soil, is the raft to deliver Russia from the flood of capitalism. On it, the discoveries of modern big industry and scientific technique are to be grafted by measures which remain his own secret—so that it can serve as the basis of a 'socialised' higher form of production. Russia can choose no other alternative: either she turns her back upon capitalist development, or she must resign herself to death and decay.[3]

---

[3] *Outlines of Our Social Economy*, p. 322. Friedrich Engels appraises the Russian situation differently. He repeatedly tries to convince Nikolayon that Russia cannot avoid a high industrial development, and that her sufferings are nothing but the typical capitalist contradictions. Thus he writes on September 22, 1892: 'I therefore hold that at present industrial production necessarily implies big industry, making use of steam power, electricity, mechanical looms and frames, and lastly the manufacture of the machines themselves by mechanical means. From the moment that railways are introduced in Russia, recourse to all these extremely modern means of production becomes inevitable. It is necessary that you should be able to mend and repair your engines, coaches, railways and the like, but to do this cheaply, you must also be in a position to make at home the things needing repair. As soon as the technique of war has become a branch of industry (armour-plated cruisers, modern artillery, machine guns, steel bullets, smokeless gun

After a crushing criticism of capitalism Nikolayon thus ends up with the same old 'populist' panacea which had as early as the fifties, though at that time with greater justification, been hailed as the 'peculiarly Russian' guarantee of a higher social development, although its reactionary character as a lifeless relic of ancient institutions had been exposed in Engels' *Fluechtlingsliteratur* in *Volksstaat* (1875). Engels wrote at the time:

'A further development of Russia on bourgeois lines would gradually destroy communal property there too, quite apart from any interference of the Russian government "with the knout and with bayonets" (as the revolutionary populists imagined). Under the pressure of taxes and usury, communal landownership is no longer a privilege, it becomes an irksome chain. The peasants frequently run away from it, either with or without their families, to seek their living as itinerant labourers, and leave the land behind. We see that communal ownership in Russia has long since passed its flower and there is every indication that its decay is approaching.'

powder, etc.) a big industry that is indispensable for the production of such items has become a political necessity for you as well. All these items cannot be made without a highly developed metal industry which on its part cannot develop unless there is a corresponding development of all other branches of production, textiles in particular' (Marx–Engels to Nikolayon, St. Petersburg, 1908, p. 75). And further in the same letter: 'So long as Russian industry depends on the home market alone, it can only satisfy the internal demand. The latter, however, can grow but slowly, and it seems to me that under present conditions of life in Russia it is even bound to decrease, since it is one of the unavoidable consequences of high industrial development that it destroys its own home market by the same process which served to create it: by destroying the bases of the peasants' domestic industry. Yet peasants cannot live without such a domestic industry. They are ruined as peasants, their purchasing power is reduced to a minimum, and unless they grow new roots in new conditions of life, unless they become proletarians, they will only represent a very small market for the newly arising plants and factories.

'Capitalist production is a phase of economic transition, full of inherent contradictions which only develop and become visible to the extent that capitalist production develops. The tendency of simultaneously creating and destroying a market is just one of these contradictions. Another is the hopeless situation that will ensue, all the sooner in a country like Russia which lacks external markets than in countries more or less fit to compete in the open world market. These latter can find some means of relief in this seemingly hopeless situation by heroic measures of commercial policy, that is to say by forcibly opening up new markets. China is the most recent market to be opened up for English commerce, and it proved adequate for a temporary revival of prosperity. That is

With these words, Engels hits right on the target of the *obshchina* problem—eighteen years before the publication of Nikolayon's principal work. If Nikolayon subsequently with renewed courage again conjured up the ghost of the *obshchina*, it was a bad historical anachronism inasmuch as about a decade later the *obshchina* was given an official burial by the state. The absolutist government which had for financial reasons tried during half a century artificially to keep the machinery of the rural community going was compelled to give up this thankless task on its own accord. The agrarian problem soon made it clear how far the old 'populist' delusion was lagging behind the actual course of economic events, and conversely, how powerfully capitalist development in Russia, mourned and cursed as still-born, could demonstrate with lightning and thunder its capacity to live and to multiply. Once

why English capital is so insistent on railroad building in China. Yet railways in China mean the destruction of the entire foundation of China's small rural enterprises and her domestic industry. In this case, there is not even a native big industry developed to compensate for this evil to some extent, and hundreds of millions will consequently find it impossible to make a living at all. The result will be mass emigration, such as the world has never yet seen, and America, Asia and Europe will be flooded with the detested Chinese. This new competitor on the labour market will compete with American, Australian and European labour at the level of what the Chinese consider a satisfactory standard of living, which is well known to be the lowest in the whole world. Well then, if the whole system of production in Europe has not been revolutionised by then, that will be the time to start this revolution' (ibid., p. 79).

Engels, though he followed Russian developments with attention and keen interest, persistently refused to take an active part in the Russian dispute. In his letter of November 24, 1894, i.e. shortly before his death, he expressed himself as follows: 'My Russian friends almost daily and weekly bombard me with requests to come forward with my objections to Russian books and reviews which not only misinterpret but even misquote the sayings of our author (Marx). My friends assure me that my intervention would suffice to put matters right. Yet I invariably and firmly refuse all such proposals because I cannot afford to become involved with a dispute held in a foreign country, in a tongue which I, at least, cannot read as easily and freely as the more familiar W. European languages, and in a literature which is at best accessible to me only in fortuitous glimpses of some fragments, and which I cannot pursue anything like systematically enough in all its stages and details without neglecting my real and serious work. There are people everywhere who, once they have taken up a certain stand are not ashamed to have recourse to misinterpreting the thoughts of others and to all kinds of dishonest manipulations for their own ends, and if that is what has happened to our author, I am afraid they will not deal more kindly with me, so that in the end I shall be compelled to interfere in the dispute, first to defend others, and then in my own defence' (ibid., p. 90).

again, and for the last time, this turn of events demonstrates in quite a different historical setting how a social critique of capitalism, which begins by doubting its capacity for development, must by a deadly logic lead to a reactionary Utopianism—both in the France of 1819 and in the Russia of 1893.[4]

---

[4] We might mention that the surviving champions of 'populist' pessimism, and Vorontsov in particular, to the last remained loyal to their views, in spite of all that happened in Russia—a fact that does more credit to their character than to their intelligence. Referring to the 1900 and 1902 crises, Vorontsov wrote in 1902: 'The doctrinaire dogma of the Neo-Marxists rapidly loses its power over people's minds. That the newest successes of the individualists are ephemeral has obviously dawned even on their official advocates. . . . In the first decade of the twentieth century, we come back to the same views about economic development in Russia that had been the legacy of the 1870's' (Cf. the review *Political Economics*, October 1902, quoted by A. Finn Yenotayevski in *The Contemporary Economy of Russia 1890–1910*, St. Petersburg, 1911, p. 2.) Even to-day, then, this last of the 'populist' Mohicans deduces the 'ephemeral character', not of his own theory, but of economic reality. What of the saying of Barrère: 'Il n'y a que les morts qui ne reviennent pas'.

21

STRUVE'S 'THIRD PERSONS' AND 'THREE WORLD EMPIRES'

We now turn to the criticism of the above opinions as given by the Russian Marxists.

In 1894, Peter v. Struve who had already given a detailed appraisal of Nikolayon's book in an essay 'On Capitalist Development in Russia',[1] published a book in Russian,[2] criticising the theories of 'populism' from various aspects. In respect of our present problem, however, he mainly confines himself to proving, against both Vorontsov and Nikolayon, that capitalism does not cause a contraction of the home market but, on the contrary, an expansion. There can be no doubt that Nikolayon has made a blunder—the same that Sismondi had made. They each describe only a single aspect of the destructive process, performed by capitalism on the traditional forms of production by small enterprise. They saw only the resulting depression of general welfare, the impoverishment of broad strata of the population, and failed to notice that economic aspect of the process which entails the abolition of natural economy and the substitution of a commodity economy in rural districts. And this is as much as to say that, by absorbing further

---

[1] Published in *Sozialdemokratisches Zentralblatt*, vol. iii, No. 1.
[2] *Critical Comments on the Problem of Economic Development in Russia.*

and further sections of formerly independent and self-sufficient producers into its own sphere, capitalism continuously transforms into commodity buyers ever new strata of people who had not before bought its commodities. In fact, the course of capitalist development is just the opposite of that pictured by the 'populists' on the model of Sismondi. Capitalism, far from ruining the home market, really sets about creating it, precisely by means of a spreading money economy.

Struve in particular refutes the theory that the surplus value cannot possibly be realised on the home market. He argues as follows: The conviction that a mature capitalist society consists exclusively of entrepreneurs and workers forms the basis of Vorontsov's theory, and Nikolayon himself operates with this concept throughout. From this point of view, of course, the realisation of the capitalist aggregate product seems incomprehensible. And Vorontsov's theory is correct in so far as it states the fact that neither the capitalists' nor the workers' consumption can realise the surplus value, so that the existence of 'third persons' must be presumed.[3] But then, is it not beyond any doubt that some such 'third persons' exist in every capitalist society? The idea of Vorontsov and Nikolayon is pure fiction 'which cannot advance our understanding of any historical process whatever by a hair's breadth'.[4] There is no actual capitalist society, however highly developed, composed exclusively of capitalists and workers.

'Even in England and Wales, out of a thousand self-supporting inhabitants, 543 are engaged in industry, 172 in commerce, 140 in agriculture, 81 in casual wage labour, and 62 in the Civil Service, the liberal professions and the like.'

Even in England, then, there are large numbers of 'third persons', and it is they who, by their consumption, help to realise the surplus value in so far as it is not consumed by the capitalists. Struve leaves it open whether these 'third persons consume enough to realise all surplus value—however that may be, 'the contrary would have to be proved'.[5] This cannot be done, he claims, for Russia, that vast country with an immense population. She, in fact, is in the fortunate position to

[3] Op. cit., p. 251.
[4] Ibid., p. 255.
[5] Ibid., p. 252.

be able to dispense with foreign markets. In this—and here Struve dips into the intellectual treasures of Professors Wagner, Schaeffle, and Schmoller—she enjoys the same privileges as the United States of America. 'If the example of the N. American Union stands for anything, it is proof of the fact that under certain circumstances capitalist industry can attain a very high level of development almost entirely on the basis of the home market.'[6]

The negligible amount of industrial exports from the U.S.A. in 1882 is mentioned in support of this statement which Struve formulates as a general doctrine: 'The vaster the territory, and the larger the population of a country, the less does that country require foreign markets for its capitalist development.' He infers from this, in direct opposition to the 'populists', 'a more brilliant future (for Russia) than for the other countries'.

On the basis of commodity production, the progressive development of agriculture is bound to create a market wide enough to support the development of Russian industrial capitalism. This market would be capable of unlimited expansion, in step with the economic and cultural progress of the country, and together with the substitution of a monetary for a natural economy. 'In this respect, capitalism enjoys more favourable conditions in Russia than in other countries.'[7]

Struve paints a detailed and highly coloured picture of the new markets which, thanks to the Trans-Siberian Railway, are opening up in

---

[6] Ibid., p. 260. 'There can be no doubt that Struve's attempt to refute what he calls the pessimist outlook on the analogy of the U.S.A. is fallacious. He says that Russia can overcome the evil consequences of the most recent capitalism just as easily as the U.S.A. But what he forgets is that the U.S.A. from the first represent a new bourgeois state, that they were founded by a petty bourgeoisie and by peasants who had fled from European feudalism to set up a purely bourgeois society. In Russia, on the other hand, we have a primitive communist foundation, a society of *gentes*, as it were, in the pre-civilised stage which, though it is already disintegrating, still serves as a material basis upon which the capitalist revolution (for it is in fact a social revolution) can take place and become effective. In America, a monetary economy had been stabilised more than a century ago, whereas a natural economy had until recently prevailed in Russia. It should be obvious therefore that this revolution in Russia is bound to be much more ruthless and violent, and accompanied by immensely more suffering than in America' (Engels to Nikolayon, October 17, 1893, *Letters . . .*, p. 85).

[7] *Critical Comments . . .*, p. 284.

Siberia, Central Asia, Asia Minor, Persia and the Balkans. But his prophetic zeal blinds him to the fact that he is no longer talking about the 'indefinitely expanding' home market but about specific foreign markets. In later years, he was to throw in his lot, in politics too, with this optimistic Russian capitalism and its liberal programme of imperialist expansion, for which he had laid the theoretical foundations when still a 'Marxist'.

Indeed, the tenor of Struve's argument is a fervent belief in the unlimited capacity for expansion of capitalist production, but the economic foundation of this optimism is rather weak. He is somewhat reticent as to what he means by the 'third persons' whom he considers the mainstay of accumulation, but his references to English occupational statistics indicate that he has in mind the various private and public servants, the liberal professions, in short the notorious *grand public* so dear to bourgeois economists when they are completely at a loss. It is this 'great public' of which Marx said that it serves as the explanation for things which the economist cannot explain. It is obvious that, if we categorically refer to consumption by the capitalists and the workers, we do not speak of the entrepreneur as an individual, but of the capitalist class as a whole, including their hangers-on— employees, Civil Servants, liberal professions, and the like. All such 'third persons' who are certainly not lacking in any capitalist society are, as far as economics is concerned, joint consumers of the surplus value for the greater part, in so far, namely, as they are not also joint consumers of the wages of labour. These groups can only derive their purchasing power either from the wage of the proletariat or from the surplus value, if not from both; but on the whole, they are to be regarded as joint consumers of the surplus value. It follows that their consumption is already included in the consumption of the capitalist class, and if Struve tries to reintroduce them to the capitalists by sleight-of-hand as 'third persons' to save the situation and help to realise the surplus value, the shrewd profiteer will not be taken in. He will see at once that this great public is nothing but his old familiar retinue of parasites who buy his commodities with money of his own providing. No, no, indeed! Struve's 'third persons' will not do at all.

Struve's theory of foreign markets and their significance for capitalist production is equally untenable. In this, he defers to the mechanist approach of the 'populists' who, along with the professors' textbooks, hold that a capitalist (European) country will first exploit the home market to the limit, and will only look to foreign markets when this is almost or completely exhausted. Then, following in the footsteps of Wagner, Schaeffle and Schmoller, Struve arrives at the absurd conclusion that a country with vast territories and a large population can make its capitalist production a 'self-contained whole' and rely indefinitely on the home market alone.[8] In actual fact, capitalist production is by nature production on a universal scale. Quite contrary to the bookish decrees issued by German scholars, it is producing for a world market already from the word go. The various pioneering branches of capitalist production in England, such as the textile, iron and coal industries, cast about for markets in all countries and continents, long before the process of destroying peasants' property, the decline of

---

[8] Professor Schmoller, amongst others, clearly reveals the reactionary aspect of the 'Three Empire Theory' (viz. Great Britain, Russia and the U.S.A.) evolved by the German professors. In his handbook of commercial policy (*Handelspolitische Säkularbetrachtung*), the venerable scholar dolefully frowns upon 'neo-mercantilism', that is to say upon the imperialist designs of the three arch-villains. 'In the interests of a higher intellectual, moral and aesthetic civilisation and social progress' he demands a strong German navy and a European Customs Union. 'Out of the economic tension of the world there arises the prime duty for Germany to create for herself a strong navy, so as to be prepared for battle in the case of need, and to be desirable as an ally to the World Powers'—which latter, however, Professor Schmoller says elsewhere, he does not wish to blame for again taking the path of large-scale colonial expansion. 'She neither can nor ought to pursue a policy of conquest like the Three World Powers, but she must be able, if necessary, to break a foreign blockade of the North Sea in order to protect her own colonies and her vast commerce, and she must be able to offer the same security to the states with whom she forms an alliance. It is the task of the Three-Partite Union (Germany, Austro-Hungary, and Italy) to co-operate with France towards imposing some restraint, desirable for the preservation of all other states, on the over-aggressive policy of the Three World Powers which constitutes a threat to all smaller states, and to ensure moderation in conquests, in colonial acquisitions, in the immoderate and unilateral policy of protective tariffs, in the exploitation and maltreatment of all weaker elements. The objectives of all higher intellectual, moral and aesthetic civilisation and of social progress depend on the fact that the globe should not be divided up among Three World Empires in the twentieth century, that these Three Empires should not establish a brutal neo-mercantilism' (*Die Wandlungen der Europäischen Handelspolitik des 19. Jahrhunderts*, 'Changes in the European Commercial Policy During the 19th Century', in *Jahrb. für Gesetzgebung, Verwaltung und Volkswirtschaft*, vol. xxiv, p. 381).

handicraft and of the old domestic industries within the country had come to an end. And again, is it likely that the German chemical or electrotechnical industries would be grateful for the sober advice not to work for five continents, as they have done from the beginning, but to confine themselves to the German home market which, being largely supplied from abroad, is evidently far from exhausted in respect of a whole lot of other German industries? Or that one should explain to the German machine industry, it should not venture yet upon foreign markets, since German import statistics are visible proof that a good deal of the demand in Germany for products of this branch is satisfied by foreign supplies? No, this schematic conception of 'foreign trade' does not help us at all to grasp the complexity of the world market with its uncounted ramifications and different shades in the division of labour. The industrial development of the U.S.A. who have already at the time of writing become a dangerous rival to Britain both on the world market and even in England herself, just as they have beaten German competition, e.g. in the sphere of electrotechnics, both in the world market and in Germany herself, has given the lie to Struve's inferences, already out-of-date when they were put on paper.

Struve also shares the crude view of the Russian 'populists' who saw hardly more than a merchant's sordid concern for his market in the international connections of capitalist economy, and its historical tendency to create a homogeneous living organism based on social division of labour as well as the countless variety of natural wealth and productive conditions of the globe. Moreover he accepts the Three Empire fiction of Wagner and Schmoller (the self-contained Empires of Great Britain, Russia and the U.S.A.) which completely ignores or artificially minimises the vital part played by an unlimited supply of means of subsistence, of raw and auxiliary materials and of labour power which is just as necessary for a capitalist industry computed in terms of a world market as the demand for finished products. Alone the history of the English cotton industry, a reflection in miniature of the history of capitalism in general, spreading over five continents throughout the nineteenth century, makes a mockery of the professors' childish pretensions which have only one real significance: to provide the theoretical justification for the system of protective tariffs.

22

BULGAKOV AND HIS COMPLETION OF MARX'S ANALYSIS

The second critic of 'populist' scepticism, S. Bulgakov, is no respecter of Struve's 'third persons' and at once denies that they form the sheet-anchor for capitalist accumulation.

'The majority of economists before Marx', he declares, 'solved the problem by saying that some sort of "third person" is needed, as a *deus ex machina*, to cut the Gordian knot, i.e. to consume the surplus value. This part is played by luxury-loving landowners (as with Malthus), or by indulgent capitalists, or yet by militarism and the like. There can be no demand for the surplus value without some such extraordinary mediators; a deadlock will be reached on the markets and the result will be over-production and crises.'[1]

'Struve thus assumes that capitalist production in its development, too, may find its ultimate mainstay in the consumption of some fantastic sort of "third person". But if this great public is essentially characterised as consuming the surplus value, whence does it obtain the means to buy?'[2]

---

[1] S. Bulgakov *On the Markets of Capitalist Production. A Study in Theory* (Moscow, 1897), p. 15.
[2] Ibid., p. 32, footnote.

For his part, Bulgakov centres the whole problem from the first in the analysis of the social aggregate product and its reproduction as given by Marx in the second volume of *Capital*. He has a thorough grasp of the fact that he must start with simple reproduction and must fully understand its working in order to solve the question of accumulation. In this context, he says, it is of particular importance to obtain a clear picture of the consumption of surplus value and wages in such branches of production as do not turn out goods for consumption, and further, to understand fully the circulation of that portion of the social aggregate product which represents used-up constant capital. This, he argues, is a completely new problem of which economists had not even been aware before Marx brought it up. 'In order to solve this problem, Marx divides all capitalistically produced commodities into two great and fundamentally different categories: the production of producer and consumer goods. There is more theoretical importance in this division than in all previous squabbles on the theory of markets.'[3]

Bulgakov, we see, is an outspoken and enthusiastic supporter of Marx's theory. The object of his study, as he puts it, is thus a critique of the doctrine that capitalism cannot exist without external markets. 'For this purpose, the author has made use of the most valuable analysis of social reproduction given by Marx in volume ii of *Capital* which for reasons unknown has scarcely been utilised in economic theory. Though this analysis cannot be taken as fully completed, we are yet of opinion that even in its present fragmentary shape it offers an adequate foundation for a solution of the market problem that differs from that adopted by Messrs. Nikolayon, V. V. and others, and which they claim to have found in Marx.'[4]

Bulgakov gives the following formulation of his solution which he has deduced from Marx himself: 'In certain conditions, capitalism may exist solely by virtue of an internal market. It is not an inherent necessity peculiar to the capitalist mode of production that the outside market be able to absorb the surplus of capitalist production. The author has arrived at this conclusion in consequence of his study of the above-mentioned analysis of social reproduction.'

[3] Ibid., p. 27.
[4] Ibid., pp. 2–3.

And now we are eager to hear the arguments Bulgakov has based on the above thesis.

At first sight, they prove surprisingly simple: Bulgakov faithfully reproduces Marx's well-known diagram of simple reproduction, adding comments which do credit to his insight. He further cites Marx's equally familiar diagram of enlarged reproduction—and this indeed is the proof we have been so anxious to find.

'Consequent upon what we have said, it will not be difficult now to determine the very essence of accumulation. The means-of-production Department I must produce additional means of production necessary for enlarging both its own production and that of Department II. II, in its turn, will have to supply additional consumption goods to enlarge the variable capital in both departments. Disregarding the circulation of money, the expansion of production is reduced to an exchange of additional products of I needed by II against additional products of II needed by I.'

Loyally following Marx's deductions, Bulgakov does not notice that so far his entire thesis is nothing but words. He believes that these mathematical *formulae* solve the problem of accumulation. No doubt we can easily imagine proportions such as those he has copied from Marx, and *if there is expanding production*, these *formulae* will apply. Yet Bulgakov overlooks the principal problem: who exactly is to profit by an expansion such as that whose mechanism he examines? Is it explained just because we can put the mathematical proportions of accumulation on paper? Hardly, because just as soon as Bulgakov has declared the matter settled and goes on to introduce the circulation of money into the analysis, he right away comes up against the question: where are I and II to get the money for the purchase of additional products? When we dealt with Marx, time and again the weak point in his analysis, the question really of consumers in enlarged reproduction, cropped up in a perverted form as the question of additional money sources. Here Bulgakov quite slavishly follows Marx's approach, accepting his misleading formulation of the problem without noticing that it is not straightforward, although he knows perfectly well that 'Marx himself did not answer this question in the drafts which were used to compile the second volume of *Capital*'. It should be all the more interesting to see what answer Marx's Russian pupil attempted to work out on his own.

'The following solution', Bulgakov says, 'seems to us to correspond best to Marx's doctrine as a whole: The new variable capital in money-form supplied by II for both departments has its commodity equivalent in surplus value II. With reference to simple reproduction, we have already seen that the capitalists themselves must throw money into circulation to realise their surplus value, money which ultimately reverts to the pocket of the very capitalist it came from. The quantity of money required for the circulation of the surplus value is determined in accordance with the general law of commodity circulation by the value of the commodities that contained it, divided by the average amount of money turnover. This same law must apply here; the capitalists of Department II must dispose of a certain amount of money for the circulation of their surplus value, and must consequently possess certain money reserves. These reserves must be ample enough for the circulation both of that portion of the surplus value which represents the consumption fund and of that which is to be accumulated as capital.'

Bulgakov further argues that it is immaterial to the question how much money is required to circulate a certain amount of commodities inside a country, whether or not some of these commodities contain any surplus value. 'In answer to the general question as to money sources inside the country, however, our solution is that the money is supplied by the producer of gold.'[5]

If a country requires more money consequent upon an 'expansion of production', the production of gold will have to be increased accordingly. So here we are again: the producer of gold is again the *deus ex machina*, just as he had been for Marx. In fact, Bulgakov has sadly disappointed us in the high hopes we had of his new solution. His 'solution' of the problem does not go a step beyond Marx's own analysis. It can be reduced to three extremely simple statements as follows: (1) Question: How much money do we need for the realisation of capitalised surplus value? Answer: Just as much as is required in accordance with the general law of commodity circulation. (2) Q.: Where do the capitalists get the money for the realisation of capitalised surplus value? A.: They are supposed to have it. (3) Q.: How did the

[5] Ibid., pp. 50, 55.

money come into the country in the first place? A.: It is provided by the producer of gold. The extreme simplicity of this method of explanation is suspicious rather than attractive.

We need not trouble, however, to refute this theory which makes the gold producer the *deus ex machina* of capitalist accumulation. Bulgakov has done it himself quite adequately. Eighty pages on, he returns to the gold producer in quite a different context, in the course of a lengthy argument against the theory of the wages fund in which he got involved for some mysterious reason. Here he suddenly displays a keen grasp of the problem:

'We know already that there is a gold producer amongst other producers. Even under conditions of simple reproduction, he increases, on the one hand, the absolute quantity of money circulating inside the country, and on the other, he buys producer and consumer goods without, in his turn, selling commodities, paying with his own product, i.e. with the general exchange equivalent, for the goods he buys. The gold producer now might perhaps render the service of buying the whole accumulated surplus value from II and pay for it in gold which II can then use to buy means of production from I and to increase its variable capital needed to pay for additional labour power so that the gold producer now appears as the real external market.

'This assumption, however, is quite absurd. To accept it would mean to make the expansion of social production dependent upon the expansion of gold production. (Hear, hear!) This in turn presupposes an increase in gold production which is quite unreal. If the gold producer were obliged to buy all the accumulated surplus value from II for his own workers, his own variable capital would have to grow by the day and indeed by the hour. Yet his constant capital as well as his surplus value should also grow in proportion, and gold production as a whole would consequently have to take on immense dimensions. (Hear, hear!) Instead of submitting this sophistical presumption to statistical tests—which in any case would hardly be possible—a single fact can be adduced which would alone refute this presupposition: it is the development of the institution of credit which accompanies the development of capitalist economy. (Hear, hear!) Credit has the tendency to diminish the amount of money in circulation (this decrease being, of course, only relative, not absolute); it is the necessary complement of a developing economy of exchange which would otherwise soon find itself hampered by a lack of coined money. I think we need not give figures in this context to prove that the rôle of money in exchange-transactions is now very small. The hypothesis is thus proved in immediate and evident disagreement with the facts and must be confuted.'[6]

Bravo! Bravissimo! This is really excellent! Bulgakov, however, thus 'confutes' also his former explanation of the question, in what way and by whom capitalised surplus value is realised. Moreover, in refuting his own statements, Bulgakov has only explained in somewhat greater detail what Marx expressed in a single word when he called the hypothesis of a gold producer swallowing up the entire surplus value of society—'absurd'.

Admittedly, Bulgakov's real solution and that of Russian Marxists in general who deal extensively with the problem must be sought elsewhere. Just like Tugan Baranovski and Ilyin [Lenin], Bulgakov underlines the fact that the opposing sceptics made a capital error with respect to the possibility of accumulation in analysing the value of the aggregate product. They, especially Vorontsov, assumed that the aggregate social product consists in consumer goods, and they all started from the false premise that consumption is indeed the object of capitalist production. This, as the Marxists now explain, is the source of the entire misunderstanding—of all the imaginary difficulties connected with the realisation of the surplus value, with which the sceptics racked their brains.

'This school created non-existent difficulties because of this mistaken conception. Since the normal conditions of capitalist production presuppose that the capitalists' consumption fund is only a part of the surplus value, and the smaller part at that, the larger being set aside for the expansion of production, it is obvious that the difficulties imagined by this (the *populist*) school do not really exist.'[7]

The unconcern with which Bulgakov here ignores the real problem is striking. Apparently it has not dawned on him that the question as to the ultimate beneficiaries, quite irrelevant so long as personal

[6] Ibid., pp. 132 ff.
[7] Ibid., p. 20.

consumption of the entire surplus value is assumed, only becomes acute on the assumption of enlarged reproduction.

All these 'imaginary difficulties' vanish, thanks to two discoveries of Marx's which his Russian pupils untiringly quote against their opponents. The first is the fact that, in terms of value, the social product is composed, not of $v + s$, but of $c + v + s$. Secondly, the ratio of c to v in this sum continually increases with the progress of capitalist production, and at the same time, the capitalised part of the surplus value as against that part of it that is consumed, is ever growing. On this basis, Bulgakov establishes a complete theory of the relations between production and consumption in a capitalist society. As this theory plays such an important part for the Russian Marxists in general, and Bulgakov in particular, it will be necessary to get better acquainted with it.

'Consumption,' Bulgakov says, 'the satisfaction of social needs, is but an incidental moment in the circulation of capital. The volume of production is determined by the volume of capital, and not by the amount of social requirements. Not alone that the development of production is unaccompanied by a growth in consumption—the two are mutually antagonistic. Capitalist production knows no other than effective consumption, but only such persons who draw either surplus value or labour wages can be effective consumers, and their purchasing power strictly corresponds to the amount of those revenues. Yet we have seen that the fundamental evolutionary laws of capitalist production tend, despite the absolute increase, to diminish the relative size of variable capital as well as of the capitalists' consumption fund. We can say, then, *that the development of production diminishes consumption*.[8] The conditions of production and of consumption are thus in conflict. Production cannot and does not expand to further consumption. Expansion, however, is an inherent fundamental law of capitalist production and confronts every individual capitalist in the form of a stern command to compete. This contradiction is negligible in view of the fact that expanding production as such represents a market for additional products. "Inherent contradictions are resolved by an extension of the outlying fields of production."[9] (Bulgakov here quotes a saying of

[8] Bulgakov's italics.
[9] *Capital*, vol. iii, p. 387.

Marx which he has thoroughly misunderstood; we shall later have occasion to deal with it once more.) 'It has just been shown how this is possible.' (A reference to the analysis of the diagram of enlarged reproduction.) 'Evidently, the greater share of the expansion is apportioned to Department I, to the production, that is to say, of constant capital, and only a (relatively) smaller part to Department II which produces commodities for immediate consumption. This change in the relations of the two departments shows well enough what part is played by consumption in a capitalist society, and it indicates where we should expect to find the most important demand for capitalist commodities.'[10] 'Even within the narrow limits of the profit motive and the crises, even on this straight and narrow path, capitalist production is capable of unlimited expansion, irrespective of, and even despite, a decrease in consumption. The Russian literature frequently points out that in view of diminishing consumption a considerable increase of capitalist production is impossible without external markets, but this is due to a wrong evaluation of the part played by consumption in a capitalist society, the failure to appreciate that consumption is not the ultimate end of capitalist production. Capitalist production does not exist by the grace of an increase in consumption but because of an extension of the outlying fields of production which in fact constitute the market for capitalist products. A whole progression of Malthusian investigators, discontented with the superficial harmony doctrine of the school of Say and Ricardo, have slaved away at a solution of the hopeless undertaking: to find means of increasing consumption which the capitalist mode of production is bound to decrease. Marx was the only one to analyse the real connections: he has shown that the growth of consumption is fatally lagging behind that of production, and must do so whatever "third persons" one might invent. Consumption and its volume then should by no means be considered as establishing the immediate limits to the expansion of production. Capitalist production atones by the crises for deviating from the true purpose of production, but it is independent of consumption. The expansion of production is alone limited by, and dependent upon, the volume of capital.'[11]

[10] Bulgakov, op. cit., p. 161.
[11] Ibid., p. 167.

The theory of Bulgakov and Tugan Baranovski is here directly attributed to Marx. In the eyes of the Russian Marxists, it is on the whole the
direct consequence of Marx's doctrine, of which it forms an organic
part. On another occasion Bulgakov says even more clearly that it is a
faithful interpretation of Marx's diagram of enlarged reproduction.
Once a country has embraced capitalist production, its internal movement develops along the following lines:

'The production of constant capital makes up the Department I of
social reproduction, thereby instituting an independent demand for
consumption goods to the extent of both its own variable capital and
the consumption fund of its capitalists. Department II in its turn starts
the demand for the products of Department I. *Thus a closed circle is already
formed at the initial stage of capitalist production, in which it depends on no external
market but is self-sufficient and can grow, of itself, as it were, by means of accumulation.*'[12]

In the hands of the Russian Marxists this theory becomes the favour-
ite stick with which to beat their opponents, the 'populist' sceptics, in
the question of markets. We can only appreciate its daring to the full
when we look at its amazing discrepancy with everyday practice, with
all the known facts of capitalist economy. A thesis pronounced so triumphantly as the purest Marxist gospel is even more deserving of our
admiration when we consider that it is grounded in an extremely
simple confusion. We shall have further occasion to deal with this
confusion when we come to the doctrine of Tugan Baranovski.

Bulgakov further develops a completely erroneous theory of foreign
commerce, based upon his misapprehension of the relations between
consumption and production in capitalist economy. A picture of
reproduction like the above in fact has no room for foreign commerce.
If capitalism forms a 'closed circle' in every country from the very
beginning, if, chasing its tail like a puppy and in complete 'self-
sufficiency', it is able of itself to create an unlimited market for its
products and can spur itself on to ever greater expansion, then every
capitalist country as such must also be a closed and self-sufficient
economic whole. In but a single respect would foreign commerce
appear reasonable: to compensate, by imports from abroad, for certain
deficiencies due to the soil and the climate, i.e. the import of raw

---

[12] Ibid., p. 210 (our italics).

materials or foodstuffs from sheer necessity. Completely upsetting the thesis of the 'populists', Bulgakov in fact advances a theory of international commerce among capitalist states which gives pride of place to the import of agricultural products, with industrial exports merely providing the requisite funds.

International traffic in commodities does not here seem to flow from the character of the mode of production but from the natural conditions of the countries concerned. This theory at any rate has not been borrowed from Marx but from the economic experts of the German bourgeoisie. Just as Struve took over from Wagner and Schaeffle his Three Empire Theory, so Bulgakov adopts from the late List (R.I.P.) the division of states on the basis of 'agriculture' and 'mixed agriculture and manufacture', or rather adapts it, in deference to the times, to the categories of 'manufacture' and 'mixed manufacture and agriculture'. Nature has afflicted the first category with a deficiency in raw materials and foodstuffs, making it thus dependent upon foreign commerce. The second category has been liberally endowed with all it needs; here foreign trade is of no account. The prototype of the first category is England, of the second—the U.S.A. The stoppage of foreign commerce would mean the economic death-blow to England, but only a temporary crisis in the U.S.A. with a guarantee of full recovery.

'Production there is capable of unlimited expansion on the basis of the internal market.'[13]

This theory, a hoary relic of German economics even now, has obviously not the least grasp of the interrelations obtaining in an international capitalist economy. It conceives of modern international trade in terms that may have been appropriate to the times of the Phoenicians. Just listen to the lecture of Professor Buecher:

'Although the liberalist era has greatly facilitated international traffic, it would be a mistake to infer from this that the period of a national economy is nearing its end, to be replaced by a period of international economy . . . Granted that we see in Europe to-day a number of small countries that are not independent nations in respect of their commodity supply, being compelled to import substantial amounts of their foodstuffs and luxuries, while their industrial productivity is in excess

[13] Ibid., p. 199.

of the national needs and creates a permanent surplus for which employment must be found in alien spheres of consumption. Yet although countries of industrial production and those producing raw materials exist side by side and depend upon one another, such "international division of labour" should not be regarded as a sign that mankind is about to attain to a higher stage of development which it would be proper to contrast, under the label of world economy, with the . . . previous stages. No stage of economic development has ever permanently guaranteed full autonomy in the satisfaction of wants. Every one of them has left certain gaps which had to be filled in by some means or other. So-called "international economy", on the other hand, has not, at any rate so far, engendered any phenomena which are essentially different from those of national economy, and we very much doubt that such phenomena will appear in the near future.'[14]

[14] K. Buecher; The Rise of National Economy (*Die Entstehung der Volkswirtschaft*), 5th edition, p. 147. Professor Sombart's theory is the most recent contribution in this field. He argues that we are not moving towards an international economy but rather farther and farther away from it. 'I maintain, on the contrary, that commercial relations to-day do not form a stronger but rather a weaker link between the civilised nations, in relation to their economy as a whole. Individual economy takes not more but rather less account of the world market than it did a hundred or fifty years ago. At least . . . it would be wrong to assume that the relative importance of international relations with regard to modern political economy is increasing. The opposite is the case.' Sombart scornfully rejects the assumption of a progressive international division of labour, of a growing need for outside markets owing to an inelastic home demand. He in his turn is convinced that 'the individual national economies will develop into ever more perfect microcosms and that the importance of the home market will increasingly surpass that of the world market for all branches of industry' (*Die Deutsche Volkswirtschaft im 19. Jahrhundert*, 2nd edition, 1909, pp. 399–420). This devastating discovery admittedly hinges on a full acceptance of the Professor's peculiar conception which, for some reasons, only considers those as 'exporting countries' who pay for their imports with a surplus of agricultural products over and above their own needs, who pay 'with the soil'. In this scheme Russia, Rumania, the U.S.A. and the Argentine are, but Germany, England and Belgium are not, 'exporting countries'. Since capitalist development will sooner or later also claim the surplus of agricultural products for the home demand in Russia and the U.S.A., it is evident that there will be fewer and fewer 'exporting countries' in the world—international economy will vanish.—Another of Sombart's discoveries is that great capitalist 'non-exporting' countries increasingly obtain 'free' imports in form of interest on exported capital—but the capital exports as well as exports of industrial commodities are of absolutely no account to Professor Sombart. 'In the course of time we shall probably get to a point where we import without exporting' (p. 422). Modern, sensational, and precious!

As far as Bulgakov is concerned, this conception at any rate results in an unexpected conclusion: his theory of the unlimited capacity for development of capitalism is confined to certain countries with favourable natural conditions. Capitalism in England is foredoomed because the world market will be exhausted before long. In the U.S.A., India and Russia it can look forward to an unlimited development because these countries are 'self-sufficient'.

Apart from these obvious peculiarities, Bulgakov's arguments about foreign commerce again imply a fundamental misconception. Against the sceptics, from Sismondi to Nikolayon, who believed that they had to take recourse to outside markets for the realisation of capitalist surplus value, he chiefly argues as follows:

'These experts obviously consider external commerce as a "bottomless pit" to swallow up in all eternity the surplus value which cannot be got rid of inside the country.'

Bulgakov for his part triumphantly points out that foreign commerce is indeed not a pit and certainly not a bottomless one, but rather appears as a double-edged sword, that exports always belong with imports, and that the two usually counterbalance one another. Thus, whatever is pushed out over one border, will be brought back, in a changed use-form, over another. 'We must find room for the commodities that have been imported as an equivalent of those exported, within the bounds of the given market, and as this is impossible, *ex hypothesi*, it would only generate new difficulties to have recourse to an external demand.'[15]

On another occasion he says that the way to realise the surplus value found by the Russian 'populists', viz. external markets, 'is much less favourable than that discovered by Malthus, v. Kirchmann and Vorontsov himself when he wrote the essay *On Militarism and Capitalism*'.[16]

---

[15] Bulgakov, op. cit., p. 132.

[16] Ibid., p. 236. A quite uncompromising version of the same view is given by V. Ilyin [Lenin]: 'The romanticists (as he calls the sceptics) argue as follows: the capitalists cannot consume the surplus value; therefore they must dispose of it abroad. I ask: Do the capitalists perhaps give away their products to foreigners for nothing, throw it into the sea, maybe? If they sell it, it means that they obtain an equivalent. If they export certain goods, it means that they import others' (*Economic Studies and Essays*, p. 2). As a matter of fact, his explanation of the part played by external commerce in capitalist production is far more correct than that of Struve and Bulgakov.

Although Bulgakov fervently copies Marx's diagram of reproduction, he here exhibits no grasp whatever of the real problem towards which the sceptics from Sismondi to Nikolayon were groping their way. He denies that foreign commerce solves the difficulty as pretended, since it again brings the surplus value that has been disposed of into the country, although in a 'changed form'. In conformity with the crude picture of v. Kirchmann and Vorontsov, he thus believes the problem to be that of destroying a certain quantity of the surplus value, of wiping it from the face of the earth. It simply does not occur to him that the real problem is the realisation of the surplus value, the metamorphosis of commodities, in fact the 'changed form' of the surplus value.

Bulgakov thus finally arrives at the same goal as Struve, though by a different route. He preaches the self-sufficiency of capitalist accumulation which swallows up its own product as Kronos swallows up his children, and breeds ever more vigorously without help from outside. Now only one further step is needed for Marxism to revert to bourgeois economics, and this, as luck would have it, was taken by Tugan Baranovski.

23

TUGAN BARANOVSKI AND HIS 'LACK OF PROPORTION'

We have left this theorist to the end, although he already developed his views in Russian in 1894, i.e. before Struve and Bulgakov, partly because he only gave his theories their mature form in German at a later date,[1] and also because the conclusions he draws from the premises of the Marxist critics are the most far-reaching in their implications.

Like Bulgakov, Tugan Baranovski starts from Marx's analysis of social reproduction which gave him the clue to this bewildering maze of problems. But while Bulgakov, the enthusiastic disciple of Marx, only sought to follow him faithfully and simply attributed his own conclusions to the master, Tugan Baranovski, on the other hand, lays down the law to Marx who, in his opinion, did not know how to turn his brilliant exposition of the reproductive process to good account. Tugan Baranovski's most important general conclusion from Marx's principles, the pivot of his whole theory, is that, contrary to the assumptions of the sceptics, capitalist accumulation is not only possible under the capitalist forms of revenue and consumption, but is, in fact,

---

[1] *Studies on the Theory and History of Commercial Crises in England* (Jena, 1901) and *Theoretical Foundations of Marxism* (1905).

completely independent of both. It is not consumption, he says, but production itself which makes for the best market. Production and the market are therefore the same, and since the expansion of production is unlimited in itself, the market, the capacity to absorb its products, has no limits either.

'The diagram quoted', he says, 'was to prove conclusively a postulate which, though simple enough, might easily give rise to objections, unless the process be adequately understood—the postulate, namely, that capitalist production creates a market for itself. So long as it is possible to expand social production, if the productive forces are adequate for this purpose, the proportionate division of social production must also bring about a corresponding expansion of the demand inasmuch as under such conditions all newly produced goods represent a newly created purchasing power for the acquisition of other goods. Comparing simple reproduction of the social capital with its reproduction on a rising scale, we arrive at the most important conclusion that in capitalist economy the demand for commodities is in a sense independent of the total volume of social consumption. Absurd as it may seem to "common-sense", it is yet possible that the volume of social consumption as a whole goes down while at the same time the aggregate social demand for commodities grows.'[2]

And again further on: 'Arising from the abstract analysis of the reproductive process of social capital we have formed the conclusion that nothing will be left over of the social product in view of the proportionate division of the social capital.'[3]

Accordingly Tugan Baranovski subjects Marx's theory of crises to a revision which he claims to have developed from Sismondi's 'overconsumption'. 'Marx is in substantial agreement with the general view that the poverty of the workers, i.e. of the great majority of the population, makes it impossible to realise the products of an ever expanding capitalist production, since it causes a decline in demand. This opinion is definitely mistaken. We have seen that capitalist production creates its own market—consumption being only one of the moments of capitalist production. In a planned social production if the leaders of

<hr>

[2] *Studies on the Theory and History* . . ., p. 23.
[3] Ibid., p. 34.

production were equipped with all *information* about the demand and with the *power* to transfer labour and capital freely from one branch of production to another, then, however low the level of social consumption, the supply of commodities would not exceed the demand.'[4]

The only circumstance which periodically causes the market to be flooded is a lack of proportion in the enlargement of production. On this assumption, therefore, Tugan Baranovski describes the course of capitalist accumulation as follows: 'What would the workers . . . produce if production were organised on proportionate lines? Obviously their own means of subsistence and production. With what object? To expand production in the second year. The production of what products? Again of means of production and subsistence for the workers—and so on *ad infinitum*.'[5]

This game of question and answer, mind you, is not a form of self-mockery, it is meant in all seriousness. 'If the expansion of production has no practical limits, then we must assume that the expansion of markets is equally unlimited, for *if social production is proportionately organised, there is no limit to the expansion of the market other than the productive forces available*.'[6]

Since production thus creates its own demand, foreign commerce of capitalist states is also assigned that peculiar mechanistic function we have already met in Bulgakov. A foreign market, for instance, is an absolute necessity for England. 'Does not this prove that capitalist production creates a surplus product for which there is no room on the internal market? Why, come to that, does England require an external market? The answer is not difficult: because a considerable part of England's purchasing power is expended on obtaining foreign commodities. The import of foreign commodities for the English home market also makes it essential to export English commodities abroad. Since England cannot manage without importing from abroad, exports are a vital condition for that country, since without them she would not be able to pay for her imports.'[7]

---

[4] Ibid., p. 333.
[5] Ibid., p. 191.
[6] Ibid., p. 231, italics in the original.
[7] Ibid., p. 305.

Here again agricultural imports are described as a stimulating and decisive factor, quite in accordance with the scheme of the German professors.

What, then, is the general line of reasoning on which Tugan Baranovski supports his daring solution of the problem of accumulation, the new revelation on the problem of crises and a whole lot of others? Hard to believe, but quite incontrovertible for all that, Tugan Baranovski's proof consists exclusively and entirely—in Marx's diagram of enlarged reproduction, no more no less. Although he repeatedly refers rather pompously to his 'abstract analysis of the reproductive process of social capital', to the 'conclusive logic' of his analysis, this entire analysis is nothing but a copy of Marx's diagram of enlarged reproduction, with a different set of figures. Nowhere in the entire works of Tugan Baranovski shall we find a trace of any other argument. In Marx's diagram, admittedly, accumulation, production, realisation and exchange run smoothly with clockwork precision, and no doubt this kind of 'accumulation' can continue *ad infinitum*, just as long, that is to say, as ink and paper do not run out. And it is this harmless written exercise with mathematical equations which Tugan Baranovski quite seriously considers a *demonstration* of such a course in real events.

'The diagrams we have adduced are bound to prove conclusively that . . .'

On another occasion he counters Hobson, who is convinced that accumulation is impossible, with the following words: 'Diagram No. 2 of the reproduction of social capital on a rising scale corresponds to the case of capital accumulation Hobson has in mind. But does this diagram show a surplus product to come into being? Far from it.'[8]

Hobson is refuted and the matter settled because 'in the diagram' no surplus product comes into being.

Admittedly, Tugan Baranovski knows quite well that in hard fact things do not work out so smoothly. There are continual fluctuations in the exchange relations and periodical crises. But these crises happen only because in the expansion of production the proper proportions are not maintained, because, that is to say, the proportions of 'diagram No. 2' are not observed in the first place. If they were, there would be

[8] Ibid., p. 191.

no crisis, and capitalist production could get along as nicely as it does on paper, in every detail. Tugan Baranovski is committed to the view that we can ignore the crises if we consider the reproductive process as a continuous process. Although the 'proportion' may be upset at any moment, yet on average it will always be re-established by different deviations, by price-fluctuations from day to day, and in the long run by periodical crises. That on the whole this 'proportion' is more or less maintained is proved by the fact that capitalist economy is still going strong—otherwise it would long ago have ended in chaos and collapse. In the long run, then, Tugan Baranovski's 'proportion' is observed by and large, and we must conclude that reality obeys 'diagram No. 2'. And since this diagram can be indefinitely extended, it follows that capitalist accumulation can also proceed *ad infinitum*.

What is striking in all this is not Tugan Baranovski's conclusion that the diagram corresponds to the actual course of events—as we have seen, Bulgakov also shared this belief; the really startling fact is that Tugan Baranovski sees no necessity for as much as inquiring whether the diagram is correct, that, instead of proving the diagram, he considers this, the arithmetical exercise on paper, as proof of the actual state of affairs. Bulgakov honestly tried to project Marx's diagram on the real concrete relations of capitalist economy and of capitalist exchange; he endeavoured to overcome the difficulties resulting from it, though without success, it is true, remaining to the last involved with Marx's analysis, which he himself recognised to be incomplete and fragmentary. But Tugan Baranovski does not need any proof, he does not greatly exercise his brains: since the arithmetical sums come out satisfactorily, and may be continued *ad lib.*, this is to him proof that capitalist accumulation can also proceed without let or hindrance—provided the said 'proportion' obtains, which it will have to do by hook or by crook, as he himself would not dream of denying.

Tugan Baranovski, however, has one indirect proof that the diagram with its strange results corresponds to, and truly reflects, reality. This is the fact that capitalist production, quite in accordance with Marx's diagram, puts human consumption second to production, that it conceives of the former as a means and of the latter as an end in itself, just as it puts human labour, the 'worker', on a par with the machine.

'Technical progress is expressed by the fact that the means of labour, the machine, increases more and more in importance as compared to living labour, to the worker himself. Means of production play an ever growing part in the productive process and on the commodity market. Compared to the machine, the worker recedes further into the background and the demand resulting from the consumption of the workers is also put into the shade by that which results from productive consumption by the means of production. The entire workings of capitalist economy take on the character of a mechanism existing on its own, as it were, in which human consumption appears as a simple moment of the reproductive process and the circulation of capitals.'[9]

Tugan Baranovski considers this discovery as a fundamental law of the capitalist mode of production, which is confirmed by a quite tangible phenomenon: with the progress of capitalist development Department I goes on growing relatively to, and at the expense of, Department II. It was Marx himself who, as we all know, set up this law in which he grounded the schematic exposition of reproduction, though in the further development of his diagram he ignored subsequent alterations for simplicity's sake. This, the automatic growth of the producer goods as compared with the consumer goods department affords Tugan Baranovski the only objective proof of his theory: that in capitalist society human consumption becomes increasingly unimportant, and production more and more an end in itself. This thesis forms the corner-stone of his entire theoretical edifice.

'In all the industrial countries', he proclaims, 'we are confronted with the same type of development—the development of national economy everywhere follows the same fundamental law. The mining industry which creates the means of production for modern industry comes more and more to the fore. The relative decrease in the export of immediately consumable manufactured goods from Britain is thus also an expression of the fundamental law governing capitalist development. The further technical progress advances, the more do consumer goods recede as compared with producer goods. Human consumption plays an ever decreasing part as against the productive consumption of the means of production.'[10]

[9] Ibid., p. 27.
[10] Ibid., p. 58.

Although this 'fundamental law' like all his other 'fundamental' laws, in so far as they mean anything at all, is borrowed ready-made from Marx, Baranovski does not rest content with this and immediately proceeds to preach the Marxist gospel to Marx himself. Scrabbling about like a blind hen, Marx has turned up another pearl—Tugan will give him that—only he does not know what to do with it. It needed a Tugan Baranovski to know how to make it useful to science, and in his hand the newly discovered law suddenly throws a new light on the whole workings of capitalist economy. This law of the expansion in the department of producer goods at the cost of that of consumer goods reveals clearly, concisely, exactly, and in measurable terms, that capitalist society attaches progressively less importance to human consumption, putting man on the same level as the means of production, and that Marx was therefore completely wrong both in assuming that man alone, not the machine, too, can be the creator of surplus value, and in saying, further, that human consumption represents a limit for capitalist production which is bound to cause periodical crises in the present, and the collapse and terrible end of capitalist economy in the near future. In short, the 'fundamental law' governing the increase of producer as compared to consumer goods reflects the singular nature of capitalist society as a whole which Marx had not understood and which to interpret happily fell to the lot of Tugan Baranovski.

We have seen above the decisive part played by the 'fundamental law' of capital in the controversy between the Russian Marxists and the sceptics. Bulgakov's remarks we already know; another Marxist already referred to, Vladimir Ilyin, expresses himself in similar terms in his polemics against the 'populists':

'It is well known that the law of capitalist production consists in the fact that the constant capital grows more rapidly than the variable capital, that is to say an ever increasing part of the newly formed capital falls to the department of social production which creates producer goods. In consequence, this department is absolutely bound to grow more rapidly than the department creating consumer goods, that is to say, the very thing happens which Sismondi declared to be "impossible", "dangerous", etc. In consequence, consumer goods make up a smaller and smaller share of the total bulk of capitalist production, and this is entirely in accordance with the historical "mission" of capitalism and its specific social structure: the former in fact consists in the development of the productive forces of society (production as an end in itself), and the latter prevents that the mass of the population should turn them to use.'[11]

In this respect, of course, Tugan Baranovski goes even farther. With his love of paradox he actually permits himself the joke of submitting a mathematical proof that accumulation of capital and expansion of production are possible even if the absolute volume of production decreases. In this connection, Karl Kautsky has pointed out, he had recourse to a somewhat dubious scientific subterfuge, namely that he shaped his daring deductions exclusively for a specific moment: the transition from simple to enlarged reproduction—a moment which is exceptional even in theory, but certainly of no practical significance whatever.[12]

[11] V. Ilyin [Lenin] 'Studies and Essays in Economics' (*Oekonomische Studien und Artikel. Zur Charakterisierung des ökonomischen Romantizismus*, St. Petersburg, 1899), p. 20.—Incidentally, the same author is responsible for the statement that enlarged reproduction begins only with capitalism. It quite escapes him that under conditions of simple reproduction, which he takes to be the rule for all pre-capitalist modes of production, we should probably never have advanced beyond the stage of the paleolithic scraper.

[12] *Die Neue Zeit*, vol. xx, part 2, *Krisentheorien*, p. 116. Kautsky's mathematical demonstration to Tugan Baranovski that consumption is bound to grow, and 'in the precise ratio as the bulk of producer goods in terms of value', calls for two comments: first, like Marx, Kautsky paid no attention to the progress in the productivity of labour so that consumption appears to have a relatively larger volume than it would in fact have. Secondly, the increase in consumption to which Kautsky here refers is only a consequence, a result of enlarged reproduction, it is neither its basis nor its aim; it is mainly due to the growth of the variable capital, the continual employment of additional workers. The upkeep of these workers, however, neither is nor ought to be the object of the expansion of reproduction—no more, for that matter, than the increasing personal consumption of the capitalist class. Kautsky's argument no doubt refutes Tugan Baranovski's pet notion: the whimsy to construe enlarged reproduction with an absolute decrease in consumption. But for all that, he does not get anywhere near the fundamental problem, the relations between production and consumption under the aspect of the reproductive process, though we are told in another passage of the same work: 'With the capitalists growing richer, and the workers they exploit increasing in numbers, they constitute between them a market for the consumer goods produced by capitalist big industry which expands continually, yet it does not grow as rapidly as the accumulation of capital and the productivity of labour, and must therefore remain inadequate.' An additional market is required for these consumer goods, a market outside their own province,

As to Tugan Baranovski's 'fundamental law', Kautsky declares it to be a mere illusion due to the fact that Tugan Baranovski considered the organisation of production only in the old countries of capitalist big industry.

'It is correct', Kautsky says, 'that with a progressive division of labour, there will be comparatively fewer and fewer factories etc. for the production of goods direct for personal consumption, together with a relative increase in the number of those which supply both the former and one another with tools, machines, raw materials, transport facilities and so on. While in original peasant economy an enterprise that cultivated the flax also made the linen with its own tools and got it ready for human consumption, nowadays hundreds of enterprises may share in the manufacture of a single shirt, by producing raw cotton, iron rails, steam engines and railway trucks that bring it to port, and so

among those occupational groups and nations whose mode of production is not yet capitalistic. This market is found and also widens increasingly, but the expansion is again too slow, since the additional market is not nearly so elastic and capable of expansion as the capitalist productive process. As soon as capitalist production has developed to the big industry stage, as in England already in the first quarter of the nineteenth century, it is capable of expanding by leaps and bounds so as soon to out-distance all expansions of the market. Every period of prosperity subsequent to a considerable extension of the market is thus from the outset doomed to an early end—the inevitable crisis. This, in brief, is the theory of crises established by Marx, and, as far as we can see, generally accepted by the "orthodox" Marxists' (ibid., p. 80). Kautsky, however, is not interested in harmonising this conception of the realisation of the aggregate product with Marx's diagram of enlarged reproduction, perhaps because, as our quotation also shows, he deals with the problem solely from the aspect of crises, regarding, in other words; the social product as a more or less homogeneous bulk of goods and ignoring the fact that it is differentiated in the reproductive process.

L. Boudin seems to come closer to the crucial point. In his brilliant review on Tugan Baranovski he gives the following formulation: 'With a single exception to be considered below, the existence of a surplus product in capitalist countries does not put a spoke in the wheel of production, not because production will be distributed more efficiently among the various spheres, or because the manufacture of machinery will replace that of cotton goods. The reason is rather that, capitalist development having begun sooner in some countries than in others, and because even to-day there are still some countries that have no developed capitalism, the capitalist countries in truth have at their disposal an outside market in which they can get rid of their products which they cannot consume themselves, no matter whether these are cotton or iron goods. We would by no means deny that it is significant if iron goods replace cotton goods as the main products of the principal capitalist countries. On the contrary, this change is of paramount importance, on. With international division of labour it will happen that some countries—the old industrial countries—can only slowly expand their production for personal consumption, while making large strides in their production of producer goods which is much more decisive for the heartbeat of economic life than the production of consumer goods. From the point of view of the nation concerned, we might easily form the opinion that producer goods can be turned out on a constantly rising scale with a more rapid rate of increase than in the production of consumer goods, and that their production is not bound up with that of the latter.'

The opinion, that producer goods can be produced independent of consumption, is of course a mirage of Tugan Baranovski's, typical of vulgar economics. Not so the fact cited in support of this fallacy: the quicker growth of Department I as compared with Department II is beyond dispute, not only in old industrial countries but wherever

but its implications are rather different from those ascribed to it by Tugan Baranovski. It indicates the beginning of the end of capitalism. So long as the capitalist countries exported commodities for the purpose of consumption, there was still a hope for capitalism in these countries, and the question did not arise how much and how long the non-capitalist outside world would be able to absorb capitalist commodities. The growing share of machinery at the cost of consumer goods in what is exported from the main capitalist countries shows that areas which were formerly free of capitalism, and therefore served as a dumping-ground for its surplus products, are now drawn into the whirlpool of capitalism. It shows that, since they are developing a capitalism of their own, they can by themselves produce the consumer goods they need. At present they still require machinery produced by capitalist methods since they are only in the initial stages of capitalist development. But all too soon they will need them no longer. Just as they now make their own cotton and other consumer goods, they will in future produce their own iron ware. Then they will not only cease to absorb the surplus produce of the essentially capitalist countries, but they will themselves produce surplus products which they can place only with difficulty' (*Die Neue Zeit*, vol. xxv, part 1, *Mathematische Formeln gegen Karl Marx*, p. 604). Boudin here broaches an important aspect of the general relations pertaining to the development of international capitalism. Further, as a logical consequence, he comes to the question of imperialism but unfortunately he finally puts the wrong kind of edge on his acute analysis by considering the whole of militarist production together with the system of exporting international capital to non-capitalist countries under the heading of 'reckless expenditure'.—We must say in parenthesis that Bouding, just like Kautsky, holds that the law of a quicker growth in the means-of-production department relative to the means-of-subsistence department is a delusion of Tugan Baranovski's.

technical progress plays a decisive part in production. It is the foundation also of Marx's fundamental law that the rate of profit tends to fall. Yet in spite of it all, or rather precisely for this reason, it is a howler if Bulgakov, Ilyin and Tugan Baranovski imagine to have discovered in this law the essential nature of capitalist economy as an economic system in which production is an end in itself and human consumption merely incidental.

The growth of the constant at the expense of the variable capital is only the capitalist expression of the general effects of increasing labour productivity. The formula c greater than v ($c > v$), translated from the language of capitalism into that of the social labour process, means only that the higher the productivity of human labour, the shorter the time needed to change a given quantity of means of production into finished products.[13]

---

[13] 'Apart from natural conditions, such as fertility of the soil, etc., and from the skill of independent and isolated producers (shown rather qualitatively in the genus than quantitatively in the mass of their products), the degree of productivity of labour, in a capitalist society, is expressed in the relative extent of the means of production that one labourer, during a given time, with the same tension of labour-power, turns into products. The mass of means of production which he thus transforms, increases with the productiveness of his labour. But those means of production play a double part. The increase of some is a consequence, that of the others a condition of the increasing productivity of labour. E.g., with the division of labour in manufacture, and with the use of machinery, more raw material is worked up in the same time and, therefore, a greater mass of raw material and auxiliary substances enter into the labour-process. That is the consequence of the increasing productivity of labour. On the other hand, the mass of machinery, beasts of burden, mineral manures, drainpipes, etc., is a condition of the increasing productivity of labour. So also is it with the means of production concentrated in buildings, furnaces, means of transport, etc. But whether condition or consequence, the growing extent of the means of production, as compared with the labour-power incorporated with them, is an expression of the growing productiveness of labour. The increase of the latter appears, therefore, in the diminution of the mass of labour in proportion to the mass of means of production moved by it, or in the diminution of the subjective factor of the labour-process as compared with the objective factor' (*Capital*, vol. i, pp. 635–6). And yet another passage: 'We have seen previously, that with the development of the productivity of labour, and therefore with the development of the capitalist mode of production, which develops the socially productive power of labour more than all previous modes of production, there is a steady increase of the mass of means of production, which are permanently embodied in the productive process as instruments of labour and perform their function in it for a longer or shorter time at repeated

This is a universal law of human labour. It has been valid in all pre-capitalist forms of production and will also be valid in the future in a socialist order of society. In terms of the material use-form of society's aggregate product, this law must manifest itself by more and more social labour time being employed in the manufacture of producer than of consumer goods. In a planned and controlled social economy, organised on socialist lines, this transformation would in fact be more rapid even than it is in contemporary capitalist economy. In the first place, rational scientific techniques can only be applied on the largest scale when the barriers of private ownership in land are abolished. This will result in an immense revolution in vast provinces of production which will ultimately amount to a replacement of living labour by machine labour, and which will enable us to tackle technical jobs on a scale quite impossible under present day conditions. Secondly, the general use of machinery in the productive process will be put on a new economic basis. At present the machine does not compete with living labour but only with that part of it that is paid. The cost of the labour power which is replaced by the machine represents the lowest limit of the applicability of the machine. Which means that the capitalist becomes interested in a machine only when the costs of its production—assuming the same level of performance—amount to less than the wages of the workers it replaces. From the point of view of the social labour process which is the only one to matter in a socialist society, the machine competes not with the labour that is necessary to maintain the worker but with the labour he actually performs. In other words, in a society that is not governed by the profit motive but aims at saving human labour, the use of machinery is economically indicated

intervals (buildings, machinery, etc.); also, that this increase is at the same time the premise and result of the development of the productivity of social labour. It is especially capitalist production, which is characterised by relative as well as absolute growth of this sort of wealth' (*Capital*, vol. i, chap. xxiii, 2). 'The material forms of existence of constant capital, the means of production, do not consist merely of such instruments of labour, but also of raw material in various stages of finished and of auxiliary substances. With the enlargement of the scale of production and the increase in the productivity of labour by co-operation, division of labour, machinery, etc., the mass of raw materials and auxiliary substances used in the daily process of reproduction, grows likewise' (*Capital*, vol. ii, p. 160).

just as soon as it can save more human labour than is necessary for making it, not to mention the many cases where the use of machinery is desirable even if it does not answer this economic minimum—for reasons of health and similar considerations, in the interest of the workers themselves. However that may be, the tension between the respective economic usefulness of the machine in (a) a capitalist, and (b) a socialist society is at least equal to the difference between labour and that part of it that is paid; it is, in other words, the precise equivalent of the whole capitalist surplus value. Consequently, if the capitalist profit motive is abolished and a social organisation of labour introduced, the marginal use of the machine will suddenly be increased by the whole extent of the capitalist surplus value, so that an enormous field, not to be gauged as yet, will be open to the triumphal march of the machine. This would be tangible proof that the capitalist mode of production, alleged to spur on to the optimum technical development, in fact sets large social limits to technical progress, in form of the profit motive on which it is based. It would show that as soon as these limits are abolished, technical progress will develop such a powerful drive that the technical marvels of capitalist production will be child's play in comparison.

In terms of the composition of the social product, this technical transformation can only mean that, compared to the production of consumer goods, the production of producer goods—measured in units of labour time—must increase more rapidly in a socialist society than it does even to-day. Thus the relation between the two departments of social production which the Russian Marxists took to reveal typical capitalist baseness, the neglect of man's need to consume, rather proves to be the precise manifestation of the progressive subjection of nature to social labour, which will become even more striking when production is organised solely with a view to human needs. The only objective proof for Tugan Baranovski's 'fundamental law' thus collapses as a 'fundamental' confusion. His whole construction, including his 'new theory of crises', together with the 'lack of proportion', is reduced to its foundations on paper: a slavish copy of Marx's diagram of enlarged reproduction.

24

THE END OF RUSSIAN 'LEGALIST' MARXISM

The Russian 'legalist' Marxists, and Tugan Baranovski above all, can claim the credit, in their struggle against the doubters of capitalist accumulation, of having enriched economic theory by an application of Marx's analysis of the social reproductive process and its schematic representation in the second volume of *Capital*. But in view of the fact that this same Tugan Baranovski quite wrongly regarded said diagram as the solution to the problem instead of its formulation, his conclusions were bound to reverse the basic order of Marx's doctrine.

Tugan Baranovski's approach, according to which capitalist production can create unlimited markets and is independent of consumption, leads him straight on to the thesis of Say–Ricardo, i.e. a natural balance between production and consumption, between supply and demand. The difference is simply that those two only thought in terms of simple commodity circulation, whilst Tugan Baranovski applies the same doctrine to the circulation of capital. His theory of crises being caused by a 'lack of proportion' is in effect just a paraphrase of Say's old trite absurdity: the over-production of any one commodity only goes to show under-production of another; and Tugan Baranovski simply translates this nonsense into the terminology used in Marx's analysis of the reproductive process. Even though he declares that, Say notwith-standing, general over-production is quite possible in the light of the circulation of money which the former had entirely neglected, yet it is in fact this very same neglect, the besetting sin of Say and Ricardo in their dealings with the problem of crises which is the condition for his delightful manipulations with Marx's diagram. As soon as it is applied to the circulation of money, 'diagram No. 2' begins to bristle with spikes and barbs. Bulgakov was caught in these spikes when he attempted to follow up Marx's interrupted analysis to a logical conclu-sion. This compound of forms of thought borrowed from Marx with contents derived from Say and Ricardo is what Tugan Baranovski modestly calls his 'attempt at a synthesis between Marx's theory and classical economics'.

After almost a century, the theory of optimism which holds, in the face of petty-bourgeois doubts, that capitalist production is capable of development, returns, by way of Marx's doctrine and its 'legalist' champions, to its point of departure, to Say and Ricardo. The three 'Marxists' join forces with the bourgeois 'harmonists' of the Golden Age shortly before the Fall when bourgeois economics was expelled from the Garden of Innocence—the circle is closed.

There can be no doubt that the 'legalist' Russian Marxists achieved a victory over their opponents, the 'populists', but that victory was rather too thorough. In the heat of battle, all three—Struve, Bulgakov and Tugan Baranovski—overstated their case. The question was whether capitalism in general, and Russian capitalism in particular, is capable of development; these Marxists, however, proved this capacity to the extent of even offering theoretical proof that capitalism can go on for ever. Assuming the accumulation of capital to be without limits, one has obviously proved the unlimited capacity of capitalism to sur-vive! Accumulation is the specifically capitalist method of expanding production, of furthering labour productivity, of developing the productive forces, of economic progress. If the capitalist mode of pro-duction can ensure boundless expansion of the productive forces, of economic progress, it is invincible indeed. The most important object-ive argument in support of socialist theory breaks down; socialist polit-ical action and the ideological import of the proletarian class struggle cease to reflect economic events, and socialism no longer appears an historical necessity. Setting out to show that capitalism is possible, this trend of reasoning ends up by showing that socialism is impossible.

The three Russian Marxists were fully aware that in the course of the dispute they had made an about-turn, though Struve, in his enthusiasm for the cultural mission of capitalism, does not worry about giving up a useful warrant.[1] Bulgakov tried to stop the gaps now made in socialist theory with another fragment of the same theory as best he could: he hoped that capitalist society might yet perish, in spite of the immanent balance between production and consumption, because of the declining profit rate. But it was he himself who finally cut away the ground from under this somewhat precarious comfort. Forgetting the straw he had offered for the salvation of socialism, he turned on Tugan Baranovski with the teaching that, in the case of large capitals, the relative decline in the profit rate is compensated by the absolute growth of capital.[2] More consistent than the others, Tugan Baranovski finally with the crude joy of a barbarian destroys all objective economic arguments in support of socialism, thus building in his own spirit 'a more beautiful world' on an ethical foundation. 'The individual protests against an economic order which transforms the end (man) into a means (production) and the means (production) into an end.'[3]

Our three Marxists demonstrated in person that the new foundations of socialism had been frail and jerry-built. They had hardly laid down the new basis for socialism before they turned their backs on it. When the masses of Russia were staking their lives in the fight for the ideals

---

[1] Struve says in the preface to the collection of his Russian essays (published in 1901): 'In 1894, when the author published his "Critical Comments on the Problem of Economic Development in Russia", he inclined in philosophy towards positivism, in sociology and economics towards outspoken, though by no means orthodox, Marxism. Since then, the author no longer sees the whole truth in positivism and Marxism which is grounded in it (!), they no longer fully determine his view of the world. Malignant dogmatism which not only browbeats those who think differently, but spies upon their morals and psychology, regards such work as a mere "Epicurean instability of mind". It cannot understand that criticism in its own right is to the living and thinking individual one of the most valuable rights. The author does not intend to renounce this right, though he might constantly be in danger of being indicted for "instability"' (*Miscellany*, St. Petersburg, 1901).

[2] Bulgakov, op. cit., p. 252.

[3] Tugan Baranovski, *Studies on the Theory and History . . .*, p. 229.

of a social order to come, which would put the end (man) before the means (production), the 'individual' went into retreat, to find philosophical and ethical solace with Kant. In actual fact, the 'legalist' bourgeois Marxists ended up just where we should expect them to from their theoretical position—in the camp of bourgeois harmonies.

Section III

The Historical Conditions
of Accumulation

25

CONTRADICTIONS WITHIN THE DIAGRAM OF ENLARGED REPRODUCTION

In the first section, we ascertained that Marx's diagram of accumulation does not solve the question of who is to benefit in the end by enlarged reproduction. If we take the diagram literally as it is set out at the end of volume ii, it appears that capitalist production would itself realise its entire surplus value, and that it would use the capitalised surplus value exclusively for its own needs. This impression is confirmed by Marx's analysis of the diagram where he attempts to reduce the circulation within the diagram altogether to terms of money, that is to say to the effective demand of capitalists and workers—an attempt which in the end leads him to introduce the 'producer of money' as a *deus ex machina*. In addition, there is that most important passage in *Capital*, volume i, which must be interpreted to mean the same.

'The annual production must in the first place furnish all those objects (use-values) from which the material components of capital, used up in the course of the year, have to be replaced. Deducting these there remains the net or surplus-product, in which the surplus-value lies. And of what does this surplus-value consist? Only of things destined to satisfy the wants and desires of the capitalist class, things which, consequently, enter into the consumption fund of the capitalists? Were that the case, the cup of surplus-value would be drained to the very dregs, and nothing but simple reproduction would ever take place.

'To accumulate it is necessary to convert a portion of the surplus-product into capital. But we cannot, except by a miracle, convert into capital anything but such articles as can be employed in the labour-process (i.e. means of production), and such further articles as are suitable for the sustenance of the labourer (i.e. means of subsistence). Consequently, a part of the annual surplus-labour must have been applied to the production of additional means of production and subsistence, over and above the quantity of these things required to replace the capital advanced. In one word, surplus-value is convertible into capital solely because the surplus-product, whose value it is, already comprises the material elements of new capital.'[1]

The following conditions of accumulation are here laid down: (1) The surplus value to be capitalised first comes into being in the natural form of capital (as additional means of production and additional means of subsistence for the workers). (2) The expansion of capitalist production is achieved exclusively by means of capitalist products, i.e. its own means of production and subsistence. (3) The limits of this expansion are each time determined in advance by the amount of surplus value which is to be capitalised in any given case; they cannot be extended, since they depend on the amount of the means of production and subsistence which make up the surplus product; neither can they be reduced, since a part of the surplus value could not then be employed in its natural form. Deviations in either direction (above and below) may give rise to periodical fluctuations and crises—in this context, however, these may be ignored, because in general the surplus product to be capitalised must be equal to actual accumulation. (4) Since capitalist production buys up its entire surplus product, there is no limit to the accumulation of capital.

Marx's diagram of enlarged reproduction adheres to these conditions. Accumulation here takes its course, but it is not in the least indicated who is to benefit by it, who are the new consumers for whose

[1] *Capital*, vol. i, pp. 593–4.

sake production is ever more enlarged. The diagram assumes, say, the following course of events: the coal industry is expanded in order to expand the iron industry in order to expand the machine industry in order to expand the production of consumer goods. This last, in turn, is expanded to maintain both its own workers and the growing army of coal, iron and machine operatives. And so on *ad infinitum*. We are running in circles, quite in accordance with the theory of Tugan Baranovski. Considered in isolation, Marx's diagram does indeed permit of such an interpretation since he himself explicitly states time and again that he aims at presenting the process of accumulation of the aggregate capital in a society consisting solely of capitalists and workers. Passages to this effect can be found in every volume of *Capital*.

In volume i, in the very chapter on 'The Conversion of Surplus-Value into Capital', he says:

'In order to examine the object of our investigation in its integrity, free from all disturbing subsidiary circumstances, we must treat the whole world as one nation, and assume that capitalist production is everywhere established and has possessed itself of every branch of industry.'[2]

In volume ii, the assumption repeatedly returns; thus in chapter 17 on 'The Circulation of Surplus-Value': 'Now, there are only two points of departure: The capitalist and the labourer. All third classes of persons must either receive money for their services from these two classes, or, to the extent that they receive it without any equivalent services, they are joint owners of the surplus-value in the form of rent, interest, etc. . . . The capitalist class, then, remains the sole point of departure of the circulation of money.'[3]

Further, in the same chapter 'On the Circulation of Money in Particular under Assumption of Accumulation': 'But the difficulty arises when we assume, not a partial, but a general accumulation of money-capital on the part of the capitalist class. Apart from this class, there is, according to our assumption—the general and exclusive domination of capitalist production—no other class but the working class.'[4]

---

[2] Ibid., p. 594, note 1.
[3] Op. cit., vol. ii, p. 384.
[4] Ibid., pp. 400–1.

And again in chapter 20: '. . . there are only two classes in this case, the working class disposing of their labour-power, and the capitalist class owning the social means of production and the money.'[5]

In volume iii, Marx says quite explicitly, when demonstrating the process of capitalist production as a whole: 'Let us suppose that the whole society is composed only of industrial capitalists and wage workers. Let us furthermore make exceptions of fluctuations of prices which prevent large portions of the total capital from reproducing themselves under average conditions and which, owing to the general interrelations of the entire process of reproduction, such as are developed particularly by credit, must always call forth general stoppages of a transient nature. Let us also make abstraction of the bogus transactions and speculations, which the credit system favours. In that case, a crisis could be explained only by a disproportion of production in various branches, and by a disproportion of the consumption of the capitalists and the accumulation of their capitals. But as matters stand, the reproduction of the capitals invested in production depends largely upon the consuming power of the non-producing classes; while the consuming power of the labourers is handicapped partly by the laws of wages, partly by the fact that it can be exerted only so long as the labourers can be employed at a profit for the capitalist class.'[6]

This last quotation refers to the question of crises with which we are not here concerned. It can leave no doubt, however, that the movement of the total capital, 'as matters stand', depends in Marx's view on three categories of consumers only: the capitalists, the workers and the 'non-productive classes', i.e. the hangers-on of the capitalist class (king, parson, professor, prostitute, mercenary), of whom he quite rightly disposes in volume ii as the mere representatives of a derivative purchasing power, and thus the parasitic joint consumers of the surplus value or of the wage of labour.

Finally, in *Theories of Surplus Value*,[7] Marx formulates his general presuppositions with regard to accumulation as follows: 'Here we have only to consider the forms through which capital passes during the

[5] Ibid., p. 488.

[6] Op. cit., vol. iii, p. 568.

[7] *Theorien* . . ., vol. ii, part 2, 'The Accumulation of Capital and Crises', p. 263.

various stages of its development. Thus we do not set out the actual conditions of the real process of production, but always assume that the commodity is sold for what it is worth. We ignore the competition of capitalists and the credit system; we also leave out of account the actual constitution of society which never consists exclusively of the classes of workers and industrial capitalists, and where there is accordingly no strict division between producers and consumers. The first category (of consumers, whose revenues are partly of a secondary, not a primitive nature, derived from profits and the wage of labour) is much wider than the second category (of producers). Therefore the manner in which it spends its income, and the extent of such income, effects very large modifications in the economic household, and especially so in the process of circulation and reproduction of capital.'

Speaking of the 'actual constitution of society', Marx here also considers merely the parasitic joint consumers of surplus value and of the wage of labour, i.e. only the hangers-on of the principal categories of capitalist production.

There can be no doubt, therefore, that Marx wanted to demonstrate the process of accumulation in a society consisting exclusively of workers and capitalists, under the universal and exclusive domination of the capitalist mode of production. On this assumption, however, his diagram does not permit of any other interpretation than that of production for production's sake.

Let us recall the second example of Marx's diagram of enlarged reproduction:

1st year:

  I. $5,000c + 1,000v + 1,000s = 7,000$ means of production
  II. $1,430c + \quad 285v + \quad 285s = \underline{2,000}$ means of subsistence
                 9,000

2nd year:

  I. $5,417c + 1,083v + 1,083s = 7,583$ means of production
  II. $1,583c + \quad 316v + \quad 316s = \underline{2,215}$ means of subsistence
                 9,798

3rd year:

  I. $5,869c + 1,173v + 1,173s = 8,215$ means of production
  II. $1,715c + \quad 342v + \quad 342s = \underline{2,399}$ means of subsistence
                10,614

4th year:

I. $6,358c + 1,271v + 1,271s = 8,900$ means of production
II. $1,858c + 371v + 371s = \underline{2,600}$ means of subsistence
$$11,500$$

Here accumulation continues year after year without interruption, the capitalists in each case consuming half of the surplus value they have gained and capitalising the other half. In the process of capitalisation, the same technical foundation, that is to say the same organic composition or division into constant and variable capital and also the same rate of exploitation (always amounting to 100 per cent) is consecutively maintained for the additional capital as it was for the original capital. In accordance with Marx's assumption in volume i of *Capital*, the capitalised part of the surplus value first comes into being as additional means of production and as means of subsistence for the workers, both serving the purpose of an ever expanding production in the two departments. It cannot be discovered from the assumptions of Marx's diagram for whose sake production is progressively expanded. Admittedly, production and consumption increase simultaneously in a society. The consumption of the capitalists increases (in terms of value, in the first year it amounts to $500 + 142$, in the second year to $542 + 158$, in the third year to $586 + 171$, and in the fourth year to $635 + 185$); the consumption of the workers increases as well; the variable capital increasing year after year in both departments precisely indicates this growth in terms of value. And yet, the growing consumption of the capitalists can certainly not be regarded as the ultimate purpose of accumulation; on the contrary, there is no accumulation inasmuch as this consumption takes place and increases; personal consumption of the capitalists must be regarded as simple reproduction. Rather, the question is: if, and in so far as, the capitalists do not themselves consume their products but 'practise abstinence', i.e. accumulate, for whose sake do they produce? Even less can the maintenance of an ever larger army of workers be the ultimate purpose of continuous accumulation of capital. From the capitalist's point of view, the consumption of the workers is a consequence of accumulation, it is never its object or its condition, unless the principles (foundations) of capitalist production are to be turned upside down. And in any case, the workers can only consume that part of the product which corresponds to the variable capital, not a jot more. Who, then, realises the permanently increasing surplus value? The diagram answers: the capitalists themselves and they alone.—And what do they do with this increasing surplus value?—The diagram replies: They use it for an ever greater expansion of their production. These capitalists are thus fanatical supporters of an expansion of production for production's sake. They see to it that ever more machines are built for the sake of building—with their help—ever more new machines. Yet the upshot of all this is not accumulation of capital but an increasing production of producer goods to no purpose whatever. Indeed, one must be as reckless as Tugan Baranovski, and rejoice as much in paradoxical statements, to assume that this untiring merry-go-round in thin air could be a faithful reflection in theory of capitalist reality, a true deduction from Marx's doctrine.[8]

Besides the analysis of enlarged reproduction roughed out in *Capital*, volume ii, the whole of Marx's work, volume ii in particular, contains a most elaborate and lucid exposition of his general views regarding the typical course of capitalist accumulation. If we once fully understand this interpretation, the deficiencies of the diagram at the end of volume ii are immediately evident.

If we examine critically the diagram of enlarged reproduction in the light of Marx's theory, we find various contradictions between the two.

To begin with, the diagram completely disregards the increasing productivity of labour. For it assumes that the composition of capital is the same in every year, that is to say, the technical basis of the productive process is not affected by accumulation. This procedure would be quite permissible in itself in order to simplify the analysis, but when we come to examine the concrete conditions for the realisation of the aggregate product, and for reproduction, then at least we must take into account, and make allowance for, changes in technique which are bound up with the process of capital accumulation. Yet if we allow for improved productivity of labour, the material aggregate of the social

---

[8] 'It is never the original thinkers who draw the absurd conclusions. They leave that to the Says and MacCullochs' (*Capital*, vol. ii, p. 451).—And—we might add—to the Tugan Baranovskis.

product—both producer and consumer goods—will in consequence show a much more rapid increase in volume than is set forth in the diagram. This increase in the aggregate of use-values, moreover, indicates also a change in the value relationships. As Marx argues so convincingly, basing his whole theory on this axiom, the progressive development of labour productivity reacts on both the composition of accumulating capital and the rate of surplus value so that they cannot remain constant under conditions of increasing accumulation of capital, as was assumed by the diagram. Rather, if accumulation continues, c, the constant capital of both departments, must increase not only absolutely but also relatively to $v+c$ or the total new value (the social aspect of labour productivity); at the same time, constant capital and similarly the surplus value must increase relatively to the variable capital—in short, the rate of surplus value, i.e. the ratio between surplus value and variable capital, must similarly increase (the capitalist aspect of labour productivity). These changes need not, of course, occur annually, just as the terms of first, second and third year in Marx's diagram do not necessarily refer to calendar years but may stand for any given period. Finally, we may choose to assume that these alterations, both in the composition of capital and in the rate of surplus value, take place either in the first, third, fifth, seventh year, etc., or in the second, sixth and ninth year, etc. The important thing is only that they are allowed for somewhere and taken into account as periodical phenomena. If the diagram is amended accordingly, the result of this method of accumulation will be an increasing annual surplus in the consumer at the expense of producer goods. It is true that Tugan Baranovski conquers all difficulties on paper: he simply constructs a diagram with different proportions where year by year the variable capital decreases by 25 per cent. And since this arithmetical exercise is successful enough on paper, Tugan triumphantly claims to have 'proved' that accumulation runs smoothly like clockwork, even if the absolute volume of consumption decreases. Even he must admit in the end, however, that his assumption of such an absolute decrease of the variable capital is in striking contrast to reality. Variable capital is in point of fact a growing quantity in all capitalist countries; only in relation to the even more rapid growth of constant capital can it be said to decrease. On the basis of what is actually happening, namely a greater yearly increase of constant capital as against that of variable capital, as well as a growing rate of surplus value, discrepancies must arise between the material composition of the social product and the composition of capital in terms of value. If, instead of the unchanging proportion of 5 to 1 between constant and variable capital, proposed by Marx's diagram, we assume for instance that this increase of capital is accompanied by a progressive readjustment of its composition, the proportion between constant and variable in the second year being 6 to 1, in the third year 7 to 1, and in the fourth year 8 to 1—if we further assume that the rate of surplus value also increases progressively in accordance with the higher productivity of labour so that, in each case, we have the same amounts as those of the diagram, although, because of the relatively decreasing variable capital, the rate of surplus value does not remain constant at the original 100 per cent—and if finally we assume that one-half of the appropriated surplus value is capitalised in each case (excepting Department II where capitalisation exceeds 50 per cent, 184 out of 285 being capitalised during the first year), the result will be as follows:

1st year:
    I. $5,000c + 1,000v + 1,000s = 7,000$ means of production
    II. $1,430c + 285v + 285s = 2,000$ means of subsistence
2nd year:
    I. $5,428\frac{4}{7}c + 1,071\frac{3}{7}v + 1,083s = 7,583$ means of production
    II. $1,587\frac{5}{7}c + 311\frac{2}{7}v + 316s = 2,215$ means of subsistence
3rd year:
    I. $5,903c + 1,139v + 1,173s = 8,215$ means of production
    II. $1,726c + 331v + 342s = 2,399$ means of subsistence
4th year:
    I. $6,424c + 1,205v + 1,271s = 8,900$ means of production
    II. $1,879c + 350v + 371s = 2,600$ means of subsistence

If this were a true picture of the accumulative process, the means of production (constant capital) would show a deficit of 16 in the second year, of 45 in the third year and of 88 in the fourth year; similarly, the means of subsistence would show a surplus of 16 in the second year, of 45 in the third year and of 88 in the fourth year.

This negative balance for the means of production may be only imaginary in part. The increasing productivity of labour ensures that the means of production grow faster in bulk than in value, in other words: means of production become cheaper. As it is use value, i.e. the material elements of capital, which is relevant for technical improvements of production, we may assume that the quantity of means of production, in spite of their lower value, will suffice for progressive accumulation up to a certain point. This phenomenon amongst others also checks the actual decline of the rate of profit and modifies it to a mere tendency, though our example shows that the decline of the profit rate would not only be retarded but rather completely arrested. On the other hand, the same fact indicates a much larger surplus of unsaleable means of subsistence than is suggested by the amount of this surplus in terms of value. In that case, we should have to compel the capitalists of Department II to consume this surplus themselves, which Marx makes them do on other occasions; in which case, and in so far as those capitalists are concerned, there would again be no accumulation but rather simple reproduction. Alternatively, we should have to pronounce this whole surplus unsaleable.

Yet would it not be very easy to make good this loss in means of production which results from our example? We need only assume that the capitalists of Department I capitalise their surplus value to a greater extent. Indeed, there is no valid reason to suppose, as Marx did, that the capitalists in each case add only half their surplus value to their capital. Advances in labour productivity may well lead to progressively increasing capitalisation of surplus value. This assumption is the more permissible in that the cheapening of consumer goods for the capitalist class, too, is one of the consequences of technological progress. The relative decrease in the value of consumable income (as compared with the capitalised part) may then permit of the same or even a higher standard of living for this class. We might for instance make good the deficit in producer goods by transferring a corresponding part of surplus value I to the constant capital of this department, a part which would otherwise be consumed, since this surplus value, like all other products of the department, originally takes the form of producer goods; $11\frac{1}{3}$; would then be transferred in the second year, 34 in the third year and

66 in the fourth year.[9] The solution of one difficulty, however, only adds to another. It goes without saying that if the capitalists of Department I relatively restrict their consumption for purposes of accumulation, there will be a proportionately greater unsaleable residue of consumer goods in Department II; and thus it becomes more and more impossible to enlarge the constant capital even on its previous technological basis. If the capitalists in Department I relatively restrict their consumption, the capitalists of Department II must relatively expand their personal consumption in proportion. The assumption of accelerated accumulation in Department I would then have to be supplemented by that of retarded accumulation in Department II, technical progress in one department by regression in the other.

These results are not due to mere chance. The adjustments we have tried out on Marx's diagram are merely meant to illustrate that technical progress, as he himself admits, must be accompanied by a relative growth of constant as against variable capital. Hence the necessity for a continuous revision of the ratio in which capitalised surplus value should be allotted to c and v respectively. In Marx's diagram, however, the capitalists are in no position to make these allocations at will, since the material form of their surplus value predetermines the forms of capitalisation. Since, according to Marx's assumption, all expansion of production proceeds exclusively by means of its own, capitalistically produced means of production and subsistence,—since there are here no other places and forms of production and equally no other consumers than the two departments with their capitalists and workers,— and since, on the other hand, the smooth working of the accumulative process depends on that circulation should wholly absorb the aggregate product of both departments, the technological shape of enlarged reproduction is in consequence strictly prescribed by the material form of the surplus product. In other words: according to Marx's diagram, the technical organisation of expanded production can and must be such as to make use of the aggregate surplus value produced in Departments I and II. In this connection we must bear in mind also that

---

[9] The figures result from the difference between the amounts of constant capital in Department I under conditions of technical progress, and under Marx's stable conditions.

both departments can obtain their respective elements of production only by means of mutual exchange. Thus the allocation to constant or variable capital of the surplus value earmarked for capitalisation, as well as the allotment of the additional means of production and subsistence (for the workers) to Departments I and II is given in advance and determined by the relations between the two departments of the diagram—both in material and in terms of value. These relations themselves, however, reflect a quite determinate technical organisation of production. This implies that, on the assumptions of Marx's diagram, the techniques of production given in each case predetermine the techniques of the subsequent periods of enlarged reproduction, if accumulation continues. Assuming, that is to say, in accordance with Marx's diagram, that the expansion of capitalist production is always performed by means of the surplus value originally produced in form of capital, and further—or rather, conversely—that accumulation in one department is strictly department on accumulation in the other, then no change in the technical organisation of production can be possible in so far as the relation of c to v is concerned.

We may put our point in yet another way: it is clear that a quicker growth of constant as compared with variable capital, i.e. the progressive metamorphosis of the organic composition of capital, must take the material form of faster expansion of production in Department I as against production in Department II. Yet Marx's diagram, where strict conformity of the two departments is axiomatic, precludes any such fluctuations in the rate of accumulation in either department. It is quite legitimate to suppose that under the technical conditions of progressive accumulation, society would invest ever increasing portions of the surplus value earmarked for accumulation in Department I rather than in Department II. Both departments being only branches of the same social production—supplementary enterprises, if you like, of the 'aggregate capitalist',—such a progressive transfer, for technical reasons, from one department to the other of a part of the accumulated surplus value would be wholly feasible, especially as it corresponds to the actual practice of capital. Yet this assumption is possible only so long as we envisage the surplus value earmarked for capitalisation purely in terms of value. The diagram, however, implies that this part of the surplus value appears in a definite material form which prescribes its capitalisation. Thus the surplus value of Department II exists as means of subsistence, and since it is as such to be only realised by Department I, this intended transfer of part of the capitalised surplus value from Department II to Department I is ruled out, first because the material form of this surplus value is obviously useless to Department I, and secondly because of the relations of exchange between the two departments which would in turn necessitate an equivalent transfer of the products of Department I into Department II. It is therefore downright impossible to achieve a faster expansion of Department I as against Department II within the limits of Marx's diagram.

However we may regard the technological alterations of the mode of production in the course of accumulation, they cannot be accomplished without upsetting the fundamental relations of Marx's diagram.

And further: according to Marx's diagram, the capitalised surplus value is in each case immediately and completely absorbed by the productive process of the following period, for, apart from the portion earmarked for consumption, it has a natural form which allows of only one particular kind of employment. The diagram precludes the cashing and hoarding of surplus value in monetary form, as capital waiting to be invested. The free monetary forms of private capital, in Marx's view, are first the money deposited gradually against the wear and tear of the fixed capital, for its eventual renewal; and secondly those amounts of money which represent realised surplus value but are still too small for investment. From the point of view of the aggregate capital, both these sources of free money capital are negligible. For if we assume that even a portion of the social surplus value is realised in monetary form for purposes of future investment, then at once the question arises: who has bought the material items of this surplus value, and who has provided the money? If the answer is: other capitalists, of course,—then, seeing that the capitalist class is represented in the diagram by the two departments, this portion of the surplus value must also be regarded as invested *de facto*, as employed in the productive process. And so we are back at immediate and complete investment of the surplus value.

Or does the freezing of one part of the surplus value in monetary form in the hands of certain capitalists mean that other capitalists will be left with a corresponding part of that surplus product in its material form? does the hoarding of realised surplus value by some imply that others are no longer able to realise their surplus value, since the capitalists are the only buyers of surplus value? This would mean, however, that the smooth course of reproduction and similarly of accumulation as described in the diagram would be interrupted. The result would be a crisis, due not to over-production but to a mere intention to accumulate, the kind of crisis envisaged by Sismondi.

In one passage of his *Theories*,[10] Marx explains in so many words that he 'is not at all concerned in this connection with an accumulation of capital greater than can be used in the productive process and might lie idle in the banks in monetary form, with the consequence of lending abroad'. Marx refers these phenomena to the section on competition. Yet it is important to establish that his diagram veritably precludes the formation of such additional capital. Competition, however wide we may make the concept, obviously cannot create values, nor can it create capitals which are not themselves the result of the reproductive process.

The diagram thus precludes the expansion of production by leaps and bounds. It only allows of a gradual expansion which keeps strictly in step with the formation of the surplus value and is based upon the identity between realisation and capitalisation of the surplus value.

For the same reason, the diagram presumes an accumulation which affects both departments equally and therefore all branches of capitalist production. It precludes expansion of the demand by leaps and bounds just as much as it prevents a one-sided or precocious development of individual branches of capitalist production.

Thus the diagram assumes a movement of the aggregate capital which flies in the face of the actual course of capitalist development. At first sight, two facts are typical for the history of the capitalist mode of production: on the one hand the periodical expansion of the whole field of production by leaps and bounds, and on the other an extremely unequal development of the different branches of production. The history of the English cotton industry from the first quarter of the eighteenth to the seventies of the nineteenth century, the most characteristic chapter in the history of the capitalist mode of production, appears quite inexplicable from the point of view of Marx's diagram.

---

[10] *Theorien über den Mehrwert*, vol. ii, part 2, p. 252.

Finally, the diagram contradicts the conception of the capitalist total process and its course as laid down by Marx in *Capital*, volume iii. This conception is based on the inherent contradiction between the unlimited expansive capacity of the productive forces and the limited expansive capacity of social consumption under conditions of capitalist distribution. Let us see how Marx describes this contradiction in detail in chapter 15 on 'Unravelling the Internal Contradictions of the Law' (of the declining profit rate):

'The creation of surplus-value, assuming the necessary means of production, or sufficient accumulation of capital, to be existing, finds no other limit but the labouring population, when the rate of surplus-value, that is, the intensity of exploitation, is given; and no other limit but the intensity of exploitation, when the labouring population is given. And the capitalist process of production consists essentially of the production of surplus-value, materialised in the surplus-product, which is that aliquot portion of the produced commodities, in which unpaid labour is materialised. It must never be forgotten, that the production of this surplus-value—and the reconversion of a portion of it into capital, or accumulation, forms an indispensable part of this production of surplus-value—is the immediate purpose and the compelling motive of capitalist production. It will not do to represent capitalist production as something which it is not, that is to say, as a production having for its immediate purpose the consumption of goods, or the production of means of enjoyment for the capitalists. (And, of course, even less for the worker. R. L.) This would be overlooking the specific character of capitalist production, which reveals itself in its innermost essence. The creation of this surplus-value is the object of the direct process of production, and this process has no other limits than those mentioned above. As soon as the available quantity of surplus-value has been materialised in commodities, surplus-value has been produced. But this production of surplus-value is but the first act of the capitalist process of production, it merely terminates the act of direct production. Capital has absorbed so much unpaid labour. With the development of the process, which expresses itself through a falling tendency of the rate of profit, the mass of surplus-value thus produced is swelled to immense dimensions. Now comes the second act of the process. The entire mass of commodities, the total product, which contains a portion which is to reproduce the constant and variable capital as well as a portion representing surplus-value, must be sold. If this is not done, or only partly accomplished, or only at prices which are below the prices of production, the labourer has been none the less exploited, but his exploitation does not realise as much for the capitalist. It may yield no surplus-value at all for him, or only realise a portion of the produced surplus-value, or it may even mean a partial or complete loss of his capital. The conditions of direct exploitation and those of the realisation of surplus-value are not identical. They are separated logically as well as by time and space. The first are only limited by the productive power of society, the last by the proportional relations of the various lines of production and by the consuming power of society. This last-named power is not determined either by the absolute productive power or by the absolute consuming power, but by the consuming power based on antagonistic conditions of distribution, which reduces the consumption of the great mass of the population to a variable minimum within more or less narrow limits. The consuming power is furthermore restricted by the tendency to accumulate, the greed for an expansion of capital and a production of surplus-value on an enlarged scale. This is a law of capitalist production imposed by incessant revolutions in the methods of production themselves, the resulting depreciation of existing capital, the general competitive struggle and the necessity of improving the product and expanding the scale of production, for the sake of self-preservation and on penalty of failure. The market must, therefore, be continually extended, so that its interrelations and the conditions regulating them assume more and more the form of a natural law independent of the producers and become ever more uncontrollable. This eternal contradiction seeks to balance itself by an expansion of the outlying fields of production. But to the extent that the productive power develops, it finds itself at variance with the narrow basis on which the conditions of consumption rest. On this self-contradictory basis it is no contradiction at all that there should be an excess of capital simultaneously with an excess of population. For while a combination of these two would indeed increase the mass of the produced surplus-value, it would at the same time intensify the contradiction between the conditions under which this surplus-value is produced and those under which it is realised.'[11]

If we compare this description with the diagram of enlarged reproduction, the two are by no means in conformity. According to the diagram, there is no inherent contradiction between the production of the surplus value and its realisation, rather, the two are identical. The surplus value here from the very beginning comes into being in a natural form exclusively designed for the requirements of accumulation. In fact it leaves the place of production in the very form of additional capital, that is to say it is capable of realisation in the capitalist process of accumulation. The capitalists, as a class, see to it in advance that the surplus value they appropriate is produced entirely in that material form which will permit and ensure its employment for purposes of further accumulation. Realisation and accumulation of the surplus value here are both aspects of the same process, they are logically identical. Therefore according to the presentation of the reproductive process in the diagram, society's capacity to consume does not put a limit to production. Here production automatically expands year by year, although the capacity of society for consumption has not gone beyond its 'antagonistic conditions of distribution'. This automatic continuation of expansion, of accumulation, truly is the 'law of capitalist production . . . on penalty of failure'. Yet according to the analysis in volume iii, 'the market must, therefore, be continually extended', 'the market' obviously transcending the consumption of capitalists and workers. And if Tugan Baranovski interprets the following passage 'this eternal contradiction seeks to balance itself by an expansion of the outlying fields of production' as if Marx had meant production itself by 'outlying fields of production', he violates not only the spirit of the language but also Marx's clear train of thought. The 'outlying fields of production' are clearly and unequivocally not production itself but consumption which 'must be continually extended'. The following passage in *Theorien über den Mehrwert*, amongst others, sufficiently shows that Marx had this in mind and nothing else: 'Ricardo therefore consistently denies the necessity for an *expansion of the market* to accompany the expansion of production and the growth of capital. The entire

---

[11] *Capital*, vol. iii, pp. 285 ff.

capital existing within a country can also be profitably used in that country. He therefore argues against Adam Smith who had set up his (Ricardo's) opinion on the one hand but also contradicted it with his usual sure instinct.'[12]

In yet another passage, Marx clearly shows that Tugan Baranovski's notion of production for production's sake is wholly alien to him: 'Besides, we have seen in volume ii part iii that a continuous circulation takes place between constant capital and constant capital (even without considering any accelerated accumulation), which is in so far independent of individual consumption, as it never enters into such consumption, but which is nevertheless definitely limited by it, because the production of constant capital never takes place for its own sake, but solely because more of this capital is needed in those spheres of production whose products pass into individual consumption.'[13]

Admittedly, in the diagram in volume ii, Tugan Baranovski's sole support, market and production coincide—they are one and the same. Expansion of the market here means extended production, since production is said to be its own exclusive market—the consumption of the workers being an element of production, i.e. the reproduction of variable capital. Therefore the limit for both the expansion of production and the extension of the market is one and the same: it is given by the volume of the social capital, or the stage of accumulation already attained. The greater the quantity of surplus value that has been extracted in the natural form of capital, the more can be accumulated; and the greater the volume of accumulation, the more surplus value can be invested in its material form of capital, i.e. the more can be realised. Thus the diagram does not admit the contradiction outlined in the analysis of volume iii. In the process described by the diagram there is no need for a continual extension of the market beyond the consumption of capitalists and workers, nor is the limited social capacity for consumption an obstacle to the smooth course of production and its unlimited capacity for expansion. The diagram does indeed permit of crises but only because of a lack of proportion within production, because of a defective social control over the productive process. It

---

[12] *Theorien* . . ., vol. ii, part 2, p. 305.
[13] *Capital*, vol. iii, p. 359.

precludes, however, the deep and fundamental antagonism between the capacity to consume and the capacity to produce in a capitalist society, a conflict resulting from the very accumulation of capital which periodically bursts out in crises and spurs capital on to a continual extension of the market.

26

THE REPRODUCTION OF CAPITAL AND ITS SOCIAL SETTING

Marx's diagram of enlarged reproduction cannot explain the actual and historical process of accumulation. And why? Because of the very premises of the diagram. The diagram sets out to describe the accumulative process on the assumption that the capitalists and workers are the sole agents of capitalist consumption. We have seen that Marx consistently and deliberately assumes the universal and exclusive domination of the capitalist mode of production as a theoretical premise of his analysis in all three volumes of *Capital*. Under these conditions, there can admittedly be no other classes of society than capitalists and workers; as the diagram has it, all 'third persons' of capitalist society—civil servants, the liberal professions, the clergy, etc.—must, as consumers, be counted in with these two classes, and preferably with the capitalist class. This axiom, however, is a theoretical contrivance—real life has never known a self-sufficient capitalist society under the exclusive domination of the capitalist mode of production. This theoretical device is perfectly admissible so long as it merely helps to demonstrate the problem in its integrity and does not interfere with its very conditions. A case in point is the analysis of simple reproduction of the aggregate social capital, where the problem itself rests upon a fiction: in a society producing by capitalist methods, i.e. a society which creates surplus value, the whole of the latter is taken to be consumed by the capitalists who appropriate it. The object is to present the forms of social production and reproduction under these given conditions. Here the very formulation of the problem implies that production knows no other consumers than capitalists and workers and thus strictly conforms to Marx's premise: universal and exclusive domination of the capitalist mode of production. The implications of both fictions are the same. Similarly, it is quite legitimate to postulate absolute dominance of capital in an analysis of the accumulation of individual capitals, such as is given in *Capital*, volume i. The reproduction of individual capitals is an element in total social reproduction but one which follows an independent course, contrary to the movements of the other elements. In consequence it will not do simply to take together the individual movements of the respective capitals in order to arrive at the total movement of social capital, since the latter is essentially different. The natural conditions of reproducing individual capitals therefore neither conform with one another, nor do they conform to the relations of the total capital. Under normal conditions of circulation, every individual capital engages in the process of circulation and of accumulation entirely on its own account, depending upon others only in so far, of course, as it is compelled to find a market for its product and must find available the means of production it requires for its specific activities. Whether the strata who afford this market and provide the necessary means of production are themselves capitalist producers or not is completely immaterial for the individual capital, although, in theory, the most favourable premise for analysing the accumulation of individual capital is the assumption that capitalist production has attained universal and exclusive domination and is the sole setting of this process.[1]

Now, however, the question arises whether the assumptions which

[1] 'If capital and the productivity of labour advance and the standard of capitalist production in general is on a higher level of development, then there is a correspondingly greater mass of commodities passing through the market from production to individual and industrial consumption, greater certainty that each particular capital will find the conditions for its reproduction available in the market' (*Theorien* . . ., vol. ii, part 2, p. 251).

were decisive in the case of individual capital, are also legitimate for the consideration of aggregate capital.

'We must now put the problem in this form: *given universal accumulation, that is to say provided that in all branches of production there is greater or less accumulation of capital*—which in fact is a condition of capitalist production, and which is just as natural to the capitalist *qua* capitalist as it is natural to the miser to amass money (but which is also necessary for the perpetuation of capitalist production)—what are the *conditions* of this universal accumulation, to what elements can it be reduced?'

And the answer: '*The conditions for the accumulation of capital are precisely those which rule its original production and reproduction in general*: these conditions being that one part of the money buys labour and the other commodities (raw materials, machinery, etc.) . . . Accumulation of new capital can only proceed therefore under the same conditions under which already existing capital is reproduced.'[2]

In real life the actual conditions for the accumulation of the aggregate capital are quite different from those prevailing for individual capitals and for simple reproduction. The problem amounts to this: If an increasing part of the surplus value is not consumed by the capitalists but employed in the expansion of production, what, then, are the forms of social reproduction? What is left of the social product after deductions for the replacement of the constant capital cannot, *ex hypothesi*, be absorbed by the consumption of the workers and capitalists—this being the main aspect of the problem—nor can the workers and capitalists themselves realise the aggregate product. They can always only realise the variable capital, that part of the constant capital which will be used up, and the part of the surplus value which will be consumed, but in this way they merely ensure that production can be renewed on its previous scale. The workers and capitalists themselves cannot possibly realise that part of the surplus value which is to be capitalised. Therefore, the realisation of the surplus value for the purposes of accumulation is an impossible task for a society which consists solely of workers and capitalists. Strangely enough, all theorists who analysed the problem of accumulation, from Ricardo and Sismondi to

---

[2] *Theorien* . . ., vol. ii, part 2, p. 250: *Akkumulation von Kapital und Krisen*. (The Accumulation of Capital and the Crises.) Marx's italics.

Marx, started with the very assumption which makes their problem insoluble. A sure instinct that realisation of the surplus value requires 'third persons', that is to say consumers other than the immediate agents of capitalist production (i.e. workers and capitalists) led to all kinds of subterfuges: 'unproductive consumption' as presented by Malthus in the person of the feudal landowner, by Vorontsov in militarism, by Struve in the 'liberal professions' and other hangers-on of the capitalist class; or else foreign trade is brought into play which proved a useful safety valve to all those who regarded accumulation with scepticism, from Sismondi to Nicolayon. Because of these insoluble difficulties, others like v. Kirchmann and Rodbertus tried to do without accumulation altogether, or, like Sismondi and his Russian 'populist' followers, stressed the need for at least putting the dampers on accumulation as much as possible.

The salient feature of the problem of accumulation, and the vulnerable point of earlier attempts to solve it, has only been shown up by Marx's more profound analysis, his precise diagrammatic demonstration of the total reproductive process, and especially his inspired exposition of the problem of simple reproduction. Yet he could not supply immediately a finished solution either, partly because he broke off his analysis almost as soon as he had begun it, and partly because he was then preoccupied, as we have shown, with denouncing the analysis of Adam Smith and thus rather lost sight of the main problem. In fact, he made the solution even more difficult by assuming the capitalist mode of production to prevail universally. Nevertheless, a solution of the problem of accumulation, in harmony both with other parts of Marx's doctrine and with the historical experience and daily practice of capitalism, is implied in Marx's complete analysis of simple reproduction and his characterisation of the capitalist process as a whole which shows up its immanent contradictions and their development (in *Capital*, vol. iii). In the light of this, the deficiencies of the diagram can be corrected. All the relations being, as it were, incomplete, a closer study of the diagram of enlarged reproduction will reveal that it points to some sort of organisation more advanced than purely capitalist production and accumulation.

Up to now we have only considered one aspect of enlarged reproduction, the problem of realising the surplus value, whose difficulties hitherto had claimed the sceptics' whole attention. Realisation of the surplus value is doubtless a vital question of capitalist accumulation. It requires as its prime condition—ignoring, for simplicity's sake, the capitalists' fund of consumption altogether—that there should be strata of buyers outside capitalist society. Buyers, it should be noted, not consumers, since the material form of the surplus value is quite irrelevant to its realisation. The decisive fact is that the surplus value cannot be realised by sale either to workers or to capitalists, but only if it is sold to such social organisations or strata whose own mode of production is not capitalistic. Here we can conceive of two different cases:

(1) Capitalist production supplies consumer goods over and above its own requirements, the demand of its workers and capitalists, which are bought by non-capitalist strata and countries. The English cotton industry, for instance, during the first two-thirds of the nineteenth century, and to some extent even now, has been supplying cotton textiles to the peasants and petty-bourgeois townspeople of the European continent, and to the peasants of India, America, Africa and so on. The enormous expansion of the English cotton industry was thus founded on consumption by non-capitalist strata and countries.[3] In England herself, this flourishing cotton industry called forth large-scale development in the production of industrial machinery (bobbins and weaving-looms), and further in the metal and coal industries and so

[3] The following figures plainly show the importance of the cotton industry for English exports:

In 1893, cotton exports to the amount of £64,000,000 made up 23 per cent, and iron and other metal exports not quite 17 per cent, of the total export of manufactured goods, amounting to £277,000,000 in all.

In 1898, cotton exports to the amount of £65,000,000 made up 28 per cent, and metal exports 22 per cent, of the total export of manufactured goods, amounting to £233,400,000 in all.

In comparison, the figures for the German Empire show the following result: In 1898, cotton exports to the amount of £11,595,000 made up 5.75 per cent of the total exports, amounting to £200,500,000. 5,250,000,000 yards of cotton bales were exported in 1898, 2,250,000,000 of them to India (E. Jaffé: *Die englische Baumwollindustrie und die Organisation des Exporthandels*. Schmoller's Jahrbücher, vol. xxiv, p. 1033).

In 1908, British exports of cotton yarn alone amounted to £13,100,000 (*Statist. Jahrb. für das Deutsche Reich*, 1910).

on. In this instance, Department II realised its products to an increasing extent by sale to non-capitalist social strata, and by its own accumulation it created on its part an increasing demand for the home produce of Department I, thus helping the latter to realise its surplus value and to increase its own accumulation.

(2) Conversely, capitalist production supplies means of production in excess of its own demand and finds buyers in non-capitalist countries. English industry, for instance, in the first half of the nineteenth century supplied materials for the construction of railroads in the American and Australian states. (The building of railways cannot in itself be taken as evidence for the domination of capitalist production in a country. As a matter of fact, the railways in this case provided only one of the first conditions for the inauguration of capitalist production.) Another example would be the German chemical industry which supplies means of production such as dyes in great quantities to Asiatic, African and other countries whose own production is not capitalistic.[4] Here Department I realises its products in extra-capitalist circles. The resulting progressive expansion of Department I gives rise to a corresponding expansion of Department II in the same (capitalistically producing) country in order to supply the means of subsistence for the growing army of workers in Department I.

Each of these cases differs from Marx's diagram. In one case, the product of Department II exceeds the needs of both departments, measured by the variable capital and the consumed part of the surplus value. In the second case, the product of Department I exceeds the volume of constant capital in both departments, enlarged though it is for the purpose of expanding production. In both cases, the surplus value does not come into being in that natural form which would make its capitalisation in either department possible and necessary. These two prototypes continually overlap in real life, supplement each other and merge.

In this contest, one point seems still obscure. The surplus of consumer goods, say cotton fabrics, which is sold to non-capitalist countries, does not exclusively represent surplus value, but, as a capitalist

---

[4] One-fifth of German aniline dyes, and one-half of her indigo, goes to countries such as China, Japan, British India, Egypt, Asiatic Turkey, Brazil, and Mexico.

commodity, it embodies also constant and variable capital. It seems quite arbitrary to assume that just those commodities which are sold outside the capitalist strata of society should represent nothing but surplus value. On the other hand, Department I clearly can in this case not only realise its surplus value but also accumulate, and that without requiring another market for its product than the two departments of capitalist production. Yet both these objections are only apparent. All we need remember is that each component of the aggregate product represents a proportion of the total value, that under conditions of capitalist production not only the aggregate product but every single commodity contains surplus value; which consideration does not prevent the individual capitalist, however, from computing that the sale of his specific commodities must first reimburse him for his outlay on constant capital and secondly replace his variable capital (or, rather loosely, but in accordance with actual practice: it must first replace his fixed, and then his circulating capital); what then remains will go down as profit. Similarly, we can divide the aggregate social product into three proportionate parts which, in terms of value, correspond to (1) the constant capital that has been used up in society, (2) the variable capital, and (3) the extracted surplus value. In the case of simple reproduction these proportions are also reflected in the material shape of the aggregate product: the constant capital materialises as means of production, the variable capital as means of subsistence for the workers, and the surplus value as means of subsistence for the capitalist. Yet as we know, the concept of simple reproduction with consumption of the entire surplus value by the capitalists is a mere fiction. As for enlarged reproduction or accumulation, in Marx's diagram the composition of the social product in terms of value is also strictly in proportion to its material form: the surplus value, or rather that part of it which is earmarked for capitalisation, has from the very beginning the form of material means of production and means of subsistence for the workers in a ratio appropriate to the expansion of production on a given technical basis. As we have seen, this conception, which is based upon the self-sufficiency and isolation of capitalist production, falls down as soon as we consider the realisation of the surplus value. If we assume, however, that the surplus value is realised outside the sphere of capitalist production, then its material form is independent of the requirements of capitalist production itself. Its material form conforms to the requirements of those non-capitalist circles who help to realise it, that is to say, capitalist surplus value can take the form of consumer goods, e.g. cotton fabrics, or of means of production, e.g. materials for railway construction, as the case may be. If one department realises its surplus value by exporting its products, and with the ensuing expansion of production helps the other department to realise its surplus value on the home market, then the fact still remains that the *social* surplus value must yet be taken as realised outside the two departments, either mediately or immediately. Similar considerations enable the individual capitalist to realise his surplus value, even if the whole of his commodities can only replace either the variable or the constant capital of another capitalist.

Nor is the realisation of the surplus value the only vital aspect of reproduction. Given that Department I has disposed of its surplus value outside, thereby starting the process of accumulation, and further, that it can expect a new increase in the demand in non-capitalist circles, these two conditions add up to only half of what is required for accumulation. There is many a slip 'twixt the cup and the lip. The second requirement of accumulation is access to material elements necessary for expanding reproduction. Seeing that we have just turned the surplus product of Department I into money by getting rid of the surplus means of production to non-capitalist circles, from where are these material elements then to come? The transaction which is the portal for realising the surplus value is also, as it were, a backdoor out of which flies all possibility of converting this realised surplus value into productive capital—one leads to the nether regions and the other to the deep sea. Let us take a closer look.

Here we use *c* in both Departments I and II as if it were the entire constant capital in production. Yet this we know is wrong. Only for the sake of simplifying the diagram have we disregarded that the *c* which figures in Departments I and II of the diagram is only part of the aggregate constant capital of society, that is to say that part which, circulating during one year, is used up and embodied in the products of one period of production. Yet it would be perfectly absurd if capitalist production— or any other—would use up its entire constant capital and create it anew in every period of production. On the contrary, we assume that the whole mass of means of production, for the periodical total renewal of which the diagram provides in annual instalments—renewal of the used-up part—lies at the back of production as presented in the diagram. With progressing labour productivity and an expanding volume of production, this mass increases not only absolutely but also relatively to the part which is consumed in production in every case, together with a corresponding increase in the efficiency of the constant capital. It is the more intensive exploitation of this part of the constant capital, irrespective of its increase in value, which is of paramount importance for the expansion of production.

'In the extractive industries, mines, etc., the raw materials form no part of the capital advanced. The subject of labour is in this case not a product of previous labour, but is furnished by Nature gratis, as in the case of metals, minerals, coal, stone, etc. In these cases the constant capital consists almost exclusively of instruments of labour, which can very well absorb an increased quantity of labour (day and night shifts of labourers, e.g.). All other things being equal, the mass and value of the product will rise in direct proportion to the labour expended. As on the first day of production, the original produce-formers, now turned into the creators of the material elements of capital—man and Nature—still work together. Thanks to the elasticity of labour-power, the domain of accumulation has extended without any previous enlargement of constant capital.—In agriculture the land under cultivation cannot be increased without the advance of more seed and manure. But this advance once made, the purely mechanical working of the soil itself produces a marvellous effect on the amount of the product. A greater quantity of labour, done by the same number of labourers as before, thus increases the fertility, without requiring any new advance in the instruments of labour. It is once again the direct action of man on Nature which becomes an immediate source of greater accumulation, without the intervention of any new capital. Finally, in what is called manufacturing industry, every additional expenditure of labour presupposes a corresponding additional expenditure of raw materials, but not necessarily of instruments of labour. And as extractive industry and agriculture supply manufacturing industry with its raw materials and those of its instruments of labour, the additional, product the former have created without additional advance of capital, tells also in favour of the latter.—General result: by incorporating with itself the two primary creators of wealth, labour-power and the land, capital acquires a power of expansion that permits it to augment the elements of its accumulation beyond the limits apparently fixed by its own magnitude, or by the value and the mass of the means of production, already produced, in which it has its being.'[5]

In addition, there is no obvious reason why means of production and consumer goods should be produced by capitalist methods alone. This assumption, for all Marx used it as the corner-stone of his thesis, is in conformity neither with the daily practice, and the history, of capital, nor with the specific character of this mode of production. In the first half of the nineteenth century, a great part of the surplus value in England was produced in form of cotton fabrics. Yet the material elements for the capitalisation of this surplus value, although they certainly represented a surplus product, still were by no means all capitalist surplus value, to mention only raw cotton from the slave states of the American Union, or grain (a means of subsistence for the English workers) from the fields of serf-owning Russia. How much capitalist accumulation depends upon means of production which are not produced by capitalist methods is shown for example by the cotton crisis in England during the American War of Secession, when the cultivation of the plantations came to a standstill, or by the crisis of European linen-weaving during the war in the East, when flax could not be imported from serf-owning Russia. We need only recall that imports of corn raised by peasants—i.e. not produced by capitalist methods—played a vital part in the feeding of industrial labour, as an element, that is to say, of variable capital, for a further illustration of the close ties between non-capitalist strata and the material elements necessary to the accumulation of capital.

Moreover, capitalist production, by its very nature, cannot be restricted to such means of production as are produced by capitalist methods. Cheap elements of constant capital are essential to the individual capitalist who strives to increase his rate of profit. In addition, the very condition of continuous improvements in labour productivity as the most important method of increasing the rate of surplus value, is

[5] *Capital*, vol. i, pp. 615–16.

unrestricted utilisation of all substances and facilities afforded by nature and soil. To tolerate any restriction in this respect would be contrary to the very essence of capital, its whole mode of existence. After many centuries of development, the capitalist mode of production still constitutes only a fragment of total world production. Even in the small Continent of Europe, where it now chiefly prevails, it has not yet succeeded in dominating entire branches of production, such as peasant agriculture and the independent handicrafts; the same holds true, further, for large parts of North America and for a number of regions in the other continents. In general, capitalist production has hitherto been confined mainly to the countries in the temperate zone, whilst it made comparatively little progress in the East, for instance, and the South. Thus, if it were dependent exclusively on elements of production obtainable within such narrow limits, its present level and indeed its development in general would have been impossible. From the very beginning, the forms and laws of capitalist production aim to comprise the entire globe as a store of productive forces. Capital, impelled to appropriate productive forces for purposes of exploitation, ransacks the whole world, it procures its means of production from all corners of the earth, seizing them, if necessary by force, from all levels of civilisation and from all forms of society. The problem of the material elements of capitalist accumulation, far from being solved by the material form of the surplus value that has been produced, takes on quite a different aspect. It becomes necessary for capital progressively to dispose ever more fully of the whole globe, to acquire an unlimited choice of means of production, with regard to both quality and quantity, so as to find productive employment for the surplus value it has realised.

The process of accumulation, elastic and spasmodic as it is, requires inevitably free access to ever new areas of raw materials in case of need, both when imports from old sources fail or when social demand suddenly increases. When the War of Secession interfered with the import of American cotton, causing the notorious 'cotton famine' in the Lancashire district, new and immense cotton plantations sprang up in Egypt almost at once, as if by magic. Here it was Oriental despotism, combined with an ancient system of bondage, which had created a sphere of activity for European capital. Only capital with its technical resources can effect such a miraculous change in so short a time—but only on the pre-capitalist soil of more primitive social conditions can it develop the ascendancy necessary to achieve such miracles. Another example of the same kind is the enormous increase in the world consumption of rubber which at present (1912) necessitates a supply of latex to the value of £50,000,000 *per annum*. The economic basis for the production of raw materials is a primitive system of exploitation practised by European capital in the African colonies and in America, where the institutions of slavery and bondage are combined in various forms.[6]

It must be noted that, when we assumed above that only the surplus product of the first or the second department is realised in a non-capitalist milieu, we were taking the most favourable case for examining Marx's schemes, a case which shows the conditions of reproduction in its purity. In reality, nothing forces us to assume that there is not a fraction of the constant and variable capital which is also realised out of the capitalist realm. Accordingly, the expansion of production as well as the replacement in kind of the materials consumed in production may be undertaken by means of products from the non-capitalist sphere. What should be clear from the above-mentioned examples is the fact that, *at least*, it is impossible that the capitalised surplus value and the corresponding part of the capitalist output can be realised within the capitalist realm; this part must be sold out of the capitalist sphere, in social strata and forms which do not produce in capitalist way.

Between the production of surplus value, then, and the subsequent period of accumulation, two separate transactions take place—that of realising the surplus value, i.e. of converting it into pure value, and that of transforming this pure value into productive capital. They are

[6] The English Blue Book on the practices of the Peruvian Amazon Company, Ltd., in Putumayo, has recently revealed that in the free republic of Peru and without the political form of colonial supremacy, international capital can, to all intents and purposes, enslave the natives, so that it may appropriate the means of production of the primitive countries by exploitation on the greatest scale. Since 1900, this company, financed by English and foreign capitalists, has thrown upon the London market approximately 4,000 tons of Putumayo rubber. During this time, 30,000 natives were killed and most of the 10,000 survivors were crippled by beatings.

both dealings between capitalist production and the surrounding non-capitalist world. From the aspect both of realising the surplus value and of procuring the material elements of constant capital, international trade is a prime necessity for the historical existence of capitalism—an international trade which under actual conditions is essentially an exchange between capitalistic and non-capitalistic modes of production.

Hitherto we have considered accumulation solely with regard to surplus value and constant capital. The third element of accumulation is variable capital which increases with progressive accumulation. In Marx's diagram, the social product contains ever more means of subsistence for the workers as the material form proper to this variable capital. The variable capital, however, is not really the means of subsistence for the workers but is in fact living labour for whose reproduction these means of subsistence are necessary. One of the fundamental conditions of accumulation is therefore a supply of living labour which can be mobilised by capital to meet its demands. This supply can be increased under favourable conditions—but only up to a certain point—by longer hours and more intensive work. Both these methods of increasing the supply, however, do not enlarge the variable capital, or do so only to a small extent (e.g. payment for overtime). Moreover, they are confined to definite and rather narrow limits which they cannot exceed owing to both natural and social causes. The increasing growth of variable capital which accompanies accumulation must therefore become manifest in ever greater numbers of employed labour. Where can this additional labour be found?

In his analysis of the accumulation of individual capital, Marx gives the following answer: 'Now in order to allow of these elements actually functioning as capital, the capitalist class requires additional labour. If the exploitation of the labourers already employed does not increase, either extensively or intensively, then additional labour-power must be found. For this the mechanism of capitalist production provides beforehand, by converting the working class into a class dependent on wages, a class whose ordinary wages suffice, not only for its maintenance, but for its increase. It is only necessary for capital to incorporate this additional labour-power, annually supplied by the working class in the shape of labourers of all ages, with the surplus means of production comprised in the annual produce, and the conversion of surplus-value into capital is complete.'[7]

Thus the increase in the variable capital is directly and exclusively attributed to the natural physical increase of a working class already dominated by capital. This is in strict conformity with the diagram of enlarged reproduction which recognises only the social classes of capitalists and workers, and regards the capitalist mode of production as exclusive and absolute. On these assumptions, the natural increase of the working class is the only source of extending the labour supply commanded by capital. This view, however, is contrary to the laws governing the process of accumulation. The natural propagation of the workers and the requirements of accumulating capital are not correlative in respect of time or quantity. Marx himself has most brilliantly shown that natural propagation cannot keep up with the sudden expansive needs of capital. If natural propagation were the only foundation for the development of capital, accumulation, in its periodical swings from overstrain to exhaustion, could not continue, nor could the productive sphere expand by leaps and bounds, and accumulation itself would become impossible. The latter requires an unlimited freedom of movement in respect of the growth of variable capital equal to that which it enjoys with regard to the elements of constant

[7] *Capital*, vol. i, p. 594. Similarly in another passage: 'One part of the surplus value, of the surplus means of subsistence produced, must then be converted into variable capital for the purpose of purchasing new labour. This can only be done if the number of workers grows or if their working time is prolonged. . . . This, however, cannot be considered a ready measure for accumulation. The working population can increase if formerly unproductive workers are transformed into productive ones, or if parts of the population who previously performed no work, such as women, children and paupers, are drawn into the process of production. Here, however, we shall ignore this aspect. Lastly, the working population can increase through an absolute increase in population. If accumulation is to proceed steadily and continuously, it must be grounded in an absolute growth of the population, though this may decline in comparison with the capital employed. An expanding population appears as the basis of accumulation conceived as a steady process. An indispensable condition for this is an average wage which is adequate not only to the reproduction of the working population but permits its continual increase' (*Theorien über den Mehrwert*, vol. ii, part 2, in the chapter on 'Transformation of Revenue Into Capital' (*Verwandlung von Revenue in Kapital*), p. 243).

capital—that is to say it must needs dispose over the supply of labour power without restriction. Marx considers that this can be achieved by an 'industrial reserve army of workers'. His diagram of simple reproduction admittedly does not recognise such an army, nor could it have room for it, since the natural propagation of the capitalist wage proletariat cannot provide an industrial reserve army. Labour for this army is recruited from social reservoirs outside the dominion of capital—it is drawn into the wage proletariat only if need arises. Only the existence of non-capitalist groups and countries can guarantee such a supply of additional labour power for capitalist production. Yet in his analysis of the industrial reserve army[8] Marx only allows for (a) the displacement of older workers by machinery, (b) an influx of rural workers into the towns in consequence of the ascendancy of capitalist production in agriculture, (c) occasional labour that has dropped out of industry, and (d) finally the lowest residue of relative over-population, the paupers. All these categories are cast off by the capitalist system of production in some form or other, they constitute a wage proletariat that is worn out and made redundant one way or another. Marx, obviously influenced by English conditions involving a high level of capitalist development, held that the rural workers who continually migrate to the towns belong to the wage proletariat, since they were formerly dominated by agricultural capital and now become subject to industrial capital. He ignores, however, the problem which is of paramount importance for conditions on the continent of Europe, namely the sources from which this urban and rural proletariat is recruited: the continual process by which the rural and urban middle strata become proletarian with the decay of peasant economy and of small artisan enterprises, the very process, that is to say, of incessant transition from non-capitalist to capitalist conditions of a labour power that is cast off by pre-capitalist, not capitalist, modes of production in their progressive breakdown and disintegration. Besides the decay of European peasants and artisans we must here also mention the disintegration of the most varied primitive forms of production and of social organisation in non-European countries.

Since capitalist production can develop fully only with complete

[8] *Capital*, vol. i, pp. 642 ff.

access to all territories and climes, it can no more confine itself to the natural resources and productive forces of the temperate zone than it can manage with white labour alone. Capital needs other races to exploit territories where the white man cannot work. It must be able to mobilise world labour power without restriction in order to utilise all productive forces of the globe—up to the limits imposed by a system of producing surplus value. This labour power, however, is in most cases rigidly bound by the traditional pre-capitalist organisation of production. It must first be 'set free' in order to be enrolled in the active army of capital. The emancipation of labour power from primitive social conditions and its absorption by the capitalist wage system is one of the indispensable historical bases of capitalism. For the first genuinely capitalist branch of production, the English cotton industry, not only the cotton of the Southern states of the American Union was essential, but also the millions of African Negroes who were shipped to America to provide the labour power for the plantations, and who later, as a free proletariat, were incorporated in the class of wage labourers in a capitalist system.[9] Obtaining the necessary labour power from non-capitalist societies, the so-called 'labour-problem', is ever more important for capital in the colonies. All possible methods of 'gentle compulsion' are applied to solving this problem, to transfer labour from former social systems to the command of capital. This endeavour leads to the most peculiar combinations between the modern wage

[9] A table published in the United States shortly before the War of Secession contained the following data about the value of the annual production of the Slave States and the number of slaves employed—for the greatest part on cotton plantations:

Year	Cotton: Dollars	Slaves
1800	5,200,000	893,041
1810	15,000,000	1,191,364
1820	26,300,000	1,543,688
1830	34,100,000	2,009,053
1840	74,600,000	2,487,255
1850	101,800,000	3,197,509
1851	137,300,000	3,200,000

(Simons, 'Class Struggles in American History'. Supplement to *Neue Zeit* (*Klassenkämpfe in der Geschichte Amerikas. Ergänzungsheft der 'Neuen Zeit'*), Nr. 7, p. 39.)

system and primitive authority in the colonial countries.[10] This is a concrete example of the fact that capitalist production cannot manage without labour power from other social organisations.

[10] Bryce, a former English Minister, describes a model pattern of such hybrid forms in the South African diamond mines: 'The most striking sight at Kimberley, and one unique in the world, is furnished by the two so-called "compounds" in which the natives who work in the mines are housed and confined. They are huge inclosures, unroofed, but covered with a wire netting to prevent anything from being thrown out of them over the walls, and with a subterranean entrance to the adjoining mine. The mine is worked on the system of three eight-hour shifts, so that the workman is never more than eight hours together underground. Round the interior of the wall are built sheds or huts in which the natives live and sleep when not working. A hospital is also provided within the inclosure, as well as a school where the work-people can spend their leisure in learning to read and write. No spirits are sold. . . . Every entrance is strictly guarded, and no visitors, white or native, are permitted, all supplies being obtained from the store within, kept by the company. The De Beers mine compound contained at the time of my visit 2,600 natives, belonging to a great variety of tribes, so that here one could see specimens of the different native types from Natal and Pondoland, in the south, to the shores of Lake Tanganyika in the far north. They come from every quarter, attracted by the high wages, usually eighteen to thirty shillings a week, and remain for three months or more, and occasionally even for longer periods . . . In the vast oblong compound one sees Zulus from Natal, Fingos, Pondos, Tembus, Basutos, Bechuanas, Gungunhana's subjects from the Portuguese territories, some few Matabili and Makalaka; and plenty of Zambesi boys from the tribes on both sides of that great river, a living ethnological collection such as can be examined nowhere else in South Africa. Even Bushmen, or at least natives with some Bushman blood in them, are not wanting. They live peaceably together, and amuse themselves in their several ways during their leisure hours. Besides games of chance, we saw a game resembling "fox and geese" played with pebbles on a board; and music was being discoursed on two rude native instruments, the so-called "Kaffir piano" made of pieces of iron of unequal length fastened side by side in a frame, and a still ruder contrivance of hard bits of wood, also of unequal size, which when struck by a stick emit different notes, the first beginning of a tune. A very few were reading or writing letters, the rest busy with their cooking or talking to one another. Some tribes are incessant talkers, and in this strange mixing-pot of black men one may hear a dozen languages spoken as one passes from group to group' (James Bryce, *Impressions of South Africa*, London, 1897, pp. 242 ff.).

After several months of work, the negro as a rule leaves the mine with the wages he has saved up. He returns to his tribe, buying a wife with his money, and lives again his traditional life. Cf. also in the same book the most lively description of the methods used in South Africa to solve the 'labour-problem'. Here we are told that the negroes are compelled to work in the mines and plantations of Kimberley, Witwatersrand, Natal, Matabeleland, by stripping them of all land and cattle, i.e. depriving them of their means

Admittedly, Marx dealt in detail with the process of appropriating non-capitalist means of production as well as with the transformation of the peasants into a capitalist proletariat. Chapter xxiv of *Capital*, vol. i, is devoted to describing the origin of the English proletariat, of the capitalistic agricultural tenant class and of industrial capital, with particular emphasis on the looting of colonial countries by European capital. Yet we must bear in mind that all this is treated solely with a view to so-called primitive accumulation. For Marx, these processes are incidental, illustrating merely the genesis of capital, its first appearance in the world; they are, as it were, travails by which the capitalist mode of production emerges from a feudal society. As soon as he comes to analyse the capitalist process of production and circulation, he reaffirms the universal and exclusive domination of capitalist production.

Yet, as we have seen, capitalism in its full maturity also depends in all respects on non-capitalist strata and social organisations existing side by side with it. It is not merely a question of a market for the additional product, as Sismondi and the later critics and doubters of capitalist accumulation would have it. The interrelations of accumulating capital and non-capitalist forms of production extend over values as well as over material conditions, for constant capital, variable capital and surplus value alike. The non-capitalist mode of production is the given historical setting for this process. Since the accumulation of capital becomes impossible in all points without non-capitalist surroundings, we cannot gain a true picture of it by assuming the exclusive and absolute domination of the capitalist mode of production. Sismondi and his school, when they attributed their difficulties entirely to the problem of realising the surplus value, indeed revealed a proper sense for the conditions vital to accumulation. Yet the conditions for augmenting the material elements of constant and variable capital are quite a different matter from those which govern the realisation of surplus value. Capital needs the means of production and the labour power of

of existence, by making them into proletarians and also demoralising them with alcohol. (Later, when they are already within the 'enclosure' of capital, spirits, to which they have just been accustomed, are strictly prohibited—the object of exploitation must be kept fit for use.) Finally, they are simply pressed into the wage system of capital by force, by imprisonment, and flogging.

the whole globe for untrammelled accumulation; it cannot manage without the natural resources and the labour power of all territories. Seeing that the overwhelming majority of resources and labour power is in fact still in the orbit of precapitalist production—this being the historical milieu of accumulation—capital must go all out to obtain ascendancy over these territories and social organisations. There is no a priori reason why rubber plantations, say, run on capitalist lines, such as have been laid out in India, might not serve the ends of capitalist production just as well. Yet if the countries of those branches of production are predominantly non-capitalist, capital will endeavour to establish domination over these countries and societies. And in fact, primitive conditions allow of a greater drive and of far more ruthless measures than could be tolerated under purely capitalist social conditions.

It is quite different with the realisation of the surplus value. Here outside consumers qua other-than-capitalist are really essential. Thus the immediate and vital conditions for capital and its accumulation is the existence of non-capitalist buyers of the surplus value, which is decisive to this extent for the problem of capitalist accumulation.

Whatever the theoretical aspects, the accumulation of capital, as an historical process, depends in every respect upon non-capitalist social strata and forms of social organisation.

The solution to this problem which for almost a century has been the bone of contention in economic theory thus lies between the two extremes of the petty-bourgeois scepticism preached by Sismondi, v. Kirchmann, Vorontsov and Nicolayon, who flatly denied accumulation, and the crude optimism advocated by Ricardo, Say and Tugan Baranovski who believed in capital's unlimited capacity for parthenogenesis, with the logical corollary of capitalism-in-perpetuity. The solution envisaged by Marx lies in the dialectical conflict that capitalism needs non-capitalist social organisations as the setting for its development, that it proceeds by assimilating the very conditions which alone can ensure its own existence.

At this point we should revise the conceptions of internal and external markets which were so important in the controversy about accumulation. They are both vital to capitalist development and yet fundamentally different, though they must be conceived in terms of social economy rather than of political geography. In this light, the internal market is the capitalist market, production itself buying its own products and supplying its own elements of production. The external market is the non-capitalist social environment which absorbs the products of capitalism and supplies producer goods and labour power for capitalist production. Thus, from the point of view of economics, Germany and England traffic in commodities chiefly on an internal, capitalist market, whilst the give and take between German industry and German peasants is transacted on an external market as far as German capital is concerned. These concepts are strict and precise, as can be seen from the diagram of reproduction. Internal capitalist trade can at best realise only certain quantities of value contained in the social product: the constant capital that has been used up, the variable capital, and the consumed part of the surplus value. That part of the surplus value, however, which is earmarked for capitalisation, must be realised elsewhere. If capitalisation of surplus value is the real motive force and aim of production, it must yet proceed within the limits given by the renewal of constant and variable capital (and also of the consumed part of the surplus value). Further, with the international development of capitalism the capitalisation of surplus value becomes ever more urgent and precarious, and the substratum of constant and variable capital becomes an ever-growing mass—both absolutely and in relation to the surplus value. Hence the contradictory phenomena that the old capitalist countries provide ever larger markets for, and become increasingly dependent upon, one another, yet on the other hand compete ever more ruthlessly for trade relations with non-capitalist countries.[11] The conditions for the capitalisation of surplus value clash increasingly with the conditions for the renewal of the aggregate capital—a conflict which, incidentally, is merely a counterpart of the contradictions implied in the law of a declining profit rate.

[11] The relations between Germany and England provide a typical example.

27

THE STRUGGLE AGAINST NATURAL ECONOMY

Capitalism arises and develops historically amidst a non-capitalist society. In Western Europe it is found at first in a feudal environment from which it in fact sprang—the system of bondage in rural areas and the guild system in the towns—and later, after having swallowed up the feudal system, it exists mainly in an environment of peasants and artisans, that is to say in a system of simple commodity production both in agriculture and trade. European capitalism is further surrounded by vast territories of non-European civilisation ranging over all levels of development, from the primitive communist hordes of nomad herdsmen, hunters and gatherers to commodity production by peasants and artisans. This is the setting for the accumulation of capital.

We must distinguish three phases: the struggle of capital against natural economy, the struggle against commodity economy, and the competitive struggle of capital on the international stage for the remaining conditions of accumulation.

The existence and development of capitalism requires an environment of non-capitalist forms of production, but not every one of these forms will serve its ends. Capitalism needs non-capitalist social strata as a market for its surplus value, as a source of supply for its means of production and as a reservoir of labour power for its wage system. For all these purposes, forms of production based upon a natural economy are of no use to capital. In all social organisations where natural economy common ownership of the land, a feudal system of bondage or anything of this nature, economic organisation is essentially in response to the internal demand; and therefore there is no demand, or very little, for foreign goods, and also, as a rule, no surplus production, or at least no urgent need to dispose of surplus products. What is most important, however, is that, in any natural economy, production only goes on because both means of production and labour power are bound in one form or another. The communist peasant community no less than the feudal *corvée* farm and similar institutions maintain their economic organisation by subjecting the labour power, and the most important means of production, the land, to the rule of law and custom. A natural economy thus confronts the requirements of capitalism at every turn with rigid barriers. Capitalism must therefore always and everywhere fight a battle of annihilation against every historical form of natural economy that it encounters, whether this is slave economy, feudalism, primitive communism, or patriarchal peasant economy. The principal methods in this struggle are political force (revolution, war), oppressive taxation by the state, and cheap goods; they are partly applied simultaneously, and partly they succeed and complement one another. In Europe, force assumed revolutionary forms in the fight against feudalism (this is the ultimate explanation of the bourgeois revolutions in the seventeenth, eighteenth and nineteenth centuries); in the non-European countries, where it fights more primitive social organisations, it assumes the forms of colonial policy. These methods, together with the systems of taxation applied in such cases, and commercial relations also, particularly with primitive communities, form an alliance in which political power and economic factors go hand in hand.

In detail, capital in its struggle against societies with a natural economy pursues the following ends:

(1) To gain immediate possession of important sources of productive forces such as land, game in primeval forests, minerals, precious stones and ores, products of exotic flora such as rubber, etc.

(2) To 'liberate' labour power and to coerce it into service.
(3) To introduce a commodity economy.
(4) To separate trade and agriculture.

At the time of primitive accumulation, i.e. at the end of the Middle Ages, when the history of capitalism in Europe began, and right into the nineteenth century, dispossessing the peasants in England and on the Continent was the most striking weapon in the large-scale transformation of means of production and labour power into capital. Yet capital in power performs the same task even to-day, and on an even more important scale—by modern colonial policy. It is an illusion to hope that capitalism will ever be content with the means of production which it can acquire by way of commodity exchange. In this respect already, capital is faced with difficulties because vast tracts of the globe's surface are in the possession of social organisations that have no desire for commodity exchange or cannot, because of the entire social structure and the forms of ownership, offer for sale the productive forces in which capital is primarily interested. The most important of these productive forces is of course the land, its hidden mineral treasure, and its meadows, woods and water, and further the flocks of the primitive shepherd tribes. If capital were here to rely on the process of slow internal disintegration, it might take centuries. To wait patiently until the most important means of production could be alienated by trading in consequence of this process were tantamount to renouncing the productive forces of those territories altogether. Hence derives the vital necessity for capitalism in its relations with colonial countries to appropriate the most important means of production. Since the primitive associations of the natives are the strongest protection for their social organisations and for their material bases of existence, capital must begin by planning for the systematic destruction and annihilation of all the non-capitalist social units which obstruct its development. With that we have passed beyond the stage of primitive accumulation; this process is still going on. Each new colonial expansion is accompanied, as a matter of course, by a relentless battle of capital against the social and economic ties of the natives, who are also forcibly robbed of their means of production and labour power. Any hope to restrict the accumulation of capital exclusively to 'peaceful competition', i.e. to regular commodity exchange such as takes place between capitalist producer-countries, rests on the pious belief that capital can accumulate without mediation of the productive forces and without the demand of more primitive organisations, and that it can rely upon the slow internal process of a disintegrating natural economy. Accumulation, with its spasmodic expansion, can no more wait for, and be content with, a natural internal disintegration of non-capitalist formations and their transition to commodity economy, than it can wait for, and be content with, the natural increase of the working population. Force is the only solution open to capital; the accumulation of capital, seen as an historical process, employs force as a permanent weapon, not only at its genesis, but further on down to the present day. From the point of view of the primitive societies involved, it is a matter of life or death; for them there can be no other attitude than opposition and fight to the finish—complete exhaustion and extinction. Hence permanent occupation of the colonies by the military, native risings and punitive expeditions are the order of the day for any colonial regime. The method of violence, then, is the immediate consequence of the clash between capitalism and the organisations of a natural economy which would restrict accumulation. Their means of production and their labour power no less than their demand for surplus products is necessary to capitalism. Yet the latter is fully determined to undermine their independence as social units, in order to gain possession of their means of production and labour power and to convert them into commodity buyers. This method is the most profitable and gets the quickest results, and so it is also the most expedient for capital. In fact, it is invariably accompanied by a growing militarism whose importance for accumulation will be demonstrated below in another connection. British policy in India and French policy in Algeria are the classical examples of the application of these methods by capitalism.

The ancient economic organisations of the Indians—the communist village community—had been preserved in their various forms throughout thousands of years, in spite of all the political disturbances during their long history. In the sixth century B.C. the Persians invaded the Indus basin and subjected part of the country. Two centuries later the Greeks entered and left behind them colonies, founded by Alexander on the pattern of a completely alien civilisation. Then the savage

Scythians invaded the country, and for centuries India remained under Arab rule. Later, the Afghans swooped down from the Iran mountains, until they, too, were expelled by the ruthless onslaught of Tartar hordes. The Mongols' path was marked by terror and destruction, by the massacre of entire villages—the peaceful countryside with the tender shoots of rice made crimson with blood. And still the Indian village community survived. For none of the successive Mahometan conquerors had ultimately violated the internal social life of the peasant masses and its traditional structure. They only set up their own governors in the provinces to supervise military organisation and to collect taxes from the population. All conquerors pursued the aim of dominating and exploiting the country, but none was interested in robbing the people of their productive forces and in destroying their social organisation. In the Moghul Empire, the peasant had to pay his annual tribute in kind to the foreign ruler, but he could live undisturbed in his village and could cultivate his rice on his *sholgura* as his father had done before him. Then came the British—and the blight of capitalist civilisation succeeded in disrupting the entire social organisation of the people; it achieved in a short time what thousands of years, what the sword of the Nogaians, had failed to accomplish. The ultimate purpose of British capital was to possess itself of the very basis of existence of the Indian community: the land.

This end was served above all by the fiction, always popular with European colonisers, that all the land of a colony belongs to the political ruler. In retrospect, the British endowed the Moghul and his governors with private ownership of the whole of India, in order to 'legalise' their succession. Economic experts of the highest repute, such as James Mill, duly supported this fiction with 'scientific' arguments, so in particular with the famous conclusion given below.[1]

---

[1] Mill, in his *History of British India*, substantiates the thesis that under primitive conditions the land belongs always and everywhere to the sovereign, on evidence collected at random and quite indiscriminately from the most varied sources (Mungo Park, Herodotus, Volney, Acosta, Garcilasso de la Vega, Abbé Grosier, Barrow, Diodorus, Strabo and others). Applying this thesis to India, he goes on to say: 'From these facts only one conclusion can be drawn, that the property of the soil resided in the sovereign; for if it did not reside in him, it will be impossible to show to whom it belonged' (James Mill, *History of British India* (4th edition, 1840), vol. i, p. 311). Mill's editor, H. H. Wilson who,

As early as 1793, the British in Bengal gave landed property to all the *zemindars* (Mahometan tax collectors) or hereditary market superintendents they had found in their district so as to win native support for the campaign against the peasant masses. Later they adopted the same policy for their new conquests in the Agram province, in Oudh, and in the Central Provinces. Turbulent peasant risings followed in their wake, in the course of which tax collectors were frequently driven out. In the resulting confusion and anarchy British capitalists successfully appropriated a considerable portion of the land.

The burden of taxation, moreover, was so ruthlessly increased that it swallowed up nearly all the fruits of the people's labour. This went to such an extreme in the Delhi and Allahabad districts that, according to the official evidence of the British tax authorities in 1854, the peasants

as Professor of Sanskrit at Oxford University, was thoroughly versed in the legal relations of Ancient India, gives an interesting commentary to this classical deduction. Already in his preface he characterises the author as a partisan who has juggled with the whole history of British India in order to justify the theories of Mr. Bentham and who, with this end, has used the most dubious means for his portrait of the Hindus which in no way resembles the original and almost outrages humanity. He appends the following footnote to our quotation: 'The greater part of the text and of the notes here is wholly irrelevant. The illustrations drawn from the Mahometan practice, supposing them to be correct, have nothing to do with the laws and rights of the Hindus. They are not, however, even accurate and Mr. Mill's guides have misled him.' Wilson then contests outright the theory of the sovereign's right of ownership in land, especially with reference to India. (Ibid., p. 305, footnote.) Henry Maine, too, is of the opinion that the British attempted to derive their claim to Indian land from the Mahometans in the first place, and he recognises this claim to be completely unjustified. 'The assumption which the English first made was one which they inherited from their Mahometan predecessors. It was that all the soil belonged in absolute property to the sovereign,—and that all private property in land existed by his sufferance. The Mahometan theory and the corresponding Mahometan practice had put out of sight the ancient view of the sovereign's rights which, though it assigned to him a far larger share of the produce of the land than any Western ruler has ever claimed, yet in nowise denied the existence of private property in land' (*Village Communities in the East and West* (5th edition, vol. 2, 1890), p. 104). Maxim Kovalevski, on the other hand, has proved thoroughly that this alleged 'Mahometan theory and practice' is an exclusively British legend. (Cf. his excellent study, written in Russian, *On the Causes, the Development and the Consequences of the Disintegration of Communal Ownership of Land* (Moscow, 1879), part i.) Incidentally, British experts and their French colleagues at the time of writing maintain an analogous legend about China, for example, asserting that all the land there had been the Emperor's property. (Cf. the refutation of this legend by Dr. O. Franke, *Die Rechisverhältnisse am Grundeigentum in China*, 1903.)

found it convenient to lease or pledge their shares in land for the bare amount of the tax levied. Under the auspices of this taxation, usury came to the Indian village, to stay and eat up the social organisation from within like a canker.[2] In order to accelerate this process, the British passed a law that flew in the face of every tradition and justice known to the village community: compulsory alienation of village land for tax arrears. In vain did the old family associations try to protect themselves by options on their hereditary land and that of their kindred. There was no stopping the rot. Every day another plot of land fell under the hammer; individual members withdrew from the family unit, and the peasants got into debt and lost their land.

The British, with their wonted colonial stratagems, tried to make it appear as if their power policy, which had in fact undermined the traditional forms of landownership and brought about the collapse of the Hindu peasant economy, had been dictated by the need to protect the peasants against native oppression and exploitation and served to safeguard their own interests.[3] Britain artificially created a landed

---

[2] 'The partitions of inheritances and execution for debt levied on land are destroying the communities—this is the formula heard nowadays everywhere in India' (Henry Maine, op. cit., p. 113).

[3] This view of British colonial policy, expounded e.g. by Lord Roberts of Kandahar (for many years a representative of British power in India) is typical. He can give no other explanation for the Sepoy Mutiny than mere 'misunderstandings' of the paternal intentions of the British rulers. '. . . the alleged unfairness of what was known in India as the land settlement, under which system the right and title of each landholder to his property was examined, and the amount of revenue to be paid by him to the paramount Power, as owner of the soil, was regulated . . . as peace and order were established, the system of land revenue, which had been enforced in an extremely oppressive and corrupt manner under successive Native Rulers and dynasties, had to be investigated and revised. With this object in view, surveys were made, and inquiries instituted into the rights of ownership and occupancy, the result being that in many cases it was found that families of position and influence had either appropriated the property of their humbler neighbours, or evaded an assessment proportionate to the value of their estates. Although these inquiries were carried out with the best intentions, they were extremely distasteful to the higher classes, while they failed to conciliate the masses. The ruling families deeply resented our endeavours to introduce an equitable determination of rights and assessment of land revenue. . . . On the other hand, although the agricultural population greatly benefited by our rule, they could not realise the benevolent intentions of a Government which tried to elevate their position and improve their prospects' (*Forty One Years in India*, London, 1901, p. 233).

aristocracy at the expense of the ancient property-rights of the peasant communities, and then proceeded to 'protect' the peasants against these alleged oppressors, and to bring this illegally usurped land into the possession of British capitalists.

Thus large estates developed in India in a short time, while over large areas the peasants in their masses were turned into impoverished small tenants with a short-term lease.

Lastly, one more striking fact shows the typically capitalist method of colonisation. The British were the first conquerors of India who showed gross indifference to public utilities. Arabs, Afghans and Mongols had organised and maintained magnificent works of canalisation in India, they had given the country a network of roads, spanned the rivers with bridges and seen to the sinking of wells. Timur or Tamerlane, the founder of the Mongol dynasty in India, had a care for the cultivation of the soil, for irrigation, for the safety of the roads and the provision of food for travellers.[4] The primitive Indian Rajahs, the Afghan or Mongol conquerors, at any rate, in spite of occasional cruelty against individuals, made their mark with the marvellous constructions we can find to-day at every step and which seem to be the work of a giant race. 'The (East India) Company which ruled India until 1858 did not make one spring accessible, did not sink a single well, nor build a bridge for the benefit of the Indians.'[5]

Another witness, the Englishman James Wilson, says: 'In the Madras

[4] In his *Maxims on Government* (translated from the Persian into English in 1783), Timur says: 'And I commanded that they should build places of worship, and monasteries in every city; and that they should erect structures for the reception of travellers on the high roads, and that they should make bridges across the rivers.

'And I commanded that the ruined bridges should be repaired; and that bridges should be constructed over the rivulets, and over the rivers; and that on the roads, at the distance of one stage from each other, Kauruwansarai should be erected; and that guards and watchmen should be stationed on the road, and that in every Kauruwansarai people should be appointed to reside . . .

'And I ordained, whoever undertook the cultivation of waste lands, or built an aqueduct, or made a canal, or planted a grove, or restored to culture a deserted district, that in the first year nothing should be taken from him, and that in the second year, whatever the subject voluntarily offered should be received, and that in the third year, duties should be collected according to the regulation' (James Mill, op. cit., vol. ii, pp. 493, 498).

[5] Count Warren, *De l'État moral de la population indigène*. Quoted by Kovalevski, op. cit., p. 164.

Province, no-one can help being impressed by the magnificent ancient irrigation systems, traces of which have been preserved until our time. Locks and weirs dam the rivers into great lakes, from which canals distribute the water for an area of 60 or 70 miles around. On the large rivers, there are 30 to 40 of such weirs . . . The rain water from the mountains was collected in artificial ponds, many of which still remain and boast circumferences of between 15 and 25 miles. Nearly all these gigantic constructions were completed before the year 1750. During the war between the Company and the Mongol rulers—and, be it said, *during the entire period of our rule in India*—they have sadly decayed.'[6]

No wonder! British capital had no object in giving the Indian communities economic support or helping them to survive. Quite the reverse, it aimed to destroy them and to deprive them of their productive forces. The unbridled greed, the acquisitive instinct of accumulation must by its very nature take every advantage of the 'conditions of the market' and can have no thought for the morrow. It is incapable of seeing far enough to recognise the value of the economic monuments of an older civilisation. (Recently British engineers in Egypt feverishly tried to discover traces of an ancient irrigation system rather like the one a stupid lack of vision had allowed to decay in India, when they were charged with damming the Nile on a grand scale in furtherance of capitalist enterprise.) Not until 1867 was England able to appreciate the results of her noble efforts in this respect. In the terrible famine of that year a million people were killed in the Orissa district alone; and Parliament was shocked into investigating the causes of the emergency. The British government has now introduced administrative measures in an attempt to save the peasant from usury. The Punjab Alienation Act of 1900 made it illegal to sell or mortgage peasant lands to persons other than of the peasant caste, though exceptions can be made in individual cases, subject to the tax collector's approval.[7] Having deliberately disrupted the protecting ties of the ancient Hindu social

---

[6] *Historical and Descriptive Account of British India* from the most remote period to the conclusion of the Afghan war by Hugh Murray, James Wilson, Greville, Professor Jameson, William Wallace and Captain Dalrymple (Edinburgh, 4th edition, 1843), vol. ii, p. 427. Quoted by Kovalevski, op. cit.

[7] Victor v. Leyden, *Agrarverfassung und Grundsteuer in Britisch Ostindien. Jahrb. f. Ges., Verw. u. Volsw.*, vol. xxxvi, no. 4, p. 1855.

associations, after having nurtured a system of usury where nothing is thought of a 15 per cent charge of interest, the British now entrust the ruined Indian peasant to the tender care of the Exchequer and its officials, under the 'protection', that is to say, of those draining him of his livelihood.

Next to tormented British India, Algeria under French rule claims pride of place in the annals of capitalist colonisation. When the French conquered Algeria, ancient social and economic institutions prevailed among the Arab–Kabyle population. These had been preserved until the nineteenth century, and in spite of the long and turbulent history of the country they survive in part even to the present day.

Private property may have existed no doubt in the towns, among the Moors and Jews, among merchants, artisans and usurers. Large rural areas may have been seized by the State under Turkish suzerainty—yet nearly half of the productive land is jointly held by Arab and Kabyle tribes who still keep up the ancient patriarchal customs. Many Arab families led the same kind of nomad life in the nineteenth century as they had done since time immemorial, an existence that appears restless and irregular only to the superficial observer, but one that is in fact strictly regulated and extremely monotonous. In summer they were wont, man, woman and child, to take their herds and tents and migrate to the sea-swept shores of the Tell district; and in the winter they would move back again to the protective warmth of the desert. They travelled along definite routes, and the summer and winter stations were fixed for every tribe and family. The fields of those Arabs who had settled on the land were in most cases the joint property of the clans, and the great Kabyle family associations also lived according to old traditional rules under the patriarchal guidance of their elected heads.

The women would take turns for household duties; a matriarch, again elected by the family, being in complete charge of the clan's domestic affairs, or else the women taking turns of duty. This organisation of the Kabyle clans on the fringe of the African desert bears a startling resemblance to that of the famous Southern Slavonic Zadruga—not only the fields but all the tools, weapons and monies, all that the members acquire or need for their work, are communal property of the clan. Personal property is confined to one suit of clothing, and in the case of a woman to the dresses and ornaments of her dowry. More valuable attire and jewels, however, are considered common property, and individuals were allowed to use them only if the whole family approved. If the clan was not too numerous, meals were taken at a common table; the women took it in turns to cook, but the eldest were entrusted with the dishing out. If a family circle was too large, the head of the family would each month ration out strictly proportionate quantities of uncooked food to the individual families who then prepared them. These communities were bound together by close ties of kinship, mutual assistance and equality, and a patriarch would implore his sons on his deathbed to remain faithful to the family.[8]

These social relations were already seriously impaired by the rule of the Turks, established in Algeria in the sixteenth century. Yet the Turkish exchequer had by no means confiscated all the land. That is a legend invented by the French at a much later date. Indeed, only a European mind is capable of such a flight of fancy which is contrary to the entire economic foundation of Islam both in theory and practice. In truth, the facts were quite different. The Turks did not touch the communal fields of the village communities. They merely confiscated a great part of uncultivated land from the clans and converted it into crownland under Turkish local administrators (Beyliks). The state worked these lands in part with native labour, and in part they were leased out on rent or against payment in kind. Further the Turks took advantage of every revolt of the subjected families and of every disturbance in the country to add to their possessions by large-scale confiscation of land, either for military establishments or for public auction, when most of it went to Turkish or other usurers. To escape from the burden of taxation and confiscation, many peasants placed themselves under the protection of the Church, just as they had done in medieval Germany. Hence

---

[8] 'When dying, the father of the family nearly always advises his children to live in unity, according to the example of their elders. This is his last exhortation, his dearest wish' (A. Hanotaux et A. Letournaux, La Kabylie et les Coûtumes Kabyles, vol. ii, 1873, 'Droit Civil', pp. 468–73). The authors, by the way, appraised this impressive description of communism in the clan with this peculiar sentence: 'Within the industrious fold of the family association, all are united in a common purpose, all work for the general interest—but no one gives up his freedom or renounces his hereditary rights. In no other nation does the organisation approach so closely to equality, being yet so far removed from communism.'

considerable areas became Church-property. All these changes finally resulted in the following distribution of Algerian land at the time of the French conquest: crownlands occupied nearly 3,750,000 acres, and a further 7,500,000 acres of uncultivated land as common property of All the Faithful (Bled-el-Islam). 7,500,000 acres had been privately owned by the Berbers since Roman times, and under Turkish rule a further 3,750,000 acres had come into private ownership, a mere 12,500,000 acres remaining communal property of individual Arab clans. In the Sahara, some of the 7,500,000 acres fertile land near the Sahara Oases was communally owned by the clans and some belonged to private owners. The remaining 57,500,000,000 acres were mainly waste land.

With their conquest of Algeria, the French made a great ado about their work of civilisation, since the country, having shaken off the Turkish yoke at the beginning of the eighteenth century, was harbouring the pirates who infested the Mediterranean and trafficked in Christian slaves. Spain and the North American Union in particular, themselves at that time slave traders on no mean scale, declared relentless war on this Moslem iniquity. France, in the very throes of the Great Revolution, proclaimed a crusade against Algerian anarchy. Her subjection of that country was carried through under the slogans of 'combating slavery' and 'instituting orderly and civilised conditions'. Yet practice was soon to show what was at the bottom of it all. It is common knowledge that in the forty years following the subjection of Algeria, no European state suffered so many changes in its political system as France: the restoration of the monarchy was followed by the July Revolution and the reign of the 'Citizen King', and this was succeeded by the February Revolution, the Second Republic, the Second Empire, and finally, after the disaster of 1870, by the Third Republic. In turn, the aristocracy, high finance, petty bourgeoisie and the large middle classes in general gained political ascendancy. Yet French policy in Algeria remained undeflected by this succession of events; it pursued a single aim from beginning to end; at the fringe of the African desert, it demonstrated plainly that all the political revolutions in nineteenth-century France centred in a single basic interest: the rule of a capitalist bourgeoisie and its institutions of ownership.

'The bill submitted for your consideration', said Deputy Humbert on June 30, 1873, in the Session of the French National Assembly as spokesman for the Commission for Regulating Agrarian Conditions in Algeria, 'is but the crowning touch to an edifice well-founded on a whole series of ordinances, edicts, laws and decrees of the Senate which together and severally have as the same object: the establishment of private property among the Arabs.'

In spite of the ups and downs of internal French politics, French colonial policy persevered for fifty years in its systematic and deliberate efforts to destroy and disrupt communal property. It served two distinct purposes: The break-up of communal property was primarily intended to smash the social power of the Arab family associations and to quell their stubborn resistance against the French yoke, in the course of which there were innumerable risings so that, in spite of France's military superiority, the country was in a continual state of war.[9] Secondly, communal property had to be disrupted in order to gain the economic assets of the conquered country; the Arabs, that is to say, had to be deprived of the land they had owned for a thousand years, so that French capitalists could get it. Once again the fiction we know so well, that under Moslem law all land belongs to the ruler, was brought into play. Just as the English had done in British India, so Louis Philippe's governors in Algeria declared the existence of communal property owned by the clan to be 'impossible'. This fiction served as an excuse to claim for the state most of the uncultivated areas, and especially the commons, woods and meadows, and to use them for purposes of colonisation. A complete system of settlement developed, the so-called *cantonments* which settled French colonists on the clan land and herded the tribes into a small area. Under the decrees of 1830, 1831, 1840, 1844, 1845 and 1846 these thefts of Arab family land were legalised. Yet this system of settlement did not actually further colonisation; it only bred wild speculation and usury. In most instances the Arabs managed to buy back the land that had been taken from them, although they were thus incurring heavy debts. French methods of oppressive taxation had the same tendency, in particular the law of June 16, 1851, proclaiming all forests to be state property, which

---

[9] 'We must lose no time in dissolving the family associations, since they are the lever of all opposition against our rule' (Deputy Didier in the National Assembly of 1851).

robbed the natives of 6,000,000 acres of pasture and brushwood, and took away the prime essential for animal husbandry. This spate of laws, ordinances and regulations wrought havoc with the ownership of land in the country. Under the prevailing condition of feverish speculation in land, many natives sold their estates to the French in the hope of ultimately recovering them. Quite often they sold the same plot to two or three buyers at a time, and what is more, it was quite often inalienable family land and did not even belong to them. A company of speculators from Rouen, e.g., believed that they had bought 50,000 acres, but in fact they had only acquired a disputed title to 3,425 acres. There followed an infinite number of lawsuits in which the French courts supported on principle all partitions and claims of the buyers. In these uncertain conditions, speculation, usury and anarchy were rife. But although the introduction of French colonists in large numbers among the Arab population had aimed at securing support for the French government, this scheme failed miserably. Thus, under the Second Empire, French policy tried another tack. The government, with its European lack of vision, had stubbornly denied the existence of communal property for thirty years, but it had learned better at last. By a single stroke of the pen, joint family property was officially recognised and condemned to be broken up. This is the double significance of the decree of the Senate dated April 22, 1864. General Allard declared in the Senate:

'The government does not lose sight of the fact that the general aim of its policy is to weaken the influence of the tribal chieftains and to dissolve the family associations. By this means, it will sweep away the last remnants of feudalism [sic!] defended by the opponents of the government bill . . . The surest method of accelerating the process of dissolving the family associations will be to institute private property and to settle European colonists among the Arab families.'[10]

The law of 1863 created special Commissions for cutting up the landed estates, consisting of the Chairman, either a Brigadier-General or Colonel, one *sous-préfet*, one representative of the Arab military

---

[10] Quoted by Kovalevski, op. cit., p. 217. Since the Great Revolution, of course, it had become the fashion in France to dub all opposition to the government an open or covert defence of feudalism.

authorities and an official bailiff. These natural experts on African economics and social conditions were faced with the threefold task, first of determining the precise boundaries of the great family estates, secondly to distribute the estates of each clan among its various branches, and finally to break up this family land into separate private allotments. This expedition of the Brigadiers into the interior of Africa duly took place. The Commissions proceeded to their destinations. They were to combine the office of judge in all land disputes with that of surveyor and land distributor, the final decision resting with the Governor-General of Algeria. Ten years' valiant efforts by the Commissions yielded the following result: between 1863 and 1873, of 700 hereditary estates, 400 were shared out among the branches of each clan, and the foundations for future inequalities between great landed estates and small allotments were thus laid. One family, in fact, might receive between 2.5 and 10 acres, while another might get as much as 250 or even 450 acres, depending on the size of the estate and the number of collaterals within the clan. Partition, however, stopped at that point. Arab customs presented unsurmountable difficulties to a further division of family land. In spite of Colonels and Brigadiers, French policy had again failed in its object to create private property for transfer to the French.

But the Third Republic, an undisguised regime of the bourgeoisie, had the courage and the cynicism to go straight for its goal and to attack the problem from the other end, disdaining the preliminaries of the Second Empire. In 1873, the National Assembly worked out a law with the avowed intention immediately to split up the entire estates of all the 700 Arab clans, and forcibly to institute private property in the shortest possible time. Desperate conditions in the colony were the pretext for this measure. It had taken the great Indian famine of 1866 to awaken the British public to the marvellous exploits of British colonial policy and to call for a parliamentary investigation; and similarly, Europe was alarmed at the end of the sixties by the crying needs of Algeria where more than forty years of French rule culminated in wide-spread famine and a disastrous mortality rate among the Arabs. A commission of inquiry was set up to recommend new legislation with which to bless the Arabs: it was unanimously resolved that there was only one lifebuoy for them—the institution of private property; that alone could save the Arab from destitution, since he would then always be able to sell or mortgage his land. It was decided therefore, that the only means of alleviating the distress of the Arabs, deeply involved in debts as they were because of the French land robberies and oppressive taxation, was to deliver them completely into the hands of the usurers. This farce was expounded in all seriousness before the National Assembly and was accepted with equal gravity by that worthy body. The 'victors' of the Paris Commune flaunted their brazenness.

In the National Assembly, two arguments in particular served to support the new law: those in favour of the bill emphasised over and over again that the Arabs themselves urgently desired the introduction of private property. And so they did, or rather the Algerian land speculators and usurers did, since they were vitally interested in 'liberating' their victims from the protection of the family ties. As long as Moslem law prevailed in Algeria, hereditary clan and family lands were inalienable, which laid insuperable difficulties in the way of anyone who wished to mortgage his land. The law of 1863 had merely made a breach in these obstacles, and the issue now at stake was their complete abolition so as to give a free hand to the usurers. The second argument was 'scientific', part of the same intellectual equipment from which that worthy, James Mill, had drawn for his abstruse conclusions regarding Indian relations of ownership: English classical economics. Thoroughly versed in their masters' teachings, the disciples of Smith and Ricardo impressively declaimed that private property is indispensable for the prevention of famines in Algeria, for more intensive and better cultivation of the land, since obviously no one would be prepared to invest capital or intensive labour in a piece of land which does not belong to him and whose produce is not his own to enjoy. But the facts spoke a different language. They proved that the French speculators employed the private property they had created in Algeria for anything but the more intensive and improved cultivation of the soil. In 1873, 1,000,000 acres were French property. But the capitalist companies, the Algerian and Setif Company which owned 300,000 acres, did not cultivate the land at all but leased it to the natives who tilled it in the traditional manner, nor were 25 per cent of the other French owners engaged in agriculture. It was simply impossible to conjure up capitalist investments and intensive agriculture overnight, just as capitalist conditions in general could not be created out of nothing. They existed only in the imagination of profit-seeking French speculators, and in the benighted doctrinaire visions of their scientific economists. The essential point, shorn of all pretexts and flourishes which seem to justify the law of 1873, was simply the desire to deprive the Arabs of their land, their livelihood. And although these arguments had worn threadbare and were evidently insincere, this law which was to put paid to the Algerian population and their material prosperity, was passed unanimously on July 26, 1873.

But even this master-stroke soon proved a failure. The policy of the Third Republic miscarried because of the difficulties in substituting at one stroke bourgeois private property for the ancient clan communism, just as the policy of the Second Empire had come to grief over the same issue. In 1890, when the law of July 26, 1873, supplemented by a second law on April 28, 1887, had been in force for seventeen years, 14,000,000 francs had been spent on dealing with 40,000,000 acres. It was estimated that the process would not be completed before 1950 and would require a further 60,000,000 francs. And still abolition of clan communism, the ultimate purpose, had not been accomplished. What had really been attained was all too evident: reckless speculation in land, thriving usury and the economic ruin of the natives.

Since it had been impossible to institute private property by force, a new experiment was undertaken. The laws of 1873 and 1887 had been condemned by a commission appointed for their revision by the Algerian government in 1890. It was another seven years before the legislators on the Seine made the effort to consider reforms for the ruined country. The new decree of the Senate refrained in principle from instituting private property by compulsion or administrative measures. The laws of February 2, 1897, and the edict of the Governor-General of Algeria (March 3, 1898) both provided chiefly for the introduction of private property following a voluntary application by the prospective purchaser or owner.[11] But there were clauses to permit a single owner, without the consent of the others, to claim private property; further, such a 'voluntary' application can be extorted at any

[11] G. Anton, *Neuere Agrarpolitik in Algerien und Tunesien. Jahrb. f. Gesetzgebung, Verwaltung und Volkswirtschaft* (1900), pp. 1341 ff.

convenient moment if the owner is in debt and the usurer exerts pressure. And so the new law left the doors wide open for French and native capitalists further to disrupt and exploit the hereditary and clan lands.

Of recent years, this mutilation of Algeria which had been going on for eight decades meets with even less opposition, since the Arabs, surrounded as they are by French capital following the subjection of Tunisia (1881) and the recent conquest of Morocco, have been rendered more and more helpless. The latest result of the French regime in Algeria is an Arab exodus into Turkey.[12]

[12] On June 20, 1912, M. Albin Rozet, on behalf of the Commission for the Reform of the 'Indigenat' (Administrative Justice) in Algeria, stated in his speech to the French Chamber of Deputies that thousands of Algerians were migrating from the Setif district, and that 1,200 natives had emigrated from Tlemcen during the last year, their destination being Syria. One immigrant wrote from his new home: 'I have now settled in Damascus and am perfectly happy. There are many Algerians here in Syria who, like me, have emigrated. The government has given us land and facilities to cultivate it.' The Algerian government combats this exodus—by denying passports to prospective emigrants. (Cf. *Journal Officiel*, June 21, 1912, pp. 1594 ff.)

28

THE INTRODUCTION OF COMMODITY ECONOMY

The second condition of importance for acquiring means of production and realising the surplus value is that commodity exchange and commodity economy should be introduced in societies based on natural economy as soon as their independence has been abrogated, or rather in the course of this disruptive process. Capital requires to buy the products of, and sell its commodities to, all non-capitalist strata and societies. Here at last we seem to find the beginnings of that 'peace' and 'equality', the *do ut des*, mutual interest, 'peaceful competition' and the 'influences of civilisation'. For capital can indeed deprive alien social associations of their means of production by force, it can compel the workers to submit to capitalist exploitation, but it cannot force them to buy its commodities or to realise its surplus value. In districts where natural economy formerly prevailed, the introduction of means of transport—railways, navigation, canals—is vital for the spreading of commodity economy, a further hopeful sign. The triumphant march of commodity economy thus begins in most cases with magnificent constructions of modern transport, such as railway lines which cross primeval forests and tunnel through the mountains, telegraph wires which bridge the deserts, and ocean liners which call at the most outlying ports. But it is a mere illusion that these are peaceful changes. Under the standard of commerce, the relations between the East India Company and the spice-producing countries were quite as piratical, extortionate and blatantly fraudulent as present-day relations between American capitalists and the Red Indians of Canada whose furs they buy, or between German merchants and the Negroes of Africa. Modern China presents a classical example of the 'gentle', 'peace-loving' practices of commodity exchange with backward countries. Throughout the nineteenth century, beginning with the early forties, her history has been punctuated by wars with the object of opening her up to trade by brute force. Missionaries provoked persecutions of Christians, Europeans instigated risings, and in periodical massacres a completely helpless and peaceful agrarian population was forced to match arms with the most modern capitalist military technique of all the Great Powers of Europe. Heavy war contributions necessitated a public debt, China taking up European loans, resulting in European control over her finances and occupation of her fortifications; the opening of free ports was enforced, railway concessions to European capitalists extorted. By all these measures commodity exchange was fostered in China, from the early thirties of the last century until the beginning of the Chinese revolution.

European civilisation, that is to say commodity exchange with European capital, made its first impact on China with the Opium Wars when she was compelled to buy the drug from Indian plantations in order to make money for British capitalists. In the seventeenth century, the East India Company had introduced the cultivation of poppies in Bengal; the use of the drug was disseminated in China by its Canton branch. At the beginning of the nineteenth century, opium fell so considerably in price that it rapidly became the 'luxury of the people'. In 1821, 4,628 chests of opium were imported to China at an average price of £265; then the price fell by 50 per cent, and Chinese imports rose to 9,621 chests in 1825, and to 26,670 chests in 1830.[1] The

---

[1] 77,379 chests were imported in 1854. Later, the imports somewhat declined, owing to increased home production. Nevertheless, China remained the chief buyer. India produced just under 6,400,000 tons of opium in 1873/4, of which 6,100,000 tons were sold to the Chinese. To-day [1912] India still exports 4,800,000 tons, value £7,500,000,000, almost exclusively to China and the Malay Archipelago.

deadly effects of the drug, especially of the cheaper kinds used by the poorer population, became a public calamity and made it necessary for China to lay an embargo on imports, as an emergency measure. Already in 1828, the viceroy of Canton had prohibited imports of opium, only to deflect the trade to other ports. One of the Peking censors commanded to investigate the question gave the following report:

'I have learnt that people who smoke opium have developed such a craving for this noxious drug that they make every effort to obtain this gratification. If they do not get their opium at the usual hour, their limbs begin to tremble, they break out in sweat, and they cannot perform the slightest tasks. But as soon as they are given the pipe, they inhale a few puffs and are cured immediately.

'Opium has therefore become a necessity for all who smoke it, and it is not surprising that under cross-examination by the local authorities they will submit to every punishment rather than reveal the names of their suppliers. Local authorities are also in some cases given presents to tolerate the evil or to delay any investigation already under way. Most merchants who bring goods for sale into Canton also deal in smuggled opium.

'I am of the opinion that opium is by far a greater evil than gambling, and that opium smokers should therefore be punished no less than gamblers.'

The censor suggested that every convicted opium smoker should be sentenced to eighty strokes of the bamboo, and anybody refusing to give the name of his supplier to a hundred strokes and three years of exile. The pigtailed Cato of Peking concludes his report with a frankness staggering to any European official: 'Apparently opium is mostly introduced from abroad by dishonest officials in connivance with profit-seeking merchants who transport it into the interior of the country. Then the first to indulge are people of good family, wealthy private persons and merchants, but ultimately the drug habit spreads among the common people. I have learnt that in all provinces opium is smoked not only in the civil service but also in the army. The officials of the various districts indeed enjoin the legal prohibition of sale by special edicts. But at the same time, their parents, families, dependants and servants simply go on smoking opium, and the merchants profit from the ban by increased prices. Even the police have been won over; they buy the stuff instead of helping to suppress it, and this is an additional reason for the disregard in which all prohibitions and ordinances are held.'[2]

Consequently, a stricter law was passed in 1833 which made every opium smoker liable to a hundred strokes and two months in the stocks, and provincial governors were ordered to report annually on their progress in the battle against opium. But there were two sequels to this campaign: on the one hand large-scale poppy plantations sprang up in the interior, particularly in the Honan, Setchuan, and Kueitchan provinces, and on the other, England declared war on China to get her to lift the embargo. These were the splendid beginnings of 'opening China' to European civilisation—by the opium pipe.

Canton was the first objective. The fortifications of the town at the main arm of the Perl estuary could not have been more primitive. Every day at sunset a barrier of iron chains was attached to wooden rafts anchored at various distances, and this was the main defence. Moreover, the Chinese guns could only fire at a certain angle and were therefore completely ineffectual. With such primitive defences, just adequate to prevent a few merchant ships from landing, did the Chinese meet the British attack. A couple of British cruisers, then, sufficed to effect an entry on September 7, 1839. The sixteen battle-junks and thirteen fire-ships which the Chinese put up for resistance were shot up or dispersed in a matter of forty-five minutes. After this initial victory, the British renewed the attack in the beginning of 1841 with a considerably reinforced fleet. This time the fleet, consisting in a number of battle-junks, and the forts were attacked simultaneously. The first incendiary rocket that was fired penetrated through the armour casing of a junk into the powder chamber and blew the ship with the entire crew sky-high. In a short time eleven junks, including the flag-ship, were destroyed, and the remainder precipitately made for safety. The action on land took a little longer. Since the Chinese guns were quite useless, the British walked right through the fortifications, climbed to a strategic position—which was not even guarded—and

---

[2] Quoted by J. Scheibert, *Der Krieg in China* (1903), vol. 2, p. 179.

proceeded to slaughter the helpless Chinese from above. The casualty list of the battle was: for the Chinese 600 dead, and for the British, 1 dead and 30 wounded, more than half of the latter having been injured by the accidental explosion of a powder magazine. A few weeks later, there followed another British exploit. The forts of Anung-Hoy and North Wantong were to be taken. No less than twelve fully equipped cruisers were available for this task. What is more, the Chinese, once again forgetful of the most important thing, had omitted to fortify the island of South Wantong. Thus the British calmly landed a battery of howitzers to bombard the fort from one side, the cruisers shelling it from the other. After that, the Chinese were driven from the forts in a matter of minutes, and the landing met with no resistance. The ensuing display of inhumanity—an English report says—will be for ever deeply deplored by the British staff. The Chinese, trying to escape from the barricades, had fallen into a moat which was soon literally filled to the brim with helpless soldiers begging for mercy. Into this mass of pros-trate human bodies, the sepoys—acting against orders, it is claimed—fired again and again. This is the way in which Canton was made receptive to commodity exchange.

Nor did the other ports fare better. On July 4, 1841, three British cruisers with 120 cannon appeared off the islands in the entrance to the town of Ningpo. More cruisers arrived the following day. In the evening the British admiral sent a message to the Chinese governor, demanding the capitulation of the island. The governor explained that he had no power to resist but could not surrender without orders from Peking. He therefore asked for a delay. This was refused, and at half-past two in the morning the British stormed the defenceless island. Within eight minutes, the fort and the houses on the shore were reduced to smouldering rubble. Having landed on the deserted coast littered with broken spears, sabres, shields, rifles and a few dead bodies, the troops advanced on the walls of the island town of Tinghai. With daybreak, reinforced by the crews of other ships which had meanwhile arrived, they proceeded to put scaling-ladders to the scarcely defended ram-parts. A few more minutes gave them mastery of the town. This splen-did victory was announced with becoming modesty in an Order of the Day: 'Fate has decreed that the morning of July 5, 1841, should be the historic date on which Her Majesty's flag was first raised over the most beautiful island of the Celestial Empire, the first European flag to fly triumphantly above this lovely countryside.'[3]

On August 25, 1841, the British approached the town of Amoy, whose forts were armed with a hundred of the heaviest Chinese guns. These guns being almost useless, and the commanders lacking in resource, the capture of the harbour was child's play. Under cover of a heavy barrage, British ships drew near the walls of Kulangau, landed their marines, and after a short stand the Chinese troops were driven out. The twenty-six battle-junks with 128 guns in the harbour were also captured, their crews having fled. One battery, manned by Tartars, heroically held out against the combined fire of three British ships, but a British landing was effected in their rear and the post wiped out.

This was the finale of the notorious Opium War. By the peace treaty of August 27, 1842, the island of Hongkong was ceded to Britain. In addition, the towns of Canton, Amoy, Futchou, Ningpo and Shanghai were to open their ports to foreign commerce. But within fifteen years, there was a further war against China. This time, Britain had joined forces with the French. In 1857, the allied navies captured Canton with a heroism equal to that of the first war. By the peace of Tientsin (1858), the opium traffic, European commerce and Christian missions were admitted into the interior. Already in 1859, however, the British resumed hostilities and attempted to destroy the Chinese fortifications on the Peiho river, but were driven off after a fierce battle in which 464 people were wounded or killed.[4]

---

[3] Ibid., p. 207.

[4] An Imperial Edict issued on the third day of the eighth moon in the tenth year of Hsien-Feng (6/9/1860) said amongst other things: 'We have never forbidden England and France to trade with China, and for long years there has been peace between them and us. But three years ago the English, for no good cause, invaded our city of Canton, and carried off our officials into captivity. We refrained at that time from taking any retaliatory measures, because we were compelled to recognise that the obstinacy of the Viceroy Yeh had been in some measure a cause of the hostilities. Two years ago, the barbarian Commander Elgin came north and we then commanded the Viceroy of Chihli, T'an Ting-hsiang, to look into matters preparatory to negotiations. But the barbarian took advantage of our unreadiness, attacking the Taku forts and pressing on to Tientsin. Being anxious to spare our people the horrors of war, we again refrained from retaliation and ordered Kuei Liang to discuss terms of peace. Notwithstanding the outrageous nature of the barbarians' demands we subsequently ordered Kuei Liang to proceed to Shanghai

After that, Britain and France again joined forces. At the end of August 1860, 12,600 English and 7,500 French troops under General Cousin-Montauban first captured the Taku forts without a single shot having been fired. Then they proceeded towards Tientsin and on towards Peking. A bloody battle was joined at Palikao, and Peking fell to the European Powers. Entering the almost depopulated and completely undefended city, the victors began by pillaging the Imperial Palace, manfully helped by General Cousin himself, who was later to become field marshal and Count of Palikao. Then the Palace went up in flames, fired on Lord Elgin's order as an imposed penance.[5]

The European Powers now obtained concessions to set up embassies

in connection with the proposed Treaty of Commerce and even permitted its ratification as earnest of our good faith.

'In spite of all this, the barbarian leader Bruce again displayed intractability of the most unreasonable kind, and once more appeared off Taku with a squadron of warships in the eighth Moon. Seng Ko Lin Ch'in thereupon attacked him fiercely and compelled him to make a rapid retreat. From all these facts it is clear that China has committed no breach of faith and that the barbarians have been in the wrong. During the present year the barbarian leaders Elgin and Gros have again appeared off our coasts, but China, unwilling to resort to extreme measures, agreed to their landing and permitted them to come to Peking for the ratification of the Treaty.

'Who could have believed that all this time the barbarians have been darkly plotting, and that they had brought with them an army of soldiers and artillery with which they attacked the Taku forts from the rear, and, having driven out our forces, advanced upon Tientsin!' (I. O. Bland and E. T. Blackhouse, *China under the Empress Dowager* (London, 1910), pp. 24–5. Cf. also in this work the entire chapter, 'The Flight to Yehol'.)

[5] These European exploits to make China receptive to commodity exchange, provide the setting for a charming episode of China's internal history: Straight from looting the Manchu Emperor's Summer Palace, the 'Gordon of China' went on a campaign against the rebels of Taiping. In 1863 he even took over command of the Imperial fighting forces. In fact, the suppression of the revolt was the work of the British army. But while a considerable number of Europeans, among them a French admiral, gave their lives to preserve China for the Manchu dynasty, the representatives of European commerce were eagerly grasping this opportunity to make capital out of these fights, supplying arms both to their own champions and to the rebels who went to war against them. 'Moreover, the worthy merchant was tempted, by the opportunity for making some money, to supply both armies with arms and munitions, and since the rebels had greater difficulties in obtaining supplies than the Emperor's men and were therefore compelled and prepared to pay higher prices, they were given priority and could thus resist not only the troops of their own government, but also those of England and France' (M. v. Brandt, 33 *Jahre in Ostasien*, 1911, vol. iii, *China*, p. 11).

in Peking, and to start trading with Tientsin and other towns. The Tchi-fu Convention of 1876 guaranteed full facilities for importing opium into China—at a time when the Anti-Opium League in England agitated against the spreading of the drug habit in London, Manchester and other industrial districts, when a parliamentary commission declared the consumption of opium to be harmful in the extreme. By all treaties made at that time between China and the Great Powers any European, whether merchant or missionary, was guaranteed the right to acquire land, to which end the legitimate arguments were ably supported by deliberate fraud.

First and foremost the ambiguity of the treaty texts made a convenient excuse for European capital to encroach beyond the Treaty Ports. It used every loophole in the wording of the treaties to begin with, and subsequently blackmailed the Chinese government into permitting the missions to acquire land not alone in the Treaty Ports but in all the provinces of the realm. Their claim was based upon the notorious barefaced distortion of the Chinese original in Abbé Delamarre's official translation of the supplementary convention with France. French diplomacy, and the Protestant missions in particular, unanimously condemned the crafty swindle of the Catholic padre, but nevertheless they were firm that the rights of French missions obtained by this fraud should be explicitly extended to the Protestant missions as well.[6]

China's entry into commodity exchange, having begun with the Opium Wars, was finally accomplished with a series of 'leases' and the China campaign of 1900, when the commercial interests of European capital sank to a brazen international dogfight over Chinese land. The description of the Dowager Empress, who wrote to Queen Victoria after the capture of the Taku forts, subtly underlines this contrast between the initial theory and the ultimate practice of the 'agents of European civilisation':

'To your Majesty, greeting!—In all the dealings of England with the Empire of China, since first relations were established between us, there has never been any idea of territorial aggrandisement on the part of Great Britain, but only a keen desire to promote the interests of her trade. Reflecting upon the fact that our country is now plunged into a

[6] Dr. O. Franke, *Die Rechtsverhältnisse am Grundeigentum in China* (Leipzig, 1903), p. 82.

dreadful condition of warfare, we bear in mind that a large proportion of China's trade, seventy or eighty per cent, is done with England; moreover, your Customs duties are the lightest in the world, and few restrictions are made at your sea-ports in the matter of foreign import- ations; for these reasons our amiable relations with British merchants at our Treaty Ports have continued unbroken for the last half century, to our mutual benefit.—But a sudden change has now occurred and gen- eral suspicion has been created against us. We would therefore ask you now to consider that if, by any conceivable combination of circum- stances, the independence of our Empire should be lost, and the Powers unite to carry out their long-plotted schemes to possess themselves of our territory'—(in a simultaneous message to the Emperor of Japan, the impulsive Tzu Hsi openly refers to 'The earth-hungry Powers of the West, whose tigerish eyes of greed are fixed in our direction'[7])—'the results to your country's interests would be disastrous and fatal to your trade. At this moment our Empire is striving to the utmost to raise an army and funds sufficient for its protection; in the meanwhile we rely on your good services to act as mediator, and now anxiously await your decision.'[8]

Both during the wars and in the interim periods, European civilisa- tion was busy looting and thieving on a grand scale in the Chinese Imperial Palaces, in the public buildings and in the monuments of ancient civilisation, not only in 1860, when the French pillaged the Emperor's Palace with its legendary treasures, or in 1900, 'when all the nations vied with each other to steal public and private property'. Every European advance was marked not only with the progress of commod- ity exchange, but by the smouldering ruins of the largest and most venerable towns, by the decay of agriculture over large rural areas, and by intolerably oppressive taxation for war contributions. There are more than 40 Chinese Treaty Ports—and every one of them has been paid for with streams of blood, with massacre and ruin.

[7] Bland and Blackhouse, op. cit., p. 338.
[8] Ibid., p. 337.

29

THE STRUGGLE AGAINST PEASANT ECONOMY

An important final phase in the campaign against natural economy is to separate industry from agriculture, to eradicate rural industries altogether from peasant economy. Handicraft in its historical beginnings was a subsidiary occupation, a mere appendage to agriculture in civilised and settled societies. In medieval Europe it became gradually independent of the *corvée* farm and agriculture, it developed into specialised occupations, i.e. production of commodities by urban guilds. In industrial districts, production had progressed from home craft by way of primitive manufacture to the capitalist factory of the staple industries, but in the rural areas, under peasant economy, home crafts persisted as an intrinsic part of agriculture. Every hour that could be spared from cultivating the soil was devoted to handicrafts which, as an auxiliary domestic industry, played an important part in providing for personal needs.[1]

---

[1] Until recently, in China the domestic industries were widely practised even by the bourgeoisie and in such large and ancient towns as Ningpo with its 300,000 inhabitants. 'Only a generation ago, the family's shoes, hats, shirts, etc., were made by the women themselves. At that time, it was practically unheard-of for a young woman to buy from a merchant what she could have made with the labour of her own hands' (Dr. Nyok-Ching Tsur, 'Forms of Industry in the Town of Ningpo' (*Die gewerblichen Betriebsformen der Stadt Ningpo*), Tuebingen, 1909, p. 51).

It is a recurrent phenomenon in the development of capitalist production that one branch of industry after the other is singled out, isolated from agriculture and concentrated in factories for mass production. The textile industry provides the textbook example, but the same thing has happened, though less obviously, in the case of other rural industries. Capital must get the peasants to buy its commodities and will therefore begin by restricting peasant economy to a single sphere—that of agriculture—which will not immediately and, under European conditions of ownership, only with great difficulty submit to capitalist domination.[2] To all outward appearance, this process is quite peaceful. It is scarcely noticeable and seemingly caused by purely economic factors. There can be no doubt that mass production in the factories is technically superior to primitive peasant industry, owing to a higher degree of specialisation, scientific analysis and management of the productive process, improved machinery and access to international resources of raw materials. In reality, however, the process of separating agriculture and industry is determined by factors such as oppressive taxation, war, or squandering and monopolisation of the nation's land, and thus belongs to the spheres of political power and criminal law no less than with economics.

Nowhere has this process been brought to such perfection as in the United States. In the wake of the railways, financed by European and in particular British capital, the American farmer crossed the Union from East to West and in his progress over vast areas killed off the Red Indians with fire-arms and bloodhounds, liquor and venereal disease, pushing the survivors to the West, in order to appropriate the land they had 'vacated', to clear it and bring it under the plough. The American farmer, the 'backwoodsman' of the good old times before the War of Secession, was very different indeed from his modern counterpart. There was hardly anything he could

[2] Admittedly, this relation is reversed in the last stages of the history of peasant economy when capitalist production has made its full impact. Once the small peasants are ruined, the entire work of farming frequently devolves on the women, old people and children, while the men are made to work for their living for capitalist entrepreneurs in the domestic industries or as wage-slaves in the factories. A typical instance is the small peasant in Wuerttemberg.

not do, and he led a practically self-sufficient life on his isolated farm.

In the beginning of the nineties, one of the leaders of the Farmers' Alliance, Senator Peffer, wrote as follows: 'The American farmer of to-day is altogether a different sort of man from his ancestor of fifty or a hundred years ago. A great many men and women now living remember when farmers were largely manufacturers; that is to say, they made a great many implements for their own use. Every farmer had an assortment of tools with which he made wooden implements, as forks and rakes, handles for his hoes and ploughs, spokes for his wagon, and various other implements made wholly out of wood. Then the farmer produced flax and hemp and wool and cotton. These fibres were prepared upon the farm; they were spun into yarn, woven into cloth, made into garments, and worn at home. Every farm had upon it a little shop for wood and iron work, and in the dwelling were cards and looms; carpets were woven, bed-clothing of different sorts was prepared; upon every farm geese were kept, their feathers used for supplying the home demand with beds and pillows, the surplus being disposed of at the nearest market town. During the winter season wheat and flour and corn meal were carried in large wagons drawn by teams of six to eight horses a hundred or two hundred miles to market, and traded for farm supplies for the next year—groceries and dry goods. Besides this, mechanics were scattered among the farmers. The farm wagon was in process of building a year or two; the material was found near the shop; the character of the timber to be used was stated in the contract; it had to be procured in a certain season and kept in the drying process a length of time specified, so that when the material was brought together in proper form and the wagon made, both parties to the contract knew where every stick of it came from, and how long it had been in seasoning. During winter time the neighbourhood carpenter prepared sashes and blinds and doors and moulding and cornices for the next season's building. When the frosts of autumn came the shoemaker repaired to the dwellings of the farmers and there, in a corner set apart to him, he made up shoes for the family during the winter. All these things were done among the farmers, and a large part of the expense was paid with products of the farm. When winter approached, the butchering season was at hand; meat for family use during the next year was prepared and preserved in the smoke house. The orchards supplied fruit for cider, for apple butter, and for preserves of different kinds, amply sufficient to supply the wants of the family during the year, with some to spare. Wheat was threshed, a little at a time, just enough to supply the needs of the family for ready money, and not enough to make it necessary to waste one stalk of straw. Everything was saved and put to use. One of the results of that sort of economy was that comparatively a very small amount of money was required to conduct the business of farming. A hundred dollars average probably was as much as the largest farmers of that day needed in the way of cash to meet the demands of their farm work, paying for hired help, repairs of tools, and all other incidental expenses.'[3]

This Arcadian life was to come to a sudden end after the War of Secession. The war had burdened the Union with an enormous National Debt,. amounting to £1,200,000, and in consequence the taxes were considerably increased. On the other hand, a feverish development of modern traffic and industry, machine-building in particular, was encouraged by the imposition of higher protective tariffs. The railway companies were endowed with public lands on an imposing scale, in order to promote railroad construction and farm-settlements: in 1867 alone, they were given more than 192,500,000 acres, and so the permanent way grew at an unprecedented rate. In 1860 it amounted to less than 31,000 miles, in 1870 it had grown to more than 53,000 miles and in 1880 to more than 93,000 miles. (During the same period—1870–1880—the permanent way in Europe had grown from 80,000 miles to 100,000 miles.) The railways and speculations in land made for mass emigration from Europe to the United States, and more than 4½ million people immigrated in the twenty-three years from 1869 to 1892. In this way, the Union gradually became emancipated from European, and in particular from British, industry; factories were set up in the States and home industries

---

[3] W. A. Peffer, *The Farmer's Side. His Troubles and Their Remedy* (New York, 1891), Part ii, 'How We Got Here', chap. i, 'Changed Conditions of the Farmer', pp. 56–7. Cf. also A. M. Simmons, *The American Farmer* (2nd edition, Chicago, 1906), pp. 74 ff.

developed for the production of textiles, iron, steel and machinery. The process of revolutionary transformation was most rapid in agriculture. The emancipation of the slaves had compelled the Southern planters to introduce the steam plough shortly after the Civil War, and new farms had sprung up in the West in the wake of the railways, which from the very beginning employed the most modern machinery and technique.

'The improvements are rapidly revolutionising the agriculture of the West, and reducing to the lowest minimum ever attained, the proportion of manual labour employed in its operations. . . . Coincident with this application of mechanics to agriculture, systematic and enlarged business aptitudes have also sought alliance with this noble art. Farms of thousands of acres have been managed with greater skill, a more economical adaptation of means to ends, and with a larger margin of real profit than many others of 80 acres.'[4]

During this time, direct and indirect taxation had increased enormously. On June 30, 1864, during the Civil War, a new finance bill was passed which is the basis of the present system of taxation, and which raised taxes on consumption and income to a staggering degree. This heavy war levy served as a pretext for a real orgy of protective tariffs in order to offset the tax on home production by customs duties.[5] Messrs. Morrill, Stevens and the other gentlemen who advanced the war as a lever for enforcing their protectionist programme, initiated the practice of wielding the implement of a customs policy quite openly and cynically to further private profiteering interests of all descriptions. Any home producer who appeared before the legislative assembly with a request for any kind

---

[4] Report of the U.S.A. Commissioner of Agriculture for the year 1867 (Washington, 1868). Quoted by Lafargue: *Getreidebau und Getreidehandel in den Vereinigten Staaten* in *Die Neue Zeit* (1885), p. 344. This essay on grain cultivation and the grain trade in the U.S.A. was first published in a Russian periodical in 1883.

[5] 'The three Revenue Acts of June 30, 1864, practically formed one measure, and that probably the greatest measure of taxation which the world has seen. . . . The Internal Revenue Act was arranged, as Mr. David A. Wells has said, on the principle of the Irishman at Donnybrook Fair: "whenever you see a head, hit it, whenever you see a commodity, tax it" ' (F. W. Taussig, *The Tariff History of the United States* (New York–London, 1888), pp. 163–4).

of special tariff to fill his own pocket saw his demands readily granted, and the tariff rates were made as high as any interested party might wish.

'The war', writes the American Taussig, 'had in many ways a bracing and ennobling influence on our national life; but its immediate effect on business affairs, and on all legislation affecting moneyed interests, was demoralising. The line between public duty and private interests was often lost sight of by legislators. Great fortunes were made by changes in legislation urged and brought about by those who were benefited by them, and the country has seen with sorrow that the honour and honesty of public men did not remain undefiled.'[6]

This customs bill which completely revolutionised the country's economic life, and remained in force unchanged for twenty years, was literally pushed through Congress in three days, and through the Senate in two, without criticism, without debate, without any opposition whatever.[7] Down to the present day it forms the basis of U.S. customs legislation.

This shift in U.S. fiscal policy ushered in an era of the most brazen parliamentary log-rolling and of undisguised and unrestrained corruption of elections, of the legislature and the press to satisfy the greed of Big Business. 'Enrichissez-vous' became the catchword of public life after the 'noble war' to liberate mankind from the 'blot of slavery'. On the stock exchange, the Yankee negro-liberator sought his fortunes in orgies of speculation; in Congress, he endowed himself with public lands, enriched himself by customs and taxes, by monopolies, fraudulent shares and theft of public funds. Industry prospered. Gone were the times when the small or medium farmer required hardly any money, when he could thresh and turn into cash his wheat reserves as the need arose. Now he was chronically in need of money, a lot of money, to pay his taxes. Soon he was forced to sell all his produce and to buy his requirements

[6] Ibid., pp. 166–7.

[7] 'The necessity of the situation, the critical state of the country, the urgent need of revenue, may have justified this haste, which, it is safe to say, is unexampled in the history of civilised countries' (ibid., p. 168).

from the manufacturers in the form of ready-made goods. As Peffer puts it:

'Coming from that time to the present, we find that everything nearly has been changed. All over the West particularly the farmer threshes his wheat all at one time, he disposes of it all at one time, and in a great many instances the straw is wasted. He sells his hogs, and buys bacon and pork; he sells his cattle, and buys fresh beef and canned beef or corned beef, as the case may be; he sells his fruit, and buys it back in cans. If he raises flax at all, instead of putting it into yarn and making gowns for his children, as he did fifty years or more ago, he threshes his flax, sells the seed, and burns the straw. Not more than one farmer in fifty now keeps sheep at all; he relies upon the large sheep farmer for the wool, which is put into cloth or clothing ready for his use. Instead of having clothing made up on the farm in his own house or by a neighbour woman or country tailor a mile away, he either purchases his clothing ready made at the nearest town, or he buys the cloth and has a city tailor make it up for him. Instead of making implements which he uses about the farm—forks, rakes, etc.—he goes to town to purchase even a handle for his axe or his mallet; he purchases twine and rope and all sorts of needed material made of fibres; he buys his cloth and his clothing; he buys his canned fruit and preserved fruit; he buys hams and shoulders and mess pork and mess beef; indeed, he buys nearly everything now that he produced at one time himself, and these things all cost money. Besides all this, and what seems stranger than anything else, whereas in the earlier time the American home was a free home, unencumbered, not one case in a thousand where a home was mortgaged to secure the payment of borrowed money, and whereas but a small amount of money was then needed for actual use in conducting the business of farming, there was always enough of it among the farmers to supply the demand. Now, when at least ten times as much is needed, there is little or none to be obtained, nearly half the farms are mortgaged for as much as they are worth, and interest rates are exorbitant. As to the cause of such wonderful changes . . . the manufacturer came with his woollen mill, his carding mill, his broom factory, his rope factory, his wooden-ware factory, his cotton factory, his pork-packing establishment, his canning factory and fruit preserving houses; the little shop on the farm has given place to the large shop in town; the wagon-maker's shop in the neighbourhood has given way to the large establishment in the city where . . . a hundred or two hundred wagons are made in a week; the shoemaker's shop has given way to large establishments in the cities where most of the work is done by machines.'[8]

Finally, the agricultural labour of the farmer himself has become machine work: 'He ploughs and sows and reaps with machines. A machine cuts his wheat and puts it in a sheaf, and steam drives his threshers. He may read the morning paper while he ploughs and sit under an awning while he reaps.'[9]

Sering estimated in the middle eighties that the necessary cash 'for a very modest beginning' of the smallest farm in the North West is £240 to £280.[10]

This revolution of American agriculture after the 'Great War' was not the end. It was only the beginning of the whirlpool in which the farmer was caught. His history brings us automatically to the second phase of the development of capitalist accumulation of which it is an excellent illustration.—Natural economy, the production for personal needs and the close connection between industry and agriculture must be ousted and a simple commodity economy substituted for them. Capitalism needs the medium of commodity production for its development, as a market for its surplus value. But as soon as simple commodity production has superseded natural economy, capital must turn against it. No sooner has capital called it to life, than the two must compete for means of production, labour power, and markets. The first aim of capitalism is to isolate the producer, to sever the community ties which protect him, and the next task is to take the means of production away from the small manufacturer.

In the American Union, as we have seen, the 'Great War' inaugurated an era of large-scale seizure of public lands by monopolist capitalist companies and individual speculators. Feverish railroad

---

[8] Peffer, op. cit., pp. 58 ff.

[9] Ibid., p. 6.

[10] 'Agricultural Competition in North America' (Die landwirtschaftliche Konkurrenz Nordamerikas) Leipzig, 1887, p. 431.

building and ever more speculation in railway shares led to a mad gamble in land, where individual soldiers of fortune and companies netted immense fortunes and even entire counties. In addition a veritable swarm of agents lured the vast flow of emigrants from Europe to the U.S.A. by blatant and unscrupulous advertising, deceptions and pretences of every description. These immigrants first settled in the Eastern States along the Atlantic seaboard, and, with the growth of industry in these states, agriculture was driven westward. The 'wheat centre' which had been near Columbus, Ohio, in 1850, in the course of the subsequent fifty years shifted to a position 99 miles further North and 680 miles further West. Whereas in 1850 51.4 per cent of the total wheat crop had been supplied by the Eastern States, in 1880 they produced only 13.6 per cent, 71.7 per cent being supplied by the Northern Central and 9 per cent by the Western States.

In 1825, the Congress of the Union under Monroe had decided to transplant the Red Indians from the East to the West of the Mississippi. The redskins put up a desperate resistance; but all who survived the slaughter of forty Red Indian campaigns were swept away like so much rubbish and driven like cattle to the West to be folded in reservations like so many sheep. The Red Indian had been forced to make room for the farmer—and now the farmer in his turn was driven beyond the Mississippi to make way for capital.

Following the railway tracks, the American farmer moved West and North-West into the land of promise which the great land speculators' agents had painted for him in glowing colours. Yet the most fertile and most favourably situated lands were retained by the companies who farmed them extensively on completely capitalistic lines. All around the farmer who had been exiled into the wilderness, a dangerous competitor and deadly enemy sprang up—the 'bonanza farms', the great capitalist agricultural concerns which neither the Old World nor the New had known before. Here surplus value was produced with the application of all the resources known to modern science and technology.

'As the foremost representative of financial agriculture we may consider Oliver Dalrymple, whose name is to-day known on both sides of the Atlantic. Since 1874 he has simultaneously managed a line of steamers on the Red River and six farms owned by a company of financiers and comprising some 75,000 acres. Each one is divided into departments of 2,000 acres, and every department is again subdivided into three sections of 667 acres which are run by foremen and gang-leaders. Barracks to shelter 50 men and stable as many horses and mules, are built on each section, and similarly kitchens, machine sheds and workshops for blacksmiths and locksmiths. Each section is completely equipped with 20 pairs of horses, 8 double ploughs, 12 horse-drawn drill-ploughs, 12 steel-toothed harrows, 12 cutters and binders, 2 threshers and 16 wagons. Everything is done to ensure that the machines and the living labour (men, horses and mules) are in good condition and able to do the greatest possible amount of work. There is a telephone line connecting all sections and the central management.

'The six farms of 75,000 acres are cultivated by an army of 600 workers, organised on military lines. During the harvest, the management hires another 500 to 600 auxiliary workers, assigning them to the various sections. After the work is completed in the fall, the workers are dismissed with the exception of the foreman and 10 men per section. In some farms in Dakota and Minnesota, horses and mules do not spend the winter at the place of work. As soon as the stubble has been ploughed in, they are driven in teams of a hundred or two hundred pairs 900 miles to the South, to return only the following spring.

'Mechanics on horseback follow the ploughing, sowing and harvesting machines when they are at work. If anything goes wrong, they gallop to the machine in question, repair it and get it moving again without delay. The harvested corn is carried to the threshing machines which work day and night without interruption. They are stoked with bundles of straw fed into the stokehold through pipes of sheet-iron. The corn is threshed, winnowed, weighed and filled into sacks by machinery, then it is put into railway trucks which run alongside the farm, and goes to Duluth or Buffalo. Every year, Dalrymple increases his land under seed by 5,800 acres. In 1880 it amounted to 25,000 acres.[11]

[11] Lafargue, op. cit., p. 345.

In the late seventies, there were already individual capitalists and companies who owned 35,000–45,000 acres of wheat land. Since the time of Lafargue's writing, extensive capitalist agriculture in America has made great strides in technique and the employment of machinery.[12]

The American farmer could not successfully compete with such capitalist enterprises. At a time when the general revolution in the conditions of finance, production and transport compelled him to give up production for personal needs and to produce exclusively for the market, the great spreading of agriculture caused a heavy fall in the prices of agricultural products. And at the precise moment when farming became dependent on the market, the agricultural market of the Union was suddenly turned from a local one into a world market, and became a prey to the wild speculations of a few capitalist mammoth concerns.

In 1879, a notable year for the history of agricultural conditions in

---

[12] The Thirteenth Annual Report of the Commissioner of Labour (Washington, 1899) tables the advantages of machinery methods over hand methods so far achieved as follows:

Type of work	Labour time per unit			
	Machine		Hand	
	hrs.	min.	hrs.	min.
Planting small corn	—	32.7	10	55
Harvesting and threshing small corn	1	—	46	40
Planting corn	—	37.5	6	15
Cutting corn	3	4.5	5	—
Shelling corn	—	3.6	66	40
Planting cotton	1	3	8	48
Cultivating cotton	12	5	60	—
Mowing grass (scythe v. mower)	1	0.6	7	20
Harvesting and baling hay	11	3.4	35	30
Planting potatoes	1	2.5	15	—
Planting tomatoes	1	4	10	—
Cultivating and harvesting tomatoes	134	5.2	324	20

Europe as well as in America, there began the mass export of wheat from the U.S.A. to Europe.[13]

Big Business was of course the only one to profit from this expanding market. The small farmer was crushed by the competition of an increasing number of extensive farms and became the prey of speculators who bought up his corn to exert pressure on the world market. Helpless in the face of the immense capitalist powers, the farmer got into debt— a phenomenon typical for a declining peasant economy. In 1890, Secretary Rusk of the U.S. Department of Agriculture sent out a circular letter with reference to the desperate position of the farmers, saying:

'The burden of mortgages upon farms, homes, and land, is unquestionably discouraging in the extreme, and while in some cases no doubt this load may have been too readily assumed, still in the majority of cases the mortgage has been the result of necessity. . . . These mortgages . . . drawing high rates of interest . . . have to-day, in the face of continued depression of the prices of staple products,

[13] Wheat exports from the Union to Europe:

Year	Million bushels	Year	Million bushels
1868–9	17.9	1885–6	57.7
1874–5	71.8	1890–1	55.1
1879–80	153.2	1899–1900	101.9

(Juraschek's *Uebersichten der Weltwirtschaft*, vol. vii, part i, p. 32).

Simultaneously, the price per bushel wheat *loco* farm (in cents) declined as follows:

1870–9	105	1896	73
1880–9	83	1897	81
1895	51	1898	58

Since 1899, when it had reached the low level of 58 cents per bushel, the price is moving up again:

1900	62	1903	78
1901	62	1904	92
1902	63		

(Ibid., p. 18).

According to the 'Monthly Returns on External Trade' (*Monatliche Nachweise über den Auswärtigen Handel*), the price (in *marks*) per 1,000 kg., was in June 1912:

Berlin	227.82	London	170.96
New York	178.08	Odessa	173.94
Mannheim	247.93	Paris	243.69

become very irksome, and in many cases threaten the farmer with loss of home and land. It is a question of grave difficulty to all those who seek to remedy the ills from which our farmers are suffering. At present prices the farmer finds that it takes more of his products to get a dollar wherewith to buy back the dollar which he borrowed than it did when he borrowed it. The interest accumulates, while the payment of the principal seems utterly hopeless, and the very depression which we are discussing makes the renewal of the mortgage most difficult.'[14]

According to the census of May 29, 1891, 2.5 million farms were deep in debt; two-thirds of them were managed by the owners whose obligations amounted to nearly £440,000.

'The situation is this: farmers are passing through the "valley and shadow of death"; farming as a business is profitless; values of farm products have fallen 50 per cent since the great war, and farm values have depreciated 25 to 50 per cent during the last ten years; farmers are overwhelmed with debts secured by mortgages on their homes, unable in many instances to pay even the interest as it falls due, and unable to renew the loans because securities are weakening by reason of the general depression; many farmers are losing their homes under this dreadful blight, and the mortgage mill still grinds. We are in the hands of a merciless power; the people's homes are at stake.'[15]

Encumbered with debts and close to ruin, the farmer had no option but to supplement his earnings by working for a wage, or else to abandon his farm altogether. Provided it had not yet fallen into the clutches of his creditors like so many thousands of farms, he could shake from off his feet the dust of the 'land of promise' that had become an inferno for him. In the middle eighties, abandoned and decaying farms could be seen everywhere. In 1887, Sering wrote:

'If the farmer cannot pay his debts to date, the interest he has to pay is increased to 12, 15 or even 20 per cent. He is pressed by the banker, the machine salesman and the grocer who rob him of the fruits of his hard work . . . He can either remain on the farm as a tenant or move further West, to try his fortunes elsewhere. Nowhere in North America have I found so many indebted, disappointed and depressed farmers as

---

[14] Peffer, op. cit., part i, 'Where We Are', chap. ii, 'Progress of Agriculture', pp. 30–1.
[15] Ibid., p. 4.

in the wheat regions of the North Western prairies. I have not spoken to a single farmer in Dakota who would not have been prepared to sell his farm.[16]

'The Commissioner of Agriculture of Vermont in 1889 reported a wide-spread desertion of farm-lands of that state. He wrote: ". . . there appears to be no doubt about there being in this state large tracts of tillable unoccupied lands, which can be bought at a price approximating the price of Western lands, situated near school and church, and not far from railroad facilities. The Commissioner has not visited all of the counties in the State where these lands are reported, but he has visited enough to satisfy him that, while much of the unoccupied and formerly cultivated land is now practically worthless for cultivation, yet very much of it can be made to yield a liberal reward to intelligent labour." '[17]

The Commissioner of the State of New Hampshire issued a pamphlet in 1890, devoting 67 pages to the description of farms for sale at the lowest figures. He describes 1,442 farms with tenantable buildings, abandoned only recently. The same has happened in other districts. Thousands of acres once raising corn and wheat are left untilled and run to brush and wood.

In order to resettle the deserted land, speculators engaged in advertising campaigns and attracted crowds of new immigrants—new victims who were to suffer their predecessors' fate even more speedily.

A private letter says: 'In the neighbourhood of railroads and markets, there remains no common land. It is all in the hands of the speculators. A settler takes over vacant land and counts for a farmer; but the management of his farm hardly assures his livelihood, and he cannot possibly compete with the big farmer. He tills as much of his land as the law compels him to do, but to make a comfortable living, he must look for additional sources of income outside agriculture. In Oregon, for instance, I have met a settler who owned 160 acres for five years, but every summer, until the end of July, he worked twelve hours a day for a dollar a day at road-making. This man, of course, also counts as one of the five million farmers in the 1890 census. Again, in the County

---

[16] Sering, op. cit., p. 433.
[17] Peffer, op. cit., pp. 34 f.

of Eldorado, I saw many farmers who cultivated their land only to feed their cattle and themselves. There would have been no profit in producing for the market, and their chief income derives from gold-digging, the felling and selling of timber, etc. These people are prosperous, but it is not agriculture which makes them so. Two years ago, we worked in Long Cañon, Eldorado County, living in a cabin on an allotment. The owner of this allotment came home only once a year for a couple of days, and worked the rest of the time on the railway in Sacramento. Some years ago, a small part of the allotment was cultivated, to comply with the law, but now it is left completely untilled. A few acres are fenced off with wire, and there is a log cabin and a shed. But during the last years all this stands empty; a neighbour has the key and he made us free of the hut. In the course of our journey, we saw many deserted allotments, where attempts at farming had been made. Three years ago I was offered a farm with dwelling house for a hundred dollars, but in a short time the unoccupied house collapsed under the snow. In Oregon, we saw many derelict farms with small dwelling houses and vegetable gardens. One we visited was beautifully made: a sturdy block house, fashioned by a master-builder, and some equipment; but the farmer had abandoned it all. You were welcome to take it all without charge.'[18]

Where could the ruined American farmer turn? He set out on a pilgrimage to follow the wheat centre and the railways. The former had shifted in the main to Canada, the Saskatchewan and the Mackenzie River where wheat can still thrive on the 62nd parallel. A number of American farmers followed—and after some time in Canada, they suffered the old fate.[19] During recent years, Canada has entered the world market as a wheat-exporting country, but her agriculture is dominated to an even greater extent by big capital than elsewhere.[20]

[18] Quoted by Nikolayon, op. cit., p. 224.

[19] 49,199 people immigrated to Canada in 1902. In 1912, the number of immigrants was more than 400,000—138,000 of them British, and 134,000 American. According to a report from Montreal, the influx of American farmers continued into the spring of the present year [1912].

[20] 'Travelling in the West of Canada, I have visited only one farm of less than a thousand acres. According to the census of the Dominion of Canada, in 1881, when the census was taken, no more than 9,077 farmers occupied 2,384,337 acres of land between them;

In Canada, public lands were lavished upon private capitalist companies on an even more monstrous scale than in the United States. Under the Charter of the Canadian Pacific Railway Company with its grant of land, private capital perpetrated an unprecedented act of robbing the public. Not only that the company was guaranteed a twenty years' monopoly of railway-building, not only that it got a building site of about 713 miles free of charge, not only that it got a 100 years' state guarantee of the 3 per cent interest on the share capital of £m. 20—to crown it all, the company was given the choice of 25 million acres out of the most fertile and favourably situated lands, not necessarily in the immediate vicinity of the permanent way, as a free gift. All future settlers on this vast area were thus at the mercy of railway capital from the very outset. The railway company, in its turn, immediately proceeded to sell off 5 million acres for ready cash to the North-West Land Company, an association of British capitalists under the chairmanship of the Duke of Manchester. The second group of capitalists which was liberally endowed with public lands was the Hudson Bay Company, which was given a title to no less than one-twentieth of all the lands between Lake Winnipeg, the U.S. border, the Rocky Mountains, and Northern Saskatchewan, for renouncing their privileges in the North-West. Between them, these two capitalist groups had gained possession of five-ninths of all the land that could be settled. A considerable part of the other lands was assigned by the State to 26 capitalist 'colonising companies'.[21] Thus the Canadian farmer was practically everywhere

accordingly, the share of an individual (farmer) amounted to no less than 2,047 acres— in no state of the Union is the average anywhere near that' (Sering, op. cit., p. 376). In the early eighties, farming on a large scale was admittedly not very widely spread in Canada. But already in 1887, Sering describes the 'Bell Farm', owned by a limited company, which comprised no fewer than 56,700 acres, and was obviously modelled on the pattern of the Dalrymple farm. In the eighties, Sering, who regarded the prospects of Canadian competition with some scepticism, put the 'fertile belt' of Western Canada at three-fifths of the entire acreage of Germany, and estimated that actually only 38,400,000 acres of this were arable land, and no more than 15,000,000 acres at best were prospective wheat land (Sering, op. cit., pp. 337–8). The Manitoba Free Press in June 1912, worked out that in summer, 1912, 11,200,000 acres were sown with spring wheat in Canada, as against 19,200,000 acres under spring wheat in the United States. (Cf. Berliner Tageblatt, Handelszeitung, No. 305, June 18, 1912.)

[21] Sering, op. cit., pp. 361 ff.

ensnared by capital and capitalist speculation. And still mass immigration continued—not only from Europe, but also from the United States!

These are the characteristics of capitalist domination on an international scale. Having evicted the peasant from his soil, it drives him from England to the East of the United States, and from there to the West, and on the ruins of the Red Indians' economy it transforms him back into a small commodity producer. Then, when he is ruined once more, he is driven from the West to the North. With the railways in the van, and ruin in the rear—capital leads the way, its passage is marked with universal destruction. The great fall of prices in the nineties is again succeeded by higher prices for agricultural products, but this is of no more avail to the small American farmer than to the European peasant.

Yet the numbers of farmers are constantly swelling. In the last decade of the nineteenth century they had grown from 4,600,000 to 5,700,000, and the following ten years still saw an absolute increase. The aggregate value of farms had during the same period risen from £150,240,000 to £330,360,000.[22] We might have expected the general increase in the price of farm produce to have helped the farmer to come into his own. But that is not so; we see that the growing numbers of tenant farmers outstrip the increase in the farming population as a whole. In 1880, the proportion of tenant farmers amounted to 25.5 per cent of the total number of farmers in the Union, in 1890 it was 28.4 per cent, in 1900 35.3 per cent, and in 1910 37.2 per cent.

Though prices for farm produce were rising, the tenant farmer was more and more rapidly stepping into the shoes of the independent farmer. And although much more than one-third of all farmers in the Union are now tenant farmers, their social status in the United States is that of the agricultural labourer in Europe. Constantly fluctuating, they are indeed wage-slaves of capital; they work very hard to create wealth for capital, getting nothing in return but a miserable and precarious existence.

In quite a different historical setting, in South Africa, the same

[22] Ernst Schultze, 'Das Wirtschaftsleben der Vereinigten Staaten', Jahrb. f. Gesetzg., Verw. u. Volkswirtschaft 1912, no. 17, p. 1724.

process shows up even more clearly the 'peaceful methods' by which capital competes with the small commodity producer.

In the Cape Colony and the Boer Republics, pure peasant economy prevailed until the sixties of the last century. For a long time the Boers had led the life of animal-tending nomads; they had killed off or driven out the Hottentots and Kaffirs with a will in order to deprive them of their most valuable pastures. In the eighteenth century they were given invaluable assistance by the plague, imported by ships of the East India Company, which frequently did away with entire Hottentot tribes whose lands then fell to the Dutch immigrants. When the Boers spread further East, they came in conflict with the Bantu tribes and initiated the long period of the terrible Kaffir wars. These god-fearing Dutchmen regarded themselves as the Chosen People and took no small pride in their old-fashioned Puritan morals and their intimate knowledge of the Old Testament; yet, not content with robbing the natives of their land, they built their peasant economy like parasites on the backs of the Negroes, compelling them to do slave-labour for them and corrupting and enervating them deliberately and systematically. Liquor played such an important part in this process, that the prohibition of spirits in the Cape Colony could not be carried through by the English government because of Puritan opposition. There were no railways until 1859, and Boer economy in general and on the whole remained patriarchal and based on natural economy until the sixties. But their patriarchal attitude did not deter the Boers from extreme brutality and harshness. It is well known that Livingstone complained much more about the Boers than about the Kaffirs. The Boers considered the Negroes an object, destined by God and Nature to slave for them, and as such an indispensable foundation of their peasant economy. So much so that their answer to the abolition of slavery in the English colonies in 1836 was the 'Great Trek', although there the owners had been compensated with £3,000,000. By way of the Orange River and Vaal, the Boers emigrated from the Cape Colony, and in the process they drove the Matabele to the North, across the Limpopo, setting them against the Makalakas. Just as the American farmer had driven the Red Indian West before him under the impact of capitalist economy, so the Boer drove the Negro to the North. The 'Free Republics' between the Orange River and the Limpopo thus were created as a protest against the designs of the English bourgeoisie on the sacred right of slavery. The tiny peasant republics were in constant guerilla warfare against the Bantu Negroes. And it was on the backs of the Negroes that the battle between the Boers and the English government, which went on for decades, was fought. The Negro question, i.e. the emancipation of the Negroes, ostensibly aimed at by the English bourgeoisie, served as a pretext for the conflict between England and the republics. In fact, peasant economy and great capitalist colonial policy were here competing for the Hottentots and Kaffirs, that is to say for their land and their labour power. Both competitors had precisely the same aim: to subject, expel or destroy the coloured peoples, to appropriate their land and press them into service by the abolition of their social organisations. Only their methods of exploitation were fundamentally different. While the Boers stood for out-dated slavery on a petty scale, on which their patriarchal peasant economy was founded, the British bourgeoisie represented modern large-scale capitalist exploitation of the land and the natives. The Constitution of the Transvaal (South African) Republic declared with crude prejudice: 'The People shall not permit any equality of coloured persons with white inhabitants, neither in the Church nor in the State.'[23]

In the Orange Free State and in the Transvaal no Negro was allowed to own land, to travel without papers or to walk abroad after sunset. Bryce tells us of a case where a farmer, an Englishman as it happened, in the Eastern Cape Colony had flogged his Kaffir slave to death. When he was acquitted in open court, his neighbours escorted him home to the strains of music. The white man frequently maltreated his free native labourers after they had done their work—to such an extent that they would take to flight, thus saving the master their wages.

The British government employed precisely the opposite tactics. For a long time it appeared as protector of the natives; flattering the chieftains in particular, it supported their authority and tried to make them claim a right of disposal over their land. Wherever it was possible, it gave them ownership of tribal land, according to well-tried methods, although this flew in the face of tradition and of the actual social organisation of the Negroes. All tribes in fact held their land

[23] Article 9.

communally, and even the most cruel and despotic rulers such as the Matabele Chieftain Lobengula merely had the right as well as the duty to allot every family a piece of land which they could only retain so long as they cultivated it. The ultimate purpose of the British government was clear: long in advance it was preparing for land robbery on a grand scale, using the native chieftains themselves as tools. But in the beginning it was content with the 'pacification' of the Negroes by extensive military actions. Up to 1879 were fought 9 bloody Kaffir wars to break the resistance of the Bantus.

British capital revealed its real intentions only after two important events had taken place: the discovery of the Kimberley diamond fields in 1869–70, and the discovery of the gold mines in the Transvaal in 1882–5, which initiated a new epoch in the history of South Africa. Then the British South Africa Company, that is to say Cecil Rhodes, went into action. Public opinion in England rapidly swung over, and the greed for the treasures of South Africa urged the British government on to drastic measures. South Africa was suddenly flooded with immigrants who had hitherto only appeared in small numbers— immigration having been deflected to the United States. But with the discovery of the diamond and gold fields, the numbers of white people in the South African colonies grew by leaps and bounds: between 1885 and 1895, 100,000 British had immigrated into Witwatersrand alone. The modest peasant economy was forthwith pushed into the background—the mines, and thus the mining capital, coming to the fore. The policy of the British government veered round abruptly. Great Britain had recognised the Boer Republics by the Sand River Agreement and the Treaty of Bloemfontein in the fifties. Now her political might advanced upon the tiny republics from every side, occupying all neighbouring districts and cutting off all possibility of expansion. At the same time the Negroes, no longer protected favourites, were sacrificed. British capital was steadily forging ahead. In 1868, Britain took over the rule of Basutoland—only, of course, because the natives had 'repeatedly implored' her to do so.[24] In 1871, the Witwatersrand diamond

---

[24] 'Moshesh, the great Basuto leader, to whose courage and statesmanship the Basutos owed their very existence as a people, was still alive at the time, but constant war with the Boers of the Orange Free State had brought him and his followers to the last stage of

fields, or West Griqualand, were seized from the Orange Free State and turned into a Crown Colony. In 1879, Zululand was subjected, later to become part of the Natal Colony; in 1885 followed the subjection of Bechuanaland, to be joined to the Cape Colony. In 1888 Britain took over Matabele and Mashonaland, and in 1889 the British South Africa Company was given a Charter for both these districts, again, of course, only to oblige the natives and at their request.[25] Between 1884 and 1887, Britain annexed St. Lucia Bay and the entire East Coast as far as the Portuguese possessions. In 1894, she subjected Tongaland. With their last strength, the Matabele and Mashona fought one more desperate battle, but the Company, with Rhodes at the head, first liquidated the rising in blood and at once proceeded to the well-tried measure for civilising and pacifying the natives: two large railways were built in the rebellious district.

The Boer Republics were feeling increasingly uncomfortable in this sudden stranglehold, and their internal affairs as well were becoming completely disorganised. The overwhelming influx of immigrants and the rising tides of the frenzied new capitalist economy now threatened to burst the barriers of the small peasant states. There was indeed a blatant conflict between agricultural and political peasant economy on the one hand, and the demands and requirements of the accumulation of capital on the other. In all respects, the republics were quite unable to cope with these new problems. The constant danger from the Kaffirs, no doubt regarded favourably by the British, the unwieldy, primitive administration, the gradual corruption of the *volksraad* in which the great capitalists got their way by bribery, lack of a police force to keep the undisciplined crowds of adventurers in some semblance of order, the absence of labour legislation for regulating and securing the exploitation of the Negroes in the mines, lack of water supplies and

distress. Two thousand Basuto warriors had been killed, cattle had been carried off, native homes had been broken up and crops destroyed. The tribe was reduced to the position of starving refugees, and nothing could save them but the protection of the British government which they had repeatedly implored' (C. P. Lucas, *A Historical Geography of the British Colonies*, part ii, vol. iv (Geography of South and East Africa), Oxford, 1904, p. 39).

[25] 'The Eastern section of the territory is Mashonaland where, with the permission of King Lobengula, who claimed it, the British South Africa Company first established themselves' (ibid., p. 72).

transport to provide for the colony of 100,000 immigrants that had suddenly sprung up, high protective tariffs which increased the cost of labour for the capitalists, and high freights for coal—all these factors combined towards the sudden and stunning bankruptcy of the peasant republics.

They tried, obstinately and unimaginatively, to defend themselves against the sudden eruption of capitalism which engulfed them, with an incredibly crude measure, such as only a stubborn and hide-bound peasant brain could have devised: they denied all civic rights to the uitlanders who outnumbered them by far and who stood for capital, power, and the trend of the time. In those critical times it was an ill-omened trick. The mismanagement of the peasant republics caused a considerable reduction of dividends, on no account to be put up with. Mining capital had come to the end of its tether. The British South Africa Company built railroads, put down the Kaffirs, organised revolts of the uitlanders and finally provoked the Boer War. The bell had tolled for peasant economy. In the United States, the economic revolution had begun with a war, in South Africa war put the period to this chapter. Yet in both instances, the outcome was the same: capital triumphed over the small peasant economy which had in its turn come into being on the ruins of natural economy, represented by the natives' primitive organisations. The domination of capital was a foregone conclusion, and it was just as hopeless for the Boer Republics to resist as it had been for the American farmer. Capital officially took over the reins in the new South African Union which replaced the small peasant republics by a great modern state, as envisaged by Cecil Rhodes' imperialist programme. The new conflict between capital and labour had superseded the old one between British and Dutch. One million white exploiters of both nations sealed their touching fraternal alliance within the Union with the civil and political disfranchisement of five million coloured workers. Not only the Negroes of the Boer Republics came away empty-handed, but the natives of the Cape Colony, whom the British government had at one time granted political equality, were also deprived of some of their rights. And this noble work, culminating under the imperialist policy of the Conservatives in open oppression, was actually to be finished by the Liberal Party itself, amid frenzied applause from the 'liberal cretins of Europe' who with sentimental pride took as proof of the still continuing creative vigour and greatness of English liberalism the fact that Britain had granted complete self-government and freedom to a handful of whites in South Africa.

The ruin of independent craftsmanship by capitalist competition, no less painful for being soft-pedalled, deserves by rights a chapter to itself. The most sinister part of such a chapter would be out-work under capitalism;—but we need not dwell on these phenomena here.

The general result of the struggle between capitalism and simple commodity production is this: after substituting commodity economy for natural economy, capital takes the place of simple commodity economy. Non-capitalist organisations provide a fertile soil for capitalism; more strictly: capital feeds on the ruins of such organisations, and although this non-capitalist milieu is indispensable for accumulation, the latter proceeds at the cost of this medium nevertheless, by eating it up. Historically, the accumulation of capital is a kind of metabolism between capitalist economy and those pre-capitalist methods of production without which it cannot go on and which, in this light, it corrodes and assimilates. Thus capital cannot accumulate without the aid of non-capitalist organisations, nor, on the other hand, can it tolerate their continued existence side by side with itself. Only the continuous and progressive disintegration of non-capitalist organisations makes accumulation of capital possible.

The premises which are postulated in Marx's diagram of accumulation accordingly represent no more than the historical tendency of the movement of accumulation and its logical conclusion. The accumulative process endeavours everywhere to substitute simple commodity economy for natural economy. Its ultimate aim, that is to say, is to establish the exclusive and universal domination of capitalist production in all countries and for all branches of industry.

Yet this argument does not lead anywhere. As soon as this final result is achieved—in theory, of course, because it can never actually happen—accumulation must come to a stop. The realisation and capitalisation of surplus value become impossible to accomplish. Just as soon as reality begins to correspond to Marx's diagram of enlarged reproduction, the end of accumulation is in sight, it has reached its limits, and capitalist production is in extremis. For capital, the standstill of accumulation means that the development of the productive forces is arrested, and the collapse of capitalism follows inevitably, as an objective historical necessity. This is the reason for the contradictory behaviour of capitalism in the final stage of its historical career: imperialism.

Marx's diagram of enlarged reproduction thus does not conform to the conditions of an accumulation in actual progress. Progressive accumulation cannot be reduced to static inter-relations and interdependence between the two great departments of social production (the departments of producer and consumer goods), as the diagram would have it. Accumulation is more than an internal relationship between the branches of capitalist economy; it is primarily a relationship between capital and a non-capitalist environment, where the two great departments of production sometimes perform the accumulative process on their own, independently of each other, but even then at every step the movements overlap and intersect. From this we get most complicated relations, divergencies in the speed and direction of accumulation for the two departments, different relations with non-capitalist modes of production as regards both material elements and elements of value, which we cannot possibly lay down in rigid formulæ. Marx's diagram of accumulation is only the theoretical reflection of the precise moment when the domination of capital has reached its limits, and thus it is no less a fiction than his diagram of simple reproduction, which gives the theoretical formulation for the point of departure of capitalist accumulation. The precise definition of capitalist accumulation and its laws lies somewhere in between these two fictions.

30

INTERNATIONAL LOANS

The imperialist phase of capitalist accumulation which implies universal competition comprises the industrialisation and capitalist emancipation of the *hinterland* where capital formerly realised its surplus value. Characteristic of this phase are: lending abroad, railroad constructions, revolutions, and wars. The last decade, from 1900 to 1910, shows in particular the world-wide movement of capital, especially in Asia and neighbouring Europe: in Russia, Turkey, Persia, India, Japan, China, and also in North Africa. Just as the substitution of commodity economy for a natural economy and that of capitalist production for a simple commodity production was achieved by wars, social crises and the destruction of entire social systems, so at present the achievement of capitalist autonomy in the *hinterland* and backward colonies is attained amidst wars and revolutions. Revolution is an essential for the process of capitalist emancipation. The backward communities must shed their obsolete political organisations, relics of natural and simple commodity economy, and create a modern state machinery adapted to the purposes of capitalist production. The revolutions in Turkey, Russia, and China fall under this heading. The last two, in particular, do not exclusively serve the immediate political requirements of capitalism; to some extent they carry over outmoded pre-capitalist claims while on the other hand they already embody new conflicts which run counter to the domination of capital. These factors account for their immense drive, but at the same time impede and delay the ultimate victory of the revolutionary forces. A young state will usually sever the leading strings of older capitalist states by wars, which temper and test the modern state's capitalist independence in a baptism by fire. That is why military together with financial reforms invariably herald the bid for economic independence.

The forward-thrusts of capital are approximately reflected in the development of the railway network. The permanent way grew most quickly in Europe during the forties, in America in the fifties, in Asia in the sixties, in Australia during the seventies and eighties, and during the nineties in Africa.[1]

Public loans for railroad building and armaments accompany all stages of the accumulation of capital: the introduction of commodity economy, industrialisation of countries, capitalist revolutionisation of agriculture as well as the emancipation of young capitalist states. For

[1] The Permanent Way (in kilometres).

Year	Europe	America	Asia	Africa	Australia
1840	2,925	4,754	—	—	—
1850	23,405	16,064	—	—	—
1860	51,862	53,955	1,393	455	376
1870	104,914	93,193	8,185	1,786	1,765
1880	168,983	174,666	16,287	4,646	7,847
1890	223,869	331,417	33,724	9,386	18,889
1900	283,878	402,171	60,301	20,114	24,014
1910	333,848	526,382	101,916	36,854	31,014

Accordingly, the increase was as follows:

	%	%	%	%	%
1840/50	710	215	—	—	—
1850/60	121	257	—	—	—
1860/70	102	73	486	350	350
1870/80	61	88	99	156	333
1880/90	32	89	107	104	142
1890/1900	27	21	79	114	27

the accumulation of capital, the loan has various functions: (a) it serves to convert the money of non-capitalist groups into capital, i.e. money both as a commodity equivalent (lower middle-class savings) and as fund of consumption for the hangers-on of the capitalist class; (b) it serves to transform money capital into productive capital by means of state enterprise—railroad building and military supplies; (c) it serves to divert accumulated capital from the old capitalist countries to young ones. In the sixteenth and seventeenth centuries, the loan transferred capital from the Italian cities to England, in the eighteenth century from Holland to England, in the nineteenth century from England to the American Republics and Australia, from France, Germany and Belgium to Russia, and at the present time [1912] from Germany to Turkey, from England, Germany and France to China, and, via Russia, to Persia.

In the Imperialist Era, the foreign loan played an outstanding part as a means for young capitalist states to acquire independence. The contradictions inherent in the modern system of foreign loans are the concrete expression of those which characterise the imperialist phase. Though foreign loans are indispensable for the emancipation of the rising capitalist states, they are yet the surest ties by which the old capitalist states maintain their influence, exercise financial control and exert pressure on the customs, foreign and commercial policy of the young capitalist states. Pre-eminently channels for the investment in new spheres of capital accumulated in the old countries, such loans widen the scope for the accumulation of capital; but at the same time they restrict it by creating new competition for the investing countries.

These inherent conflicts of the international loan system are a classic example of spatio-temporal divergencies between the conditions for the realisation of surplus value and the capitalisation thereof. While realisation of the surplus value requires only the general spreading of commodity production, its capitalisation demands the progressive supercession of simple commodity production by capitalist economy, with the corollary that the limits to both the realisation and the capitalisation of surplus value keep contracting ever more. Employment of international capital in the construction of the international railway network reflects this disparity. Between the thirties and the sixties of the nineteenth century, railway building and the loans necessary for it mainly served to oust natural economy, and to spread commodity economy—as in the case of the Russian railway loans in the sixties, or in that of the American railways which were built with European capital. Railway construction in Africa and Asia during the last twenty years, on the other hand, almost exclusively served the purposes of an imperialist policy, of economic monopolisation and economic subjugation of the backward communities. As regards Russia's railroad construction in Eastern Asia, for instance, it is common knowledge that Russia had paved the way for the military occupation of Manchuria by sending troops to protect her engineers working on the Manchurian railway. With the same object in view, Russia obtained railway concessions in Persia, Germany in Asia Minor and Mesopotamia, and Britain and Germany in Africa.

In this connection, we must deal with a misunderstanding concerning the capital investments in foreign countries and the demand of these countries for capital imports. Already in the early twenties of the last century, the export of British capital to America played an important part, being largely responsible for the first genuine industrial and commercial crises in England in 1825. Since 1824, the London stock exchange had been flooded with South American stocks and shares. During the following year, the newly created states of South and Central America raised loans in London alone for more than £20,000,000, and in addition, enormous quantities of South American industrial shares and similar bonds were sold. This sudden prosperity and the opening up of the South American markets in their turn called forth greatly increased exports of British commodities to the Latin Americas. British commodity exports to these countries amounted to £2,900,000 in 1821 which had risen to £6,400,000 by 1825.

Cotton textiles formed the most important item of these exports; this powerful demand was the impetus for a rapid expansion of British cotton production, and many new factories were opened. In 1821, raw cotton to the value of £m. 129 was made up in England, and in 1826 the amount had risen to £m. 167.

The situation was thus fraught with the elements of a crisis. Tugan Baranovski raises the question: 'But from where did the South American countries take the means to buy twice as many commodities in 1825 as in 1821? The British themselves supplied these means. The loans floated on the London stock exchange served as payment for imported goods. Deceived by the demand they had themselves created, the British factory-owners were soon brought to realise by their own experience that their high expectations had been unfounded.'[2]

He thus characterises as 'deceptive', as an unhealthy, abnormal economic phenomenon the fact that the South American demand for English goods had been brought about by British capital. Thus uncritically he took over the doctrine of an expert with whose other theories he wished to have nothing in common. The opinion had been advanced already during the English crisis of 1825 that it could be explained by the 'singular' development of the relations between British capital and South American demand. None other than Sismondi had raised the same question as Tugan Baranovski and given a most accurate description of events in the second edition of his *Nouveaux Principes*:

'The opening up of the immense market afforded by Spanish America to industrial producers seemed to offer a good opportunity to relieve British manufacture. The British government were of that opinion, and in the seven years following the crisis of 1818, displayed unheard-of activity to carry English commerce to penetrate the remotest districts of Mexico, Columbia, Brazil, Rio de la Plata, Chile and Peru. Before the government decided to recognise these new states, it had to protect English commerce by frequent calls of battleships whose captains had a diplomatic rather than a military mission. In consequence, it had defied the clamours of the Holy Alliance and recognised the new republics at a moment when the whole of Europe, on the contrary, was plotting their ruin. But however big the demand afforded by free America, yet it would not have been enough to absorb all the goods England had produced over and above the needs of consumption, had not their means for buying English merchandise been suddenly increased beyond all bounds by the loans to the new republics. Every American state borrowed from England an amount sufficient to consolidate its government. Although they were capital loans, they were immediately spent in the course of the year like income, that is to say they were used up entirely to buy English goods on behalf of the treasury, or to pay for those which had been dispatched on private

[2] Tugan Baranovski, *Studies on the Theory and History of Commercial Crises in England*, p. 74.

orders. At the same time, numerous companies with immense capitals were formed to exploit all the American mines, but all the money they spent found its way back to England, either to pay for the machinery which they immediately used, or else for the goods sent to the localities where they were to work. As long as this singular commerce lasted, in which the English only asked the Americans to be kind enough to buy English merchandise with English capital, and to consume them for their sake, the prosperity of English manufacture appeared dazzling. It was no more income but rather English capital which was used to push on consumption: the English themselves bought and paid for their own goods which they sent to America, and thereby merely forwent the pleasure of using these goods.'[3]

From this Sismondi drew the characteristic conclusion that the real limits to the capitalist market are set by income, i.e. by personal consumption alone, and he used this example as one more warning against accumulation.

Down to the present day, the events which preceded the crisis of 1825 have remained typical for a period of boom and expansion of capital, and such 'singular commerce' is in fact one of the most important foundations of the accumulation of capital. Particularly in the history of British capital, it occurs regularly before every crisis, as Tugan Baranovski himself showed by the following facts and figures: the immediate cause of the 1836 crisis was the flooding of the American market with British goods, again financed by British money. In 1834, U.S. commodity imports exceeded exports by £m. 1.2 but at the same time their imports of precious metal exceeded exports by nearly £m. 3.2. Even in 1836, the year of the crisis itself, their surplus of imported commodities amounted to £m. 10.4, and still the excess of bullion imported was £m. 1. This influx of money, no less than the stream of goods, came chiefly from England, where U.S. railway shares were bought in bulk. 1835/6 saw the opening in the United States of sixty-one new banks with a capital of £m. 10.4, predominantly British. Again, the English paid for their exports themselves. The unprecedented industrial boom in the Northern States of the Union, eventually

---

[3] Sismondi, *Nouveaux Principes* . . ., vol. i, book iv, chap. iv: 'Commercial Wealth Follows the Growth of Income', pp. 368–70.

leading to the Civil War, was likewise financed by British capital, which again created an expanding market for British industry in the United States.

And not only British capital—other European capitals also made every possible effort to take part in this 'singular commerce'. To quote Schaeffle, in the five years between 1849 and 1854, at least £m. 100 were invested in American shares on the various stock exchanges of Europe. The simultaneous revival of world industry attained such dimensions that it culminated in the world crash of 1857.—In the sixties, British capital lost no time in creating similar conditions in Asia as well as the United States. An unending stream was diverted to Asia Minor and East India, where it financed the most magnificent railroad projects. The permanent way of British India amounted in 1860 to 844 miles, in 1870 to 4,802 miles, in 1880 to 9,361 miles and in 1890 to 16,875 miles. This at once increased the demand for British commodities. No sooner had the War of Secession come to a close, than British capital again flowed into the United States. It again paid for the greater part of the enormous railroad constructions in the Union during the sixties and seventies, the permanent way amounting in 1850 to 8,844 miles, in 1860 to 30,807 miles, in 1870 to 53,212 miles, in 1880 to 94,198 miles, and in 1890 to 179,005 miles. Materials for these railways were also being supplied by England—one of the main causes for the rapid development of the British coal and iron industries and the reasons why these industries were so seriously affected by the American crises of 1866, 1873 and 1884. What Sismondi considered sheer lunacy was in this instance literally true: the British with their own materials, their own iron etc., had built railroads in the United States, they had paid for the railways with their own capital and only forwent their 'use'. In spite of all periodical crises, however, European capital had acquired such a taste for this madness, that the London stock exchange was seized by a veritable epidemic of foreign loans in the middle of the seventies. Between 1870 and 1875, loans of this kind, amounting to £m. 260, were raised in London. The immediate consequence was a rapid increase in the overseas export of British merchandise. Although the foreign countries concerned went periodically bankrupt, masses of capital continued to flow in. Turkey, Egypt, Greece, Bolivia, Costa Rica, Ecuador, Honduras, Mexico, Paraguay, Peru, St.

Domingo, Uruguay, and Venezuela completely or partially suspended their payments of interest in the late seventies. Yet undeterred by this, the fever for exotic state loans burst out again at the end of the eighties—the South American states and South African colonies were lent immense quantities of European capital. In 1874, for instance, the Argentine Republic borrowed as much as £m. 10 and the loan had risen to £m. 59 by 1890.

England built railways with her own iron and coal in all these countries as well, paying for them with her own capital. In 1885, the Argentine permanent way had been 1,952 miles, in 1893 it was 8,557 miles.

Exports from England were rising accordingly:

	1886	1890
	£m.	£m.
Iron	21.8	31.6
Machinery	10	16.4
Coal	9	19

British total exports (mainly to the Argentine) amounted to £m. 4.7 in 1885 and to £m. 10.7 a mere four years later.

At the same time, British capital flowed into Australia in the form of state loans. At the end of the eighties the loans to the three colonies Victoria, New South Wales and Tasmania amounted to £m. 112, £m. 81 of which were invested in railway construction. The permanent way of Australia extended over 4,900 miles in 1880, and over 15,600 miles in 1895.

Britain, supplying capital and materials for these railways, was also embroiled in the crises of 1890 in the Argentine, Transvaal, Mexico, Uruguay, and in that of 1893 in Australia.

The following two decades made a difference only in so far as German, French and Belgian capital largely participated with British capital in foreign investments, while railway construction in Asia Minor had been financed entirely by British capital from the fifties to the late eighties. From then on, German capital took over and put into execution the tremendous project of the Anatolian railway. German capital investments in Turkey gave rise to an increased export of German goods to that country.

In 1896, German exports to Turkey amounted to £m. 1.4, in 1911 to £m. 5.65. To Asiatic Turkey, in particular, goods were exported in 1901 to the value of £m. 0.6 and in 1911 to the value of £m. 1.85. In this case, German capital was used to a considerable extent to pay for German goods, the Germans forgoing, to use Sismondi's term, only the pleasure of using their own products.

Let us examine the position more closely:

Realised surplus value, which cannot be capitalised and lies idle in England or Germany, is invested in railway construction, water works, etc. in the Argentine, Australia, the Cape Colony or Mesopotamia. Machinery, materials and the like are supplied by the country where the capital has originated, and the same capital pays for them. Actually, this process characterises capitalist conditions everywhere, even at home. Capital must purchase the elements of production and thus become productive capital before it can operate. Admittedly, the products are then used within the country, while in the former case they are used by foreigners. But then capitalist production does not aim at its products being enjoyed, but at the accumulation of surplus value. There had been no demand for the surplus product within the country, so capital had lain idle without the possibility of accumulating. But abroad, where capitalist production has not yet developed, there has come about, voluntarily or by force, a new demand of the non-capitalist strata. The consumption of the capitalist and working classes at home is irrelevant for the purposes of accumulation, and what matters to capital is the very fact that its products are 'used' by *others*. The new consumers must indeed realise the products, pay for their use, and for this they need money. They can obtain some of it by the exchange of commodities which begins at this point, a brisk traffic in goods following hard on the heels of railway construction and mining (gold mines, etc.). Thus the capital advanced for railroad building and mining, together with an additional surplus value, is gradually realised. It is immaterial to the situation as a whole whether this exported capital becomes share capital in new independent enterprises, or whether, as a government loan, it uses the mediation of a foreign state to find new scope for operation in industry and traffic, nor does it matter if in the first case some of the companies are fraudulent and fail in due course, or if in the second case the borrowing state finally goes bankrupt, i.e. if the owners sometimes lose part of their capital in one way or another. Even the country of origin is not immune, and individual capitals frequently get lost in crises. The important point is that capital accumulated in the old country should find elsewhere new opportunities to beget and realise surplus value, so that accumulation can proceed. In the new countries, large regions of natural economy are open to conversion into commodity economy, or existing commodity economy can be ousted by capital. Railroad construction and mining, gold mining in particular, are typical for the investment of capitals from old capitalist countries in new ones. They are pre-eminently qualified to stimulate a brisk traffic in goods under conditions hitherto determined by natural economy and both are significant in economic history as mile-stones along the route of rapid dissolution of old economic organisations, of social crises and of the development of modern conditions, that is to say of the development of commodity economy to begin with, and further of the production of capital.

For this reason, the part played by lending abroad as well as by capital investments in foreign railway and mining shares is a fine sample of the deficiencies in Marx's diagram of accumulation. In these instances, enlarged reproduction of capital capitalises a surplus value that has already been realised (in so far as the loans or foreign investments are not financed by the savings of the petty bourgeoisie or the semi-proletariat). It is quite irrelevant to the present field of accumulation, when, where and how the capital of the old countries has been realised so that it may flow into the new country. British capital which finds an outlet in Argentine railway construction might well in the past have been realised in China in the form of Indian opium. Further, the British capital which builds railways in the Argentine, is of English origin not only in its pure value-form, as money capital, but also in its material form, as iron, coal and machinery; the use-form of the surplus value, that is to say, has also come into being from the very beginning in the use-form suitable for the purposes of accumulation. The actual use-form of the variable capital, however, labour power, is mainly foreign: it is the native labour of the new countries which is made a new object of exploitation by the capital of the old countries. If we want to keep our investigation all on one plane, we may even assume that the labour power, too, has the same country of origin as the capital. In point of fact new discoveries, of gold mines for instance, tend to call forth mass emigration from the old countries, especially in the first stages, and are largely worked by labour from those countries. It might well be, then, that in a new country capital, labour power and means of production all come from the same capitalist country, say England. So it is really in England that all the material conditions for accumulation exist—a realised surplus value as money capital, a surplus product in productive form, and lastly labour reserves. Yet accumulation cannot proceed here: England and her old buyers require neither railways nor an expanded industry. Enlarged reproduction, i.e. accumulation, is possible only if new districts with a non-capitalist civilisation, extending over large areas, appear on the scene and augment the number of consumers.

But then, who are these new consumers actually; who is it that realises the surplus value of capitalist enterprises which are started with foreign loans; and who, in the final analysis, pays for these loans? The international loans in Egypt provide a classical answer.

The internal history of Egypt in the second half of the nineteenth century is characterised by the interplay of three phenomena: large-scale capitalist enterprise, a rapidly growing public debt, and the collapse of peasant economy. Until quite recently, *corvée* prevailed in Egypt, and the Wali and later the Khedive freely pursued their own power policy with regard to the condition of landownership. These primitive conditions precisely offered an incomparably fertile soil for the operations of European capital. Economically speaking, the conditions for a monetary economy had to be established to begin with, and the state created them by direct compulsion. Until the thirties, Mehemet Ali, the founder of Modern Egypt, here applied a method of patriarchal simplicity: every year, he 'bought up' the fellaheen's entire harvest for the public exchequer, and allowed them to buy back, at a higher price, a minimum for subsistence and seed. In addition he imported cotton from East India, sugar cane from America, indigo and pepper, and issued the fellaheen with official directions what to plant and how much of it. The government again claimed the monopoly for cotton

and indigo, reserving to itself the exclusive right of buying and selling
these goods. By such methods was commodity exchange introduced in
Egypt. Admittedly, Mehemet Ali also did something towards raising
labour productivity. He arranged for dredging of the ancient canalisation, and above all he started the work of the great Kaliub Nile dams
which initiated the series of great capitalist enterprises in Egypt. These
were to comprise four great fields: (1) irrigation systems, in which the
Kaliub works built between 1845 and 1853 take first place—quite
apart from unpaid forced labour, they swallowed up £m. 2.5 and incidentally proved quite useless at first; (2) routes for traffic—the most
important construction which proved ultimately detrimental to Egypt
being the Suez Canal; (3) the cultivation of cotton, and (4) the production of sugar cane. With the building of the Suez Canal, Egypt became
caught up in the web of European capitalism, never again to get free of
it. French capital led the way with British capital hard on its heels. In
the twenty years that followed, the internal disturbances in Egypt were
coloured by the competitive struggle between these two capitals.
French capital was perhaps the most peculiar exponent of the European
methods of capital accumulation at the expense of primitive conditions. Its operations were responsible for the useless Nile dams as well
as for the Suez Canal. Egypt first contracted to supply the labour of
20,000 serfs free of charge for a number of years, and secondly to take
up shares in the Suez Company to the tune of £m. 3.5, i.e. 40 per cent
of the company's total capital. All this for the sake of breaking through
a canal which would deflect the entire trade between Europe and Asia
from Egypt and would painfully affect her part in this trade. These
£m. 3.5 formed the nucleus for Egypt's immense national debt which
was to bring about her military occupation by Britain twenty years later.
In the irrigation system, sudden transformations were initiated: the
ancient *sakias*, i.e. bullock-driven water-wheels, of which 50,000 had
been busy for 7 months in the year in the Nile delta alone, were
partially replaced by steam pumps. Modern steamers now plied on the
Nile between Cairo and Assuan. But the most profound change in the
economic conditions of Egypt was brought about by the cultivation of
cotton. This became almost epidemic in Egypt when, owing to the
American War of Secession and the English cotton famine, the price per
short ton rose from something between £30 and £40 to £200–£250.

Everybody was planting cotton, and foremost among all, the Viceroy and his family. His estates grew fat, what with large-scale land robbery, confiscations, forced 'sale' or plain theft. He suddenly appropriated villages by the score though without any legal excuse. Within an incredibly short time, this vast demesne was brought under cotton, with the result that the entire technique of Egyptian traditional agriculture was revolutionised. Dams were thrown up everywhere to protect the cotton fields from the seasonal flooding of the Nile, and a comprehensive system of artificial irrigation was introduced. These waterworks together with continuous deep ploughing—a novel departure for the fellah who had until then merely scratched his soil with a plough dating back to the Pharaohs—and finally the intensive labours of the harvest made between them enormous demands on Egypt's labour power. This was throughout the same forced peasant labour over which the state claimed to have an unrestricted right of disposal; and thousands had already been employed on the Kaliub dams and the Suez Canal and now the irrigation and plantation work to be done on the viceregal estates clamoured for this forced labour. The 20,000 serfs who had been put at the disposal of the Suez Canal Company were now required by the Khedive himself, and this brought about the first clash with French capital. The company was adjudged a compensation of £m. 3.35 by the arbitration of Napoleon III, a settlement to which the Khedive could all the more readily agree, since the very fellaheen whose labour power was the bone of contention were ultimately to be mulcted of this sum. The work of irrigation was immediately put in hand. Centrifugal machines, steam and traction engines were therefore ordered from England and France. In their hundreds, they were carried by steamers from England to Alexandria and then further. Steam ploughs were needed for cultivating the soil, especially since the rinderpest of 1864 had killed off all the cattle, England again being the chief supplier of these machines. The Fowler works were expanded enormously of a sudden to meet the requirements of the Viceroy for which Egypt had to pay.[4]

---

[4] Engineer Eyth, a representative of Fowler's, tells us: 'Now there was a feverish exchange of telegrams between Cairo, London and Leeds.— "When can Fowler's deliver 150 steam ploughs?"—Answer: "Working to capacity, within one year."—"Not good enough.

But now Egypt required yet a third type of machine, cotton gins and presses for packing. Dozens of these gins were set up in the Delta towns. Like English industrial towns, Sagasis, Tanta, Samanud and other towns were covered by palls of smoke and great fortunes circulated in the banks of Alexandria and Cairo.

But already in the year that followed, this cotton speculation collapsed with the cotton prices which fell in a couple of days from 27d. per pound to 15d., 12d., and finally 6d. after the cessation of hostilities in the American Union. The following year, Ismail Pasha ventured on a new speculation, the production of cane sugar. The forced labour of the fellaheen was to compete with the Southern States of the Union where slavery had been abolished. For the second time, Egyptian agriculture was turned upside down. French and British capitalists found a new field for rapid accumulation. 18 giant sugar factories were put on order in 1868–9 with an estimated daily output of 200 short tons of sugar, that is to say four times as much as that of the greatest then existing

---

Expect unloading Alexandria by spring 150 steam ploughs."—A.: "Impossible."—The works at that time were barely big enough to turn out 3 steam ploughs per week. N.B. a machine of this type costs £2,500 so that the order involved £m. 3.75. Ismail Pasha's next wire: "Quote cost immediate factory expansion. Viceroy willing foot bill."—You can imagine that Leeds made hay while the sun shone. And in addition, other factories in England and France as well were made to supply steam ploughs. The Alexandria warehouses, where goods destined for the viceregal estates were unloaded, were crammed to the roof with boilers, wheels, drums, wire-rope and all sorts of chests and boxes. The second-rate hostelries of Cairo swarmed with newly qualified steam ploughmen, promoted in a hurry from anvil or share-plough, young hopefuls, fit for anything and nothing, since every steam plough must be manned by at least one expert pioneer of civilisation. Wagonloads of this assorted cargo were sent into the interior, just so that the next ship could unload. You cannot imagine in what condition they arrived at their destination, or rather anywhere but their destination. Ten boilers were lying on the banks of the Nile, and the machine to which they belonged was ten miles further. Here was a little heap of wire-rope, but you had to travel another 20 hours to find the appropriate pulleys. In one place an Englishman who was to set up the machines squatted desolate and hungry on a pile of French crates, and in another place his mate had taken to native liquor in his despair. Effendis and Katibs, invoking the help of Allah, rushed to and fro between Siut and Alexandria and compiled endless lists of items the names of which they did not even know. And yet, in the end, some of this apparatus was set in motion. In Upper Egypt, the ploughs belched steam—civilisation and progress had made another step forward' (*Lebendige Kräfte, 7 Vorträge aus dem Gebiete der Technik*, Berlin, 1908, p. 21).

plant. Six of them were ordered from England, and twelve from France, but England eventually delivered the lion's share, because of the Franco-German war. These factories were to be built along the Nile at intervals of 6.2 miles (10 km.), as centres of cane plantations of an area comprising 10 sq. km. Working to full capacity, each factory required a daily supply of 2,000 tons of sugar cane. Fellaheen were driven to forced labour on the sugar plantations in their thousands, while further thousands of their number built the Ibrahimya Canal. The stick and *kourbash* were unstintingly applied. Transport soon became a problem. A railway network had to be built round every factory to haul the masses of cane inside, rolling stock, funiculars, etc., had to be obtained as quickly as possible. Again these enormous orders were placed with English capital. The first giant factory was opened in 1872, 4,000 camels providing makeshift transport. But it proved to be simply impossible to supply cane in the quantities required by the undertaking. The working staff was completely inadequate, since the fellah, accustomed to forced labour on the land, could not be transformed overnight into a modern industrial worker by the lash of the whip. The venture collapsed, even before many of the imported machines had been installed. This sugar speculation concluded the period of gigantic capitalist enterprise in Egypt in 1873.

What had provided the capital for these enterprises? International loans. One year before his death in 1863, Said Pasha had raised the first loan at a nominal value of £m. 3.3 which came to £m. 2.5 in cash after deduction of commissions, discounts, etc. He left to Ismail Pasha the legacy of this debt and the contract with the Suez Canal Company, which was to burden Egypt with a debt of £m. 17. Ismail Pasha in turn raised his first loan in 1864 with a nominal value of £m. 5.7 at 7 per cent and a cash value of £m. 4.85 at 8¼ per cent. What remained of it, after £m. 3.35 had been paid to the Suez Canal Company as compensation, was spent within the year, swallowed up for the greater part by the cotton gamble. In 1865, the first so-called Daira-loan was floated by the Anglo-Egyptian Bank, on the security of the Khedive's private estates. The nominal value of this loan was £m. 3.4 at 9 per cent, and its real value £m. 2.5 at 12 per cent. In 1866, *Fruehling & Goschen* floated a new loan at a nominal value of £m. 3 and a cash value of £m. 2. The Ottoman Bank floated another in 1867 of nominally £m. 2, really

£m. 1.7. The floating debt at that time amounted to £m. 30. The Banking House Oppenheim & Neffen floated a great loan in 1868 to consolidate part of this debt. Its nominal value was £m. 11.9 at 7 per cent, though Ismail could actually lay hands only on £m. 7.1 at 13½ per cent. This money made it possible, however, to pay for the pompous celebrations on the opening of the Suez Canal, in presence of the leading figures in the Courts of Europe, in finance and in the demi-monde, for a madly lavish display, and further, to grease the palm of the Turkish Overlord, the Sultan, with a new baksheesh of £m. 1. The sugar gamble necessitated another loan in 1870. Floated by the firm of Bischoffsheim & Goldschmidt, it had a nominal value of £m. 7.1 at 7 per cent, and its cash value was £m. 5. In 1872/3 Oppenheim's floated two further loans, a modest one amounting to £m. 4 at 14 per cent and a large one of £m. 32 at 8 per cent which reduced the floating debt by one-half, but which actually came only to £m. 11 in cash, since the European banking houses paid it in part by bills of exchange they had discounted.

In 1874, a further attempt was made to raise a national loan of £m. 50 at an annual charge of 9 per cent., but it yielded no more than £m. 3.4. Egyptian securities were quoted at 54 per cent of their face value. Within the thirteen years after Said Pasha's death, Egypt's total public debt had grown from £m. 3.293 to £m. 94.110,[5] and collapse was imminent.

These operations of capital, at first sight, seem to reach the height of madness. One loan followed hard on the other, the interest on old loans was defrayed by new loans, and capital borrowed from the British and French paid for the large orders placed with British and French industrial capital.

While the whole of Europe sighed and shrugged its shoulders at Ismail's crazy economy, European capital was in fact doing business in Egypt on a unique and fantastic scale—an incredible modern version of the biblical legend about the fat kine which remains unparalleled in capitalist history.

In the first place, there was an element of usury in every loan, anything between one-fifth and one-third of the money ostensibly lent sticking to the fingers of the European bankers. Ultimately, the

---

[5] Cf. Evelyn Baring, Earl of Cromer, Egypt Today (London, 1908), vol. i, p. 11.

exorbitant interest had to be paid somehow, but how—where were the means to come from? Egypt herself was to supply them; their source was the Egyptian fellah—peasant economy providing in the final analysis all the most important elements for large-scale capitalist enterprise. He provided the land since the so-called private estates of the Khedive were quickly growing to vast dimensions by robbery and blackmail of innumerable villages; and these estates were the foundations of the irrigation projects and the speculation in cotton and sugar cane. As forced labour, the fellah also provided the labour power and, what is more, he was exploited without payment and even had to provide his own means of subsistence while he was at work. The marvels of technique which European engineers and European machines performed in the sphere of Egyptian irrigation, transport, agriculture and industry were due to this peasant economy with its fellaheen serfs. On the Kaliub Nile dams and on the Suez Canal, in the cotton plantations and in the sugar plants, untold masses of peasants were put to work; they were switched over from one job to the next as the need arose, and they were exploited to the limit of endurance and beyond. Although it became evident at every step that there were technical limits to the employment of forced labour for the purposes of modern capital, yet this was amply compensated by capital's unrestricted power of command over the pool of labour power, how long and under what conditions men were to work, live and be exploited.

But not alone that it supplied land and labour power, peasant economy also provided the money. Under the influence of capitalist economy, the screws were put on the fallaheen by taxation. The tax on peasant holdings was persistently increased. In the late sixties, it amounted to £2 5s. per *hectare*, but not a farthing was levied on the enormous private estates of the royal family. In addition, ever more special rates were devised. Contributions of 2s. 6d. per *hectare* had to be paid for the maintenance of the irrigation system which almost exclusively benefited the royal estates, and the fellah had to pay 1s. 4d. for every date tree felled, 9d. for every clay hovel in which he lived. In addition, every male over 10 years of age was liable to a head tax of 6s. 6d. The total paid by the fellaheen was £m. 2.5 under Mehemet Ali, £m. 5 under Said Pasha, and £m. 8.15 under Ismail Pasha.

The greater the debt to European capital became, the more had to be extorted from the peasants.[6] In 1869 all taxes were put up by 10 per cent and the taxes for the coming year collected in advance. In 1870, a supplementary land tax of 8s. per hectare was levied. All over Upper Egypt people were leaving the villages, demolished their dwellings and no longer tilled their land—only to avoid payment of taxes. In 1876, the tax on date palms was increased by 6d. Whole villages went out to fell their date palms and had to be prevented by rifle volleys. North of Siut, 10,000 fellaheen are said to have starved in 1879 because they could no longer raise the irrigation tax for their fields and had killed their cattle to avoid paying tax on it.[7]

Now the fellah had been drained of his last drop of blood. Used as a leech by European capital, the Egyptian state had accomplished its function and was no longer needed. Ismail, the Khedive, was given his congé; capital could begin winding up operations.

Egypt had still to pay 394,000 Egyptian pounds as interest on the Suez Canal shares for £m. 4 which England had bought in 1875. Now British commissions to 'regulate' the finances of Egypt went into action. Strangely enough, European capital was not at all deterred by the desperate state of the insolvent country and offered again and again to grant immense loans for the salvation of Egypt. Cowe and Stokes proposed a loan of £m. 76 at 9 per cent for the conversion of the total debt, Rivers Wilson thought no less than £m. 103 would be necessary. The Crédit Foncier bought up floating bills of exchange by the million, attempting, though without success, to consolidate the total debt by a loan of £m. 91. With the financial position growing hopelessly desperate, the time drew near when the country and all her productive forces was to become the prey of European capital. October 1878 saw the

---

[6] Incidentally, the money wrested from the Egyptian fellah further fell, by way of Turkey, to European capital. The Turkish loans of 1854, 1855, 1871, 1877 and 1886 were based on the contributions from Egypt which were increased several times and paid direct into the Bank of England.

[7] 'It is stated by residents in the Delta', reports *The Times* of March 31, 1879, 'that the third quarter of the year's taxation is now collected, and the old methods of collection applied. This sounds strangely by the side of the news that people are starving by the roadside, that great tracts of country are uncultivated, because of the physical burdens, and that the farmers have sold their cattle, the women their finery, and that the usurers are filling the mortgage offices with their bonds, and the courts with their suits of foreclosure' (quoted by Th. Rothstein, *Egypt's Ruin*, 1910, pp. 69–70).

representatives of the European creditors landing in Alexandria. British and French capital established dual control of finances and devised new taxes; the peasants were beaten and oppressed, so that payment of interest, temporarily suspended in 1876, could be resumed in 1877.[8]

Now the claims of European capital became the pivot of economic life and the sole consideration of the financial system. In 1878, a new commission and ministry were set up, both with a staff in which Europeans made up one-half. In 1879, the finances of Egypt were brought under permanent control of European capital, exercised by the *Commission de la Dette Publique Égyptienne* in Cairo. In 1878, the Tshifliks, estates of the viceregal family, which comprised 431,100 acres, were converted into crown land and pledged to the European capitalists as collateral for the public debt, and the same happened to the Daira lands, the private estates of the Khedive, comprising 485,131 acres, mainly in Upper Egypt; this was, at a later date, sold to a syndicate. The other estates for the greatest part fell to capitalist companies, the Suez Canal Company in particular. To cover the cost of occupation, England requisitioned ecclesiastical lands of the mosques and schools. An opportune pretext for the final blow was provided by a mutiny in the Egyptian army, starved under European financial control while European officials were drawing excellent salaries, and by a revolt engineered among the Alexandrian masses who had been bled white. The British military occupied Egypt in 1882, as a result of twenty years' operations of Big Business, never to leave again. This was the ultimate and final step in the process of liquidating peasant economy in Egypt by and for European capital.[9]

It should now be clear that the transactions between European loan

[8] 'This produce', wrote the correspondent of *The Times* from Alexandria, 'consists wholly of taxes paid by the peasants in kind, and when one thinks of the poverty-stricken, overdriven, under-paid fellaheen in their miserable hovels, working late and early to fill the pockets of the creditors, the punctual payment of the coupon ceases to be wholly a subject of gratification' (quoted by Rothstein, op. cit., p. 49).

[9] Eyth, an outstanding exponent of capitalist civilisation in the primitive countries, characteristically concludes his masterly sketch on Egypt, from which we have taken the main data, with the following imperialist articles of faith: 'What we have learnt from the past also holds true for the future. Europe must and will lay firm hands upon those countries which can no longer keep up with modern conditions on their own, though this will not be possible without all kinds of struggle, when the difference between right and wrong will become blurred, when political and historical justice will often enough mean

capital and European industrial capital are based upon relations which are extremely rational and 'sound' for the accumulation of capital, although they appear absurd to the casual observer because this loan capital pays for the orders from Egypt and the interest on one loan is paid out of a new loan. Stripped of all obscuring connecting links, these relations consist in the simple fact that European capital has largely swallowed up the Egyptian peasant economy. Enormous tracts of land, labour, and labour products without number, accruing to the state as taxes, have ultimately been converted into European capital and have been accumulated. Evidently, only by use of the *kourbash* could the historical development which would normally take centuries be compressed into two or three decades, and it was just the primitive nature of Egyptian conditions which proved such fertile soil for the accumulation of capital.

As against the fantastic increase of capital on the one hand, the other economic result is the ruin of peasant economy together with the growth of commodity exchange which is rooted in the supreme exertion of the country's productive forces. Under Ismail's rule, the arable and reclaimed land of Egypt grew from 5 to 6.75 million acres, the canal system from 45,625 to 54,375 miles and the permanent way from 256.25 to 1,638 miles. Docks were built in Siut and Alexandria, magnificent dockyards in Alexandria, a steamer-service for pilgrims to Mecca was introduced on the Red Sea and along the coast of Syria and Asia Minor. Egypt's exports which in 1861 had amounted to £4,450,000 rose to £m. 14.4 in 1864; her imports which under Said Pasha amounted to £m. 1.2 rose under Ismail to between £m. 5 and £m. 5.5. Trade which recovered only in the eighties from the opening up of the Suez Canal amounted to £m. 8.15 worth of imports and £m. 12.45 worth of exports in 1890, but in 1900 the figures were £m. 144 for imports and £m. 12.25 for exports, and in 1911— £m. 27.85 for imports and £m. 26.85 for exports. Thanks to this development of commodity economy which expanded by leaps and

disaster for millions and their salvation depend upon what is politically wrong. All the world over, the strongest hand will make an end to confusion, and so it will even on the banks of the Nile' (op. cit., p. 247). Rothstein has made it clear enough what kind of 'order' the British created 'on the banks of the Nile'.

bounds with the assistance of European capital, Egypt herself had fallen a prey to the latter. The case of Egypt, just as that of China and, more recently, Morocco, shows militarism as the executor of the accumulation of capital, lurking behind international loans, railroad building, irrigation systems, and similar works of civilisation. The Oriental states cannot develop from natural to commodity economy and further to capitalist economy fast enough and are swallowed up by international capital, since they cannot perform these transformations without selling their souls to capital. Their feverish metamorphoses are tantamount to their absorption by international capital.

Another good recent example is the deal made by German capital in Asiatic Turkey. European capital, British capital in particular, had already at an early date attempted to gain possession of this area which marches with the ancient trade route between Europe and Asia.[10]

In the fifties and sixties, British capital built the railway lines Symrna–Aydin–Diner and Smyrna–Kassaba–Alasehir, obtained the concession to extend the line to Afyon Karahisar and also leased the first tract for the Anatolian railway Ada–Bazar–Izmid. French capital gradually came to acquire influence over part of the railway building during this time. In 1888, German capital appeared on the scene. It took up 60 per cent of the shares in the new merger of international interests, negotiated principally with the French capitalist group represented by the *Banque Ottomane*. International capital took up the remaining 40 per cent.[11] The Anatolian Railway Company, a Turkish company, was founded on the 14th Redsheb of the year 1306 (March 4, 1889)

[10] Already in the early twenties of the last century, the Anglo-Indian government commissioned Colonel Chesney to investigate the navigability of the River Euphrates in order to establish the shortest possible connection between the Mediterranean and the Persian Gulf, resp. India. After detailed preparations and a preliminary reconnaissance in winter 1831, the expedition proper set out in 1835/7. In due course, British staff and officials investigated and surveyed a wider area in Eastern Mesopotamia. These efforts dragged on until 1866 without any useful results for the British government. But at a later date Great Britain returned to the plan of connecting the Mediterranean with India by way of the Gulf of Persia, though in a different form, i.e. the Tigris railway project. In 1879, Cameron travelled through Mesopotamia for the British government to study the lie of the land for the projected railway (Max Freiherr v. Oppenheim, *Vom Mittelmeer zum Persischen Golf durch den Hauran, die Syrische Wüste und Mesopotamien*, vol. ii, pp. 5 and 36).

[11] S. Schneider, *Die Deutsche Bagdadbahn* (1900), p. 3.

with the *Deutsche Bank* for principal backer, to take over the railway lines between Ada–Bazar and Izmid, running since the early seventies, as also the concession for the Izmid–Eskisehir–Angora line (525 miles). It was further entitled to complete the Ada–Bazar–Scutari line and branch lines to Brussa, in addition to building the supplementary network Eskisehir–Konya (278 miles) on the basis of the 1893 concession, and finally to run a service from Angora to Kaisari (264 miles). The Turkish government gave the company a state guarantee of annual gross earnings amounting to £412 per km. on the Ada–Bazar line and of £600 per km. on the Izmid–Angora lines. For this purpose it wrote over to the *Administration de la Dette Publique Ottomane* the revenue from tithes in the *sandshaks* of Izmid, Ertoghrul, Kutalia and Angora, with which to make up the gross earnings guaranteed by the government. For the Angora–Kaisari line the government guaranteed annual gross earnings of 775 Turkish pounds, i.e. £712 per km., and 604 Turkish pounds, i.e. approximately £550, provided, in the latter case, that the supplementary grant per km. did not exceed 219 Turkish pounds (£200 a year). The government was to receive a quarter of the eventual surplus of gross earnings over the guaranteed amount. The *Administration de la Dette Publique Ottomane* as executor of the government guarantee collected the tithes of the *sandshaks* Trebizonde and Gumuchhane direct and paid the railway company out of a common fund which was formed of all the tithes set aside for this purpose. In 1898, the Eskisehir–Konya maximum grant was raised from 218 to 296 Turkish pounds.

In 1899, the company obtained concessions to build and run a dockyard at Ada–Bazar, to issue writs, to build corn-elevators and store-rooms for goods of every description, further the right to employ its own staff for loading and unloading and, finally, in the sphere of customs policy, the creation of a kind of free port.

In 1901, the company acquired a concession for the Baghdad railway Konya–Baghdad–Bazra–Gulf of Persia (1,500 miles) which connects with the Anatolian line by the Konya–Aregli–Bulgurlu line. For taking up this concession, a new limited company was founded which placed the order of constructing the line, at first to Bulgurlu, with a Building Company registered in Frankfort-on-the-Main.

Between 1893 and 1910, the Turkish government gave additional grants—£1,948,000 for the Ada–Bazar–Angora line and 1,800,000

Turkish pounds for the Eskisehir–Konya line—a total of £3,632,000.[12]
Finally, by the concession of 1907, the company was empowered to
drain the Karavirar Lake and to irrigate the Konya plain, these works to
be executed within six years at government expense. In this instance,
the company advanced the government the necessary capital up to
£780,000 at 5 per cent interest, repayable within thirty-six years. In
return the Turkish government pledged as securities: (1) an annual
sum of 25,000 Turkish pounds, payable from the surplus of the tithes'
fund assigned to the *Administration de la Dette Publique Ottomane* to cover the
railway grants and other obligations; (2) the residual tithes over the last
5 years in the newly irrigated regions; (3) the net proceeds from the
working of the irrigation systems, and (4) the price of all reclaimed or
irrigated land that was sold. For the execution of this work, the Frank-
fort company had formed a subsidiary company 'for the irrigation of
the Konya plain' with a capital of £m. 5.4 to take this work in hand.

In 1908 the company obtained the concession for extending the
Konya railway as far as Baghdad and the Gulf of Persia, again with
inclusion of a guaranteed revenue.

To pay for this railway grant, a German Baghdad railway loan was
taken up in three instalments of £m. 2.16, £m. 4.32 and £m. 4.76
respectively, on the security of the aggregate tithes for the *vilayets* Aydin,
Baghdad, Mossul, Diarbekir, Ursa and Alleppo, and the sheep-tax in the
vilayets Konya, Adana, Aleppo, etc.[13]

[12] Saling, *Börsenjahrbuch* 1911/12, p. 2211.
[13] Ibid., pp. 360–1. Engineer Pressel of Wuerttemberg, who as assistant to Baron v. Hirsch
was actively engaged in these transactions in European Turkey, neatly accounts for the
total grants towards railway-building in Turkey which European capital wrested from
the Turkish government:

	Length in km.	Paid guarantee in francs
3 lines in European Turkey	1888.8	33,099,352
Turkish permanent way in Asia completed before 1900	2313.2	53,811,538
Commissions and other costs connected with the guaranteed railway grants paid to the A.D.P.O.		9,351,209
Total		96,262,099

Continued overleaf

The foundation of accumulation here becomes quite clear. German capital builds railways, ports and irrigation works in Asiatic Turkey; in all these enterprises it extorts new surplus value from the Asiatics whom it employs as labour power. But this surplus value must be realised together with the means of production from Germany (railway materials, machinery, etc.). How is it done? In part by commodity exchange which is brought about by the railways, the dockyards, etc., and nurtured in Asia Minor under conditions of natural economy. In part, i.e. in so far as commodity exchange does not grow quickly enough for the needs of capital, by using force, the machinery of the state, to convert the national real income into commodities; these are turned into cash in order to realise capital plus surplus value. That is the true object of the revenue grants for independent enterprises run by foreign capital, and of the collateral in the case of loans. In both instances so-called tithes (*ueshur*), pledged in different ways, are paid in kind by the Turkish peasant and these were gradually increased from about 12 to 12½ per cent. The peasant in the Asiatic *vilayet* must pay up or else his tithe would simply be confiscated by the police and the central and local authorities. These tithes, themselves a

Footnote 13 continued

All this refers only to the period before 1899; not until that date were the revenue grants paid in part. The tithes of no less than 28 out of the 74 *sandshaks* in Asiatic Turkey had been pledged for the revenue grants, and with these grants, between 1856 and 1900, a grand total of 1,576 miles of rails had been laid down in Asiatic Turkey. Pressel, the expert, by the way gives an instance of the underhand methods employed by the railway company at Turkish expense; he states that under the 1893 agreement the Anatolian company promised to run the railway to Baghdad via Angora, but later decided that this plan of theirs would not work and, having qualified for the guarantee, left the line to its fate and got busy with another route via Konya. 'No sooner have the companies succeeded in acquiring the Smyrna–Aydin–Diner line, than they will demand the extension of this line to Konya, and the moment these branch lines are completed, the companies will move heaven and earth to force the goods traffic to use these new routes for which there are no guarantees, and which, more important still, need never share their takings, whereas the other lines must pay part of their surplus to the government, once their gross revenue exceeds a certain amount. In consequence, the government will gain nothing by the Aydin line, and the companies will make millions. The government will foot the bill for practically the entire revenue guarantee for the Kassaba–Angora line, and can never hope to profit by its contracted 25 per cent share in the surplus above £600 gross takings' (W. V. Pressel, *Les Chemins de Fer en Turquie d'Asie* (Zurich, 1900), p. 7).

manifestation of ancient Asiatic despotism based on natural economy, are not collected by the Turkish government direct, but by tax-farmers not unlike the tax-collectors of the *ancien régime*; that is to say the expected returns from the levy in each *vilayet* are separately auctioned by the state to tax-farmers. They are bought by individual speculators or syndicates who sell the tithes of each *sandshak* (district) to other speculators and these resell their shares to a whole number of smaller agents. All these middlemen want to cover their expenses and make the greatest possible profit, and thus, by the time they are actually collected, the peasants' contributions have swollen to enormous dimensions. The tax-farmer will try to recoup himself for any mistake in his calculations at the expense of the peasant, and the latter, nearly always in debt, is impatient for the moment when he can sell his harvest. But often, after cutting his corn, he cannot start threshing for weeks, until indeed the tax-farmer deigns to take his due. His entire harvest is about to rot in the fields, and the tax-farmer, usually a grain merchant himself, takes advantage of this fact and compels him to sell at a low price. These tax-collectors know how to enlist the support of the officials, especially the Muktars, the local headmen, against complaining malcontents.[14]

Along with the taxes on salt, tobacco, spirits, the excise on silk, the fishing dues, etc., the tithes are pledged with the *Conseil de l'Administration de la Dette Publique Ottomane* to serve as security for the railway grant and the loans. In every case the *Conseil* reserves to itself the right to vet the tax-farmers' contracts and stipulates for the proceeds of the tithe to be paid directly into the coffers of its regional offices. If no tax-farmer can be found, the tithes are stored in kind by the Turkish government; the warehouse keys are deposited with the *Conseil* which then can sell the tithes on its own account.

Thus the economic metabolism between the peasants of Asia Minor, Syria and Mesopotamia on the one hand and German capital on the other proceeds in the following way: in the *vilayets* Konya, Baghdad, Bazra, etc., the grain comes into being as a simple use-product of primitive peasant economy. It immediately falls to the tithe-farmer as a state levy. Only then, in the hands of this latter, does it become a

---

[14] Charles Moravitz, *Die Türkei im Spiegel ihrer Finanzen* (1903), p. 84.

commodity, and, as such, money which falls to the state. This money is nothing but converted peasant grain; it was not even produced as a commodity. But now, as a state guarantee, it serves towards paying for the construction and operation of railways, i.e. to realise both the value of the means of production and the surplus value extorted from the Asiatic peasants and proletariat in the building and running of the railway. In this process further means of production of German origin are used, and so the peasant grain of Asia, converted into money, also serves to turn into cash the surplus value that has been extorted from the German workers. In the performance of these functions, the money rolls from the hands of the Turkish government into the coffers of the *Deutsche Bank*, and here it accumulates, as capitalist surplus value, in the form of promoters' profits, royalties, dividends and interests in the accounts of Messrs. Gwinner, Siemens, Stinnes and their fellow directors, of the shareholders and clients of the *Deutsche Bank* and the whole intricate system of its subsidiary companies. If there is no tax-farmer, as provided in the concessions, then the complicated meta-morphoses are reduced to their most simple and obvious terms: the peasant grain passes immediately to the *Administration de la Dette Publique Ottomane*, i.e. to the representatives of European capital, and becomes already in its natural form a revenue for German and other foreign capital: it realises capitalist surplus value even before it has shed its use-form for the Asiatic peasant, even before it has become a commodity and its own value has been realised. This is a coarse and straight-forward metabolism between European capital and Asiatic peasant economy, with the Turkish state reduced to its real rôle, that of a political machinery for exploiting peasant economy for capitalist purposes,—the real function, this, of all Oriental states in the period of capitalist imperialism. This business of paying for German goods with German capital in Asia is not the absurd circle it seems at first, with the kind Germans allowing the shrewd Turks merely the 'use' of their great works of civilisation—it is at bottom an exchange between German capital and Asiatic peasant economy, an exchange performed under state compulsion. On the one hand it makes for progressive accumulation and expanding 'spheres of interest' as a pretext for fur-ther political and economic expansion of German capital in Turkey. Railroad building and commodity exchange, on the other hand, are fostered by the state on the basis of a rapid disintegration, ruin and exploitation of Asiatic peasant economy in the course of which the Turkish state becomes more and more dependent on European capital, politically as well as financially.[15]

---

[15] 'Incidentally, in this country everything is difficult and complicated. If the government wishes to create a monopoly in cigarette paper or playing cards, France and Austro-Hungary immediately are on the spot to veto the project in the interest of their trade. If the issue is oil, Russia will raise objections, and even the Powers who are least concerned will make their agreement dependent on some other agreement. Turkey's fate is that of Sancho Panza and his dinner: as soon as the minister of finance wishes to do anything, some diplomat gets up, interrupts him and throws a veto in his teeth' (Moravitz, op. cit., p. 70).

31

PROTECTIVE TARIFFS AND ACCUMULATION

Imperialism is the political expression of the accumulation of capital in its competitive struggle for what remains still open of the non-capitalist environment. Still the largest part of the world in terms of geography, this remaining field for the expansion of capital is yet insignificant as against the high level of development already attained by the productive forces of capital; witness the immense masses of capital accumulated in the old countries which seek an outlet for their surplus product and strive to capitalise their surplus value, and the rapid change-over to capitalism of the pre-capitalist civilisations. On the international stage, then, capital must take appropriate measures. With the high development of the capitalist countries and their increasingly severe competition in acquiring non-capitalist areas, imperialism grows in lawlessness and violence, both in aggression against the non-capitalist world and in ever more serious conflicts among the competing capitalist countries. But the more violently, ruthlessly and thoroughly imperialism brings about the decline of non-capitalist civilisations, the more rapidly it cuts the very ground from under the feet of capitalist accumulation. Though imperialism is the historical method for prolonging the career of capitalism, it is also a sure means of bringing it to a swift conclusion. This is not to say that capitalist development must be actually driven to this extreme: the mere tendency towards imperialism of itself takes forms which make the final phase of capitalism a period of catastrophe.

Classical economics, in its period of storm and stress, had had high hopes of a peaceful development of the accumulation of capital and of a trade and industry which can only prosper in times of peace, evolving the orthodox Manchester ideology of the harmony of interests among the world's commercial nations on the one hand, and between capital and labour on the other. These hopes were apparently justified in Europe by the short period of Free Trade in the sixties and seventies, which was based upon the mistaken doctrine of the English Free Traders that the only theoretical and practical condition for the accumulation of capital is commodity exchange, that the two are identical. As we have seen, Ricardo and his whole school identified accumulation and its reproductive conditions with simple commodity production and the conditions of simple commodity circulation. This was soon to become even more obvious in the practices of the common Free Trader. The special interests of the exporting Lancashire cotton manufacturers in Manchester determined the entire line of argument of the Cobden League. Their principal object was to get markets, and it became an article of faith: 'Buy from foreign countries and thus in turn sell our industrial product, our cotton goods, on the new markets.' Cobden and Bright demanded Free Trade and cheaper foodstuffs in particular in the interest of consumption; but the consumer was not the worker who eats the bread, but the capitalist who consumes labour power.

This teaching never expressed the interests of capitalist accumulation as a whole. In England herself it was given the lie already in the forties, when the harmony of interests of the commercial nations in the East were proclaimed to the sound of gunfire in the Opium Wars which ultimately, by the annexation of Hongkong, brought about the very opposite of such harmony, a system of 'spheres of interest'.[1] On the

---

[1] And not only in England. 'Even in 1859, a pamphlet, ascribed to Diergardt of Viersen, a factory owner, was disseminated all over Germany, urging that country to make sure of the East-Asiatic markets in good time. It advocated the display of military force as the

European Continent, Free Trade in the sixties did not represent the interests of industrial capital, because the foremost Free Trade countries of the Continent were still predominantly agrarian with a comparatively feeble development of industry. Rather, the policy of Free Trade was implemented as a means for the political reconstruction of the Central European states. In Germany, under Bismarck and Manteuffel, it was a peculiarly Prussian lever for ousting Austria from the *Bund* and the *Zollverein* and to set up the new German Empire under Prussian leadership. Economically speaking, the mainstays of Free Trade were in this case the interests both of commercial capital, especially in the Hansa towns to whom international trade was vital, and of agrarian consumers; among industry proper, it was otherwise. The iron industry was won over only with difficulty and in exchange for the abolition of the Rhine tolls. But the cotton industry in Southern Germany remained irreconcilable and clung to protective tariffs. In France, 'most favoured nations' clause' agreements, the basis of the Free Trade system all over Europe, were concluded by Napoleon III without the consent, and even against the will, of parliament, industrialists and agrarians, who constituted an absolute majority, being in favour of protective tariffs. The government of the Second Empire only took the course of commercial treaties as an emergency measure—Britain accepted it as such—in order to get round political opposition in France and to establish Free Trade behind the back of the legislature by international action. The first principal treaty between England and France simply rode

only means for getting commercial advantages from the Japanese and the Eastern Asiatic nations in general. A German fleet, built with the people's small savings, had been a youthful dream, long since brought under the hammer by Hannibal Fischer. Though Prussia had a few ships, her naval power was not impressive. But in order to enter into commercial negotiations with Eastern Asia, it was decided to equip a ship. Graf zu Eulenburg, one of the ablest and most prudent Prussian statesmen, was appointed chief of this mission which also had scientific objects. Under most difficult conditions he carried out his commission with great skill, and though the plan for simultaneous negotiations with the Hawaiian islands had to be given up, the mission was otherwise successful. Though the Berlin press of that time knew better, declaring whenever a new difficulty was reported, that it was only to be expected, and denouncing all expenditure on naval demonstrations as a waste of the taxpayers' money, the ministry of the new era remained steadfast, and the harvest of success was reaped by the ministry that followed' (W. Lotz, *Die Ideen der deutschen Handelspolitik*, p. 80).

rough-shod over public opinion in France.[2] Two imperial decrees abolished the old system of French protective tariffs which had been in force from 1853 to 1862. With scant observance of the formalities they were 'ratified' in 1863. In Italy, Free Trade was a prop of Cavour's policy, depending as it did on French support. Under pressure of public opinion, an inquiry was made in 1870 which revealed that those most intimately concerned were hostile to the policy of Free Trade. In Russia, finally, the tendency towards Free Trade in the sixties was but the first step towards creating a broad basis for commodity economy and industry on a large scale, coming at the same time as the abolition of serfdom and the construction of a railway network.[3]

[2] Following on the preliminary discussion between Michel Chevalier and Richard Cobden on behalf of the French and English governments, 'official negotiations were shortly entered upon and were conducted with the greatest secrecy. On January 1, 1860, Napoleon III announced his intentions in a memorandum addressed to M Fould, the Minister of State. This declaration came like a bolt from the blue. After the events of the past year, the general belief was that no attempt would be made to modify the tariff system before 1861. Feelings ran high, but all the same the treaty was signed on January 23' (Auguste Devers, *La politique commerciale de la France depuis 1860. Schriften des Vereins für Sozialpolitik*, vol. 51, p. 136).

[3] Between 1857 and 1868, the revision along liberal lines of the Russian tariffs and the ultimate writing-off of the insane system of *kantrin* with regard to protective tariffs were a manifestation and corollary of the progressive reforms which the disastrous Crimean wars had made inevitable. But the reduction of customs duties reflected the concern of the landowning gentry who, both as consumers of foreign goods and as producers of grain for export, were interested in unrestricted commerce between Russia and Western Europe. The champion of agrarian interests, the 'Free Economic Association' stated: 'During the last sixty years, between 1822 and 1882, agriculture, Russia's largest producer, was brought to a precarious position owing to four great setbacks. These could in every case be directly attributed to excessive tariffs. On the other hand, the thirty-two years between 1845 and 1877 when tariffs were moderate went by without any such emergency, in spite of three foreign wars and one civil war [meaning the Polish insurrection of 1863—R. L.], every one of which proved a greater or less strain on the financial resources of the state' (*Memorandum of the Imperial Free Economic Association on Revising Russian Tariffs* (St. Petersburg, 1890), p. 148). As late as the nineties, then, the scientific spokesman of the Free Trade Movement, the said 'Free Economic Association', had to agitate against protective tariffs as a 'contrivance to transplant' capitalist industry to Russia. In a reactionary 'populist' spirit, it denounced capitalism as a breeding ground for the modern proletariat, 'those masses of shiftless people without home or property who have nothing to lose and have long been in ill repute' (p. 191). This is proof enough that until most recent times the Russian champions of Free Trade, or at least of moderate tariffs, did

Thus the very inception of an international system of Free Trade shows it to be just a passing phase in the history of capitalist accumulation, and it shows up the fallacy of attributing the general reversion to protective tariffs after the seventies simply to a defensive reaction against English Free Trade.[4]

Such an explanation is vitiated by the fact that both in Germany and France the leaders in the reversion to protective tariffs were the agrarian interests, that the measures were directed not against British but against American competition, and that not England but Germany constituted the chief danger to the rising home industry in Russia, and France to that in Italy. Nor was Britain's monopoly the cause for the world-wide depression which prevailed since the seventies and induced the desire for protective tariffs. We must look deeper for the reasons responsible for the change of front on the question of protective tariffs. The doctrine of Free Trade with its delusion about the harmony of interests on the world market corresponded with an outlook which conceived of everything in terms of commodity exchange. It was abandoned just as soon as big industrial capital had become sufficiently established in the principal countries of the European Continent to look to the conditions for its accumulation. As against the mutual interests of capitalist countries, these latter bring to the fore the antagonism engendered by the competitive struggle for the non-capitalist environment.

not to any appreciable extent represent the interests of industrial capital. Cf. also K. Lodyshenski: *The History of the Russian Tariffs* (St. Petersburg, 1886), pp. 239–58.

[4] This is also the opinion of F. Engels. In one of his letters to Nikolayon, on June 18, 1892, he writes: 'English authors, blinded by their patriotic interests, completely fail to grasp why the whole world so stubbornly rejects England's example of free trade and adopts in its place the principle of protective tariffs. Of course, they simply dare not admit even to themselves that the system of protective tariffs, by now almost universal, is merely a defensive measure against English free trade which was instrumental in perfecting England's industrial monopoly. Such a defence policy may be more or less reasonable—in some cases it is downright stupid, as for instance in Germany who under the system of free trade had become a great industrial power and now imposes protective tariffs on agricultural products and raw materials, thus increasing the cost of her industrial production. In my view this universal reversion to protective tariffs is not a mere accident but the reaction against England's intolerable industrial monopoly. The form which this reaction takes, as I said before, may be wrong, inadequate and even worse, but its historical necessity seems to me quite clear and obvious' (*Letters* of Karl Marx and Frederick Engels to Nikolayon (St. Petersburg, 1908), p. 71).

When the Free Trade era opened, Eastern Asia was only just being made accessible by the Chinese wars, and European capital had but begun to make headway in Egypt. In the eighties the policy of expansion became ever stronger, together with a policy of protective tariffs. There was an uninterrupted succession of events during the eighties: the British occupation of Egypt, Germany's colonial conquests in Africa, the French occupation of Tunisia together with the Tonkin expedition, Italy's advances in Assab and Massawa, the Abyssinian war and the creation of a separate Eritrea, and the English conquests in South Africa. The clash between Italy and France over the Tunisian sphere of interest was the characteristic prelude to the Franco-Italian tariff war seven years later, by which drastic epilogue an end was made to the Free Trade harmony of interests on the European Continent. To monopolise the non-capitalist areas at home and abroad became the warcry of capital, while the free-trade policy of the 'open door' specifically represented the peculiar helplessness of non-capitalist countries in the face of international capital and the natural equilibrium which was aimed at by its competition in the preliminary stage of the partial or total occupation of these areas as colonies or spheres of interest. As the oldest capitalist Empire, England alone could so far remain loyal to Free Trade, primarily because she had long had immense possessions of non-capitalist areas as a basis for operations which afforded her almost unlimited opportunities for capitalist accumulation. Until recently, she had thus in fact been beyond the competition of other capitalist countries. These, in turn, universally strove to become self-sufficient behind a barrier of protective tariffs; yet they buy one another's commodities and come to depend ever more one upon another for replenishing their material conditions of reproduction. Indeed, protective tariffs have by now completely lost their use for technical development of the productive forces, all too often being the instrument for the artificial conservation of obsolete productive methods. The inherent contradictions of an international policy of protective tariffs, exactly like the dual character of the international loan system, are just a reflection of the historical antagonism which has developed between the dual interests of accumulation: expansion, the realisation and capitalisation of surplus value on the one hand, and, on the other, an outlook which conceives of everything purely in terms of commodity exchange.

This fact is evidenced particularly in that the modern system of high protective tariffs, required by colonial expansion and the increasing inner tension of the capitalist medium, was also instituted with a view to increasing armaments. The reversion to protective tariffs was carried through in Germany as well as in France, Italy, and Russia, together with, and in the interests of, an expansion of the armed services, as the basis for the European competition in armaments which was developing at that time, first on land, and then also at sea. European Free Trade, with its attendant continental system of infantry, had been superseded by protective tariffs as the foundation and supplement of an imperialist system with a strong bias towards naval power.

Thus capitalist accumulation as a whole, as an actual historical process, has two different aspects. One concerns the commodity market and the place where surplus value is produced—the factory, the mine, the agricultural estate. Regarded in this light, accumulation is a purely economic process, with its most important phase a transaction between the capitalist and wage labourer. In both its phases, however, it is confined to the exchange of equivalents and remains within the limits of commodity exchange. Here, in form at any rate, peace, property and equality prevail, and the keen dialectics of scientific analysis were required to reveal how the right of ownership changes in the course of accumulation into appropriation of other people's property, how commodity exchange turns into exploitation and equality becomes class-rule.

The other aspect of the accumulation of capital concerns the relations between capitalism and the non-capitalist modes of production which start making their appearance on the international stage. Its predominant methods are colonial policy, an international loan system—a policy of spheres of interest—and war. Force, fraud, oppression, looting are openly displayed without any attempt at concealment, and it requires an effort to discover within this tangle of political violence and contests of power the stern laws of the economic process.

Bourgeois liberal theory takes into account only the former aspect: the realm of 'peaceful competition', the marvels of technology and pure commodity exchange; it separates it strictly from the other aspect: the realm of capital's blustering violence which is regarded as more or less incidental to foreign policy and quite independent of the economic sphere of capital.

In reality, political power is nothing but a vehicle for the economic process. The conditions for the reproduction of capital provide the organic link between these two aspects of the accumulation of capital. The historical career of capitalism can only be appreciated by taking them together. 'Sweating blood and filth with every pore from head to toe' characterises not only the birth of capital but also its progress in the world at every step, and thus capitalism prepares its own downfall under ever more violent contortions and convulsions.

32

MILITARISM AS A PROVINCE OF ACCUMULATION

Militarism fulfils a quite definite function in the history of capital, accompanying as it does every historical phase of accumulation. It plays a decisive part in the first stages of European capitalism, in the period of the so-called 'primitive accumulation', as a means of conquering the New World and the spice-producing countries of India. Later, it is employed to subject the modern colonies, to destroy the social organisations of primitive societies so that their means of production may be appropriated, forcibly to introduce commodity trade in countries where the social structure had been unfavourable to it, and to turn the natives into a proletariat by compelling them to work for wages in the colonies. It is responsible for the creation and expansion of spheres of interest for European capital in non-European regions, for extorting railway concessions in backward countries, and for enforcing the claims of European capital as international lender. Finally, militarism is a weapon in the competitive struggle between capitalist countries for areas of non-capitalist civilisation.

In addition, militarism has yet another important function. From the purely economic point of view, it is a pre-eminent means for the realisation of surplus value; it is in itself a province of accumulation. In examining the question who should count as a buyer for the mass of products containing the capitalised surplus value, we have again and again refused to consider the state and its organs as consumers. Since their income is derivative, they were all taken to belong to the special category of those who live on the surplus value (or partly on the wage of labour), together with the liberal professions and the various parasites of present-day society ('king, professor, prostitute, mercenary'). But this interpretation will only do on two assumptions: first, if we take it, in accordance with Marx's diagram, that the state has no other sources of taxation than capitalist surplus value and wages,[1] and secondly, if we regard the state and its organs as consumers pure and simple. If the issue turns on the personal consumption of the state organs (as also of the 'mercenary') the point is that consumption is partly transferred from the working class to the hangers-on of the capitalist class, in so far as the workers foot the bill.

Let us assume for a moment that the indirect taxes extorted from the workers, which mean a curtailment of their consumption, are used entirely to pay the salaries of the state officials and to provision the regular army. There will then be no change in the reproduction of social capital as a whole. Both Departments II and I remain constant because society as a whole still demands the same kind of products and in the same quantities. Only v as the commodity of 'labour power' has changed in value in relation to the products of Department II, i.e. in relation to the means of subsistence. This v, the same amount of money representing labour power, is now exchanged for a smaller amount of

---

[1] Dr. Renner indeed makes this assumption the basis of his treatise on taxation. 'Every particle of value created in the course of one year is made up of these four parts: profit, interest, rent, and wages; and annual taxation, then, can only be levied upon these' (*Das arbeitende Volk und die Steuern*, Vienna, 1909). Though Renner immediately goes on to mention peasants, he cursorily dismisses them in a single sentence: 'A peasant e.g. is simultaneously entrepreneur, worker, and landowner, his agricultural proceeds yield him wage, profit, and rent, *all in one.*' Obviously, it is an empty abstraction to apply simultaneously all the categories of capitalist production to the peasantry, to conceive of the peasant as entrepreneur, wage labourer and landlord all in one person. If, like Renner, we want to put the peasant into a single category, his peculiarity for economics lies in the very fact that he belongs neither to the class of capitalist entrepreneurs nor to that of the wage proletariat, that he is not a representative of capitalism at all but of simple commodity production.

means of subsistence. What happens to the products of Department II which are then left over? Instead of the workers, the state officials and the regular army now receive them. The organs of the capitalist state take over the workers' consumption on the same scale exactly. Although the conditions of reproduction have remained stable, there has been a redistribution of the total product. Part of the products of Department II, originally intended entirely for the consumption of the workers as equivalent for v, is now allocated to the hangers-on of the capitalist class for consumption. From the point of view of social reproduction, it is as if the relative surplus value had in the first place been larger by a certain amount which is added on to the consumption of the capitalist class and its hangers-on.

So far the crude exploitation, by the mechanism of indirect taxation, of the working class for the support of the capitalist state's officials amounts merely to an increase of the surplus value, of that part of it, that is to say, which is consumed. The difference is that this further splitting off of surplus value from variable capital only comes later, after the exchange between capital and labour has been accomplished. But the consumption by the organs of the capitalist state has no bearing on the realisation of *capitalised* surplus value, because the additional surplus value for this consumption—even though it comes about at the workers' expense—is created afterwards. On the other hand, if the workers did not pay for the greater part of the state officials' upkeep, the capitalists themselves would have to bear the entire cost of it. A corresponding portion of their surplus value would have to be assigned directly to keeping the organs of their class-rule, either at the expense of production which would have to be curtailed accordingly, or, which is more probable, it would come from the surplus value intended for their consumption. The capitalists would have to capitalise on a smaller scale because of having to contribute more towards the immediate preservation of their own class. In so far as they shift onto the working class (and also the representatives of simple commodity production, such as peasants and artisans) the principal charge of their hangers-on, the capitalists have a larger portion of surplus value available for capital-isation. But as yet *no opportunities for such capitalisation* have come into being, no new market, that is to say, for the surplus value that has become available, in which it could produce and realise new commodities. But when the monies concentrated in the exchequer by taxation are used for the production of armaments, the picture is changed.

With indirect taxation and high protective tariffs, the bill of militarism is footed mainly by the working class and the peasants. The two kinds of taxation must be considered separately. From an economic point of view, it amounts to the following, as far as the working class is concerned: provided that wages are not raised to make up for the higher price of foodstuffs—which is at present the fate of the greatest part of the working class, including even the minority that is organised in trade unions, owing to the pressure of cartels and employers' organisations[2]—indirect taxation means that part of the purchasing power of the working class is transferred to the state. Now as before the variable capital, as a fixed amount of money, will put in motion an appropriate quantity of living labour, that is to say it serves to employ the appropriate quantity of constant capital in production and to produce the corresponding amount of surplus value. As soon as capital has completed this cycle, it is divided between the working class and the state: the workers surrender the state part of the money they received as wages. Capital has wholly appropriated the former variable capital in its material form, as labour power, but the working class retains only part of the variable capital in the form of money, the state claiming the rest. And this invariably happens after capital has run its cycle between capitalist and worker; it takes place, as it were, behind the back of capital, at no point impinging direct on the vital stages of the circulation of capital and the production of surplus value, so that it is no immediate concern of the latter. But all the same it does affect the conditions for the reproduction of capital as a whole. The transfer of some of the purchasing power from the working class to the state entails a proportionate decrease in the consumption of means of subsistence by the working class. For capital as a whole, it means producing a smaller quantity of consumer goods for the working class, provided that both variable capital (in the form of money and as labour

[2] It would go beyond the scope of the present treatise to deal with cartels and trusts as specific phenomena of the imperialist phase. They are due to the internal competitive struggle between individual capitalist groups for a monopoly of the existing spheres for accumulation and for the distribution of profits.

power) and the mass of appropriated surplus value remain constant, so that the workers get a smaller share of the aggregate product. In the process of reproduction of the entire capital, then, means of subsistence will be produced in amounts smaller than the value of the variable capital, because of the shift in the ratio between the value of the variable capital and the quantity of means of subsistence in which it is realised, with the money wages of labour remaining constant, according to our premise, or at any rate not rising sufficiently to offset the increase in the price of foodstuffs. This increase represents the level of indirect taxation.

How will the material relations of reproduction be adjusted? When fewer means of subsistence are needed for the renewal of labour power, a corresponding amount of constant capital and living labour becomes available which can now be used for producing other commodities in response to a new effective demand arising within society. It arises from the side of the state which has appropriated, by way of tax legislation, the part wanting of the workers' purchasing power. This time, however, the state does not demand means of subsistence (after all that has already been said under the heading of 'third persons', we shall here ignore the demand for means of subsistence for state officials which is also satisfied out of taxes) but it requires a special kind of product, namely the militarist weapons of war on land and at sea.

Again we take Marx's second diagram of accumulation as the basis for investigating the ensuing changes in social reproduction:

I. $5,000c + 1,000v + 1,000s = 7,000$ means of production
II. $1,430c + 285v + 285s = 2,000$ means of subsistence

Now let us suppose that, owing to indirect taxation and the consequent increase in the price of means of subsistence, the working class as a whole reduces consumption by, say, a 100 value units of the real wages. As before, the workers receive $1,000v + 285v = 1,285v$ in money, but for this money they only get means of subsistence to the value of 1,185. The 100 units which represent the tax increase in the price of foodstuffs go to the state which receives in addition military taxes from the peasants, etc., to the value of 150 units, bringing the total up to 250. This total constitutes a new demand—the demand for armaments. At present, however, we are only interested in the 100 units taken from the workers' wages. This demand for armaments to the value of 100 must be satisfied by the creation of an appropriate branch of production which requires a constant capital of 71.5 and a variable capital of 14.25, assuming the average organic composition outlined in Marx's diagram.

$$71.5c + 14.25v + 14.25s = 100 \text{ weapons of war}$$

This new branch of production further requires that 71.5 means of production be produced and about 13 means of subsistence, because, of course, the real wages of the workers are also less by about one-thirteenth.

You could counter by saying that the profit accruing to capital from this new expansion of demand is merely on paper, because the cut in the actual consumption of the working class will inevitably result in a corresponding curtailment of the means of subsistence produced. It will take the following form for Department II:

$$71.5c + 14.25v + 14.25s = 100$$

In addition, Department I will also have to contract accordingly, so that, owing to the decreasing consumption of the working class, the equations for both departments will be:

$$
\begin{aligned}
\text{I.} \quad & 4{,}949c && + 989.75v + 989.75s = 6{,}928.5 \\
\text{II.} \quad & 1{,}358.5c && + 270.75v + 270.75s = 1{,}900
\end{aligned}
$$

If, by the mediation of the state, the same 100 units now call forth armament production of an equal volume with a corresponding fillip to the production of producer goods, this is at first sight only an extraneous change in the material forms of social production: instead of a quantity of means of subsistence a quantity of armaments is now being produced. Capital has won with the left hand only what it has lost with the right. Or we might say that the large number of capitalists producing means of subsistence have lost the effective demand in favour of a small group of big armament manufacturers.

But this picture is only valid for individual capital. Here it makes no difference indeed whether production engages in one sphere of activity or another. As far as the individual capitalist is concerned, there are no departments of total production such as the diagram distinguishes. There are only commodities and buyers, and it is completely immaterial to him whether he produces instruments of life or instruments of death, corned beef or armour plating.

Opponents of militarism frequently appeal to this point of view to show that military supplies as an economic investment for capital merely put profit taken from one capitalist into the pocket of another.[3] On the other hand, capital and its advocates try to overpersuade the working class to this point of view by talking them into the belief that indirect taxes and the demand of the state would only bring about a change in the material form of reproduction; instead of other commodities cruisers and guns would be produced which would give the workers as good a living, if not a better one.

One glance at the diagram shows how little truth there is in this argument as far as the workers are concerned. To make comparison easier, we will suppose the armament factories to employ just as many workers as were employed before in the production of means of subsistence for the working class. 1,285 units will then be paid out as wages, but now they will only buy 1,185's worth of means of subsistence.

All this looks different from the perspective of capital as a whole. For

---

[3] In a reply to Vorontsov, Professor Manuilov, for example, wrote what was then greatly praised by the Russian Marxists: 'In this context, we must distinguish strictly between a group of entrepreneurs producing weapons of war and the capitalist class as a whole. For the manufacturers of guns, rifles and other war materials, the existence of militarism is no doubt profitable and indispensable. It is indeed quite possible that the abolition of the system of armed peace would spell ruin for Krupp. The point at issue, however, is not a special group of entrepreneurs but the capitalists as a class, capitalist production as a whole.' In this connection, however, it should be noted that 'if the burden of taxation falls chiefly on the working population, every increase of this burden diminishes the purchasing power of the population and hence the demand for commodities'. This fact is taken as proof that militarism, under the aspect of armament production, does indeed 'enrich one group of capitalists, but at the same time it injures all others, spelling gain on the one hand but loss on the other' (*Vesnik Prava*, Journal of the Law Society (St. Petersburg, 1890), no. 1, 'Militarism and Capitalism').

this the 100 at the disposal of the state, which represent the demand for armaments, constitute a new market. Originally this money was variable capital and as such it has done its job, it has been exchanged for living labour which produced the surplus value. But then the circulation of the variable capital was stopped short, this money was split off, and it now appears as a new purchasing power in the possession of the state. It has been created by sleight of hand, as it were, but still it has the same effects as a newly opened market. Of course for the time being capital is debarred from selling 100 units of consumer goods for the working class, and the individual capitalist considers the worker just as good a consumer and buyer of commodities as anyone else, another capitalist, the state, the peasant, foreign countries, etc. But let us not forget that for capital as a whole the upkeep of the working class is only a necessary evil, only a means towards the real end of production: the creation and realisation of surplus value. If it were possible to extort surplus value without giving labour an equal measure of means of subsistence, it would be all the better for business. To begin with indirect taxation has the same effects as if—the price of foodstuffs remaining constant—the capitalists had succeeded in depressing wages by a hundred units without detracting from the work performed, seeing that a lower output of consumer goods is equally the inevitable result of continuous wage cuts. If wages are cut heavily, capital does not worry about having to produce fewer means of subsistence for the workers, in fact it delights in this practice at every opportunity; similarly, capital as a whole does not mind if the effective demand of the working class for means of subsistence is curtailed because of indirect taxation which is not compensated by a rise in wages. This may seem strange because in the latter case the balance of the variable capital goes to the exchequer, while with a direct wage cut it remains in the capitalists' pockets and—commodity prices remaining equal—increases the relative surplus value. But a continuous and universal reduction of money wages can only be carried through on rare occasions, especially if trade union organisation is highly developed. There are strong social and political barriers to this fond aspiration of capital. Depression of the real wage by means of indirect taxation, on the other hand, can be carried through promptly, smoothly and universally, and it usually takes time for protests to be heard; and besides, the opposition is

confined to the political field and has no immediate economic reper-
cussions. The subsequent restriction in the production of means of
subsistence does not represent a loss of markets for capital as a whole
but rather a saving in the costs of producing surplus value. Surplus
value is never realised by producing means of subsistence for the
workers—however necessary this may be, as the reproduction of living
labour, for the production of surplus value.

But to come back to our example:

I. $5,000c + 1,000v + 1,000s = 7,000$ means of production
II. $1,430c + 285v + 285s = 2,000$ means of subsistence

At first it looks as if Department II were also creating and realising
surplus value in the process of producing means of subsistence for the
workers, and Department I by producing the requisite means of production. But if we take the social product as a whole, the illusion
disappears. The equation is in that case:

$$6,430c + 1,285v + 1,285s = 9,000$$

Now, if the means of subsistence for the workers are cut by 100
units, the corresponding contraction of both departments will give us
the following equations:

I. $4,949c + 989.75v + 989.75s = 6,928.5$
II. $1,358.5c + 270.75v + 270.75s = 1,900$

and for the social product as a whole:

$$6,307.5c + 1,260.5v + 1,260.5s = 8,828.5$$

This looks like a general decrease in both the total volume of production and in the production of surplus value—but only if we contem-
plate just the abstract quantities of value in the composition of the total
product; it does not hold good for the material composition thereof.
Looking closer, we find that nothing but the upkeep of labour is in
effect decreased. Fewer means of subsistence and production are now

being made, no doubt, but then, they had had no other function save to maintain workers. The social product is smaller and less capital is now employed—but then, the object of capitalist production is not simply to employ as much capital as possible, but to produce as much surplus value as possible. Capital has only decreased because a smaller amount is sufficient for maintaining the workers. If the total cost of maintaining the workers employed in the society came to 1,285 units in the first instance, the present decrease of the social product by 171.5—the difference of $(9,000-8,828.5)$—comes off this maintenance charge, and there is a consequent change in the composition of the social product:

$$6,430c + 1,113.5v + 1,285s = 8,828.5$$

Constant capital and surplus value remain unchanged, and only the variable capital, paid labour, has diminished. Or—in case there are doubts about constant capital being unaffected—we may further allow for the event that, as would happen in actual practice, concomitant with the decrease in means of subsistence for the workers there will be a corresponding cut in the constant capital. The equation for the social product as a whole would then be:

$$6,307.5c + 1,236v + 1,285s = 8,828.5$$

In spite of the smaller social product, there is no change in the surplus value in either case, and it is only the cost of maintaining the workers that has fallen.

Put it this way: the value of the aggregate social product may be defined as consisting of three parts, the total constant capital of the society, its total variable capital, and its total surplus value, of which the first set of products contains no additional labour, and the second and third no means of production. As regards their material form, all these products come into being in the given period of production— though in point of value the constant capital had been produced in a previous period and is merely being transferred to new products. On this basis, we can also divide all the workers employed into three mutually exclusive categories: those who produce the aggregate constant capital of the society, those who provide the upkeep for all the workers, and finally those who create the entire surplus value for the capitalist class.

If, then, the workers' consumption is curtailed, only workers in the second category will lose their jobs. Ex *hypothesi*, these workers had never created surplus value for capital, and in consequence their dismissal is therefore no loss from the capitalist's point of view but a gain, since it decreases the cost of producing surplus value.

The demand of the state which arises at the same time has the lure of a new and attractive sphere for realising the surplus value. Some of the money circulating as variable capital breaks free of this cycle and in the state treasury it represents a new demand. For the technique of taxation, of course, the order of events is rather different, since the amount of the indirect taxes is actually advanced to the state by capital and is merely being refunded to the capitalists by the sale of their commodities, as part of their price. But economically speaking, it makes no difference. The crucial point is that the quantity of money with the function of variable capital should first mediate the exchange between capital and labour power. Later, when there is an exchange between workers and capitalists as buyers and sellers of commodities respectively, this money will change hands and accrue to the state as taxes. This money, which capital has set circulating, first fulfils its primary function in the exchange with labour power, but subsequently, by mediation of the state, it begins an entirely new career. As a new purchasing power, belonging with neither labour nor capital, it becomes interested in new products, in a special branch of production which does not cater for either the capitalists or the working class, and thus it offers capital new opportunities for creating and realising surplus value. When we were formerly taking it for granted that the indirect taxes extorted from the workers are used for paying the officials and for provisioning the army, we found the 'saving' in the consumption of the working class to mean that the workers rather than the capitalists were made to pay for the personal consumption of the hangers-on of the capitalist class and the tools of their class-rule. This charge devolved from the surplus value to the variable capital, and a corresponding amount of the surplus value became available for purposes of capitalisation. Now we see how the taxes extorted from the workers afford capital a new opportunity for accumulation when they are used for armament manufacture.

On the basis of indirect taxation, militarism in practice works both ways. By lowering the normal standard of living for the working class, it ensures both that capital should be able to maintain a regular army, the organ of capitalist rule, and that it may tap an impressive field for further accumulation.[4]

We have still to examine the second source of the state's purchasing power referred to in our example, the 150 units out of the total 250 invested in armaments. They differ essentially from the hundred units considered above in that they are not supplied by the workers but by the petty bourgeoisie, i.e. the artisans and peasants. (In this connection, we can ignore the comparatively small tax-contribution of the capitalist class itself.)

The money accruing to the state as taxes from the peasant masses— as our generic term for all non-proletarian consumers—was not originally advanced by capital and has not split off from capital in circulation. In the hand of the peasant it is the equivalent of goods that have been realised, the exchange value of simple commodity production. The state now gets part of the purchasing power of the non-capitalist consumers, purchasing power, that is to say, which is already free to realise the surplus value for capitalist accumulation. Now the question arises, whether economic changes will result for capital, and if so, of what nature, from diverting the purchasing power of such strata to the state for militarist purposes. It almost looks as if we had come up against yet another shift in the material form of reproduction. Capital will now produce an equivalent of war materials for the state instead of producing large quantities of means of production and subsistence for peasant consumers. But in fact the changes go deeper. First and foremost, the state can use the mechanism of taxation to mobilise much

---

[4] Ultimately, the deterioration of the normal conditions under which labour power is renewed will bring about a deterioration of labour itself, it will diminish the average efficiency and productivity of labour, and thus jeopardise the conditions for the production of surplus value. But capital will not feel these results for a long time, and so they do not immediately enter into its economic calculations, except in so far as they bring about more drastic defensive measures of the wage labourers in general.

larger amounts of purchasing power from the non-capitalist consumers than they would ordinarily spend on their own consumption.

Indeed the modern system of taxation itself is largely responsible for forcing commodity economy on the peasants. Under pressure of taxes, the peasant must turn more and more of his produce into commodities, and at the same time he must buy more and more. Taxation presses the produce of peasant economy into circulation and compels the peasants to become buyers of capitalist products. Finally, on a basis of commodity production in the peasant style, the system of taxation lures more purchasing power from peasant economy than would otherwise become active.

What would normally have been hoarded by the peasants and the lower middle classes until it has grown big enough to invest in savings banks and other banks is now set free to constitute an effective demand and an opportunity for investment. Further the multitude of individual and insignificant demands for a whole range of commodities, which will become effective at different times and which might often be met just as well by simple commodity production, is now replaced by a comprehensive and homogeneous demand of the state. And the satisfaction of this demand presupposes a big industry of the highest order. It requires the most favourable conditions for the production of surplus value and for accumulation. In the form of government contracts for army supplies the scattered purchasing power of the consumers is concentrated in large quantities and, free of the vagaries and subjective fluctuations of personal consumption, it achieves an almost automatic regularity and rhythmic growth. Capital itself ultimately controls this automatic and rhythmic movement of militarist production through the legislature and a press whose function is to mould so-called 'public opinion'. That is why this particular province of capitalist accumulation at first seems capable of infinite expansion. All other attempts to expand markets and set up operational bases for capital largely depend on historical, social and political factors beyond the control of capital, whereas production for militarism represents a province whose regular and progressive expansion seems primarily determined by capital itself.

In this way capital turns historical necessity into a virtue: the ever fiercer competition in the capitalist world itself provides a field for accumulation of the first magnitude. Capital increasingly employs militarism for implementing a foreign and colonial policy to get hold of the means of production and labour power of non-capitalist countries and societies. This same militarism works in a like manner in the capitalist countries to divert purchasing power away from the non-capitalist strata. The representatives of simple commodity production and the working class are affected alike in this way. At their expense, the accumulation of capital is raised to the highest power, by robbing the one of their productive forces and by depressing the other's standard of living. Needless to say, after a certain stage the conditions for the accumulation of capital both at home and abroad turn into their very opposite—they become conditions for the decline of capitalism.

The more ruthlessly capital sets about the destruction of non-capitalist strata at home and in the outside world, the more it lowers the standard of living for the workers as a whole, the greater also is the change in the day-to-day history of capital. It becomes a string of political and social disasters and convulsions, and under these conditions, punctuated by periodical economic catastrophes or crises, accumulation can go on no longer.

But even before this natural economic impasse of capital's own creating is properly reached it becomes a necessity for the international working class to revolt against the rule of capital.

Capitalism is the first mode of economy with the weapon of propaganda, a mode which tends to engulf the entire globe and to stamp out all other economies, tolerating no rival at its side. Yet at the same time it is also the first mode of economy which is unable to exist by itself, which needs other economic systems as a medium and soil. Although it strives to become universal, and, indeed, on account of this its tendency, it must break down—because it is immanently incapable of becoming a universal form of production. In its living history it is a contradiction in itself, and its movement of accumulation provides a solution to the conflict and aggravates it at the same time. At a certain stage of development there will be no other way out than the application of socialist principles. The aim of socialism is not accumulation but the satisfaction of toiling humanity's wants by developing the productive forces of the entire globe. And so we find that socialism is by its very nature an harmonious and universal system of economy.

Index

Routledge Classics
Get inside a great mind

The Road to Serfdom
F. A. Hayek

'This book has become a true classic: essential reading for everyone who is seriously interested in politics in the broadest and least partisan sense.'
Milton Friedman

The Road to Serfdom remains one of the all-time classics of twentieth-century intellectual thought. For over half a century, it has inspired politicians and thinkers around the world, and has had a crucial impact on our political and cultural history. Addressing economics, fascism, history, socialism and the Holocaust, Hayek unwraps the trappings of socialist ideology. He reveals to the world that little can result from such ideas except oppression and tyranny.

Hb: 0–415–25543–0   Pb: 0–415–25389–6

The Protestant Ethic and the Spirit of Capitalism
Max Weber

'One of the most renowned and controversial works of modern social science.'
Anthony Giddens

Max Weber's best-known and most controversial work, *The Protestant Ethic and the Spirit of Capitalism*, first published in 1904, remains to this day a powerful and fascinating read. It contends that the Protestant ethic made possible and encouraged the development of capitalism in the West. Widely considered as the most informed work ever written on the social effects of advanced capitalism, it holds its own as one of the most significant books of the twentieth century.

Hb: 0–415–25559–7   Pb: 0–415–25406–X

For these and other classic titles from Routledge, visit
www.routledgeclassics.com

Some titles not available in North America

Routledge Classics
Get inside a great mind

The Open Society and Its Enemies
Karl Popper

'One of the great books of the century.'
The Times

Written in political exile during the Second World War and first published in 1945, Karl Popper's *The Open Society and Its Enemies* is one of the most influential books of the twentieth century. Hailed by Bertrand Russell as a 'vigorous and profound defence of democracy', its now legendary attack on the philosophies of Plato, Hegel and Marx exposed the dangers inherent in centrally planned political systems. It is a work that demands to be read both today and in years to come.

Volume I: The Spell of Plato
Hb: 0–415–29062–7   Pb: 0–415–23731–9

Volume II: Hegel and Marx
Hb: 0–415–29063–5   Pb: 0–415–27842–2

Marxism and Literary Criticism
Terry Eagleton

'Terry Eagleton is that rare bird among literary critics – a real writer.'
Colin McCabe, The Guardian

A wonderfully clear introduction to the application of Marx's theories to the study of literature. Short and very well-written, it provides a survey of major twentieth-century literary theorists, including Marcuse, Jameson and Lukács. In this ground-breaking work, Eagleton applies viewpoints central to Marxist thought to his analysis. Through this, he is able to show the part that Marxist criticism has to play in defining the crucial link between literature and historical condition.

Hb: 0–415–28583–6   Pb: 0–415–28584–4

For these and other classic titles from Routledge, visit
www.routledgeclassics.com

Routledge Classics
Get inside a great mind

The Political Unconscious
Narrative as a socially symbolic act
Fredric Jameson

'Fredric Jameson is generally considered to be one of the foremost contemporary English-language Marxist literary and cultural critics.'
Douglas Kellner

In this ground-breaking and influential study Fredric Jameson explores the complex place and function of literature within culture. At the time Jameson was actually writing the book, in the mid- to late seventies, there was a major reaction against deconstruction and post-structuralism. As one of the most significant literary theorists of the time, Jameson found himself in the unenviable position of wanting to defend his intellectual past yet keep an eye on the future. With this book he carried it off beautifully.

Hb: 0–415–28750–2   Pb: 0–415–28751–0

One-Dimensional Man
Studies in the ideology of advanced industrial society
Herbert Marcuse

'A bitter cry for social protest, fortified by uncommon erudition and rationality.'
Newsweek

One of the most important texts of modern times, Herbert Marcuse's analysis and image of a one-dimensional man in a one-dimensional society has shaped many young radicals' ways of seeing and experiencing life. As Douglas Kellner notes in his Introduction, Marcuse's greatest work was 'a damning indictment of contemporary Western societies, capitalist and communist.' Yet it also expressed the hope of a radical philosopher that human freedom and happiness could be greatly expanded beyond the regimented thought and behaviour prevalent in the established society.

Hb: 0–415–28976–9   Pb: 0–415–28977–7

For these and other classic titles from Routledge, visit
www.routledgeclassics.com